Like a River Glorious

Like a River Glorious

The Biography of John Paul Newport

Karen O'Dell Bullock

1845BOOKS

© 2022 by 1845 Books, an imprint of Baylor University Press
Waco, Texas 76798

All Rights Reserved. No part of this publication may be reproduced, stored in a retrieval system, or transmitted, in any form or by any means, electronic, mechanical, photocopying, recording, or otherwise, without the prior permission in writing of Baylor University Press.

Cover and book design by Kasey McBeath
Cover art courtesy of Unsplash/K. Mitch Hodge

Baylor University Press is grateful for the generous support of the Newport Foundation in the publication of this book.

The Library of Congress has cataloged this book under paperback ISBN 978-1-4813-1606-4.

Library of Congress Control Number: 2022933281

Printed case ISBN: 978-1-4813-1614-9

*This volume is lovingly dedicated to
Martha, Frank, and John Paul
and their extended families
and
to the members of the
John Paul Newport Foundation
whose love and devotion remain steadfast*

And to my wonderful father, William H. O'Dell (1930–2021)

Contents

Preface   ix

Prologue   1

1   Headwaters Deep in Missouri Soil   7

2   An Ozark Boy and His Cumberland Girl   15

3   Streams of Knowledge   33
       1939–1949

4   Widening Currents   53
       1949–1959

5   The Long Rolling River   69
       1959–1971

6   Navigating Rapids   89
       1971–1994

7   The River Joins the Sea   125
       1994–2000

8   Nourishing Waters   141
       The Thought of John Paul Newport

9   Enduring Legacy   151
       1949–2000 and Beyond

Epilogue   181

Appendix A: The Bibliography of John Paul Newport   189

Appendix B: Philosophy of Religion Doctoral Students Supervised by John Paul Newport   195

Appendix C: John Paul Newport (1917–2000)
   Memorial Service   197
      Broadway Baptist Church, Fort Worth, Texas

Notes   203
Bibliography   283

Preface

Tolle, lege: "Take up and read."
St. Augustine of Hippo[1]

In 2012, the John Paul Newport Foundation commissioned me to write its official biography of John Newport (1917–2000), the late and influential philosopher and apologist who taught for more than half a century in Baptist life. Born in Missouri, he studied with the best minds of his day. He became legendary as a Baptist statesman, scholar, peacemaker, and transformational professor who supervised more than fifty Ph.D. students in philosophy, apologetics, theology, biblical studies, and world religions. Many of those former students now teach in faculties around the globe.

John Newport was also a churchman in pulpits across the southland, as interim pastor in more than 150 churches in four states, and as one who engaged college and seminary students to use their minds for Christ's Kingdom. His best-known book, *Life's Ultimate Questions*, synthesized the most-often-asked questions about what it *means* to live as human beings, and anchored his responses in a reasoned, philosophical, and biblical worldview, making him perhaps the first in Baptist life to work in this area. He was an open, approachable, scholarly, and constructive evangelical, inviting Baptists to engage with the world of ideas, other Christians, and people of non-Christian faiths.

While Newport taught for fifty years (1949–1999) at four Baptist institutions and Rice University, he spent most of his career at Southwestern Baptist Theological Seminary, having known seven of its nine presidents and served under five. He never knew B. H. Carroll, who died just before he was born, nor the latest, Adam Greenway, who took office nineteen years after his death. At Southwestern, he chaired the philosophy department and served as vice president of academic affairs and provost. He was the special consultant to the president—Russell Dilday, his former student—when Dilday was terminated without cause. John led the faculty during some of its most difficult days. The story of his life and work unfolds in these pages.

Before he died in 2000, John Newport had gathered together eight boxes of autobiographical materials, separated these from his 168 boxes of personal and academic papers, and was in the process of writing his own story. I have spent the last eight years reading and researching in his files. The records are exhaustive, including thousands of handwritten letters and files dating back to the early 1940s. These are a detailed chronicling of not only John's career, but also the theological and philosophical changes that took place in the twentieth century and the controversies that fractured Baptists across the South during his lifetime.

Meticulously precise, John Newport kept diaries, journals, even sermon lists with places preached, topics covered, and biblical references used, and a record of all telephone calls and appointments he scheduled during his career. From these accounts, his life could almost be reconstructed on a daily basis from early 1940, when he left home for college, to his death in 2000. My guiding principle has been to consult Newport's notes and initial narratives, as these aided in knowing how, in his final months, he was reflecting on his own journey. Like an archivist who receives a collection to catalog, I have maintained the provenance of his boxes in the way that he arranged them. In addition, I was also able to research in Newport's vast personal library, numbering more than twenty thousand volumes, most of which was housed at B. H. Carroll Theological Institute in Irving, Texas, before moving to The Texas Collection and University Archives, Baylor University, Waco, Texas.

I owe deep gratitude to many people without whose help this project could not have been completed. I thank the John Paul Newport Foundation members for their kind invitation to write this biography and their long-suffering patience, for this work took longer than we had all anticipated. I appreciate B. H. Carroll's generous six-week sabbatical to complete the manuscript in the summer of 2020. I am indebted to several archivists for finding facts and information I needed: Taffy Hall, Director of The Southern Baptist Historical Library and Archives in Nashville,

Tennessee; Jill Botticelli, Archivist of the B. H. Carroll Center for Baptist Heritage and Mission at Southwestern Baptist Theological Seminary in Fort Worth, Texas; and Don Day, Librarian of the B. H. Carroll Theological Institute in Irving, Texas. I owe much to the Baylor editorial team and their marvelous editing and design skills: Cade Jarrell, Maddee Barbier, Kasey McBeath, and Jenny Hunt.

I am also deeply grateful to Dr. Larry Ashlock, who as a constant friend sacrificially read and copy edited this manuscript while writing one of his own. His unwavering encouragement enabled the project from its first moment to its last. Finally, I am thankful to my family who, with cheerful support, allowed me uninterrupted time to write, especially to the Grands—Noah, Nathanael, Chloe, Sophia, Emma, and Obadiah—who delayed many adventures without complaining until the book was finished.

As I see it, the most fitting metaphor for John Newport's life is a mighty, rushing, powerful river, sweeping along in its robust current all of life's knowledge and human experience. The river runs its course, rushing ever onward until it meets the sea, its intended destination. There is something consequential and eternal about our lives, and this truth informs the purpose of John Newport's existence. This volume seeks to share that purpose. The title of this work, then, is taken from the first line of a hymn text by Frances Ridley Havergal (1836–1879), the pastor's daughter, scholar, and poet, whose life was permeated with her passionate love of Jesus. I believe John would have liked that.

> Like a river glorious is God's perfect peace,
> over all victorious in its bright increase: perfect,
>   yet still flowing fuller every day;
> perfect, yet still growing deeper all the way.
> Stayed upon Jehovah, hearts are fully blest,
> finding, as he promised, perfect peace and rest.[2]

Prologue

> I have sought to show evangelicals the coherence
> and viability of their beliefs.
>
> **John Paul Newport**

John Paul Newport (1917–2000) was almost too complex a man to squeeze between the covers of a book. Born in a small Missouri town in 1917, his adult career spanned the entire second half of the twentieth century. His life paralleled catastrophic global events, major world wars, the terms of fifteen presidents, from Woodrow Wilson to Bill Clinton, and the cleaving of American Protestant denominations, including Baptists. He never yearned to be famous, yet by the time of his death, he had become widely known beyond the Baptist circles of his younger years.

Like his peers, such as Billy Graham in evangelism, F. F. Bruce in New Testament studies, Francis Schaeffer in theology and philosophy, Carl F. H. Henry and J. I. Packer in theology, John Newport was known as a constructive, conservative evangelical. His academic area was philosophy, but he had a penchant for collecting all theological disciplines into his dialogical bag, for he believed that they all connected. He spent his life trying to show people how they actually did. He was one of the few Southern Baptists in his day to swing wide the doors of the Baptist House and step out to shake hands with other Christians in the new evangelical community that was evolving from the 1940s through the end of the century.

Poetically speaking, if John Newport were a crisp, trumpet reveille call, he would signal a new dawn. If he were a table, he would be broad enough for everyone to find a seat from which their voice could be heard.

If he were a banquet, he would provide a smorgasbord of viewpoints to be offered for discussion, meaningful exploration, and the discovery of truth-claims. If he were a bridge, he would connect a chasm, across which clashing sides could meet at center, find concord, and resolve conflict. If John Newport were a mighty river, he would sweep along all of his knowledge, fed by the tributaries of his life, all experiences, all known realities, to carve canyons and channels with his powerful, deep current. The river's course would leave a monumental imprint, changing the landscape through which it flowed. The man John Paul Newport was such a force.

The topography that contained this river is the key to understanding Newport's life and the motivating impulses that drove his work. In the period in which he lived, vast changes were taking place within the world, across America, and in the churches of her land. Newport was a conservative Christian philosopher and apologist, investing his vast scholarship in twentieth-century Protestantism in America. The historical literature concerning this development is extensive, but a concise orientation may be helpful for understanding the different phases of American Protestantism's changes.[1] This context is significant when considering the impact of Newport's life and work.

Historians concur that Protestants were shocked by change at the beginning of the twentieth century when they were forced to confront the rise of modernism.[2] When the World Parliament of Religions met in Chicago in 1893, several new, non-Christian religions made their appearances. Along with these new belief systems, the weight of "new science," or Darwinism, German biblical higher criticism, and the Social Gospel movement began to reveal fractures within the landscape of American Christianity.[3] By the turn of the century, Protestant Christians had begun to lean toward either "Modernist" or "Conservative" approaches to these changes. Fea unfolds four phases of the relationship among conservatives that eventuated into what became, by the mid-twentieth century, the evangelical and fundamentalist movements. This began with the Presbyterians and Old Princetonian theology.

The first development was the late nineteenth-century *irenic* phase (1893–1919), which followed on the heels of Dwight L. Moody's (1837–1899) interdenominational evangelism and the beginning of the Holiness movement, and led up to World War I. This period is characterized by the attempts of nineteenth-century Protestants to address the rising theological modernism that was now influencing their denominations.

The period includes the 1910 publication of *The Fundamentals: A Testimony to the Truth*, an open and concerned response toward theological modernism.[4] *The Fundamentals* included twelve volumes of theological essays devoted to providing a "testimony" to what the representative authors believed to be the fundamental principles of evangelical faith. Marsden has argued that, at the time of its publication, *The Fundamentals* represented the consensus of religious thought in America.[5] A peaceable, tolerant spirit pervaded theological conservativism in these days, even though its denominational leaders were deeply aware of looming threats to their own theological and denominational unity. The term "Fundamentalist" had not yet been coined.[6]

The *militant* phase (1920–1936) encompassed the "fundamentalist-modernist controversies," as conservatives increasingly expressed their opposition to the "new" theology. The toleration of the former period was no more. Now the language used was "anti-modernist," "anti-liberal," even "militant fundamentalism" as a self-describing moniker for those who were now "doing battle" against modernism. America was at war with Germany, who was considered the "enemy," and war metaphors pervaded everyday speech. "Liberal theology" was thought to be a destructive force upon the tenets of traditional "orthodox theology," and even as political war broke out across Europe, religious war erupted in Protestant America. The term "fundamentalist," and the militancy now associated with the term, appeared in America by 1920, where the battles were now fought *within* mainline denominations, with neither party willing to surrender control to the opposing forces.[7] As a general rule, at the close of this era, modernists had co-opted mainline denominations and their institutions, particularly Presbyterians and Northern Baptists, along with massive cultural and intellectual changes that were becoming part of the fiber of the nation on the brink of World War II.

The third phase was *divisive* (1941–1960), when fundamentalism split into "evangelical" and "separatist" factions. During the 1940s, two distinct national, interdenominational entities evolved. One group, fully intending to continue the "anti-modernist battle," organized the American Council of Christian Churches (ACCC) in 1941, led by a faction who had left their respective denominations for more conservative stances on theology.[8] The ACCC was characterized by its opposition to modernism, the National Council of Churches (NCC), and to those who were open to dialogue with these entities.

The other group was represented by those who held a more open-minded, "positive" approach to modernism so that ideas and theology could be engaged for the purposes of productive conversations. This group felt that the term "fundamentalist" had been scarred by the rancor of the previous period and wished no longer to be identified with the negative aspects of the term. This group founded the National Association of Evangelicals (NAE) in April 1942, and the new term "evangelicals" gained popular acceptance by conservatives who were intentionally taking a middle path between the extremes of the militant fundamentalists and modern liberals.[9] The NAE continued to uphold the same fundamentalist doctrinal core; however, they felt uncomfortable about the militant isolation from culture. They believed that Jesus came to deal with the physical well-being, in addition to the more serious spiritual well-being, of the people he met. They knew that vital Christianity must *engage* culture to be an effective transformative agent *of* culture.

The last phase, that of *separatism*, has continued from 1950 to the present, where the self-designation of fundamentalism is used primarily by Protestants who remove themselves from mainstream American culture and religion. In this period, Harold J. Ockenga coined the term "neo-evangelicalism" to describe a new version of conservatism that presented classic fundamentalist doctrine in a fresh, non-polemical light accompanied with an emphasis on original scholarship and social concern. New institutions, like Fuller Theological Seminary, a new generation of university-trained evangelical scholars, and new journals like *Christianity Today* began to distinguish the movement from the continued negativism associated with "fundamentalism."[10]

By 1955, Carl F. H. Henry had defined neo-evangelicalism in strictly doctrinal terms, calling a neo-evangelical anyone who was committed to "biblical authority, the holiness of God, a revealing God, a creating, supernatural God, man as created in God's image, the sinfulness of man, the love of God, the death of Christ, the new birth, social action, and the return of Christ."[11] The separatist fundamentalist leadership agreed with these statements, except for that of social action, which they perceived to be linked with the "Social Gospel" movement and was therefore to be avoided.[12] The latter group also continued to foster an aggressive anti-modernism and ecclesiastical separation within their ranks.

From the 1960s through the 1980s, the fundamentalist view of separation led to divisions within the group, especially with the ascendancy of personality-oriented alliances. Leaders such as Carl McIntire, John R. Rice, Bob Jones Sr., Bob Jones Jr., and Jerry Falwell ultimately distanced and even separated from each other. "What was once a unified coalition against modernism, neo-evangelicalism, and Billy Graham," Fea states, "fragmented into a fundamentalist civil war."[13]

By the third quarter of the twentieth century, many fundamentalists in the Southern Baptist Convention had coalesced around a small group of leaders, named themselves a "Conservative Resurgence," and turned their attention to gaining control of Southern Baptist seminaries and convention structures. Their rallying cry was to establish "inerrancy," an Old Princetonian Presbyterian approach to scriptural authority, as the method by which to ensure the reliability of the biblical text.[14]

In the same period, but in a larger arena, evangelicals continued to flourish. A precise statement of their convictions was signed as a covenant by more than 3,700 evangelical leaders from 150 countries, gathering in Lausanne, Switzerland, for the ten-day Lausanne Congress on World Evangelization in July 1974. The covenant described what evangelicals believed and what they hoped to do in the name of Christ in the world.[15]

This milieu, then, particularly the last two phases of Protestant conservative development and the last half of the twentieth century, is the context of Newport's life and ministry. Like canyon walls that guide a river's course, the events of evangelicalism's mediating progress as it engaged both the separatist fundamentalists on one hand, and the broader religious and secular worlds on the other, also informed Newport's trajectory. In his day, as a Baptist from the southland, and a voice both to and for Southern Baptists, Newport knew and interacted with the principal leaders, scholars, and thinkers of all sides of these movements, earning a respected place among them.[16] This was no small feat.

The present volume seeks to do more than to recount John Newport's walk upon the earth. It also explores the question of whether John Newport's life and legacy has contributed anything of singular and lasting significance to Baptist life in the twentieth and twenty-first centuries. If so, what might be the nature of that contribution, how was it unique, and what factors made it remarkable? This story will demonstrate that John Paul Newport was a link among his days, an ambassador who joined Southern Baptists and the larger Baptist family to the wider evangelical and religious worlds. He was perhaps the first among Baptists to work with a new concept in philosophy of religion circles, a "biblical worldview." Further, his unique and remarkable training, his statesmanship, his decades of teaching and generational legacy of influence, and his masterful approach to applied philosophy all were singular and significant contributions to Baptist and evangelical life.[17] It is to the fascinating tale of John Paul Newport that this volume now turns.

1
Headwaters Deep in Missouri Soil

> How wonderful it is that nobody need wait a single moment
> before starting to improve the world.
>
> Anne Frank[1]

The life of the remarkable John Paul Newport begins in the rural and beautiful setting of Buffalo, nestled on the northern slope of the Ozark mountain range in southwest Missouri. Born in the first decade of the twentieth century and possessed from his earliest days with a keen sense of observation, John would grow to embrace his world from within this exceptional framework. Unique geographical, cultural, spiritual, and familial influences melded into a rich learning environment for the small and curious child, and, as he recounted in later years, provided his initial and foundational intellectual orientation to the world.

The Land

When the first descendants of Europeans pushed into this area in the early 1800s, they found a vast wilderness of great scenic beauty inhabited by wild animals and Native Americans. Small communities of Osage, Delaware, Shawnee, and Miami hunted turkey, quail, duck, goose, elk, and deer in this pristine paradise. The western sectors of what later came to be known as Dallas County, Missouri, were composed of rugged hills, rushing streams, and some of the largest caves and springs in North America. The Niangua River, near Buffalo, was later to form one of the important arms of the Lake of the Ozarks.[2] This was the spot that Newport's ancestors called home.

Missouri State Map

A Homestead Called "Buffalo"

Missouri won statehood in 1821, and soon hundreds of immigrants from Kentucky, Tennessee, and the rest of the new states crossed its borders to stake their holdings. A decade later, Mark Reynolds moved his family from the Nashville area and settled the first claim on a beautiful prairie in the southwest region. He built a homestead, found a stake left by some earlier traveler on one of the Blue Mounds, and mounted a skeleton of a buffalo head upon it. This buffalo head became a landmark, and as the nearby settlement grew, it was simply called "Buffalo."[3] Because of the vast numbers, religious preferences, and predominant culture of its new citizens, the state of Missouri over time became distinctly American, Protestant, and Anglo. The families of Morrow and Newport were of this stock.

The Morrows

About two miles north of the Buffalo town square still stands the old Morrow family community, 1,500 acres of beautiful rolling prairies and rocky foothills. This land was settled in the year 1843 by the maternal great-grandfather of John Newport, William Lockhart Morrow (1817–1898).[4]

William Lockhart and Sarah Lydia Brown Morrow

After he had helped his father's family to resettle from Tennessee to Ozark, near Springfield, William set out at the age of twenty-five to find his own way. He traveled north a distance of thirty miles and determined that the verdant region of the state near Buffalo, north of Springfield, was to be his new home. Once his land was acquired and his homestead established, he returned to Durant, Mississippi, to court the girl he loved. William and Sarah Lydia Brown married in 1844.[5] She was twenty-one, and William twenty-seven, when they packed their wedding gifts to trundle the 445 wagon miles from Mississippi to their new homestead in Missouri.[6]

Within five years, Buffalo became a thriving community, and William Morrow was among its leading citizens. His land lay just beyond the Buffalo township limits. He served as Dallas County postmaster and treasurer, and as a leading layman in the Methodist Church that he had helped to build upon land he and Sarah had donated. He opened a mercantile business, purchasing goods in St. Louis and transporting them by wagon to Buffalo.[7] By 1859, on the eve of the Civil War, William and Sarah were parents to a dozen children. They had six of their own and took into their care William's six youngest siblings after his father and stepmother died in a cholera epidemic that passed through the Ozarks in 1849.[8]

The Civil War brought much danger to the Morrows of Buffalo. Guerilla warfare waged by radicals on both sides of the conflict ravaged the civilian population, and murder, violence, thievery, and arson were rampant.[9] Despite the harrowing hardships of this period, William and his family returned to Buffalo following the war and began to resettle their lives. They thrived. William began to purchase land, amassing some fifteen hundred acres in the region.[10] He served as county treasurer from 1858–1860 and, in 1880, was elected to represent Dallas County in the state legislature, serving two terms until 1882. In 1888, William sold his family business to his son, William L. Jr., and retired from the concerns of commerce, living another decade as an honored citizen of Missouri and a devout leader in his Methodist church.[11]

George Washington and Mary Ann Welch Morrow

The youngest son and third child of William and Sarah was George Washington Morrow (1863–1952), who was born and reared in Buffalo and continued in the family business of his father and brothers. The Morrows were well-respected as grocery, general merchandise, and hardware providers in their region of the state for at least four generations. George married Mary Ann Welch Van der Voort (Vanderford, 1867–1972) in 1887, and they had one daughter, Mildred Dupont Morrow, who would become John's mother. It was this grandmother, Mary Ann, who shared with John her maternal heritage, originally from Holland, through Illinois, and her paternal heritage from the Welch families of Cambridge and Wales.[12] It was also this daughter Mildred who connected the families of Morrow to the Newports when she met and married Marvin Jackson (Jack) Newport, whose people had migrated from England to Tennessee to Buffalo many generations before.

The Newports

Like the Morrows, the Newports were long-standing residents of Dallas County, Missouri. The ancestor who left England to come to the New World was John Richard Newport (1697–1746), who had married his wife Elizabeth Harriet Burnett (1697–1746) in 1742 in St. Mark's Parish and settled in the Orange County area of the Virginia Colony. Their son, Reverend Richard Newport (1744–1825), married Hannah Hines (1767–1847)[13] and settled in Tennessee in Knox County, where Richard served the rest of his days as a pastor. Their son Calvin Newport followed in his father's Baptist ministry footsteps.

Calvin Newport was born in Bull Run, northwest of Knoxville, in 1806. He was reared as the son of a pastor and was trained in theology and Scripture. He became a well-known and respected Baptist pastor, like his father before him. He married Margaret Abel, from Wythe County, Virginia, in 1828, and together they had six children.[14] Among them was John Newport's paternal great-grandfather, John David Newport.

John David and Harriet Narcissus Bennett Newport

Sometime around 1850, about seven years after Buffalo had been established, members of the Newport and Bennett families migrated to Missouri from Roane County, Tennessee.[15] John David Newport (1832–1907), along with his parents and eight of his siblings, was among the travelers. When he was twenty years old, he met Harriet Narcissus Bennett (1837–1891), whose family had also come from Roane County, near Knoxville. They married in 1852 and had eleven children together.[16] Moses Calvin was their firstborn, and the grandfather of John Newport.

Moses Calvin Newport and Sarah Ellen Brooks

Moses Calvin was born in 1855 and grew up on the farm along with his father and siblings. He was a wanderer, dreaming of other places and unexplored wildernesses. He was also finely skilled in the raising of cattle and horses. As a young man, he began to travel with his brothers to the northwest to sell livestock. He met Sarah Ellen Brooks, also of Dallas County, Missouri, at home in Buffalo, where she was a teacher at the school there. He was very impressed with her culture, background, and family.

Sarah Ellen's father, Matthew Brooks, had been born about 1833 in Lancashire, north of Liverpool, England. He had come to New York as a young man, where he had studied hard and finished medical school, even though his family had rejected him for migrating to America. Upon his graduation, he moved to Wisconsin, where he took up the practice of medicine. Here he met and married Mary Achsa West in 1855. She had been born in 1832 in Castle Creek, Broome County, New York, and had been reared a devout Baptist, as were all of her West family. Matthew and Mary then moved to Bourbon, Kansas, where he served as a pioneer physician. Sarah Ellen was born in 1857. Just months afterwards, while he was attending patients during an epidemic of influenza, Matthew also contracted the virus and died. On his deathbed, he requested that his only child be sent back to Wisconsin, where her relatives, the Wests, would provide for her education.

After Dr. Brooks died, Sarah's mother, Mary Achsa, married John William Barrick in 1859, and she and John moved to Dallas County.[17] When Sarah Ellen was twelve years old, her father's wish was fulfilled when she was sent to live in Wisconsin with her mother's relatives. There she finished grade school, high school, and attended college. With her education complete, she moved back to Buffalo and became a teacher. Ellen, as she was called, was accomplished, intelligent, witty, and cultured. She met the dashing, adventurous Moses Calvin Newport and they married in 1879.

In later years, John Newport would write that his grandfather Moses was a "restless man" with a constant urge to "go west!" Moses would often travel to Oregon and Washington and stay a year or more before returning home, trading in livestock and enjoying the freedom of the untamed, vast forests and coasts of the northwest territory. Sarah Ellen spent many years as a traveling companion to Moses. In fact, of their five children, the first two, Lloyd and Roy, were born in Clatsop, Oregon, while their last three, Ola, Marvin, and Achsa, were born in Buffalo.[18] Marvin would become John Newport's father. As John Newport grew to adulthood, he knew and loved his paternal Grandmother Ellen, who was extremely influential in his life. She is the one God used to affirm his call to the ministry.[19]

Marvin Jackson (Jack) and Mildred Dupont Morrow Newport

The two people who joined the refined Methodist Morrows with the cultured Baptist Newports were Marvin "Jack" Newport and Mildred Dupont Morrow. They met in Buffalo and married in August 1916. The two families were very close and amiable, including aunts and uncles, grandparents and great-grandparents, on both sides.[20] They were prominent families and well-respected in the region. Jack and Mildred had four children: John, Russell E., Jack Winston, and Mary Ellen.

Marvin continued in the same business as his mother's family, owning several variety or "five and dime" stores, as they were then called, in southern Missouri and northern Arkansas. Jack Newport's stores were called "Newport" and "Ben Franklin," and he and Sam Walton were in the same business, both having grown up in the Ozarks and in the merchandise business.[21]

The family remembers Jack as a stalwart, strict, hardworking man. He did not have a college education, but was intelligent, determined, and empathetic to those around him. Known as a soul-winner and an energetic member of the First Baptist Church, he was magnanimous with his time, influence, and finances, supporting church, community, businesses, and culture in the city. Marvin valued education at all levels and worked industriously to provide the necessities of life for his family, which for him included higher education for his children. His successful business was the result of wisdom, conscientiousness, and skill. John's mother, Mildred, was gentle, very kind, and loved unconditionally. Appreciating music and culture, she played the piano and organ, was deeply involved in the activities of their Baptist church, like her husband, and nurtured the hearts and minds of her children. Marvin and Mildred were wonderful people who loved their Lord and their family well.

Heritage as Foundation

John Newport's foundational perspectives were shaped by generations of family values: strong faith, hard work, faithful marriages, loving families, the pursuit of education, positive change, and progressive ideas. Of long-living and industrious stock, John Newport's people on both sides of the family were upright, conscientious, and devoutly Christian. His lineage was filled with people who transformed their surroundings and brought benefit to others.

The Morrows were of Methodist roots and the Newports were predominately Baptists. These two traditions helped John to see the things of God from more than one perspective. His heritage stemmed from Europe, England, Holland, the Northwest, the Appalachians, and the Ozarks. His grandfather and uncles explored the wildernesses of the west and brought back their knowledge and appreciation of still more ancient wisdom, ways of learning, and cultures. All of these rivulets of heritage coalesced into the stream that birthed John and his siblings.

Conscious of these geographical, cultural, spiritual, and familial influences upon his thinking and early development, in later years, as John took pen to paper to retrace his life, he began here, in the seedbed of what he would later shape into his biblical worldview, and counted his background as a treasure. He was Eurocentric and Protestant and American. He was a son of dark Missouri soil, yet he was not bound to the land itself. His opportunities came from the other realms—from commerce, culture, and education—and he took full advantage of these gifts that others had established so securely for him.

John, six months old, at Christmas in 1917

2
An Ozark Boy and His Cumberland Girl

> All that happens to us, including our humiliations, our misfortunes,
> our embarrassments, all is given to us as raw material, as clay,
> so that we may shape our art.
>
> **J. L. Borges**[1]

Not far from Springfield and Bolivar, Missouri, lay the small town of Buffalo, population 833, and the seat of Dallas County, where Marvin Jack and Mildred Morrow Newport settled after their marriage.[2] Here John Paul Newport was born at home on 16 June 1917. He was welcomed into their strong, evangelical Christian family. Each of them had experienced "new birth" and loved the Bible and its teachings. Their relationships with Christ were the center of their existence together, and as their family grew, they instilled a love of Jesus and the Scriptures into the life of their firstborn son and his siblings.[3] The man John Newport became was shaped by his earliest, sometimes intangible, though indelible influences: his intimate childhood home and relationships, his life-changing conversion, and his primary and secondary educations that laid the bedrock upon which his later life emerged. John's call to ministry, his seminary training, and his choice of a life partner were further significant influences.

John and his brother Russell in 1921

John's maternal grandparents were models of godly living. John remembered how, as a child, he would bundle up on cold, dark, Ozark nights and walk beside his maternal grandfather, George Washington Morrow, to prayer meetings, the path lit by the flickering glow of a lantern his grandfather held aloft to light the way. He would never forget his mother's worn Scofield Bible, family prayers at meals and evenings, and the consistent, deep spiritual and moral values of all of his parents, grandparents, and relatives.[4] This home and community fostered a love for Christ and an abiding confidence in both experiential faith and the truth of God's Word.

John's parents loved people. His father, Jack, was known by everyone in the county. As a strong deacon in the Baptist Church, Jack modeled churchmanship for his family. Each week, the Newports attended not only two Sunday services, but Sunday School, Training Union, Wednesday night Bible Study, prayer, teacher, and committee meetings too. He and Mildred served on several committees and supported all of the local, state, and national Baptist mission causes. They gave regularly of offerings, time, and skills to support God's work. With consistent empathy, most of the time behind the scenes, Jack and Mildred would care for families who were struggling or who had fallen on hard times. They funded the education of young "preacher boys," sent young people to Baptist Student Union conventions, and distributed Gideon Bibles. With a quiet and pastoral manner, Jack would visit in homes, let his pastor know of those for whom he was praying for salvation, and request visits for those who needed Christ's comfort. Quiet and industrious, upright and devoted, Jack and Mildred were bedrocks of their Buffalo church and community.

Jack loved to hunt and fish and was proud when his children and later grandchildren shared his love of outdoors.[5] John's mother, Mildred was gentle, very kind, and loved unconditionally. Her culture was evident in her well-kept home, her love of music, her skill with the piano and organ. She, too, was involved in the activities of their Baptist church and excelled in the nurturing of her children and the formation of their character.

Conversion and Transformation

In the fall of 1927, when John was ten years old, he attended a series of revival meetings at his home Baptist church in Buffalo. The church, as was the custom in those days, would enter into a "season of revival," holding weeks of prayer before the scheduled week of meetings. The children would be taught the plan of salvation from the New Testament and the names of all children above eight years of age would be placed on a special prayer list for the upcoming revival services. John studied along with the other children and was captivated, for the first time, by the truths of Christ's life and work. John later wrote:

> The evangelist took one week to preach the horrors of being lost now and in eternity. Then he told of God sending Christ to die for us and raising him to God's right hand to give *power*. He told us the Holy Spirit was convicting us. The altar call was given. As a ten-year-old lad, I went forward to accept Christ as my personal Savior.[6]

Soon afterward, he was baptized on a cold, fall afternoon in the nearby Greasy Creek. His Methodist cousins, "who had been sprinkled as infants," he later said, "made much sport of me for belonging to a religious group that required such an inconvenient ceremony."[7]

John (middle), Russell (left), and Jack (right) in 1930

John's father and mother were conscientious about the spiritual growth and development of their three sons. Evangelism and missions permeated their lives, John would later recall. His Baptist fellowship was aflame with New Testament and prophetic studies that provided an urgent motivation for reaching the non-churched and those without knowledge of Christ. When John was a teenager, his mother often took the three brothers to Baptist Hill, an encampment located in Mt. Vernon, Missouri. Encircled by the bend of the beautiful "Big Spring," where John and his brothers canoed and swam, and close to Rebel's Bluff for hiking treks, this was a place to hear God speak. It was at Baptist Hill that John first heard L. R. Scarborough preach when Scarborough was in his prime. His famous sermon, "Lost," was one John never forgot.[8]

In his mid-teens, John began to take on an intense desire for learning that was remarkable, even in this family that valued education so highly. John had an obsession for reading and this set him apart, even as a child.[9] He excelled in the public schools of Buffalo, where he attended all grades through high school. His teachers found in John a keen mind and an avid and unusual curiosity for most subjects. He loved language arts and rhetoric, science and social studies, enjoyed music and mathematics, and honed his skills, fostered by Baptist Young People's Union at church, both to debate and communicate well.[10] He was an athlete, playing most sports with ease, although basketball was his favorite game both in high school and in college.

University Days and Call to Ministry

When the time came for John to earn his bachelor's degree, he was presented with two strong colleges from which to choose. John's maternal side of the family, devoutly Methodist, urged him to attend the Methodist Central College of Missouri (now Central Methodist University), in Fayette, founded in 1854. Since John was a Baptist, however, he chose instead to earn his undergraduate degree from William Jewell College in Liberty, Missouri, which had a long tradition dating back to 1849 when it sat at the edge of the American wilderness.

William Jewell was associated at the time with the American Baptist Convention (formerly Northern Baptist Convention), and Dr. John F. Herget, a Baptist minister, served as its president from 1928 to 1942. Because of a strong recommendation from Lawrence Cleland of Buffalo, Dr. Herget drove 250 miles to meet and invite the young John Newport to study at William Jewell and to offer him an academic scholarship. John accepted.

John's Methodist cousins good-naturedly ribbed him about his choice. Most of John's ministerial student friends did too, for they had chosen to attend non-Baptist institutions. August Hinz, for example, enrolled at Colgate Rochester, and Bernard Magruder went to Yale, where "Baptist Student Union announcements were booed in Chapel" at the time, wrote John later in life. When W. O. Vaught, who served as the state director of Baptist Student Union, first came to Yale, the students published a "yellow sheet" deriding him.[11] John's mind was set, however, despite the ridicule. He neither agreed with, nor was intimidated by, those who thought that conservative, Bible-centered education was outmoded.[12]

William Jewell College

John enrolled at William Jewell College in the fall of 1934. It was located 155 miles northwest of Buffalo in a 200-acre rural setting, in a suburb of one of the most colorful Midwestern cities, Kansas City, known as "the Springboard to the West." Here, college life was new and "exciting almost beyond description," he wrote home, and offered avenues of learning that both ignited and challenged John's mind and captured his emotions. He became involved in campus politics, joined the basketball team, and even, against his better judgment, he admitted, pledged to a fraternity. The church and his personal spiritual growth, he said, faded to the periphery of his life.[13] He began to drift.

John studied hard, engrossed with history, literature, the arts, and philosophy. He learned to read and write better and polished his speaking skills. From the demanding English assignments and courses providing historical and cultural perspectives to the opportunities to join a national debate tour, his college life prepared him for graduate study and his future. The diverse student body afforded him wide-ranging friendships. Because of the relatively small size of the student body, opportunities for numerous student leadership positions opened to him.

In his rare free moments, John ambled the countryside and thought about life and its meaning. The Scopes Trials of 1925, held in Dayton, Tennessee, were as fresh to his college mind as they had been as an eight-year-old boy when he had heard the sessions with his family in the evenings, broadcasted by radio to every home in America.[14] During this time, he also met a friend whose father was a physician and was introduced to the world of medicine. This new realm fascinated him. Finally, he had for some time been aware that the Unity School's World Headquarters was located not far from his college, near Kansas City.[15] Now, however, the worldview disseminated by the Unity School, with its close associations with Christian Science, New Thought, and mind-body healings, contained ideas with which he not only learned, but wrestled. John would later cite these fertile ideas, as well as many examples of "great divides between perspectives and denominations" that shaped his life and thinking during this period.[16]

World War I Era

While John lived in the college dorm, played basketball, expanded his thinking, and made the library his second home, the world was engaged in escalating turmoil, events rapidly unfolding in alarming ways. In the White House, President Franklin D. Roosevelt, president from 1933 to 1945,[17] paced the Oval Office in his first term, seeking relief from the Great Depression that had devastated America's economy and dropped her national production by 80 percent. He had signed into law the New Deal in 1933, bent on restoring relief for the unemployed and the poor, recovering the economy to normal levels, and reforming the financial system in order to prevent another collapse in the future.[18]

Amidst the deprivation of economic ravages, the cultural heartbeats of America in New York City and Hollywood, California, were unsure whether the public either could afford or would choose to attend theaters. Despite predictions to the contrary, the nation's people flocked to the movies during the Depression, as entertainments seemed to help ease the burdens of everyday workers. After all, Roosevelt had encouraged citizens to live as normally as possible. These were the years of Hollywood's evolution from silent films to "talkies," the growing influence of film media, and movie stars like Jean Harlow, Katharine Hepburn, Cary Grant, and Clark Gable. The nail-biter movie *King Kong* hit the screens in 1933, followed by the popular comedy *Bringing Up Baby* in 1938, and *Stagecoach* the following year.

At the same time, beyond the borders of the United States, global events were building like ominous black thunderclouds. Mussolini mobilized Italian armies following his takeover of Abyssinia in 1935, preparing to seize more territory. Hitler's rise to power in Germany, his buildup to his invasion of Austria in 1938, and of Poland the year after, only foreshadowed the atrocities that would come in the next decade. Britain's Prime Minister, Neville Chamberlain, and France's Premier, Édouard Daladier, in an attempt to prevent further German aggression, tried a reasonable approach of appeasement with disappointing results. Every day, the radio reported the darkening news to the students at William Jewell. For a young man, intent upon his studies, these were tense times in which to live.

Debate Team

John was well aware of the events unfolding across the world. He had been invited to join the National Eastern Debate Tour in 1937–1938 and immersed himself in research focusing upon global political, economic, and military events in order to present his arguments. So that the William Jewell debate team could save on travel and event expenses during these lean years, they generally lodged in fraternity houses on the campuses they visited. John shared later that he was disheartened and repulsed by some of the extremes of drunkenness and sexual immorality he witnessed.[19] Nonetheless, the debate tour was life-changing for John in other ways, flooding his mind with new experiences and avenues of thought, both of which he drank in and processed intellectually.

He traveled to Center College, Kentucky, Florida's Rollins College near Orlando, and colleges in Georgia and North Carolina. At Dartmouth College, his interest in Orozco, the Mexican muralist, was aroused when he viewed the newly completed mural of Mexican culture in the Baker Library on campus. Then he traveled to Michigan and Indiana, noting cultural differences along the way and trying to discover their sources. When John's team debated George Washington University in Washington, D.C., something remarkable happened. John was serving that year as president of the National Student Congress and had the pleasure of interviewing President Franklin Delano Roosevelt for twenty minutes.[20]

The team debated Yale, and then Harvard, where the dean of Harvard Law School, himself a graduate of William Jewell College, interviewed John for a possible scholarship and admission to study for a law degree. As John shared about his background, his parents' concern for spiritual values, and his own interest in service organizations, the dean replied firmly, "We don't give [the slightest concern] about these influences. We are chiefly interested in your intellectual abilities."[21] The dean promptly awarded John a three-year scholarship to Harvard Law School, about the same time that he was honored as a regional finalist for the Rhodes Scholars program.

Meanwhile, a small group of Christian young people on campus at William Jewell, active in the Baptist Student Union (BSU), became concerned about John's spiritual condition. For almost a year these young men and women prayed for him in their daily prayer meetings. Through a friendship formed with one of the young women in this group, John was invited to and attended the state BSU convention, and because of the messages he heard there, his heart began to return to the God of his earlier years. Although he was not a ministerial student at the time, the spiritual perspectives that had been his heritage and earliest experiences, combined with those undergirded and enhanced by William Jewell's religion courses, chapel programs, devout professors, and the Christian atmosphere of the school, began to crystallize into what became the focus of his life. John's mind and heart locked in to following Christ.

Call to Ministry

One week in 1937, George W. Truett, the famous pastor of the First Baptist Church of Dallas, Texas, and a Baptist statesman, came to the Baptist church in Liberty to preach a series of revival services.[22] Some of the

John at William Jewell College, 1937

fraternity brothers attended and sat in the balcony to jeer. When a number of them were converted, however, John was struck by the Spirit's power of transformation in their lives, and this added to his enlarging confidence in God's plan for the world in general and his life in particular.

Another significant week in John's pilgrimage back to the faith of his childhood happened just following his graduation from college in the spring of 1938. He had earned his Bachelor of Arts degree in History in May of that year. The next month, as a graduation present, John was given a trip to the Southern Baptist Student Union Conference at Ridgecrest, North Carolina. There, John saw more than a thousand young people, just as attractive as those he had observed in the fraternities and sororities on his debate tours. John was amazed, impacted by their joyful exuberance and steady faithfulness to Christ. They were aware of the world's crises and expressed deep concerns about the moral and spiritual needs of the world.

In contrast with the debauchery he had earlier witnessed on college campuses across the eastern portion of the United States, these young men and women were used by God to shape John's future vocational calling. It was at this meeting at Ridgecrest that John committed his life to what was then termed "putting Christ first."[23]

Seminary Days

In the following weeks, the state BSU director, W. O. Vaught, asked John to give his testimony in several services of youth revivals in the state of Missouri. Less than a month before he was to leave for law school, John came under the conviction that God was calling him into the Christian ministry. At that late date, and at the last minute, Vaught helped John to be admitted to Southern Seminary in Louisville, even though his Harvard room had already been secured and the down payment on his tuition paid. John packed his bags and moved to Louisville instead. Noting later that he was ill prepared for the ministry, John wrote,

> I knew little about the Bible. I had no Greek or Hebrew. I hardly knew anyone on campus. I grew discouraged. In fact, I wrote to the law school and asked if I could still be accepted on the scholarship. Fortunately, a campus revival was held and in that context I realized that I had neglected my personal devotional life in the midst of academic study. I also realized that I was full of self-pity and was not even taking advantage of the opportunities for Christian service that were available to me.[24]

John leaped into ministry with all the fervor of his being. His next few months were consumed with the youth evangelism movement that was sweeping the Southern Baptist Convention at the time. In his first year of seminary, John volunteered to serve as codirector of the City-Wide Youth Revival. He then became involved in preaching and organizing so many youth revivals that a seminary faculty graduate committee warned him that he would have to choose between staying in his graduate program or becoming a full-time evangelist. He then settled into routines of classes, preparation, writing, and ministry. From 1939 to 1943, he became pastor of two churches simultaneously: the Crab Orchard Baptist Church and the Drakes Creek Baptist Church, both near Louisville.

John Newport's Ordination Certificate, 1939

Crab Orchard Baptist Church Crusade, John Newport, Pastor, c. 1940

In his third year of seminary, as America was on the brink of war, he met someone who would change the course of his life—the elegant Miss Eddie Belle Leavell.

The Cumberland Girl

Eddie Belle Leavell was the daughter of the renowned Dr. Frank Hartwell and Martha Maria Boone Leavell.[25] Her parents were both devout Southern Baptists. In fact, Eddie Belle's father was the middle child of nine famous Leavell brothers from Oxford, Mississippi, most of whom were full-time Southern Baptist preachers, missionaries, teachers, or denominational workers.[26]

Eddie Belle was the eldest child, born on 12 June 1919 in Memphis, Tennessee, into this illustrious family. Her younger sister, Mary Martha Leavell, was born more than three years later on 2 January 1923, and their youngest brother, Frank Hartwell Leavell Jr., arrived almost on Eddie Belle's ninth birthday on 16 June 1928, after the family had moved to Nashville, the headquarters of the Southern Baptist Convention (SBC).[27] Eddie Belle was reared to care for other people, beginning with her siblings.

Eddie Belle's home life was unique. As she grew, she became accustomed to a father who frequently traveled and whose primary passion was focused upon ministries to college students. Her childhood and teenage years were spent at home, focused on family, church life, the larger Baptist denomination, and education. As the daughter of a prominent SBC leader, she watched her father's vibrant devotion to Christ and the church and purposed to walk in similar traces. She longed, from her earliest years, to "make a difference; to be of service to others," which was her lifelong and oft-stated desire.[28]

Eddie Belle remained living at home in Nashville during her first two years of college, attending the historic women's Ward-Belmont College, now Belmont University, from 1937 to 1938. While she was a student there, she was a member of both the Math Club and the Angkor Club, the latter of which was based upon the culture and ideals of India, and known for its athleticism, scholarship, and citizenship.[29] Graduating in 1938 with a general degree, she turned her energies toward pursuing further education.

Eddie Belle moved to Raleigh, North Carolina, where she attended the all-female Meredith College for two years, graduating in the spring of 1941 with a degree in English.[30] During her junior and senior years at Meredith, Eddie Belle was active in many clubs: the Baptist Student

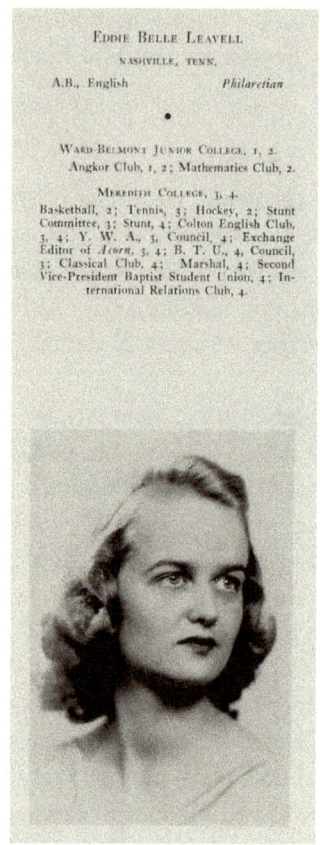

Eddie Belle Leavell at Meredith College in 1940

Union, The Colton English Club, where she served as "Exchange Editor" both years for the campus paper "The Acorn," and the Helen Hull Law Classical Club. She also served as Chief Marshall of the Philaretian Literary Society. She shot archery and played tennis and team sports—lacrosse, basketball, and field hockey. Accomplished, athletic, and scholarly, interested in law, mathematics, and international topics, able to write and communicate well, this Baptist daughter of Frank and Martha Leavell brought distinction to her family's reputation.

Following her graduation, as war was raging across Europe, Eddie Belle was twenty-two years old and serving as a social worker in Davidson County, Tennessee, when John met her at Ridgecrest Baptist Assembly in the summer of 1941.[31] Reared to be scrupulously honest and devoted to the honor of her family, this upright, determined, and thoroughly Southern girl was as graceful as she was lovely. She was exceptionally bright, with manners and social grace to rival any queen. Eddie Belle was an unusual young woman. Her keen intellect, her commitment to Christ, an intense longing to be of service to others, and a profound curiosity about the world made her instantly attractive to John. As soon as he met her at the student conference, John was smitten.

Almost at once, John was convinced that she was the one he wanted to share his life with. He found himself captivated by her mind and vivacity. She understood him, listened to him, and conversed with deep insight about matters of the mind and heart. She loved the same things about which he was passionate. Later he would remark that she was his "enabler, a companion of the years, the love of his life, and the real Baptist in the family with a vital sense of the liberty found in Christ."[32] Eddie Belle was John's equal in every way. They were married on 14 November 1941 at the First Baptist Church of Nashville, her home church, where John's brother, Russell, served as best man. John and Eddie Belle honeymooned nearby in Gatlinburg.

Influences of First Pastorates and Family Life

Their first home together was in Kentucky, where John continued his studies at Southern Baptist Theological Seminary and Eddie Belle shared the ministry load as the pastor's new wife at the Crab Orchard and Drakes Creek Baptist churches. Following John's graduation in 1942 with his Master of Theology degree, he stayed to earn a Doctor in Theology degree, which he completed in 1945 just as the last months of the war were drawing to a close. His degree was in New Testament with an emphasis in apocalyptic literature of the Bible and the Intertestamental Period.

John and Eddie Belle then moved to Clinton, Mississippi, where John was called to pastor the Clinton Baptist Church that stood adjacent to the Mississippi College campus, the premier Baptist college in the state. Both townspeople and university students and faculty were members of this church, where John learned the complexities of thoughtful interaction in the midst of evolving academic advances. Many, many college students questioned their pastor about the problems of suffering, evil, and the occult. John studied thoughtfully, trying his best to answer their questions. From these sessions came his popular series, "Skeptic and Apologist," in the periodical *The Baptist Student*. The editor defined an apologist, in this series, as "one who gives a spirited defense of the faith capable of holding its own among all other systems of knowledge."[33] John authored several articles in these years to address these questions of faith. During these fruitful days of ministry, a daughter, Martha Ellen, was born to John and Eddie Belle on 24 January 1946.

Later that year, John moved to Edinburgh, Scotland, where he began to work on his Ph.D. at the University of Edinburgh.[34] Eddie Belle and Martha settled with her mother and father in Nashville, Tennessee, until John could finish his term of studies. This was a wonderful and poignant season for Eddie Belle to spend with her parents, for her father died in 1949 while she was with them.

Upon his return from Scotland, John and Eddie answered a call from the Immanuel Baptist Church in Tulsa, where he served as pastor from 1948 to 1949. Frank Marvin was born on 1 November 1948 as the ministry was flourishing.[35] From 1949 to 1951, the Newport family lived in Waco, Texas, where John taught at Baylor University as an associate professor and director of graduate studies in religion. During the next academic year, from 1951 to 1952, John moved his family to New Orleans, where he taught as associate professor of philosophy of religion and New Testament at the New Orleans Baptist Theological Seminary.

Their final move of this period was to Southwestern Baptist Theological Seminary in Fort Worth, Texas, where John joined the faculty as associate professor of philosophy of religion in the fall of 1952. Fort Worth was their home when John and Eddie Belle welcomed their third and last child into the family on 2 April 1954. This son was given his father's name, John Paul Newport Jr.[36] John served at Southwestern for the rest of his career, except for a year's sabbatical at Harvard, studying under Paul Tillich, in 1958 to 1959, and the three years he spent at Rice University, in the Harry Chavanne Endowed Chair of Religion, in Houston, Texas.

It was John's teaching career at Southwestern Seminary that would define both his ministry and academic investment. From 1952 until his retirement in 1990, and for another teaching decade following, John Newport's influence in classrooms, pulpits, lecterns, and in the hearts of his students was monumental. Through the second half of the twentieth century, Newport became a resounding voice for an evangelical Christian apologetic, one of the few in Baptist life at the time, known for his weaving of disparate strands of knowledge from various intellectual disciplines into a "coherent, comprehensive, creative, and fulfilling biblical worldview"[37] which he sought to incarnate and share with others.

Before John stepped in front of a lectern, however, he sought to train his mind. From what sources did young John Newport turn for this preparation? For answers, one must trace the thought-mentors that filled the reservoirs of John's soul and guided him to understand the swirling layers of the world through the lens of biblical authenticity. It is to an examination of these various unusual and creative streams of thought that the next chapter turns. The year he enrolled in seminary was 1939.

3
Streams of Knowledge
1939–1949

> Wear the old coat and buy the new book.
>
> **Rev. Austin Phelps**[1]

Even as a young man, John Newport had an insatiable quest for knowledge. He valued his years at William Jewell, for there his world had widened, his faith had both declined and then matured rapidly, his abilities to read, focus, and analyze had been sharpened, and his skills in oratory and apologetics were honed. When God called him into the gospel ministry, however, he felt that he had not been adequately equipped to fulfill his vocation. He needed further training.

He turned from his previously planned trajectory of law, and his Harvard scholarship, and enrolled instead at the Southern Baptist Theological Seminary (SBTS) in Louisville, Kentucky. He intentionally steered his life and future into the current of lifelong learning in biblical studies, theology, philosophy, and the world of ideas. His six years of study and ministry, between 1939 and 1946 in Louisville, and the year from 1946 to 1947 in Edinburgh, Basel, and Zurich, together with his subsequent pastorates, fed this current, which became swifter and deeper by the year. A closer examination of Newport's intellectual mentors helps to inform the scholar he became just a few years later.

The Southern Baptist Theological Seminary

When John moved to Louisville, Kentucky, before he was even married, he found an intellectual and theological home with the faculty at SBTS. With his endless appetite for books and an unquenchable curiosity, learning was sheer joy. He spent a great deal of time, apart from sermon preparation and ministry focus, thinking about what he was reading, searching out other students and faculty members to discuss new ideas he was processing, and synthesizing the new with the familiar.

He was extremely disciplined, setting strict times for study and rarely varying his schedule. He developed patterns during these years that would serve him the rest of his days. Rising early each morning, he would spend several hours in Bible reading and sermon study. In between classes and afterward, he would study additional hours, often leaving the supper table to return to his work before retiring to bed.

In the classrooms of Southern Seminary, five professors became lifelong intellectual mentors, influencing John's approaches to Scripture, theology, religions, and the cultures of the world's inhabitants. In later years he recalled their monumental investment in the development of his mind: H. C. Goerner, William Hersey Davis, James McKee Adams, W. O. Carver, and Gaines Dobbins. The writing of E. Y. Mullins also influenced him.

John took his first philosophy course with Henry Cornell Goerner (1908–1998), his missions professor, who later became famous as an executive with the Foreign Mission Board of the SBC and perhaps the most influential authority on global missions and evangelism during the first half of the twentieth century.[2] This young professor lit John's passion for comparative religions, one that remained a central focus of his teaching and study through the years.

William Hersey Davis (1887–1950) was another of John's mentors. Davis was professor of New Testament Interpretation at Southern from 1920 to 1948.[3] Known as a keen scholar, he had coauthored *A New Short Grammar of the Greek Testament* (1931) with his department chair, Archibald Thomas Robertson, and focused his teaching on the grammatical-historical method of textual interpretation. When Robertson died in 1934, Davis became head of the New Testament department. In the last decade of Davis' life, he became John Newport's New Testament professor and prompted John's interest in his doctoral research topic.[4]

John sat under the teaching of other influential professors as well. James McKee Adams (1886–1945) was a theologian, biblical lecturer, enthusiastic professor of Biblical Backgrounds, and author of numerous textbooks. When John hosted his first tour to the Middle East in 1955, he took Adams' four volumes along to provide the content for his lectures.[5]

William Owen Carver (1868–1954), the famous missiologist, was also one of John's professors. Joining the faculty as a New Testament professor from 1896 until his retirement in 1943,[6] he offered a course in comparative religions in 1899 and opened the missions department in 1900, which he then directed for almost a half a century. He was a recognized authority in his field, ecumenically and theologically progressive, and one of the first named to the American theological committee of the World Council on Faith and Order in 1948. From this scholar's large heart and broadened perspective, John learned the benefits of ecumenical dialogue and a sense of shared respect when religious questions arise between persons of different faith traditions. This respectful dialogue became a characteristic of John Newport as well.

When John enrolled in Gaines Stanley Dobbins' (1886–1978) class, Dobbins was already legendary across the SBC for his work in church administration, pastoral care, missions, evangelism, and Christian education. His emphasis upon each person's value as a human being created in the image of God was a hallmark of every aspect of his scholarship and teaching. John was astounded at the number of Dobbins' publications in the area of practical Christianity and appreciated Dobbins' expertise as a pioneer of church growth.[7] His book, *Evangelism According to Christ*, was John's handbook on soul-winning in the local church when he became a full-time pastor following his graduation.

John often stated that during these years he was persuaded by the writings of E. Y. Mullins (1860–1928), the famous Baptist minister, SBTS president, theologian, and professor.[8] As the acknowledged Baptist leader across the southland, Mullins had a profound influence. During his tenure as president of the SBC from 1921 to 1924, and as president of the Baptist World Alliance in 1928, Mullins became known for his firm but conciliatory manner that invited dialogue between factious groups.

Mullins' philosophical approach deeply informed John's thinking. In Mullins' *The Axioms of Religion*, John was introduced to the comprehensive view of all knowledge, which preserved the Christian scholar from having to choose between faith and reason, Scripture and science. In addition,

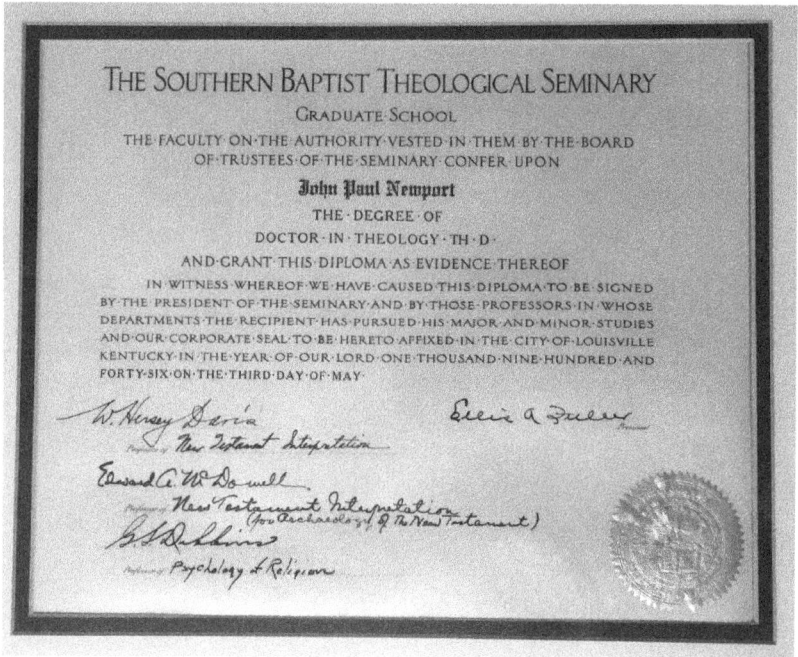

John Newport's Th.D. Diploma from Southern Seminary, 1946

Mullins' strong Calvinistic stance also impacted John to the extent that, when he took his degree from the University of Edinburgh, he explored Calvin's use of the linguistic and historic principles of biblical exegesis.

After graduating from Southern Seminary, where John had earned his M.Th. in 1942 and his Th.D. four years later, he received a letter from Clinton, Mississippi, with an invitation to become pastor of the Baptist church in the heart of that university town. The Newports accepted the invitation with joy.

Clinton, Oklahoma, and Mississippi College

When John and Eddie Belle drove up to the Clinton Baptist Church, they noticed immediately that it was directly across the street from the campus of Mississippi College. Here, John discovered the rich diversity and excitement of pastoring in a university setting, where ministering to faculty and students had both unique challenges and joys.

John became friends with dozens of professors and students, and many of these asked for help with their struggles about relating Enlightenment thought, secular humanism, and preliminary New Age ideas to their own academic areas of study. Many of them were finishing degrees at secular universities that were entrenched in these new ideas.[9] The tensions of alternative perspectives were sweeping through international academic circles as postwar Europeans learned to reconcile their disparate philosophies. John was determined in his soul to explore these larger ideas and to help his friends to understand their implications. He became convinced that he should train further in the fields of philosophy of religion, philosophical theology, or Christian apologetics.

Across the months, as John pastored and maintained close friendships with the faculty of Mississippi College, they encouraged him toward further study. He felt that the academic areas of apologetics and philosophy would be needed as the South became less isolated and as America became a stronger global power, interacting with the world's evolving political ideologies. When the war ended with the unconditional surrenders of Germany on 8 May 1945 and by Japan on 2 September 1945, the way was opened for John to turn his dream of focused study into reality.

John and Eddie Bell decided that John should pursue a course of study in Scotland and that Eddie Belle and tiny baby Martha Ellen

John (left), Navy Lieutenant Russell Newport (right), and their mother (in car)

would remain in Nashville in the home of her parents, with an occasional visit to Springfield to stay with the Newports. Eddie Belle hoped to join John for a time in Scotland after he was settled. The enthusiastic endorsement and support of both sets of parents added the final benediction. John resigned as pastor of the church, and he and Eddie Belle spent a few days at his parents' home in Springfield. He packed and arranged the finances he would need for his study before he traveled to New York to board ship.

Edinburgh, 1946–1947 and 1953

Newport set sail on 5 September 1946 aboard the *John Ericson*, outbound from New York Harbor to England's Plymouth Harbour, arriving at 6:00 a.m. nine days later. John traveled by rail to London to meet Reverend Stanley Plunkett, a Baptist pastor, and his Baptist deacon brother-in-law, Dr. C. W. J. Claydon. John was invited to stay in Elm Lodge in Half Moon Lane, the home of Claydon, for two days and nights. The two gentlemen hosted John to a tour of the area and John was astounded; he was dismayed to observe both the vast destruction caused by incendiary bombs and the depth of deprivation experienced by the people.

On 16 September, John departed London for Edinburgh on the 10:00 a.m. train and arrived by nightfall, pulling into the station at the foot of Castle Rock. For almost two weeks the family of Reverend Callum Patterson, pastor of the Bristo Baptist Church in the city, hosted John at their home at 25 Orchard Road South.[10] He wrote of those days, "I have eaten all of my meals here . . . they have used up much of their precious food and fuel for my comfort. Mr. Patterson's salary is 1,600 pounds per year. I cannot force them to accept one cent of money for these eight days."[11]

During the last week of September, John moved to Number 10 Carleton Terrace to take up room and board in the home of Mrs. Marie Evans.[12] After a few days of sightseeing and settling in, he then enrolled in New College, Edinburgh University, to earn a Ph.D. in the philosophy of religion. By 1 October he was in thrall to a busy schedule. He attended twenty-four lectures each week across six mornings. In the afternoons, he took German with Dr. Galzen, who had recently served as chaplain to the German Prisoner of War Camp, housed at Duff House, along the Banffshire coast in northeast Scotland.[13]

New College, Edinburgh

John Newport was keen to settle down to study. New College was recognized as one of the most renowned centers of postgraduate theological studies in the world, and its prestigious faculty was unmatched. Celebrating the centennial anniversary of its founding in 1946, the ethos of New College, embodying both tradition and modernity, fed John's desire to be saturated by wider knowledge and trained under the best minds he could find.[14]

The years immediately following the Great War were a time of change in the faculty at New College, marking a significant divide in the college's history. Students had left for battle and never returned. Replacements of students and faculty had dwindled during the years between the wars, and optimism seemed to have been shattered. A more sober mood had descended upon the churches and theology of Scotland.

During the privations of World War II, however, differing religious bodies joined forces, leading to an increased sense of cooperation between them, and this new spirit now defined the amalgamated faculty of New College. These were remarkable days for students, who gleaned the best from both distinguished faculties in a fresh chapter. Perhaps no other time was as propitious for John Newport to travel and study in Scotland than the years immediately following the Second War.

The wild beauty of "The Mound's" environs also drew from him a soul-song of poetic romanticism. In that magnificent and ancient city, rooted upon and arising from immense, imposing rock crags, John absorbed a rich culture common to both his family and early America. The gray castle walls and vivid moss of Arthur's Seat, the buoyant feel of peat-packed moors, and carved monuments, standing as silent sentinels across the centuries, opened his senses and fed his imagination. On rainy and bone-chilling days, John holed up in the university's libraries, reading historical, theological, and philosophical tomes and conversing with other students and faculty. These days nurtured his soul, which became indelibly stamped by makers of human history—David Hume, whose statue stood between St. Giles Kirk and the Castle atop the Royal Mile, and John Knox, reformer and preacher at St. Giles, in whom Newport was particularly interested.[15]

At New College, John was convinced that, better to understand the roots of Protestantism, he must engage in intensive study in the areas of biblical language, epistemology, and biblical literature, as they all related to the Protestant Reformation in general and John Calvin in particular. He noted a number of distinguished and famous scholars with whom he studied, each of whom poured into John's fertile mind and seeking heart those ideas that would shape his vocational calling and approach to scholarship.

Among those with whom he studied was professor of divinity John Baillie (1886–1960), a renowned theologian and minister of the Church of Scotland, who specialized in exploring the relationship of the knowledge of God to spiritual and moral experience.[16] With this elder philosopher-theologian, John Newport observed the art of statesmanship and conciliation. John Baillie was instrumental as the Convener of the Church of Scotland's General Assembly's "Commission for the Interpretation of God's Will in the Present Crisis" (the "Baillie Commission") that reported to the Assembly from 1941 to 1945. In this role, and as moderator of the General Assembly in 1943, Baillie guided that body as it considered its mission to the world following the war. John was a witness to the recasting of Christian truths as the world moved forward from the horrors of war and respected Baillie's efforts to lead his denomination to be strategic about addressing vast needs across the globe.

Another powerful influence upon John's thinking was the legendary professor of Christian dogmatics, Thomas Forsyth Torrance (1913–2007), who was known for his work relating science to theology, his many systematic theology volumes, and his translation of both Karl Barth's thirteen-volume, six-million-word *Church Dogmatics* (1956–1960) and Calvin's *New Testament Commentaries* (1964–1968).[17] Torrance's mind was formidable, yet he was a gentle soul, an ordained minister in the Church of Scotland and a reconciler of conflicting opinions on points of doctrine between faith traditions. Almost the same age, John Newport appreciated the keen insight afforded him by this young giant of a thinker. He also studied with G. T. Thompson, who worked with Torrance in the later translation of Barth's and Calvin's works.

James Stuart Stewart (1896–1990), known as one of the best preachers of the twentieth century, also impacted John's thinking in two areas—the art of building a sermon in order to communicate biblical truth and his translation of Schleiermacher's major work.[18] When John arrived as a student, Stewart was in his prime and had just resigned as pastor of Morningside Church to become professor of New Testament language, literature, and theology at New College. He made Christian orthodoxy both fascinating and applicable to daily life. Stewart's sermons emphasized a high view of the authority of Scripture and the supremacy of Jesus Christ as the incarnate God-Man. John was fresh from the pastorate himself, and his regular dialogues with Stewart and hearing Stewart preach crystallized John's ideal of the scholar-pastor. As an interim pastor for the rest of his life in more than fifty churches, John never forgot the deep influence that a scholar wields when he steps, prepared by study and the power of the Holy Spirit, into the pulpit. He had seen it firsthand in James Stewart.

William Manson (1882–1965) became John's New Testament and biblical criticism mentor from whom John learned much about broader approaches to interpreting the text than he had previously experienced.[19] It was this openness to understanding how other scholars thought and used methods of research that would come to characterize Newport's writing and thinking in later years. In two other offices down the hall from Manson and Stewart were the famous scholars Norman W. Porteous (1898–2003) and Oliver Shaw Rankin (1885–1954), both giants among Old Testament studies. Porteous, as chair of Hebrew and Semitic languages until his retirement in 1968, together with his roles as dean of the faculty and principal of New College, had postulated that an anonymous author wrote the book of Daniel during the persecution under the reign of Antiochus IV Epiphanes. He also taught the centrality of what the Old Testament itself calls "knowledge of God," by which it means non-speculative practicality resulting in right behavior.[20] Rankin held the chair of Old Testament language, literature, and theology and he sparked John's curiosity about Judaism with a special intensity. His work, focused on the ancient Semitic languages and the celebrations surrounding Hanukah, enlivened and enhanced John's respect for the Jewish faith tradition.[21]

John also became more appreciative of his own Christian and Protestant Reformation faith traditions as he learned from John Henderson Seaforth Burleigh (1894–1985), professor of ecclesiastical history and imminent author of the history of the Kirk of Scotland. His volume was required reading for all students who attended New College from its publication date of 1930 through the next three generations, including Newport. W. S. Tindal, one of the earliest sociologists in Great Britain at the time, influenced John to examine the cultures of particular peoples, including religions, death rituals, beliefs in afterlife, and customs. He had just moved to New College and was serving as chair of Christian sociology at New College when John arrived.

One of the most outstanding of all of John Newport's acquaintances at New College, however, was the Scottish philosopher, John Macmurray

(1891–1976), whose life and thought changed the course of twentieth-century political science, religion, education, and philosophy.[22] As a philosopher, Macmurray held views that diverted from the predominant themes of his day. He focused upon the primacy in human life of action as over against theory, and "his primary criticism of the Western philosophical tradition is that it begins from a theoretical, rather from than a practical, standpoint. In *The Self as Agent*, he critiques and corrects Descartes' 'I think' with 'I *do*,' a construction of the Self existing first and foremost as an agent of action in the world."[23]

With part of his mind, Newport was distinguishing between Western and European approaches to philosophy. With the other, he was pining for a reunion with Eddie Belle and Martha Ellen. To keep his mind from becoming distracted over their absence, as John sat in the libraries poring over books, absorbing and processing new ideas and information, he also made time for fresh experiences that opened his horizons in other ways.

One example was to observe how the Church of Scotland was strategically engaging with the arts and media as an attempt to reengage younger generations following World War II. Recasting drama as the "weapon of enlightenment," the Church of Scotland experimented with novel ways to relay the Christian message in an emerging culture where the roles of traditional religion and Christian morality in the midst of the war had declined in importance.[24] The arts became one of the Church's answers "to the problem of our changing world," which was becoming more secularized each year.[25] In 1946, the Church of Scotland officially welcomed the arts by opening its own theater in Edinburgh, called the Gateway Theatre, in Leith Walk. The Church also closely allied itself the following year with the new Edinburgh Festival of Music and Drama, inaugurated in August 1947.[26]

John absorbed into his coalescing worldview this focus upon, and incorporation of, the arts as an effective expression of Christianity. While attending the Festival and theater, he was eager to learn from and appreciate this bridge between Christianity and secular culture. Art was a powerful tool that used the senses to communicate deep truths. Other examples of this kind of investigation were his travels in Great Britain and Europe during these months abroad, where he absorbed the art, architecture, and culture of places he had previously only read about and dreamed of seeing. His views of the world were indeed expanding rapidly.

In December 1946, John traveled with a group to London, and then to Oxford, to attend the Students' Theological Conference. He explored the cobblestone streets of Oxford and visited the museums and libraries and quads of the universities and colleges. He wrote voluminous notes of places he visited and their histories, the people he met, and how these threads of knowledge wove themselves into and through his life.[27] He filled his "Diary Letters" with each day's activities, cited famous graduates, inventors, artists, statesmen, and scientists from these ivy-clad halls of learning and sent them home to Eddie Belle, who then forwarded them to his parents. He was homesick, but in every letter home, written each week on Sunday afternoon, he expressed gratitude to his parents and family who enabled the gift of this season of study.[28]

Christmas that year was a lonely one. John returned from Oxford on 23 December and spent the holiday remembering former family celebrations. He wrote, "I certainly thought about you on Christmas Day. In my mind's eye I pictured the Christmas tree and the good times you had. We have always had happy Christmas seasons at home. I shall never forget them . . . my mouth waters every time I think of quail breasts."[29]

Eddie Belle and Martha, 1946

John visited Tyndale House, Cambridge, for a theological conference between 31 December and 2 January at the invitation of its Warden, Sir Norman Anderson, the famous scholar of Arab studies and war hero, in whose home John lodged. He wrote of this visit:

> I do believe that this was one of the highest spiritual and intellectual weeks I have ever experienced. I always have thought that such a group of men existed—but I had never found them before. An Evangelical movement of great potentiality is arising in this country and this group is the fountainhead. A number of prominent laymen are supporting it financially and have bought the Tyndale House in Cambridge as the headquarters. I do not believe that I shall ever be the same again after such a week.[30]

More good news followed during the winter term in Edinburgh. John received word in January 1947 that he had been accepted at the universities of Basel and Zurich in Switzerland to study during the late spring and summer term, though Professor John Baillie had advised John to study in Basel first, because the best theological faculty in Europe was currently there. Baillie had promised that John would get full transfer credit at Edinburgh's New College for the terms taken at Basel by way of an exchange partnership between the two institutions. Intrigued by the neo-orthodox developments in the universities of Basel and Zurich at the time, John was elated with this opportunity.

Basel and Zurich, 1947

The tuition was high, at forty pounds for the three months, about $3,000, but John thought he could economize by not taking meals at the boarding house and eating in his room. He planned ahead, securing an apartment for the fall term in Edinburgh before packing his bags, during the Easter break in March, to travel to Switzerland. With his Swiss passport and visa in hand, and during one of the worst blizzards in the history of Scotland, John left Edinburgh by train and arrived in Basel almost a week later to commence an intensive study of German with Frau Dr. Dück-Tobler. He had three weeks before classes began in April.[31] Basel University was the second-oldest German-speaking university in Europe, and famous teachers had included Paracelsus, Erasmus, and Nietzsche. John wanted to be prepared to learn as much as possible of this second language so that, when he attended lectures, he would not miss a syllable.

John was enraptured with the beauty of Switzerland. Basel was the only city of major importance along the entire course of the Rhine River that remained in good condition after World War II. Here, after the hideous ravages of destruction he had witnessed elsewhere, and the privations of England and Scotland, he found in Basel a medieval city with its monuments intact and its historic continuity unbroken. As he absorbed its cultural offerings, he grew more excited each day about the prospect of meeting and learning from internationally recognized scholars.

In Basel, a week before the beginning of the term, John moved into the Theological *Alumneum, Bebelstrasse*, International Hostel, under the direction of the famous New Testament scholar Oscar Cullman (1902–1999), one of Europe's most famous Christian theologians. Trained in the Lutheran tradition and known for his successful work in ecumenical dialogue, Cullman impressed Newport with the necessity of a listening posture when attempting to understand other faith traditions or to resolve theological conflicts.[32] John spent many hours with Cullman, asking questions, exchanging ideas, and coming to know him as a friend. In later years, he would absorb the volumes Cullman wrote and correspond with him about their contents. John's own view of the value of ecumenism was solidified under Cullman.

Relieved to find that meals were included in this accommodation, he also enjoyed the fellowship of other ministerial students from Denmark, Hungary, Paris, Germany, and many other European cities. In a letter home, dated 28 April 1947, John wrote of Martin Nieden, his roommate: "Men are here from many countries. At the same table are a man who was in the German army and two young men who led in the French Resistance movement. That could only happen in the Kingdom of Christ." He went on to say that he was relearning the art of "doing without." He said he had no radio, took one bath every ten days, walked everywhere he went, and enjoyed no heat. "I certainly long to see all of you again. I sometimes wonder why I was fortunate in my family and country. Europe is in a terrible state and the Germans are practically starving. This German friend here was half-starved when he came. He eats like a wolf now and is trying to build his system up. He has almost no possessions."[33]

Professor Cullman took the students as a group to concerts, museums, and art galleries. At the cost of fifty American dollars, some of the students took a seven-day trip to Italy. They traveled in third-class accommodations within Switzerland and second-class in Italy, staying in cheaper hotels and eating plain fare. They visited Milan, Venice, Bologna, Florence, Rome, and Genoa. On their way home, they were entertained by the mother of one of the students in her beautiful chalet in Gryon, Switzerland. On another long weekend, the *Alumneum* was closed, and the group attended a conference of theological students from various universities in a chateau on Thuner Lake near Interlaken.

German was the only language spoken both in class and at the Theological *Alumneum*. John threw himself into an intense schedule of classes and study and added Greek and Latin to his German language study. Here he studied with the Swiss theologian Karl Barth, leader of the Confessing Church that resisted Hitler's influence upon the existing churches in Germany. Barth was regarded as perhaps the greatest Protestant theologian of the twentieth century.[34] Barth dominated Europe's postwar theology, rejecting both nineteenth-century liberalism and extreme conservative views in favor of his "theology of the Word," a dialectical approach.

During the time John Newport was interacting with Barth in Basel, Barth was writing the Darmstadt Statement of 1947, which attributed to Germany the greatest measure of guilt and responsibility for both the Third Reich and Second World War and called for both German penitence and reconciliation with churches abroad. From his relationship with Barth, John's high view of God's sovereignty was confirmed and his mind was opened to the complex processes involved in reconciliation, both personally and nationally, as well as to the realities and consequences of corporate sin. John also met and studied with Karl Ludwig Schmidt (1891–1956), the German theologian and professor of New Testament studies at the University of Basel, before studying in Zurich for a few months. Here, he met Emil Brunner and Carl Jung, two more famous scholars who informed his thinking.

John commuted once a week to the University of Zurich to study under Karl Barth's contemporary, Emil Brunner (1889–1966), a famous Swiss systematic theologian.[35] John's commute into Zurich each week was easy by train, but his trek up the hill to the university, sitting high above the city overlooking the River Limmat, was a steep climb. Brunner had just returned from Scotland, where he had taught a year and delivered the distinguished Gifford Lectures at the University of St. Andrews in 1946 and 1947. These lectures, "Christianity and Civilization," held immediately following World War II's armistice, addressed

"Foundations" and "Specific Problems." Brunner argued his conviction that only Christianity is capable of furnishing the basis of a civilization that can rightly be described as human. It was Brunner's contention, however, that building and living in a Christian civilization is so complex that it forces Christians to use a new kind of approach that begins with and seeks to examine foundational questions.

Such foundational questions address and include the problems of truth, time, meaning, humankind in the universe, personality and humanity, justice, freedom, and creativity. From Brunner, John received a deeper and broader perspective of how the Protestant faith of the Reformers had both influenced the philosophy of religion and paved a way for the future. John keenly listened and processed Brunner's ideas through his own fertile mind that captured and later used some of these same categories for his own book, *Life's Ultimate Questions* (1989).[36]

The last of the European scholars with whom John studied was Carl Jung (1875–1961),[37] Swiss psychiatrist and psychotherapist who was for many years a close friend and colleague of Sigmund Freud. Jung founded analytical psychology and the psychological notions of "individuation" as the central process of human development, the "collective unconscious," including the "archetype," the "complex," and "synchronicity." Of particular fascination to Newport were Jung's explorations of Eastern and Western philosophy and the occult as these are related to sociology. Jung's influence upon the "psychologization of religion," spirituality in general, and the New Age movement was profound, as Jung saw the human psyche as "by nature religious."[38] From these tangential areas of studies, Jung was convinced that holistic human development and growth, which he called "individualization," must of necessity include a spiritual component. John found this study to be keenly significant to his own research on cults. In the future, as John researched these concepts for himself and increased his understanding, he spent much time and personal funds purchasing and collecting religious objects, venerated by different cultures throughout the world, to illustrate the common yearning that humankind has expressed to find God.

John was also aware of the complexity of the human experience and wanted to learn all he could about how the roles of spirituality, religious expression, and the "collective unconscious" of all humankind meshed with a holistic view of reality. A new term was emerging that seemed to capture the imaginations of scholars—a "worldview"—and John began to think through the implications of what might constitute a "biblical worldview" in which all of reality was grounded in the authority of special revelation.

John wrapped up his work in mid-July and took a wandering route back to Edinburgh. What he saw was critical to his evolving understanding of the world. He absorbed the classical cultural centers and museums of these regions, most of which were beginning to recover and rebuild after the war's devastation. John saw, firsthand, the rubble-filled streets and the ravaged cities, the shells of buildings hollowed by bombs and mortar-fire. He noted the faces of the men, women, and children full of sorrow and misery. His heart and mind never forgot these images that provided a wrenching pool of sympathy for those who suffer.

Having these observations and experiences as a maturing scholar introduced John indeed to the European roots of his culture, which was one of the primary purposes for which he had left the United States to learn. The unexpected and more deeply ingrained lessons, however, emerged from the stark dichotomies of the human condition: both war and peace; evil and good; the disregard and the valuing of human life; the loss and preservation of cultural identity; the discarding and cherishing of faith in crises; and the anguished questions postwar Europeans were asking concerning the meaning of life.

After John's period of study in Switzerland, Eddie Belle and Martha Ellen sailed across the Atlantic to join him for the last remaining months of the year in Edinburgh. The little family took up residence in the home of Professor Burleigh in one of the finest residential districts in the city. Their student apartment was comprised of a large sitting room, a large bedroom, a smaller bedroom, and a kitchenette. John was thrilled to have his family together again and turned his energies to completing his residential study so that they could return to the United States by Christmas.[39] He would write his dissertation back home.

John's course of study drew to a close at the end of December 1947. They packed their belongings, shipped crates of books homeward, said goodbyes to dear friends, and boarded the *Queen Mary*, a Cunard White Star ocean liner, outbound from Southampton to New York, on 19 December.[40] This had been a glorious interlude of scholarship, the light of which would remain undimmed for the rest of his life.[41]

Streams of Knowledge 49

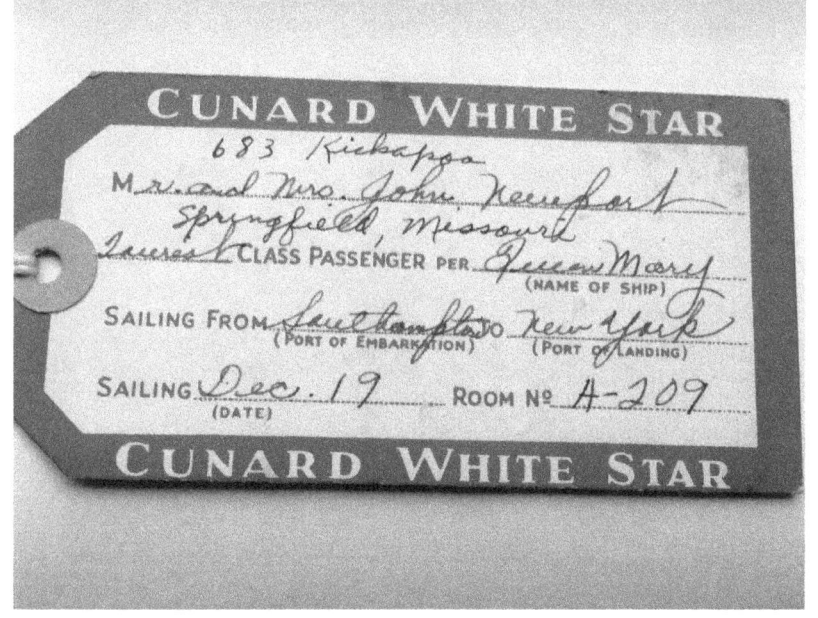

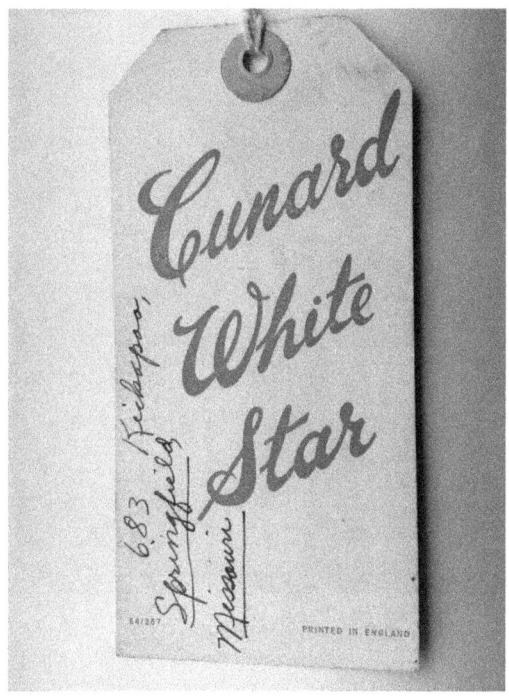

Queen Mary Passenger Tickets Home, December 1947, back and front

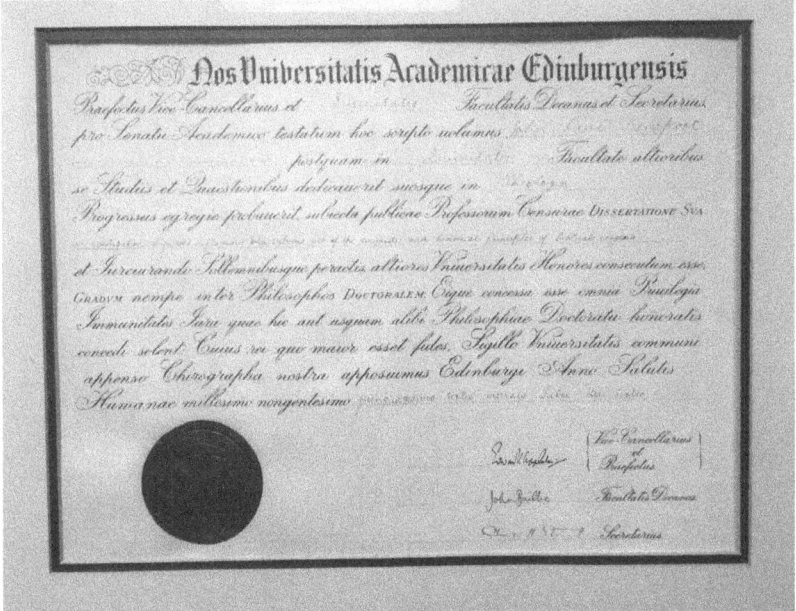

Newport's University of Edinburgh Diploma, 1953

Immanuel Baptist Church, Native American Culture, and Oral Roberts

A subdued and more mature John Newport returned with his family from Scotland in December 1947 to become pastor of the Immanuel Baptist Church in Tulsa, Oklahoma. The contrast was palpable. The state's relatively flat topography, Native American culture, and western ethos replaced the rugged and bracing beauty of Scotland's highlands. Yet the people were similar: hardy, industrious, open, and warm-hearted. John was eager to put his new knowledge into practice, and the church received him well. Frank Marvin was born on 1 November 1948 as the ministry was flourishing. Attendance at Sunday School each week totaled more than nine hundred, with four hundred in Training Union.[42] While he pastored this thriving downtown church, his recent experiences enriching both pulpit and classrooms, John said he was drawn to two areas of consuming interest. The first was the Native American Indian culture of the region,[43] and the second was the ministry and teachings of a fellow pastor in the area—Oral Granville Roberts (1918–2009).[44]

Born within six months of and living almost a decade longer than John Newport, American Methodist-Pentecostal televangelist Oral Roberts was John's contemporary. He was preaching part-time in churches and holding tent revivals in the area when John moved to Tulsa. It was a year earlier, in 1947, that Roberts had revealed that he had received a vision that changed his ministry. As his preaching began to focus on what Roberts called "seed faith," the "prosperity gospel," and "abundant life" teachings, Roberts became increasingly known as a fiery preacher, charismatic healer, entrepreneur, and controversial leader in American Christian circles in the twentieth century. Later, he founded the Oral Roberts Evangelistic Association and Oral Roberts University. As his family and ministry were firmly entrenched in the Tulsa area, Roberts and his evolving brand of Christianity offered both opportunities for dialogue and theological challenges for John Newport in his pastoral role. Gracious and polished, John Newport spent slightly more than a year in the pulpit at Immanuel before he received an invitation from Waco, Texas, to come join Baylor University's faculty. John and Eddie Belle accepted, and this move was to launch John's five-decade-long teaching career.

4
Widening Currents

1949–1959

*The words of the mouth are deep waters,
but the fountain of wisdom is a rushing stream.*

Proverbs 18:4 (NIV)

Following the sustained anxiety and national efforts to help to end the devastations of World War II, the next two decades in America exploded into frenetic activity. The new dance step, "Be Bop," had emerged in 1945 as a reaction to the "Swing." The next year, the Broadway musical "Annie Get Your Gun" produced more hits than had any previous show in entertainment history. George Balanchine formed the New York City Ballet in 1948, the same year Eero Saarinen established the huge General Motors Technical Center in Warren, Michigan. Cole Porter wrote "Kiss Me Kate" as television first appeared and sales skyrocketed. Upon the death of Franklin Delano Roosevelt, Harry S. Truman became the thirty-third president during the Berlin airlift and Cold War escalation.

In other fields, American scientists perfected the electronic computer (Electronic Numerical Integrator and Calculator), chemist Willard Libby discovered radiocarbon dating, physicist John Bardeen made the first transistor at Bell Laboratories, and astronomer George Garrow proposed the "Big Bang" theory of the universe. In addition, medical researchers at Ohio State University used cobalt-60 to treat cancer patients in 1949, the same year George Orwell published his futuristic novel *Nineteen Eighty-Four*.

The estimated worldwide population in 1950 was 2.5 million. That year, the first doctor was called by radio pager from a golf course, antihistamines arrived on the market as popular remedies for colds and allergies, and Britain and France were first linked by television. On 25 June, the Korean War erupted when communist North Korea invaded South Korea, and General Douglas MacArthur commanded the United Nations troops, comprised largely of Americans and South Koreans. The next year introduced the first heart-lung machine and transistorized hearing aid, while Salinger's *The Catcher in the Rye* and Dylan Thomas' poetry were both published.

Across the globe in 1952, as Dwight D. Eisenhower became president in the nation's capital, Elizabeth II assumed the throne of Great Britain and Northern Ireland. King Farouk I of Egypt abdicated his sovereignty, and Jawaharlal Nehru took the stage as leader of India's new independent democratic republic. In science and technology, the first sex-change operation was successfully conducted, the first pocket-sized transistor radios were marketed, and ultra-wide screens were installed in motion-picture cinemas across America. More sobering, the first major nuclear accident occurred at a reactor in Deep River, Ottawa, in Canada, even as the hydrogen bomb was being tested in America.

In the months to come, the Korean War would end in 1953 with an armistice signed at Panmunjom, and climbers Edmund Hillary and Tenzing Norgay would conquer Mount Everest. Joseph Stalin would die, and the dominant Nikita Khrushchev would succeed him. Cigarette smoking would be blamed for lung cancer, and American virologist Jonas Edward Salk would develop the polio vaccine and thereby increase the chance of better health for succeeding generations of the world's inhabitants.[1]

These were heady days to be alive, as the optimistic Newports packed their belongings and moved from Tulsa to Texas. For the next decade, they immersed themselves in the stimulating atmosphere of academia and campus life in three states, as John accepted invitations to teach at Baylor University, New Orleans Baptist Theological Seminary, and Southwestern Baptist Theological Seminary. At the end of this decade, John also took his first sabbatical leave to teach at Boston University and to conduct further study at Harvard Divinity School and the Massachusetts Institute of Technology. This was a significant decade in John Newport's life, for it introduced him to cutting-edge theological scholarship that challenged and sharpened his own beliefs in ways he could not have foreseen. It also introduced him to the classroom, where he would spend the rest of his life.

Early Teaching

John had discovered within himself a deep love of teaching. Surrounded by his beloved books and opportunities to engage with students and colleagues in meaningful dialogue each day, he found his life's purpose and calling and reveled in it. His reputation soon grew as a kind, generous, courteous, and brilliant young professor. His first invitation to join a faculty came from Baylor University, the oldest educational institution in the state of Texas.[2]

Baylor University, Waco, Texas, 1949–1951

At Baylor, John taught for two academic years as an associate professor and director of graduate studies in religion. He taught undergraduates their survey courses in religion, biblical history, and interpretation. In his solitary moments, he continued to read avidly, often losing himself as he absorbed and processed information at an accelerated pace. Fresh from his pastorate in Oklahoma, he was also writing, applying what he was teaching to the lay men and women in local churches.[3] At Baylor, he was also preaching regularly on Sundays in the pulpits of churches large and small. He desired to stay connected to the local churches and the members who were seeking to follow God more closely.

Here in the Southwest, as in Oklahoma, John was once again exposed to new cultures and learning. He traced the Baptist heritage of Texas through the dramatic history of Texas' beginnings. He was also exposed, for the first time, to what became for him a lifelong passion—the culture of South America. Baylor's then president, William R. White, sent John to the Rio Grande Valley of Texas to speak at a college commencement service on behalf of the university. John took the opportunity to cross over the nation's southern border to explore Matamoros, Mexico. John was immediately captivated by its landscape, heritage, culture, and people. As he briefly experienced life there, he began to synthesize this new knowledge with the European culture in which he had so recently been immersed. The differences were obvious; yet, as John noted later, similarities also began to emerge that contributed to his evolving worldview. He determined to return to South America and to study more deeply.

Meanwhile, in his first semester of college-level teaching, the young professor Newport met for the first time a bright young freshman student who walked into his classroom one morning. His name was Russell Dilday. Neither knew at the time that this classroom encounter would forge a solid friendship that would last the entirety of their lives. Even though Newport was an "unknown entity," Dilday later recalled, and an upperclassman had warned him against taking such risks, the new student enrolled in New Testament III under Newport. He found Newport to be "erudite without being pedantic," "fresh without being trendy," and "creative without an obvious straining to be novel." He was entertaining and humorous, and his content was both scholarly and practical, something the students appreciated deeply.[4]

The two years progressed quickly through the academic cycle of scheduling classes, advising students, registration, writing lectures, teaching, testing and grading, evaluating courses and programs, and planning for future course offerings. At the same time, he was completing his dissertation, submitting chapters and writing late into the nights. He spoke of early morning risings at 3:00 or 4:00 a.m. and the ceaseless duties of being a professor. John was also traveling much in this period, riding trains and local buses through long days and nights to preach revivals and fill pulpits of churches across the United States. These trips took him away from home a great deal, and Eddie Belle held the family together while he was away. Eddie Belle spent some time in late 1949 with her parents in Nashville. She was there with little Martha and baby Frank when her father passed away on 7 December 1949.

The two years in Waco were a whirlwind. Toward the end of the spring term of 1951, another invitation arrived in the mail. John was asked to come to teach graduate seminary courses at the newly reorganized and renamed New Orleans Baptist Theological Seminary.[5] After several weeks of prayer and consideration, although they loved Waco and the university and the people of that city, the Newports felt God's leadership to go. Once again, Eddie and John assembled the boxes for moving.

New Orleans Baptist Theological Seminary, New Orleans, Louisiana, 1951–1952

John relocated his family to New Orleans in the late summer of 1951, just in time for the start of the new academic year. Roland Quinche Leavell (1891–1963), one of Eddie Belle's famous nine Baptist uncles, served as president of the seminary at the time. John took up his duties

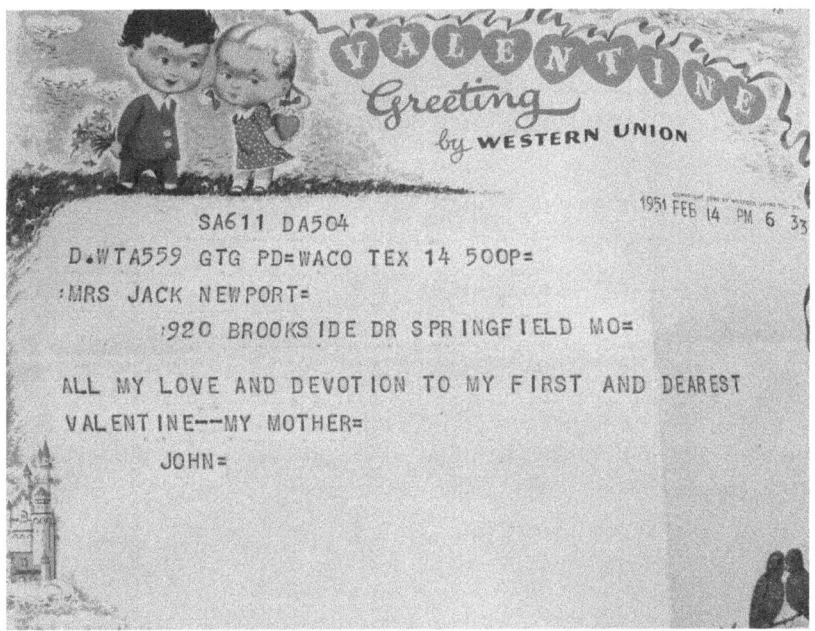

John's Valentine cable sent to his mother, 1951

as associate professor of philosophy of religion and New Testament. He also taught biblical history and interpretation, as he had at Baylor, only this time at the graduate level. In this vibrant city along the Mississippi River, John and Eddie Belle absorbed its French culture, including its Evangeline tradition brought by Acadians to New Orleans in the eighteenth century,[6] its steamboats, distinctive jazz music, Louisiana cuisine, religious expressions, and arts.

In New Orleans John felt fortunate indeed, for across the city, six miles to the southeast, Tulane University and its notable faculty were easily accessible. Here John learned more about the emerging New Age movement as he became immersed in the academic life of the city. He and Eddie Belle attended public lectures and debates, concerts, and receptions. As a member of the seminary faculty, John also spoke in many churches and at civic events, often where Tulane University and medical faculty were numbered among the audience. He wrote and presented research papers in order to dialogue with the faculty at Tulane as well. He also published a peer-reviewed article on new developments in New Testament theology in January 1952.[7]

While teaching, preaching, and writing, John took time to travel to New York City to pay his respects and attend the funeral of the famous philosopher, psychologist, and educational reformer, John Dewey (1859–1952), on 4 June 1952.[8] As a scholar-practitioner himself, Newport was an advocate of Dewey's "learning by doing" philosophy and appreciative of Dewey's wide global perspectives. He had read Dewey's thoughts on epistemology, ethics, arts, metaphysics, and his support of experimental intelligence, and admired Dewey's staunch defense of democracy.

It was following this trip to New York in the summer of 1952 that Newport received a call that would change the remainder of his life. Southwestern Baptist Theological Seminary was in need of a philosophy professor. John and Eddie Belle, sensing a call from God in this direction and excited about the possibilities, agreed to move back to Texas and plant their lives in the seminary's faculty, students, churches of the state, and the intellectual community of Fort Worth.

Southwestern Baptist Theological Seminary, Fort Worth, Texas, 1952–1958

When John joined the faculty of Southwestern Seminary as associate professor of philosophy of religion, he followed Albert Venting, philosopher from 1921 to 1937, and Stewart A. Newman, who came in 1936 and served in the same capacity until 1952. Newman had just accepted an invitation to join the first faculty of the Southeastern Baptist Theological Seminary in Wake Forest, North Carolina, which was founded in 1950 and held its first term of classes the next year.[9] With Newport's experience at Baylor and New Orleans standing him in good stead, he filled the vacuum that Newman had left behind and took up his responsibilities with great energy and excitement.

When Newport arrived on campus, only one faculty member remained from the tenure of Southwestern's first president, B. H. Carroll (1908–1914), and its first years in Fort Worth. This was W. W. Barnes, professor of Church History (1913–1953, and faculty chairman 1926–1948). From Lee Rutland Scarborough's term as president (1915–1942), several faculty members remained: Robert A. Baker, Church History (1942–1981); Floy Barnard, Educational Arts (1933–1960, Dean 1944–1960); E. L. Carlson, Old Testament (1921–1964); W. L. House, Educational Administration (1933–1955); T. B. Maston, Christian Ethics (1922–1963); Edwin McNeely, Voice (1920–1963), and his wife, Wayne McNeely, Piano

John Newport, c. 1953

(1919–1956); Jesse James Northcutt, Preaching (1939–1945, 1950–1979, Dean 1953–1972, Vice president 1973–1979); J. M. Price, Principles of Religious Education (1915–1956); and Ray Summers, New Testament (1938–1959, Dean 1949–1953).

Newport's accession to the faculty came during the last year of Dr. E. D. Head's presidency.[10] Head had suffered a heart attack in January 1952, following his return from a preaching crusade to Japan in the late fall of 1951. He recovered well and returned to his duties by March to fulfill his heavy responsibilities for another year. Head then announced his retirement in March 1953 to be effective 1 August, just as Newport was completing his first full academic year.

Head's decade had been a fruitful tenure, in which many distinguished professors joined the faculty ranks and became Newport's colleagues, some of them for the rest of his life: A. Donald Bell, Psychology (1951–1960, 1963–1972); Ann Bradford, Childhood Education (1945–1970); Henry Clifton Brown, Preaching (1947–1973); Ralph

Churchill, Religious Journalism (1944–1970); Gladys Day, Organist (1952–1978); Huber Lelland Drumwright Jr., New Testament (1951–1959, 1960–1980, Dean 1973–1980); R. Othal Feather, Educational Administration (1947–1970); Cal Guy, Missions (1946–1982); Joe Davis Heacock, Educational Administration (1944–1973, Dean 1956–1973); W. Boyd Hunt, Theology (1944–1946, 1953–1999); Gracie Knowlton, Educational Arts (1947–1971); Jack W. MacGorman, New Testament (1948–2001); James McKinney, Voice (1950–1994, Dean 1956–1994); Alpha Melton, Social Work (1945–1971); Franklin Segler, Pastoral Ministry (1951–1972); Ralph L. Smith, Old Testament (1949–1996); and Curtis Vaughan, New Testament (1950–1987, 1989–1995).[11]

At that time, the campus hill was an expanse of parched, dry, and treeless ground, covered in Johnson grass. Construction work on the new building sites and unfinished classrooms filled the air with sounds of machinery, concrete mixers, and hammering. No air conditioning was to be found. Students from those days remember sitting in the institutional-green painted basement classrooms of Scarborough Hall in the new Carroll Memorial building in narrow, connected, swing-topped desks. Whenever a latecomer joined the class, the whole row of students would gather their papers and books, flip up and fold back their desktops, and stand to their feet as the tardy one struggled across the row and found his or her seat. In summers, the students in white shirts and ties, and professors in suits, would swelter in the classrooms, relieved only if a slight breeze blew through the high, narrow window slits of the mostly underground floor.[12]

These were difficult days in other ways. The student body was growing rapidly, which was at once a blessing and a challenge. President Head reported to the SBC that the teachers were lecturing to "congregations" rather than classes. The semester he took office in 1942, a total of twenty-three full-time professors taught 760 students enrolled that year. Upon Head's retirement in 1953, forty-two full-time faculty members taught 2,160 students, including 1,354 in the School of Theology, 749 in the School of Religious Education, and 124 in the School of Sacred Music.[13] Although the faculty had grown by 83 percent, the sheer size of the student body, which had swelled by 184 percent, continued to stretch new classrooms to capacity. The student-teacher ratio was one to fifty.[14]

The election of Southwestern Seminary's fourth president, Dr. J. Howard Williams (1953–1958), a fifty-nine-year-old Baptist pastor who had served Texas Baptists as Executive Secretary, saw no diminished growth during his tenure. Williams was winsome, warm-hearted, and exuded graciousness. He was also a formidable administrator. He set his sights to raise ten million dollars in his first five years, with half going to faculty accessions, student housing, and campus improvements, and the other half to endowment.

Williams instituted a massive campus improvement plan, which resulted in several new buildings, the renovation of other structures, and the addition of air conditioning to classrooms in Memorial Hall. In the next few years, thirty-seven new professors joined the faculty, and salaries slowly increased. Retirement, insurance, and housing plans were put in place, and the *Southwestern Journal of Theology* was founded in 1958, with James Leo Garrett, professor of systematic theology, as its managing editor. The Memorial Building expanded on both sides with wings, called Fleming and Scarborough, and the library was enlarged. Married students moved into newly built apartments just across Seminary Drive from the campus, which the trustees named the "J. Howard Williams Student Village" in honor of the president who made students his priority. A trailer park was added for student housing, and duplexes were finished to host missionary families on furlough. A student center and an infirmary were fitted out in one wing of the Memorial Building until new structures could be built for these purposes. Finally, President Williams continued to add faculty who helped to lower the teacher to student ratio considerably. The conclusion of World War II brought many students, with G.I. Bill funds in hand, to enroll in classes on Seminary Hill. As a result, the student body doubled its enrollment in less than three years.[15]

During these early years at Southwestern, while John was scrambling to teach classes, grade papers and tests, and preach each Sunday and most Wednesday evenings at churches across the state and nation, John and Eddie Belle welcomed their third and last child into the family on 2 April 1954. This son was given his father's name—John Paul Newport Jr.[16] Eddie Belle admirably filled the roles of both mother and father during these years, seeing to it that the children and she were happily and regularly involved in the Broadway Baptist Church near downtown Fort Worth, with all of its programs, services, and ministry service opportunities.

In 1955, John organized an overseas travel group for the first time, something he and Eddie Belle would enjoy doing together annually for the next forty years. The first of twenty-five such trips took a group of about fifty participants to study the background regions of "Eurocentric culture" found in Egypt, Israel, Jordan, Syria, Lebanon, Turkey, and Greece. John prepared extensive notes of each region's history, geography, significance for cultural formation, and famous events and personalities associated with every tour stop. He delivered these with enthusiasm.

John wrote two articles upon his return. The first was addressed to students in colleges and universities. He felt a great longing to help them to experience the depth of faith and commitment that he himself had experienced as a young adult student. He wrote "Skeptic and Apologist" in 1956, and in the following year, a more scholarly article that was published in volume one of the *Encyclopedia of Southern Baptists*. It addressed authority and the Bible, a topic that was already producing squalls of discontent and dividing leaders within the SBC. Newport wrote:

> The authority of the Bible is both objective and subjective. It is a divinely inspired and authoritative historical record and interpretation of God's revelation in history and thus constitutes an objective authority in religion. Yet it exerts its authority in an internal and subjective manner. It is a living and pulsating Book[,] which is used by the Holy Spirit to constrain without compelling and to lead without forcing.

The article affirmed the reliability of the Bible in all of its parts and its authority as the basis for all doctrinal formulations and practice of the Christian faith. This was a deep conviction that, for Newport, would never be in doubt.[17]

Before John knew it, the year 1958 was approaching with two wonderful events to enjoy, even though the first would bring an unexpected loss. The first was the celebration of Southwestern Baptist Theological Seminary's fiftieth anniversary, which J. Howard Williams had been planning since the spring of 1954. Each of the three schools set aside a full week to celebrate the event with special scholarly speakers: the School of Religious Education during 17–21 February; the School of Theology on 17–21 March; and the School of Church Music during 14–18 April, all in 1958. The festivities were to include the entire Southern Baptist Convention when it met in Houston on 22 May.

Before this final meeting took place, however, J. Howard Williams suffered a fatal heart attack and died on 20 April. This was a real blow to the seminary family, who was aware that he had battled a heart condition but had not expected this sudden loss. The five years of his tenure had been beneficial to the life of the seminary, especially its students, for whom he was ever dreaming of plans to enrich their lives.[18] While the seminary family mourned and the board of trustees gathered to plan the next steps, John received news that lifted his spirits.

The second significant event of 1958 was the opportunity to study on sabbatical leave. John had made inquiries, applied for, and now received word that a fellowship was to be his. He had won the Seatlantic Fund from the Rockefeller Foundation to study at Harvard University and its divinity school for the academic year of 1958–1959. Given the task of Associate Field Work director for Harvard Divinity School while he studied, and another invitation to be a lecturer for the Boston University School of Theology, John faced a full schedule. He and Eddie Belle packed the family and made plans to be away for the year, not knowing who would become president of the seminary in their absence.

In Cambridge, Massachusetts, Harvard Divinity School had just founded its Center for the Study of World Religions. John was keen to explore the relationship between religion and culture, a fascination that had been growing for some time, and one that would stay with him the rest of his career. With his rather extensive background in multicultural observations and research, John found this year of exploration to be one of the most exciting and stimulating intellectual experiences of his life. He took the chance to study both Far Eastern religions and the overlapping disciplines of religion and the arts. In fact, the background for Newport's first book, *Theology and Contemporary Art Forms*, was formulated here at Harvard, and a decade later, after much expansion of content, the book was published in 1970. He was also led to understand the uniqueness of the distinctive "biblical worldview" under the leadership of several notable scholars at three institutions of higher learning in and near Boston, Massachusetts.

Harvard University, MIT, and Boston University, 1958–1959

When John Newport walked onto the Harvard campus in the fall of 1958, he met and became friends with several members of the faculties of both of the university and divinity schools. Some of these were of the older generation, and others were younger and bringing fresh perspectives to the Harvard ethos. He made arrangements to study with several of these scholars. Together they fostered Newport's cognitive creativity, deepened his knowledge and understanding bases, and influenced his thinking for his future years, especially in the realms of multicultural studies, world religions, art, preaching, and philosophy.

One of the scholars with whom John was most excited to learn was Robert Henry Lawson Slater (1896–1984), first professor of world religions and founder of the new Harvard Divinity School Center for the Study of World Religions.[19] He served as its director from 1960 to 1964. Slater's skills in facilitating dialogue among people of different religions and races, interpreting cultures to cultures, and elucidating mankind's various ways of seeing the world and living in it made him a model of scholarly informed, intelligent, and creative involvement in the task of communication and cooperation across borders and continents. John benefited greatly from his friendship with this gentle scholar, who resonated at such deep levels with his own approach and worldview.

Anther faculty member influenced his thinking about multiculturalism. Krister Olofson Stendahl (1921–2008) was a Swedish theologian who had just joined Harvard's divinity school faculty in 1954 as a professor of New Testament. He later went on to become dean of the divinity school (1968–1979) before moving to his home country as the Church of Sweden's Bishop of Stockholm (1984–1988).[20] John appreciated Stendahl's beautiful use of language, extraordinary sensitivity to the perspectives of differing cultures, and his ability to communicate gracefully to people of varied beliefs, traits that would later characterize John's own work within interfaith contexts.

An especial delight to John Newport was the friendship of George Buttrick (1892–1980),[21] the famous pastor of the Madison Avenue Presbyterian Church in New York City, and, since 1955, professor of Christian Morals at Harvard. He had brought his inimitable preaching style to his sermons prepared for Harvard University students. He published a book of these sermons in 1959, *Sermons Preached in a University Church*, as John was studying there. Newport listened to many of Buttrick's sermons and formed a friendship that would last many years, even when Buttrick came later to teach homiletics at the Southern Baptist Theological Seminary in the late 1970s.

In a similar vein, Newport was eager to learn from a newcomer to the Harvard Divinity School faculty, one who had recently stepped into the role of dean following the resignation of Douglas Horton in 1957 to lead the World Council of Churches' Faith and Order Commission. Samuel

Howard Miller (1900–1968)²² had recently been pastor of the Old Cambridge Baptist Church for twenty-five years and brought fresh pastoral perspectives to the Divinity School, steeped as it was in scholarly erudition. As the new dean, he formed the Department of the Church, which offered courses in the relationship of the church to society and sponsored a fieldwork program in mental hospitals and prisons for prospective ministers. He stressed the development of ministers in the image he had set for himself—an awareness of and ability to deal with social problems—at a time when this was far from the concern of most members of the Divinity School faculty.

Much to Newport's delight, Miller also expressed his love of life through an appreciation of art and literature. He brought artists to lecture at the Divinity School and sponsored monthly exhibitions of their work. From Miller, Newport learned ways to train pastors in a type of relational ministry that was also alert to social problems, tasks that he felt must be conveyed and apprehended by each generation of ministers. He also explored more deeply the synthesis between the practice of ministry, religious expression, and art.

Other scholars who impacted John's view of interfaith and multicultural studies were John Luther Adams (1901–1994)²³ and Harvey Gallagher Cox Jr. (1929–present).²⁴ John Adams had been teaching Christian ethics at Harvard for just two years when Newport first met him. His emphasis upon society and culture and the works of Paul Tillich, Ernst Troeltsch, and Karl Holl focused on the theology of social ethics. This intrigued Newport, who had many conversations with Adams and counted him among those whose work and teaching impacted him most the year he was in the Boston area.

Newport met Harvey Cox, the Baptist pastor, when Cox was teaching at Andover Newton Theological School, just seven miles from Boston city center. Cox had joined the faculty of Andover Newton in 1957, and Newport worked with him as he was helping to direct the field work for Harvard Divinity School. As they spent time together, sharing in common their love for Latin America and its cultures, Cox became another friend. Later, Cox joined the faculty of Harvard Divinity School as Hollis Research Professor of Divinity and focused his teaching on the theological developments in world Christianity, particularly in Latin America, and liberation theology, areas Newport also researched.

Newport studied under two notable theologian-ethicists during the year. The first was Joseph Francis Fletcher (1905–1991).[25] Fletcher became associated with the theory of situational ethics and was a pioneer of bioethics by the early 1960s. He had already published his work advocating euthanasia and, by the time Newport met him, Fletcher was already teaching on the moral questions behind such controversial practices as abortion, cloning, eugenics, and voluntary euthanasia. These fascinating and then-cutting-edge topics spawned questions that Newport would later address in his *Life's Ultimate Questions*.

The second ethicist was Paul L. Lehman (1906–1994),[26] who was known for two significant aspects of his life—he was the closest American friend and soul mate of Dietrich Bonhoeffer and he was a leading Christian ethicist. He and Bonhoeffer had met when they were both students at Union Theological Seminary in New York. In 1939, on Bonhoeffer's second trip to the United States, Lehman took Dietrich to the harbor to embark upon the last scheduled steamer to leave New York Harbor for Germany, where he was already a leading figure, with Barth, in the Confessing Church of Protestants who were resisting Hitler's regime.[27] Lehman had also studied under Karl Barth and Reinhold Niebuhr.

Fletcher, Lehman, and Newport had stimulating conversations about their teachers, how new philosophies and advances in medical technology seemed to be changing long-held assumptions about moral choices, and how best to communicate to and with people of differing perspectives. Even at this earlier stage in Fletcher's career, he and his ideas challenged Newport's worldview and assumptions. A good balancing influence, then, were the theologians with whom John studied and with whom his ideas were more congruent.

The two biblical scholars who impacted John's life most were George Ernest Wright (1909–1974),[28] Parkman Professor of Divinity, leading Old Testament scholar and biblical archaeologist, and Frank Moore Cross (1921–2012), Hancock Professor of Hebrew and Other Oriental Languages at Harvard University.[29] Wright was known as an expert in dating pottery and leading archaeological digs in the Palestinian region. Frank Cross was also renowned for his preservation, study, translation, and expertise in the Dead Sea Scrolls which, from 1953 forward, became his life's work and resulted in his later publication *Canaanite Myth and the Hebrew Epic* (1973).

Newport was captivated with Wright and Cross' adventurous tales and loved to converse with them about their travels and discoveries, as their links to Kathleen Kenyon and her excavation of Jericho between 1951 and 1958 made for lively discussions and almost weekly news. He soaked up this information like a sponge. As authors of dozens of books and journal, encyclopedic, and commentary articles about the lands of the Bible, their formidable scholarship served to supply additional material for Newport's teaching lectures for the tours he would continue to conduct to these very regions.

Finally, during this year in Harvard, two prominent philosophers impacted John's thinking the most: John Daniel Wild (1902–1972),[30] professor of philosophy, and Paul Johannes Tillich (1886–1965),[31] one of only five "University Professors" at Harvard Divinity School, who taught philosophical theology. Wild was two years from moving on to Northwestern University, but he was still a leading faculty member at Harvard and important to Newport's thought because of his emphases upon existentialism and phenomenology, both concepts with which Newport continued to dialogue and follow for the rest of his career.

It was the erudition of Paul Tillich that particularly captivated John's attention, however. John was so fascinated by him that John later undertook to write a book on his life and thought. Tillich was perhaps the theologian with the widest horizon among the great theologians of the twentieth century, since his approach was historical, intercultural, interdisciplinary, and interreligious. Tillich wanted to recreate a meaningful link between Christianity and contemporary society by reintroducing the truth of the absoluteness of God and the Christian message, particularly into the chaos of postwar Europe. This was contrary to the message of liberal Protestantism at the time, which robbed Christianity of its essence.

Tillich also linked the Christian message to social justice. He asserted that the absolute God was present in all of life and that religion was a necessary dimension of every culture. John Newport had read Tillich's first two volumes of *Systematic Theology* (1951, 1957) and his *Dynamics of Faith* (1957), and his soul resonated with much he had read. His friendship with Paul Tillich would begin here and continue until Tillich's death six years later. Many of his writings and ideas, however, would live on in Newport's own teaching and writing.

One other relationship from this year was important to John. Not far from the campus of Harvard lay the sprawling campus of Massachusetts Institute of Technology (MIT). Here John also met and befriended Huston Cummings Smith (1919–2016), chair of the department of philosophy and already considered a premier scholar on world religions.[32] They shared the same age and interests regarding how people practiced their religious beliefs. Smith had just published a book that would sell more than two million copies in the next fifty years, *The Religions of Man* (later retitled *World's Religions*, 1958), a comparative religions and mystical traditions textbook. As a world traveler and a sensitive filterer of religious tenets and expressions, Smith helped to shape the academic conversation about comparative religion, interfaith dialogue, and religious tolerance in the twentieth century. John was a beneficiary of this friend's journey of faith and drew upon his work when he wrote his own world religions lectures, articles, and books.

Ever ready to learn, explore, and investigate, John also delved into the beliefs and practices of Transcendentalism, Christian Science, and Swedenborg while he was in Boston, since the city was where members of the American Literary Transcendentalist school, like Ralph Waldo Emerson (1803–1882), Henry David Thoreau (1817–1862), and Nathaniel Hawthorne (1804–1864), had lived and worked a century before and where the "Mother Church" of Christian Science was located.

He and the family enjoyed New England's heritage. The rich beauty of its verdant hills and its colorful leaves reminded him of his boyhood home. Traveling through the eight-state New England region allowed him the time to relive the Puritan heritage of America's earliest days and gave him an even greater appreciation for his own family's heritage. His family joined him for jaunts and visits to his research sites, spending time with him in a more relaxed setting. This was a year for making memories.[33]

As the summer of 1959 came to a close, the Newports turned their faces homeward. John was intellectually richer by far than he had been when he had commenced his journey. At forty-two years old, his currents of knowledge were both wide and deep, sweeping him forward and propelling him toward mature scholarship. This year had been a most invigorating study sabbatical. With renewed purpose and excitement, John packed his expanded mind along with the family's baggage into the car and returned to Fort Worth. He was ready to teach again.

5
The Long Rolling River
1959–1971

> I am reading six books at once, the only way of reading;
> since, as you will agree, one book is only a single unaccompanied note,
> and to get the full sound, one needs ten others at the same time.
>
> **Virginia Woolf**[1]

John was forty-two years old when he returned to take up his responsibilities at Southwestern Seminary. Building upon the foundation laid by his faculty predecessors in philosophy, Albert Venting, who taught from 1921 to 1937 and Stewart A. Newman from 1936 to 1952, Newport took the next few years to develop a strong, integrated biblical philosophy.[2] During this decade, his own worldview crystallized, and he found that touring the world and teaching at other faculties had heightened his experiential as well as cognitive learning. In the fall of 1959, fresh from his time away and full of New England's intellectual bounty, John made his students his first priority.

Southwestern Baptist Theological Seminary, 1959–1971

John began to teach philosophy classes almost exclusively in this new season. This time, however, he had help. Milton Ferguson joined the faculty as professor of philosophy of religion in 1959, coinciding with John's return. These two became close friends and shared the department's teaching load until 1973.

Even though John Newport had been thoroughly grounded in a biblical foundation since childhood, which had remained with him thus far, he still searched through the 1950s and early 1960s for a philosophical direction, a point of reference, an encompassing *weltanschauung* that would serve as his organizational framework for thinking and teaching. He had written and privately published various compilations of notes for his students to use in his courses across the years. His four-volume *A Guide to a Christian Philosophy of Religion* was an anthology of many views, while his two-volume *Questions People Ask about a Christian Philosophy of Religion* reflected more of his own thinking on key issues and philosophical perspectives. In addition, his *A Guide to Religious Authority and Biblical Interpretation in the Thought of John Calvin* drew from his research in Edinburgh, and *Biblical Interpretation and the Modern Mind* explored options in epistemology.[3] None of these had satisfied Newport as a definitive textbook, especially since he had returned from Harvard. While he taught, he thought; his mind began to synthesize once again as he interacted with and engaged the minds of students.

Newport loved the dialogical model of learning best. Appearing the first day of class with a bulging briefcase and an arm full of books, he would introduce the course in his commanding voice and embark upon a semester's conversation that was far-reaching, intellectually stimulating, and challenging—all without loosening the biblical moorings he held to be essential. He taught and supervised many students and spent extra hours, often in his study after dinner, grading exams and research papers, guiding doctoral students, and evaluating dissertations. His new article, "Religion and Morals," in the *Baptist Student* magazine was published in 1959 just as he arrived back on campus.[4] Added to these academic tasks were the many committee and administrative responsibilities he undertook and the deepening of the relationship John was forging with his old friend, but new president, Robert Ernest Naylor (1909–1999), who had shouldered the mantle of presidential leadership in 1958 while John was away on sabbatical leave.

Robert Naylor was no stranger to Fort Worth or the seminary, having served as pastor of the Travis Avenue Baptist Church in Fort Worth for six years and as a member of the seminary board of trustees since 1941. He had actually been chairman of that body for three years when the news came that the previous president, Dr. J. Howard Williams, had died.[5] Robert had served with such distinction that the trustee search committee was convinced of his abilities and prevailed upon him to become the fifth president of Southwestern. He accepted on 22 June 1958. By that time, John had already left for Cambridge and Boston. Upon his return a year later, Naylor's presidency, which would last a full two decades, was in full swing, and a number of advances were underway.

Teaching under Naylor's Tenure, 1958–1978

Many changes took place when Naylor became president. His contacts across the SBC and his ability to engender trust with donors and leaders aided the seminary's explosive growth during his term of office. The trustee board was strengthened.[6] An administrative restructuring brought greater efficiency in operation when vice presidents were added to share the administrative load. Under Naylor's leadership, the school received a larger share of SBC funding and saw the completion of the Naylor Student Center (1965), the Walsh Medical Clinic (1968), the president's home (1971), the Naylor Children's Building (1973), and the Slover Recreation and Aerobics Center (1979). Older buildings were renovated, classroom space opened for use, and student housing expanded. Each month seemed to bring new sounds and sights as the building projects across campus moved toward completion. Southwestern was a busy place. Each effort undergirded the primary and significant task of SWBTS—the student learning that teachers fostered in the classrooms.

When Naylor moved into the president's office in 1958, a total of 2,395 students were enrolled in the classes of fifty-three faculty members. By the time of his retirement in 1978, two decades later, that teaching cadre numbered 125 men and women serving as professors, teaching assistants, adjunct teachers, and guest professors.[7] Naylor brought several outstanding scholars and practitioners to the seminary's faculty during these years and encouraged the accrediting agencies to recognize the quality of their teaching.

Newport's colleagues, most of whom became lifelong friends and who were appointed to the theology ranks during this period, were: Robert O. Coleman, Biblical Backgrounds (1958); William L. Hendricks, Theology (1958); Kenneth Chafin, Evangelism (1959); G. Lacoste Munn, New Testament (1959); D. David Garland, Old Testament (1959); Huber L. Drumwright, New Testament (1951–1959, and after 1960); Harry Leon McBeth, Church History (1962); Thomas C. Urrey, New Testament (1963); William Pinson Jr., Christian Ethics (1963); Roy J. Fish, Evangelism (1965); F. B. Huey, Old Testament

(1965); Clyde J. Fant, Preaching (1966); William B. Tolar, Biblical Backgrounds (1967); Larry L. Walker, Old Testament (1967); John J. Kiwiet, Theology (1968); Gerald E. Marsh, Pastoral Ministry (1969); Farrar Patterson, Preaching (1969); David F. D'Amico, Church History (1970); Douglas Ezell, Preaching (1970); Bert B. Dominy, Theology (1970); J. N. "Boo" Heflin, Old Testament (1972); Jimmie Nelson, Old Testament (1972); Yandall C. Woodfin, Philosophy of Religion (1960–1967, and after 1973); James W. Eaves, Evangelism (1973); J. David Fite, Pastoral Ministry and Continuing Education (1973); Justice C. Anderson, Missions (1974); Harold Freeman, Preaching (1974); W. Oscar Thompson, Evangelism (1974); Ebbie C. Smith, Christian Ethics and Missions (1975); Scott L. Tatum, Preaching (1975); L. Russ Bush, Philosophy of Religion (1975); Al Fasol, Preaching (1975); Lorin L. Cranford, New Testament (1976); Bobby E. Adams, Christian Ethics (1976); James A. Brooks, New Testament (1976); Harry B. Hunt Jr., Old Testament (1976); R. Bruce Corley, New Testament (1976); and Thomas J. Nettles, Church History (1976).[8]

While John was teaching several classes a semester, he quickly resumed a frenetic pace of pulpit and conference speaking, revivals, student retreats, laymen's institutes, training seminars, club and banquet speeches, and writing. With the expanded faculty, John was able to focus on the academic discipline he loved best—philosophy. He taught a variety of courses at the master and doctoral levels. He offered courses in philosophy of religion and philosophical theology; epistemology, religious authority, and religious language; religion and contemporary art forms; religion and American thought, including American literature, pragmatism, and process philosophy; and contemporary European philosophies of religion, such as existentialism and phenomenology. Other courses were in the academic areas of primitive, Middle Eastern, and Far Eastern religions; Mysticism, including Eastern and Western categories; occult studies; religion and science, including faith and nature; theology and philosophies of history; evil and suffering; and the philosophies of eschatology.[9]

Newport's Developing Worldview

Finally, in 1963, Newport formulated a sharp, biblical worldview. His student course text that year included his *Biblical Philosophy and the Modern Mind*, which contained his newly published article by the same name.[10] In this article, Newport defined his new biblical philosophy, a decided shift

Frank, Martha, John
The John Newports

Martha, Frank, and Johnny, 1962

from his former objective philosophical approach and traditional apologetics. No longer was he searching for his strategic organizational principle. The impetus for this crystallizing, he said, was his relationship with G. Ernest Wright, with whom he had studied at Harvard, and Wright's emphasis upon realism.[11] It was Wright who talked to John about synthesizing the two fields of biblical theology and philosophy.

Wright was a student of the famous archaeologist William Foxwell Albright (1891–1971) and one of his most accomplished students, renowned in his own right. W. F. Albright, linguist and biblical scholar, was on faculty at Johns Hopkins and had exerted considerable influence on key thinkers within the new "Biblical Theology Movement." This movement was a largely North American phenomenon that sprang up after World War II and ended in the 1960s.[12] Albright had penned no volumes specifically on biblical theology, but his students had done so with distinction. Wright, a professor at Harvard Divinity School, field archaeologist, and founder of the periodical *Biblical Archaeologist*, exemplified the priority of history and archaeology to Old Testament theology. He was also, from 1961 until his death, the Parkman Professor and the curator of the Semitic Museum. In his book, *The God Who Acts*, Wright argued that:

> Biblical theology is first and foremost a theology of recital in which Biblical man confesses his faith by reciting the formative events of his history as the redemptive handiwork of God. The *realism* [author's emphasis] of the Bible consists in its close attention to the facts of history and of tradition because these facts are the facts of God.[13]

It is generally understood that the Biblical Theology movement, with its interest in biblical history and archaeology, emerged as a more objective approach than the dominant Old Testament higher-critical approaches and sought a middle ground in early twentieth-century debates between modernists and fundamentalists, the former characteristically dismissing or minimizing the authority of the Bible and the latter taking a literalistic stance in these matters.[14]

While in Cambridge, Newport had many conversations with Wright, who urged him "to develop a distinctively biblical philosophy following the structures of the biblical mind and the centrality of history and covenant."[15] Before John had met Wright at Harvard, he had, in his own words, taken "a neutral, objective approach. After, I began with the Christian faith and biblical key-categories, then turned to dialogue." He said, "I began with history plus existence, then proceeded to revelation and to reason, and from reason to dialogue with world religions, art, science, etc."[16]

Before John left Cambridge, Professor Wright invited John to his home. Wright's concern was the possibility of developing a more "adequate approach to the teaching of philosophy of religion in evangelical seminaries." He argued that a unique biblical approach might be used to answer philosophical inquiries. Wright and Newport discussed how this approach could be developed and implemented. John later said that this session with Wright was the impetus to his changed direction.[17] In his personal research and classrooms, then, Newport made his shift. In the next two decades, John would pen and present his more comprehensive and maturing biblical worldview for wider audiences.

During these years, visitors to Newport's seminary or home office routinely found his desk piled with books, articles, magazines, and journals, and almost hidden by the stacks, John himself, preparing a sermon or scholarly presentation or manuscript. He was a voracious reader, a habit cultivated in childhood and carried through to his last weeks of life. When he walked the campus, his nose was in a book. While descending stairs, he read. When riding to the airport, he sat in the back seat, absorbed in the latest volume. On trains, planes, and automobiles, he would rather read than converse or take in the scenery. He took arms full of books to class with slips of tissue marking the pages he wished to note. He was obsessed with the written word and tried to read every new addition to the library so that he could dialogue with peers and experts and students about the latest ideas. Confronting him in the hallway, or arriving early for class, or visiting him in his office would like as not precipitate the question, "Have you read . . . ?"

During these years, John was also writing, producing several articles for publication, most of which dealt with scriptural authority and the intersection between religion and art. He also penned a chapter tribute to his beloved friend, J. Howard Williams, for whom he felt deep respect and admiration.[18] John pored over travel itineraries and guidebooks to places he wished to explore, always tied to information he felt he must learn. At this time, he particularly longed to study in Asia. He sensed that if he were to understand and deal with philosophical developments, particularly mysticism and New Age groups, he would need to study the writings and philosophies of, experience the cultures of, and engage with the people of the Far and Middle East. He needed to become acquainted with "eastern thought." Thus, in the summer of 1963, John organized and guided a tour to some of these places, and included his daughter, Martha, in the company. They toured Russia, Egypt, and the Middle East, which opened a larger world for Martha.[19]

Early in 1965, John had the opportunity to apply for another study leave for the academic year of 1965–1966, made possible because another faculty member, who was intending to take leave, was unable to do so. John received word that he had won a research grant to become a postdoctoral visiting scholar at Union Theological Seminary and Columbia University in New York City. Since this leave was now assured, he also made further inquiries about a travel tour to take place during the summer prior to his sabbatical. With help from the SBC Foreign Mission Board in

John Newport, c. 1963

John Newport teaching in Taiwan, 1965

Richmond and a recommendation by his friend, Robert Slater, John made plans to travel to Thailand, Taiwan, Korea, Japan, and the Hindu Benares University, and made contacts to visit in Iran. His dream to investigate the Far East was becoming a reality at last.

This trip further opened Newport's eyes and mind to the wonders of ancient civilizations and the complex intermingling of theological, philosophical, and cultural roots of other world religions. He learned lessons from alternative religious traditions and the practices of Buddhists, Hindus, Muslims, followers of Confucianism, and other peoples. This firsthand knowledge supplemented his thinking, research, and writing about emerging world religions and became a focus of several scholarly addresses, articles, and books in the next decade.[20] As John ended his summer travel of 1965, after a trip home, he arrived in New York and took up his study routine at Union and Columbia that fall.

Union Theological Seminary and Columbia, New York City, 1965

John's sojourn in New York City was a joy for him, personally. The city's eclectic and diverse voices hummed in its museums and sang in its streets. The notes wove a palpable harmony of music, drama, art, conversation, and scholarly discourse. Their choruses energized him. The faculties at Union Theological Seminary and Columbia University received him well in his role as a postdoctoral visiting scholar. John was given a small office and was introduced to the faculties of each school. The purpose of his year of study was to investigate several areas of academic and applied theology, including philosophical theology, religion and contemporary arts, Jewish philosophy, and social ethics. Since John had several professors in mind from whom he wished to learn, he began to seek them out in typical Newport fashion. He made an appointment to visit, and then invited them to share a meal. Almost immediately, he cultivated the acquaintance of three fiery and famous Christian ethicists, each of whom had gained a reputation for outspoken involvement in politics.

The first of these was the president of Union Theological Seminary, John Coleman Bennett (1902–1995), called "Dr. Bennett" because of the more than twenty honorary doctorates conferred upon him by mid-career.[21] With Bennett, John was able to discuss social ethics and ecumenism and note firsthand the dynamic and profound interchange between theology, ethics, and culture in the life of this activist-scholar.

Another prominent faculty member was Karl Paul Reinhold Niebuhr (1892–1971), the older brother of Richard Niebuhr, late theological ethicist for many decades at Yale University, whom John had met while on sabbatical leave in New England.[22] Reinhold was an ethicist, shaper of public policy and international political relations, and one of the most powerful social activists of the twentieth century. Reinhold was in the last years of his life when John Newport met him and took him to restaurants, where they had conversations over dinner about his brother and philosophy and life.

Reinhold's complex philosophy, based upon the fallibility of humankind, the absurdity of human pretensions, and the biblical teaching that one should love God and one's neighbor, continued to pervade his thinking. Reinhold rejected utopian idealism, which asserts that greater reasoning, education, and technological conquests of nature make for moral progress. He also dismissed the notion that, because nations and peoples are inherently selfish, therefore, selfishness cannot be overcome. Instead, he believed that politics is the rational direction of the irrationalities of human beings.

He challenged intellectual men and women to cooperate to lend their learning toward solving the practical problems of power and social justice. To a man like John Newport, whose worldview was also based upon the biblical truth of mankind's sinful condition and the need for holistic redemption, Reinhold's applied theology both affirmed his thinking and inspired him to be a link in the training of global and collaborative solution-seekers.

The third outspoken ethicist was the Methodist pastor-scholar Tom Faw Driver (1925–present),[23] the Paul J. Tillich Professor of Theology and Culture. Driver's cross-disciplinary and ecumenical career united three principal areas of Newport's own interests: modern theological thought in relation to culture; ritual, religion, and theater as modes of performance; and the rejection of war and the advocacy of nonviolent resistance to evil. In many ways, sans the activism of Driver's later life, Newport's career of eclectic interests was similar to that of Tom Driver. Newport interacted with colleagues whose academic foci evolved with the continuous modulations of culture and ideas. Like these intellectual mentors, John also seemed always to be seeking the next perplexing question to unravel and solve and pursued each ensuing topic with a consuming passion.[24]

Never satiated and always processing his new learning, Newport made the acquaintance of another intellectual giant he had hoped to meet, John Macquarrie (1919–2007), the Scottish-born, Anglican philosopher-theologian. Macquarrie had recently come to Union Theological Seminary in 1962 as professor of systematic theology.[25] They were roughly the same age and shared a love of Scotland. Macquarrie's recent co-translation of Martin Heidegger's *Sein und Zeit* (*Being and Time*, 1962) into English and his deft explanations of the pedantic philosopher's work to English audiences drew Newport to him. Macquarrie was also a facile commentator on the work of Rudolf Bultmann, an added bonus.

Macquarrie had written an article, published in 1964, called "Christianity and Other Faiths,"[26] which asserted that, while rejecting syncretism, truth-value could reside in other faith traditions. He believed that people of faith should respect and even learn from each other's beliefs. In the year John was at Union, Macquarrie was also writing a manuscript, published as *Principles of Christian Theology* the following year, the thesis of which attempted to bridge existentialism with orthodox Christian thought. Newport was fond of Macquarrie, enjoyed their stimulating conversations, and followed his career from this point forward. He too was open to learning from people of other faiths.

One of John's intentions in coming to Union was also to engage with a trio of selected biblical scholars during his stay in New York. John had written an article in 1952 called "New Developments in New Testament Theology," and another article on the subject of biblical interpretation was then fermenting in his mind.[27] He wanted to consult with two eminent leaders in the field of New Testament studies, Frederick Clifton Grant (1891–1974)[28] and William David Davies (1911–2001).[29] Frederick Grant was the Edward Robinson Professor Emeritus of Biblical Theology at Union Theological Seminary, an author, and part of an international circle of leading New Testament scholars. He was one of nine who had translated and published the Revised Standard Version of the Bible in 1952, including Henry J. Cadbury (Harvard University), Walter Russell Bowie (Union Theological Seminary), Millar Burrows (Yale University, joined the team in 1938), Clarence T. Craig (Oberlin Graduate School of Theology), Edgar J. Goodspeed (University of Chicago), James Moffatt (Union Theological Seminary, died in 1944), Luther A. Weigle (Yale University), and Abdel R. Wentz (Lutheran Theological Seminary).

Grant had introduced form criticism to America and argued in his 1957 book, *The Gospels: Their Origin and Growth*, that Matthew, Mark, and Luke drew from a single collection of stories, testimonies, and other information. John was able to schedule several sessions with Grant to discuss the new form criticism in New Testament research and its implications for other theological disciplines. To read a unit of text and attempt to determine its meaning for the original readers, even perhaps before it was inserted into the biblical narrative, had the potential to impact profoundly the intertextual conversations between the Old and New Testament scholars, the historical study of biblical literature, linguistics, and hermeneutics. With much to process from Grant's conversations, Newport sought out the second New Testament scholar he wished to consult—W. D. Davies.

Davies had been at Union a decade, and John Newport met him just months before Davies left Union to return to Duke University. Davies had developed a significant friendship with Reinhold Niebuhr at Union and, across the street at the Jewish Theological Seminary of America, with Louis Finkelstein, Abraham Joshua Heschel, and Saul Lieberman. He also was a close colleague of Salo Wittmayer Baron of Columbia University, which was down the hill from Union. Davis had a single passion with two foci: the first was the Jewish background of the New Testament, and the second was the theological implications of this background, particularly the tensions between law and gospel in Paul's writings. Davies introduced John Newport to Abraham Joshua Heschel (1907–1972), professor of Jewish mysticism, who was the third scholar with whom John had longed to study.[30]

Known as one of the foremost Jewish theologians and philosophers of the twentieth century and a leader in the American civil rights movement, Abraham Heschel was almost sixty years old when he and John, younger by a decade, became friends. Abraham had just launched his seventh book, *Who Is Man?*, in early June 1965. The primary focus of Heschel's work was that encountering the Divine, or "ineffable," is a fundamental experience common to humankind, and that no religious tradition can claim to have the sum of religious truth. He examined the human search for spirituality and questions about doubt and faith in his earlier volumes, *Man Is Not Alone* (1951), his philosophy of religion, and *God in Search of Man* (1955), his philosophy of Judaism, and called for a careful and correct synthesis of both intention and observance for persons of faith. John Newport was keen to absorb a greater understanding of Christian roots from this enigmatic intellectual giant. They spent many days together, walking paths in Central Park and discussing the philosophical roots of faith together.

Of enduring joy to Newport was the friendship he made with Daniel Day Williams (1910–1973),[31] professor of theology at Union and specialist in process theology. Newport remained in dialogue with this brilliant scholar for the remainder of Williams' life and counted his time with Daniel as a gift. All of these scholars, with their specialties in New Testament, Jewish philosophy, and process theology, enhanced Newport's understanding of both new developments in New Testament studies, the process of biblical interpretation, and the significance of Judaism to Christianity's theological moorings. These were valuable months that provided deep wisdom for John's later teaching and scholarship.

Southwestern Again, 1966-1971

Upon returning to Fort Worth from his sabbatical in New York, John found Southwestern alive with excitement. Old students were returning to campus and new students had been enrolled in his absence.[32] President Naylor had been working with an industrious and responsible board of trustees that had added substantively to a positive ethos and an ambitious building plan for the campus. The two-storied, spacious Robert E. Naylor Student Center was finished in 1965, and the numbers of faculty had increased. After John had met his new colleagues, settled into his full teaching schedule, begun mentoring his students again, and attending committee meetings, he drove to the campus of Texas Christian University across the city and applied for admittance. John intended to earn another master's degree.

Master of Arts, Texas Christian University

John wanted to deepen his own philosophical understanding of linguistic analysis and religious language. He had discovered a weakness in his understanding and wished to make this an area of academic strength instead. Especially helpful in his investigations were professors Ted Klein and Alvin Nelson of TCU's faculty, and the writings of the elder statesman in philosophy, Arthur Campbell Garnett, just retiring after twenty-eight years at the University of Wisconsin.[33] Klein was a relative newcomer to TCU's faculty, joining its ranks as a young scholar in 1963, fresh from Yale, where he had earned his Ph.D. in 1958. Klein taught philosophy and worked alongside John. Alvin Nelson and John were the same age and had been working on many of the same topics as well. Alvin had earned his B.A. and M.A. from the University of Nebraska and his Ph.D. from Ohio State University. He had come to TCU in 1960 from the faculty of Yonkers College in New York, where he had held the C. M. Fiske chair of philosophy and psychology. Klein, Nelson, and Newport were members of the same academic societies and had become good friends. Both of these scholars provided new insights and advised John on his master's thesis, "Representative Contemporary Attempts to Establish the Meaningfulness and Uniqueness of Religious and Biblical Language," which was approved and granted in 1968.

John also noted that, in these years following his sabbatical, A. C. Garnett had influenced his thinking about metaphysics. Garnett's *Reality and Value*, originally published in 1937, addressed the importance of the theory of values that rests on a general metaphysical understanding, founded upon a comprehensive view of all aspects of the world. Garnett argued against absolutist theories; instead, he offered a realistic one that encompassed a proposition of space and time and considered value as an object of immediate intuition. These great philosophical questions fed into discussions of the philosophy of religion and of science because Garnett distinguished between spiritual values and other values on the ground that spiritual values are not subjective to satiety, while other values are. He contended that one's knowledge of mind is as direct and reliable as one's knowledge of the physical world.

As he was exploring and processing his responses to these leading areas of philosophical inquiry, John was consistently preaching and speaking. In the single year of 1968, for example, excluding his tour lectures when he was away from 17 June through 2 August, he spoke 112 times in churches and civic clubs.[34] He spoke at pastors' meetings and evangelism and student conferences. He delivered sermons on Sundays and Wednesday nights. He taught January Bible studies, held revivals, and was guest speaker for banquets, community gatherings, college and seminary chapels, and business retreats. He attended and spoke at state and national Baptist conventions and gatherings. He regularly took buses or trains or drove from one destination and traveled through the night to arrive at his next engagement.

John's reputation as a scholar was growing. He began to receive honors as he engaged with a widening circle of Baptists and evangelicals. In 1967,

William Jewell College, his alma mater, conferred upon him the honorary Doctor of Letters degree. That same year and the next, he served as president of the American Academy of Religion, Southwestern Division. He was a member of the Southwestern Philosophical Association and the Society of Biblical Literature and Exegesis, and frequently attended the Baptist World Alliance annual gatherings each summer.

Despite his heavy speaking and teaching schedules, in his personal life John remained devoted to his family. When he was away from home, he faithfully wrote to his mother and father once a week and kept Eddie Belle's mailbox full of letters, writing her and the children each day. In these letters, John sent newspaper clippings, bulletins of church services, and church newsletters, sharing the details of what had happened and who he had met at each event. He kept up with the children's and Eddie Belle's well-being, responded to her family and local news, and reminded her of his love for them.[35] In turn, Eddie Belle sent John letters in advance to arrive in his hotel rooms, or at churches where he would preach, so that he would have them waiting when he walked through the door.[36]

Next to his family, and students, and being with the people of God in church settings, John loved travel. So did Eddie Belle. Always planning their next travel destination together, they scheduled two exciting projects for the end of this decade—the "World Tours" as John called them. The first was from "East to West," and the second was from "West to East."

Around the World Tours of 1968 and 1970

John and Eddie Belle Newport organized a tour during the summer of 1968. Eddie Belle handled the logistics, a role she seemed born to do, and John delivered the lectures and added historical and cultural background to each stop. They toured cities in Japan, China, Thailand, India, Egypt, Lebanon, Israel, Greece, Italy, Switzerland, Paris, and England, in twelve countries in almost seven weeks. About thirty friends, laypersons from churches, students from the seminary, and other interested individuals jumped at the chance to explore the world with these affable and gracious hosts. Participants strolled ancient cities, visited historical sites, and saw, through John's eyes and mind, the importance of what they were experiencing. His exhaustive lecture notes from these trips cover cultural, linguistic, historical, and spiritual background. They were also full of little-known facts and curiosities, delivered in John's inimitable style. That year, John and Eddie Belle took their middle son, Frank, who was nineteen and a college student.

Just two years later in 1970, John and William Tolar, professor of Old Testament and archeology, codirected a similar tour, this time beginning in Scotland and traveling through Norway, Sweden, Finland, the U.S.S.R., Romania, Turkey, Cyprus, Israel, India, Thailand, Hong Kong, Japan, and back home through Hawaii. This trip took in fourteen countries in a little more than five weeks. Bill Tolar, with his rapid-fire Louisiana drawl and eyes that twinkled in fun, was a popular teacher at Southwestern, and had gained a following. His knowledge of all things pertaining to the Holy Land was vast and his congenial, humorous, and vivacious personality made him a splendid host. John and Bill shared the lectures, alternating the subject matter to suit their respective expertise.[37] This is the year that John and Eddie Belle's sixteen-year-old son, John Jr., accompanied the group. By the end of this year, each of the Newport children had experienced an international tour.

Shifts in American and Christian Culture

As John returned home, his writing accelerated and a new volume was released in 1971, *Theology and Contemporary Art Forms*,[38] based in part upon what he had observed in churches and communities and museums in Mexico, England, Scotland, Europe, the Far East, Middle East, and Near East. His personal experience of Scotland's postwar resurgence of significant, new, and meaningful religious expressions had caused him to rethink how Christians could share their faith effectively in fresh mediums and symbols. The next year, Newport's fascinating book, *Demons, Demons, Demons*, was published. When released, the volume sparked dozens of invitations to speak in churches, student groups, and seminars. This volume had hit a nerve. The American culture had changed in the 1960s and early 1970s and its religious landscape with it.

American Cultural Changes

In 1961, the Cuban Bay of Pigs attempt to overthrow Fidel Castro failed. In 1962, Russia's buildup of nuclear missile bases on that island continued the Cold War's escalation. The same year, East Germany sealed sixty-eight of the eighty crossings between East and West Berlin and erected the Berlin Wall. In 1963, U.S. President Kennedy was shot by Lee Harvey Oswald, and Martin Luther King Jr. led a peaceful march of 250,000 people on

Washington, D.C. to demand equal civil rights. In Asia, although there had been conflict in Vietnam since the 1950s, U.S. Navy vessels were attacked by North Vietnamese torpedo boats in 1964. War erupted. By the next August, more than 125,000 U.S. troops were actively serving in Vietnam. Mao Tse Tung's Cultural Revolution began in 1965 and, in 1966, the first pictures of the moon's surface were transmitted from Russia's unmanned spacecraft, Luna 9, and shown on television. In 1968, both Martin Luther King Jr. and Robert F. Kennedy were assassinated. It seemed the whole world was politically unstable.

In science, the laser came into use in 1961. The next year, after the Russians had successfully sent Yuri Gagarin to orbit the earth in his capsule, Vostok 3KA, then-President Kennedy launched the Apollo Project to put a U.S. astronaut on the moon by the end of the decade, for the United States was racing for prominence in space exploration and achievements. John Glenn became the first American in space the following year. Quasars and quarks were discovered, as were rotating neutron stars. In 1968, Apollo 8 made the first manned orbit of the moon, and the next year, on 20 July, Neil Armstrong was the first human being to step foot on its surface. President Kennedy's dream had been realized, although he had not lived to see it.

In medicine, British immunologists discovered antibodies in 1963, and American physician J. D. Hardy performed the first successful lung transplant. This precipitated global transplant research that resulted in Dr. Christian Barnard's first successful heart transplant in 1967 in Cape Town, South Africa. Medicare was signed into law in 1965. Closer to home, cultural revolutions overturned America. The Civil Rights Acts of 1960 and 1964 protected the voting rights of African American citizens and guaranteed equal treatment in public accommodation, education, and employment. The Peace Corps was launched, even as anti-war protestors rioted in America's streets.

Rock and roll music demanded the cessation of war, and "draft-dodgers" fled across the nation's borders to escape service in the military. A "hippie" counterculture arose, centered in its early days on the east and west coasts. A music festival was held on 15–18 August 1969 on Max Yasgur's 600-acre dairy farm in Bethel, New York, about forty miles southwest of Woodstock. This event became an iconic symbol of the younger generation's dissatisfaction with American politics and war policies. Billed as "an Aquarian Exposition: 3 Days of Peace & Music," this rock festival attracted more than 400,000 participants. In California, hippies took over the Haight-Ashbury district of San Francisco, near Golden Gate Park, and created an anti-war, anti-establishment commune there, a social experiment in which drugs, music, and countercultural ideals were practiced. Their peace-agenda "Flower Power" and "Make Love, Not War" slogans were plastered across windows and cars.

A local self-described "community anarchist" group, called The Diggers, believed in both a free society and the good in human nature. To express their belief, they established a free store, gave out free meals daily, and built a free medical clinic, which was the first of its kind, all of which relied on volunteers and donations. Members of the bands Jefferson Airplane and Grateful Dead and singer Janis Joplin all lived there. Thousands of young people left their homes, streaming from every state, to join the movement, which peaked about 1967 when the last residents staged a "funeral" for the hippie movement in October.[39]

Christian Cultural Changes

In Christian circles, a similar movement with a different focus took a parallel path. The Youth Revival movement of the 1940s, especially Intervarsity Fellowship, organized in 1941, Billy Graham's influence upon the formation of the 1946 Youth for Christ International organization, and Bill Bright's 1951 Campus Crusades had captured the hearts of evangelical young people in churches and schools across the nation. These revivals and discipleship ministries had provided opportunities and training for spiritual conversions and growth. John Newport and his brother Russell had served as a preacher-musician team for several such crusades and revivals.[40]

In the late 1960s and throughout the 1970s, however, these Christian young people, who had grown up in the same culture that had produced the hippies, found a faith response that was uniquely countercultural as well. The movement started on the West Coast when several rock band members, like Chuck Girard, Tommy Coomes, Jay Truax, Fred Field, Keith Green, and Barry McGuire, were converted and began sharing with others the radical transformation they had experienced in Christ. They began to write music to reflect their new faith. This new music spread like wildfire and unified the movement. First called "Jesus People" by the press, and "Jesus Freaks" by the hippies, they were concerned about their own generation, were witnesses to its degeneration and hopelessness, and tried to be of help.[41]

The Jesus People movement was one of the few in American history with no recognized leader. Chuck Smith of the Calvary Chapel in Costa Mesa, California, was an early preacher who taught hundreds of young people each week and baptized them, upon their confession of faith in Jesus Christ, in the ocean. He and friends would launch the first contemporary Christian music label, Maranatha! Music, in 1971 as an outlet for the Jesus Music bands playing at Calvary Chapel. Many music groups developed out of this, and some became the voices of the Jesus People movement, most notably Barry McGuire, Love Song, Second Chapter of Acts, Petra, Randy Stonehill, Andrae Crouch and the Disciples, Nancy Honeytree, and Larry Norman.

They played a new, folk-rock style of hymns and worship songs influenced by their own salvation and the experience of being together as a younger generation under the leadership of God's Spirit. Coffee houses with black lights and readings of Christian poetry, art exhibitions, and contemporary Christian concerts entered into the culture of evangelical life, accompanied by drums and guitars in worship services. In the next decades, jeans would replace suits, tall stools would replace pulpits, and technology would arrive to help proclaim the Gospel in corporate worship and spawn another "war" of a worship kind. All of this was in the future as of yet. In 1970, the movement was just beginning. Some of these young people, however, had sensed a call to local church ministry and were now applying for admission to seminaries. Dozens of them were coming to Southwestern. John Newport was keenly aware of the cultural shifts in both Christian circles and in their broader contexts. His own children were of this very generation. As he anticipated and analyzed and interpreted the meanings of the shifts as they were happening, he wrote books at a steady pace to respond to what he was seeing, beginning in the 1970s and continuing into the 1990s.[42]

The 1960s and 1970s at Southwestern

For several years, each of the three schools at Southwestern Seminary had engaged in intensive self-study that resulted in strengthened curricula, new degrees, and the addition of new faculty. In the School of Religious Education, the Doctor of Religious Education was phased out and replaced with an improved Doctor of Education in 1965, and the addition of faculty specialists in age-graded study, curriculum, church building, and finances led to 143 new courses, of which sixty-two were at the doctoral level. The old degree, Associate in Religious Education, became the Diploma in Religious Education, and the Master of Religious Education was strengthened substantially. A Graduate Specialist in Religious Education was added for those students who wanted to concentrate in a particular area.

In the School of Theology, a professional doctorate, the new Doctor of Ministry degree, was added in 1972, and the former Doctor of Theology became the Doctor of Philosophy in 1973. In the School of Church Music, the Doctor of Church Music, established in 1961, had become the Doctor of Musical Arts in 1964, and students could minor in either of the schools of Theology or Religious Education. The old Master of Church Music branched into two possible degrees: the Master of Church Music, for students who sensed a call to serve the local church, or the Master of Music, for those who wanted to teach in college or university faculties. All schools were accredited by the Association of Theological Schools (ATS) and the Southern Association of Colleges and Schools (SACS).

In May 1971, the farsighted and harmonious seminary trustees approved the purchase of the seminary's first computer, which quickly became an efficient tool for many activities of the seminary. This machine helped with the administrative tasks of student registration and scheduling, business office transactions, library acquisitions, alumni records, and long-range planning. Southwestern also turned its attention to requests from pastors in other areas who needed training. Administrators planned for the opening of extension centers in the next few semesters.[43]

In the offing was the retirement announcement of President Robert Naylor, but that would not happen until 1976 and was still unknown at the time. As the decade of the 1960s passed and the calendar stood at 1970, John Newport began making arrangements for his next academic study leave. This time, he decided to study in Houston with the faculty of Rice University for the fall of 1971 and the academic year of 1972–1973. Rice University was to play a significant role in John's career and become his second academic home.

6
Navigating Rapids
1971–1994

> Reading furnishes the mind only with materials of knowledge;
> it is thinking that makes what we read ours. We are of the ruminating kind.
>
> **John Locke**[1]

John Newport petitioned for and received a half-year sabbatical leave for the fall of 1971 to study at Rice University in Houston. In visits to the Southwestern campus, Carl F. H. Henry had told John that one of the greatest needs in religious scholarship was for evangelicals to gain appointments in secular universities. Henry had encouraged John to remain open to such opportunities. Before long, through a series of providential circumstances, John's study leave evolved into an invitation to fill an endowed chair with full tenure at Rice.

Rice University, Fall 1971, 1972–1973, and 1976–1979

The Rice Department of Religious Studies had eleven professors when John and Eddie Belle moved some of their belongings into their new residence in the late summer of 1971. John was seen as the representative evangelical of the group. The other men had a variety of religious backgrounds. The visiting professorship proved to be a significant juncture in both John's approach to controversy and intellectual pursuits. He learned critical skills he would use the remainder of his life.

In the context of Rice's stimulating intellectual atmosphere, John served peaceably and cooperated with those with whom he might disagree. This did not mean that John either altered his own views or turned a blind eye to unorthodox beliefs he encountered. What he did learn was the importance of dialogue. Much more mature now at fifty-five, he assimilated his experiences, past and present, and addressed new challenges and questions with depth and precision. He was called upon to offer a conservative, evangelical position at more assemblies of scholars and wider religious audiences than he had ever been previously and to dialogue afterward. In public, academic, religious, civic, and other venues, John sharpened and practiced his abilities to think, process, and deliver thoughtful answers, adapting them to his varied audiences.

John Newport at Rice University in 1972

For example, at this time, both at Rice and in the Academy of Religion meetings, John was noting a strong move toward pluralism. There was a tendency to move religion into the private world of one's values and preferences, where questions of truth and falsity were deemed inappropriate to ask. John quoted Lesslie Newbigin as saying that "the central issue in the pluralistic approach to religion is the abandonment of the belief that it is possible to know the truth. It is true that the human mind cannot totally comprehend God. God is hidden, even in his revelation. But this true statement is used to disqualify any firm affirmation of truth."[2] John was concerned about this trend.

The years at Rice forced John to deal with the research bibliographies and movements of New Age, the occult, futurology, and the critiques of scholars, such as Paul Tillich. During this period, John's letters attest to his heavy teaching, writing, and speaking schedules. He worked fifteen hours a day, writing books late into the nights that would be published in the next years on the occult and new consciousness developments. He also wrote several journal articles.[3] He was in high demand as a speaker, combining his academic work with interim pastorates, revivals, student conferences, church study series, seminars, and college lectureships. As they settled in and forged deep friendships with the faculty and the congregation of the South Main Baptist Church, where he and Eddie Belle had become members, they decided to stay in Houston for the time being.

John had for some time been keen to study with Niels Nielsen Jr., chairman of the department of religious studies at Rice University.[4] These two scholars were almost the same age and shared a love of travel and a similar approach to philosophy. As members of the same academic societies, the American Philosophical Association, the American Academy of Religion, and the American Society for the Study of Religion, they had seen each other several times annually, corresponded, and become friends. John had a book in mind and sought Nielsen's input to aid in its early stages of organization and design.[5] While he was in Houston, John maintained his guest professorships, touring, and his many speaking engagements.

Golden Gate Guest Professor, South American Tours, and Southwestern 1972–1973

During the summer of 1972, John took a brief teaching assignment as guest professor at the Golden Gate Baptist Theological Seminary in Mill Valley, California, the youngest of the six seminaries of the Southern Baptist

Convention.⁶ He and Eddie Belle enjoyed the exquisite beauty of the campus on Strawberry Point overlooking Richardson Bay, across the Golden Gate Bridge from San Francisco. They experienced its impenetrable morning mists, climbed Mt. Tamalpais, strolled the redwood forest trails nearby, and fell asleep to the sounds of mournful foghorns and the sweep of lighthouse beams warning ships to avoid the coastline rocks. On weekends, they visited San Francisco and delighted in its famed Chinatown, street trolleys, and fishing wharfs. John spoke in churches, encouraging Baptists and making new friends. The faculty and students loved him.

During the summer of 1973, John and Eddie Belle hosted a tour to South America. They visited the countries, people, and cultures of Colombia, Peru, Chile, Argentina, Brazil, and Venezuela.⁷ On these trips, John invariably purchased objects of art and religious objects and wrote historical and theological lectures to accompany the daily stops. These countries fascinated John. His firsthand knowledge of their religions and his interpretation for Western minds, complete with illustrative objects for enhanced understanding, captured the imaginations of students from all walks of life.

In 1973, John was back again at Southwestern Seminary, where he picked up his responsibilities, continuing his training of doctoral students and teaching a full load, all while working on and finishing other manuscripts for publication. He remained there, hosting Middle Eastern tours with Eddie Belle each summer until 1976. During this time, John saw that the perception of the nature of the Bible and its interpretation were becoming increasing points of tension in both evangelical and SBC circles.

He wrote a semi-popular book entitled *Why Christians Fight Over the Bible* (1974), hoping to alleviate the developing tension. In this book, he developed a dialectical evangelical approach. He had been exposed both to radical higher criticism and narrow fundamentalism. Fortunately, he had studied with and learned from scholars in various locations the possibility of a balanced and constructive evangelical approach. He was desperately seeking for what he later called an "evangelical balance."⁸ During the 1960s and 1970s, Newport was invited to teach at Oklahoma State University, Southwest Missouri State University, Southern Seminary, Southeastern Seminary, and Northern Seminary, but Southwestern Seminary's rare combination of the experiential and the scholarly kept him in Fort Worth.

When Rice University offered John Newport the tenured Harry Chavanne Endowed Chair of Religion professorship to begin in the academic year of 1976–1977, however, John accepted. This move came as a surprise and dismay to many of the faculty at Southwestern. Dr. Naylor was contemplating, and then announced, his retirement from the presidency in November 1976 to become effective in August 1978.[9] Naylor felt that John's vast experience, stature, and abilities were needed at this time in the seminary's life. Nevertheless, despite his disappointment, Naylor expressed his full support of John's decision. John had also received many letters from Southwestern faculty members indicating their prayer for him and longing for his return to Southwestern.[10]

For John, to be on the faculty at Rice was stimulating, even challenging. He felt he walked a razor's edge when he contemplated how the two schools were situated on the spectrum of reason and faith. He saw Rice as more heavily weighted toward the mind and wished for more emphasis of faith. At the same time, he saw Southwestern Seminary's strength centered in faith, but sometimes longed for a greater openness in matters of reason and a willingness to engage and dialogue thoughtfully with wider scholarship. In his role at Rice that first summer, John put his head down and worked sixteen-hour days, writing, preparing lectures for the fall, and facilitating the department's business during the summer when its director, Niels Nielsen, was away.[11]

Presidential Transition at Southwestern

Meanwhile, in Fort Worth, as August 1978 neared, Robert Naylor's tenure as president was drawing to a close. The Southwestern trustees had put into place several measures that indicated their deep appreciation for his leadership as president. They had formed a committee that year to honor the retiring president and make provisions for his needs afterward. For twenty years the seminary had experienced unprecedented growth. President Naylor had secured additional funding from the Southern Baptist Convention and received many large private gifts and bequests for buildings and endowment. He had strengthened the faculty, assured the school's accreditation, and seen to the renovation of older buildings on campus and the building of new ones. He had provided housing for the students and added classrooms as the student enrollment was exploding. He had restructured the administration, resulting in the appointment of deans and better efficiency in the development and financial offices. He had acquired computers to manage the business, enrollment, and transcript processes. He had been a stabilizing factor in the convention controversies in the 1960s and 1970s.[12] His had been a remarkable presidency.

A nominating committee of the trustees sought many months to find a man whose background and stature had prepared him to take up the presidency of Southwestern. On 2 November 1977, with eight months left until Naylor's retirement date, James E. Carter, chairman of the committee, brought a recommendation to the trustees that Russell H. Dilday Jr., pastor of the Second-Ponce de Leon Baptist Church in Atlanta, Georgia, be named the sixth president of the seminary.[13]

Russell Dilday was born in 1930 in Amarillo, Texas, into a devout Christian family. His father was a strong educator and denominational leader among Texas Baptists. Russell earned degrees at Baylor University and Southwestern Seminary, including his Ph.D. in philosophy under the supervision of John Newport. He then served as pastor of two Texas churches, Antelope and Clifton, before he was called to Tallowood Baptist Church in Houston in 1959. After a decade there, he moved to Atlanta, Georgia, to pastor the historic Second-Ponce de Leon Baptist Church. In the meanwhile, the SBC had learned to respect his leadership. Russell served on the executive committee of the Georgia Baptist Convention (1970–1975), as moderator of the Atlanta Baptist Association (1973–1974), president of the Atlanta Baptist Association's Pastor's Conference (1974–1975), and second vice president of the SBC (1970–1971). He had demonstrated his scholarship and academic expertise by authoring two books, writing articles for many periodicals, and serving on the faculty of Baylor University and as a trustee of Baylor, San Marcos Academy, and Pace Academy in Georgia. He had also been president of the trustees of the SBC's Home Mission Board (1974–1976) and a member of the SBC's Missions Challenge Committee that articulated the seventy-five-year mission plan for the denomination.

Strong, articulate, capable, handsome, and personable, Russell was well-suited for this role. He and his wife Betty had three children, all of whom were students at Baylor in Texas. Robert, Nancy, and Ellen were glad to see their parents return home to Fort Worth. After his unanimous election by the Southwestern Seminary trustees on 22 November 1977, the trustees rose to their feet in unanimous applause. Russell would move to Fort Worth by the first of the year and begin work as president-elect. Betty would stay in Atlanta to prepare their home for sale and then join Russell in the early spring of 1978. With the new year, Russell spent January and

February in the American Management Association Executive Development Program for a thorough grounding in management and finance. From March through May, he spent his time in conferences with Robert Naylor and faculty members. On 1 June, Dilday assumed full responsibility as president and, on 1 August 1978, Dr. Naylor was named president-emeritus. The transition was complete.[14] As early as March, Russell was planning for his new leadership team. John Newport, still teaching at Rice, was among his top picks.

The Hesitation

As early as the fall of 1977, after Dilday's election, still-president Naylor and Russell Dilday had approached John about returning to the faculty in the triple roles of vice president of academic affairs, provost, and faculty responsibilities. John had initially agreed to return, and Southwestern had announced the news joyfully. His return had been published in the *Baptist Standard*. Friends had sent letters to John congratulating him on his return. By early March 1978, however, in handwritten letters to both Robert Naylor and Russell Dilday, John admitted that he must withdraw his acceptance. The blow was palpable for Southwestern, especially for Robert Naylor, John's friend, who was concerned about both John's uncharacteristic vacillation of mind and the school's reputation.

John's touching lines in letters to both Robert and Russell, written on 23 March 1978 from his home in Houston, revealed his deeply divided mind and personal agony at the thought that he had hurt either of the two men whom he loved. "This is the most difficult letter I have ever written," John penned to Russell.

> I love Southwestern and appreciate more than words can express all she has meant to me. Southwestern solidified in me a unique evangelical and missionary perspective. She gave me the opportunity to teach and develop friendships with some of Baptists' outstanding young people, such as yourself. This letter is especially difficult because I am convinced that you are God's unique person for Southwestern at this time.[15]

John went on to explain that he had answered the invitation quickly while speaking at a Southwestern Academy meeting in Los Alamos. Eddie Belle was visiting family in Kentucky at the time. Upon reflection and prayer, however, John now felt that his best thinking and writing and speaking could take place in Houston at present, where the circles of scholarship were wider and platforms for speaking had enlarged. He said that his evangelical, Baptist, and moral convictions had been both sharpened and deepened in this secular context. "In other words, I believe that I have found here a unique opportunity to witness and serve the Baptist and evangelical causes in another dimension than I have known before. I do not think that my opportunity will compare with my twenty-three years at Southwestern, but this is different and I believe that I would be making a mistake to leave it now."[16]

There was another consideration. John was now sixty-one years old and he had watched his children grow into fine adults. Eddie Belle had flourished in Houston. He explained to Russell that, although she was willing to follow the direction in which John felt he should go, she had found challenges and opportunities to develop more of her own identity and talents. She was arranging international tours at least twice a year, was involved in church and club activities, and had made many deep friendships. John understood and openly spoke of his family's sacrifices. He said, "For years Eddie Belle has given herself to the home and children while I worked seven days a week and studied and traveled to supply and speak . . . Her desires and preferences have weighed heavily upon me."[17] John and Eddie Belle stayed in Houston for the time being.[18]

Russell and Robert Naylor continued to extend open-armed invitations to return to Southwestern, trusting John's discernment. Dilday met with John four times, outlining his vision for Southwestern. Dilday had shared that he wanted John to help him develop that critical but difficult balance between faith and reason. John wrote in later years that the more he considered Dilday's desire in prayer, the more he "felt that this was his dream. This should be my spiritual home," he said. "What is the biblical focus that enables us to balance out faith and reason? Futurologists say that in this pluralistic and chaotic world, we must find a central focus around which to build our lives. Biblical scholars are almost unanimously agreed that the central focus of the Bible is the Kingdom of God. I have increasingly found this to be the focus for my life and ministry."[19] John and Eddie Belle both sensed that it was time to think about returning to Southwestern.

Return to Southwestern

During the fall of 1978, while John was still immersed in his teaching responsibilities at Rice but continuing to teach doctoral seminars and supervise students at Southwestern, John allowed his name to be brought before the trustees for a vote. The trustees met on 24 October 1978 to deliberate Dilday's new appointments and administrative recommendations. Four vice presidents were elected. Vice president for business affairs, Wayne Evans, remained in his role. John Seelig's title was changed to vice president for public affairs. The vice president for student affairs was currently vacant but was to be filled soon. The last of the vice presidents, upon the retirement of Jesse J. Northcutt, was to be John Paul Newport, who would return from teaching at Rice University and take up his teaching responsibilities on 1 January 1979 and the role of vice president of academic affairs and provost on 1 August. One last appointment was the role of executive vice president, which was filled by Lloyd Elder.

As vice president for academic affairs and provost, Newport would supervise the work of the deans of the theology, church music, and religious education schools. He would also oversee the directors of the libraries, admissions, and continuing education, as well as add and evaluate faculty and staff in all three schools. He was to take responsibility for curriculum, act as a liaison between the deans and president and trustees, preside at faculty meetings, chair the Advanced Studies Council and Curriculum Council, direct all areas of academic research, appoint all faculty committees, and supervise the accreditation of the institution. Finally, he was to help the president design new programs to enhance the seminary's mission and represent the president and the seminary at denominational, academic, and theological functions and conferences, including speaking. This was an enormous responsibility that John was prepared to assume. Robert Naylor wrote to his old friend, "I just want to tell you how pleased I am that you are coming back to the Seminary. There is nothing new in saying that, and yet through all of the time in between, you know that I have always been warm and kind toward the thought that you might one day return."[20] And return he did.

Newport at SWBTS Under Dilday, 1979-1990

I am a lover of liberty. I will not and I cannot serve a party.

Desiderius Erasmus of Rotterdam[21]

When John returned to SWBTS in January 1979, he received hearty greetings from faculty, staff, and students. He felt he had returned home. He promptly resumed both his teaching load and collegial friendship with Yandall Woodfin (1973-1994), who was now professor of philosophy.

John in Faculty Meeting, 1979

From this point, John served on the faculty as professor of philosophy until his retirement in 1990 and then afterward for another five years until 1995. His role as vice president for academic affairs, from August 1979, also continued until his retirement in 1990, after which time and until his death in 2000, he served as Special Consultant to the President for both Russell Dilday (1978-1994) and Kenneth Shell Hemphill (1994-2003).

Newport and Colleagues

The deans who worked with John those first years were Huber L. Drumwright (1951-1981) and William B. Tolar (1967-2001) of the School of Theology; James C. McKinney (1940-1994) of the School of Church Music; and Jack D. Terry (1969-present) of the School of Religious Education. John also worked with Jeter Basden (1981-1989); Keith C. Wills (1959-1985), director of libraries; Justice C. Anderson (1974-1998), director of the World Missions and Church Growth Center; J. David Fite (1973-2000), director of continuing education; and, beginning in 1981, the directors of the Children's Center, David C. White, and the Center for Christian Communication Studies, Darrel Baergen.

In his first faculty retreat speech in 1979, Dilday stated that good leadership is characterized by the shared processes of decision-making without shirking the president's personal responsibility. He wanted his leadership to be marked by a harmonious coordination of a team in order to avoid adversarial roles of factionalism. Dilday soon earned the unanimous appreciation of administration, faculty, and staff. As his right hand, Newport exemplified this style of leadership. Major decisions—such as agreeing on the selection of new deans, directors, and faculty, or the establishment of new degrees, programs, or centers—were made by polling the faculty.[22]

Nearly all of Newport's letters to Russell Dilday during these years contain names of faculty members, pastors, or denominational leaders that Newport was recommending to his president. Newport brought a wide swath of contacts, made throughout the years, and was an invaluable asset to the institution in this regard. Southwestern was in dire need of new faculty, since one of Dilday's goals was to lower the teacher-student ratio. In 1978, the year he took office, the full-time student number in the three schools was 2,978. In 1981, just three years later, that number had reached 3,317. Students were earning diplomas and graduating in greater numbers as well, climbing to 875 graduates in the academic year of 1981–1982. Dilday and the trustees added several new faculty members between 1978 and 1982, and Newport had recommended them all.[23]

In the School of Theology, fifteen new faculty joined its ranks: James Leo Garrett in Theology (1949–1959; and 1979–1997); George H. Gaston in Pastoral Ministry (1979–1983); Thomas D. Lea in New Testament (1979–1999); Thomas V. Brisco in Biblical Backgrounds and Archaeology (1980–2003); Guy Greenfield in Christian Ethics (1980–1991); George L. Kelm in Biblical Backgrounds and Archaeology (1980–1993); Dan Gentry Kent in Old Testament (1980–1999); William David Kirkpatrick in Theology (1980–2006); Robert B. Sloane Jr. in Theology (1980–1983); Bill Bellinger in Old Testament (1981–1984); William M. Tillman Jr. in Christian Ethics (1981–1998); Joel C. Gregory in Preaching (1982–1985); Malcolm McDow in Evangelism (1982–2005); Doyle L. Young in Church History (1982–1993); and Earl R. Martin in Missions and World Religions (1982–1987).[24]

In the School of Religious Education, Dilday and Newport recommended to the trustees five new faculty: Bob W. Brackney in Social

Work (1979–1999); B. A. "Pat" Clendinning Jr. in Psychology and Counseling (1979–1996); William A. Budd Smith in Foundations of Education (1979–2003); Jerry A. Privette in Educational Administration (1980–2001); and Robert P. Raus in Church Recreation (1980–1995). Five more faculty were added to the School of Church Music in these years. William Mac Davis Jr. was elected to teach Music Theory and Composition (1979–2011), and Sue Biggs King specialized in Vocal Instruction, first as a resident teacher from 1959 to 1979, and then elected to faculty from 1979 to 1999. Elizabeth R. McKinney was a Piano resident instructor from 1967 to 1979, and then was elected to faculty from 1979 to 1993. C. David Keith came to teach Conducting (1980–2007), and William J. Reynolds was elected to teach Church Music (1980–1998).[25] Faculty meetings were moved to larger rooms to accommodate the swelling numbers. A sense of fresh hope settled over the campus. It was a new day.

Campus Advances

The trustees, working with the senior leadership of the school, also provided additional benefits for the well-being of the faculty and staff. Annual cost of living raises were put in place, along with allowances extended for faculty development, sabbatical leaves, and attendance at professional meetings. Improved medical, tenure, and retirement policies were adopted. The trustees realized that part of their responsibility to ensure the flourishing of the school's mission was to care for the exceptional faculty who were investing their lives and scholarship in Southwestern and her students.

The campus was buzzing about the new professors, the growing student population, and the expanded housing, classroom, recreation, health, and children's spaces. The new recreation center provided indoor basketball and handball courts, a swimming pool, saunas, and weightlifting rooms. Outdoors, there were football and soccer fields, a playground for children, and walking paths. The counseling center offered a place for psychology and counseling students to see clients while under supervision and to provide help to the community.

The Medical Center provided much-needed healthcare for seminary families. The new library was going up on the east side of the Memorial Building on campus. Beneath all of the positive changes that were taking place, however, remaining tensions concerning the perceived threat of liberalism, or modernism, came from some sectors in the convention and continued to build almost weekly. Like the slow swirls of turbulent clouds gaining strength overhead, or the acceleration of a river raft as it nears the narrowing waterfall, these mounting stressors became daily and constant realities throughout the remainder of both Dilday's and Newport's tenures at Southwestern.

Rising Waters

John, as one of four vice presidents, felt himself congruently aligned with Russell Dilday. Their jobs were increasingly beset by sociological and theological revolutions that were already beginning to manifest themselves. These revolutions came to affect the Southern Baptist Convention and all of its agencies. Segments of the SBC were sympathetic with more moderate theological emphases. Conversely, other segments of the denomination were calling for, in John's words, "a more overt reactionary, fundamentalist-conservative approach" to differences in the way that Baptists dealt with questions about doctrine, theology, and interpretation of Scripture.

Dilday contended that there was a better approach to these differences, which he called "Constructive Creative Evangelicalism." Without questioning the authority of Scripture, he noted that the *Baptist Faith and Message* statement of 1963 allowed for three different theological approaches. The preamble and the article on education allowed for a certain amount of Christian freedom in theological enterprise. The last part of the confession, articles eleven through seventeen, had statements on education, evangelism, social order, and war and peace. These articles were in line with long-standing Southern cultural emphases concerning the practical side of Kingdom work. The section on traditional doctrines, articles one through ten, was quite conservative in form and content. These articles emphasized that correct doctrinal elaboration is essential to Christian faith. Generationally aware, Dilday felt that churches needed to avoid error in the same fashion as the ways in which they embraced truth.

Dilday believed that these convention-adopted articles of faith furnished guidelines for Southwestern Seminary and Southern Baptists to be leaders in the new approach that was already taking place in what was called "New-Evangelicalism." Schools like Wheaton, Fuller, Trinity, and Gordon-Conwell were moving in this direction, and the new approach was evidenced in the maturing ministry of Billy Graham.[26] John noted in later years that in a 1993 publication, Al Mohler, new president at Southern

Seminary, had stated that the "future shape of the SBC must avoid the twin dangers of obscurantist, angry, and separatist fundamentalism on the right and revisionist compromise on the left."[27] This was a prophetic statement. There were reasons to be concerned.

To help Southwestern move beyond the more reactionary, fundamentalist-conservative ideology, Dilday suggested that John attend the first National Inerrancy Conference to be held in San Diego in 1980. He asked John to search out constructive, creative evangelicals who could be brought to Southwestern to model this approach. At the conference, John said he had "misgivings about the approach of Tim LaHaye and Franky Schaeffer," the son of the better-known Francis Schaeffer. In contrast, John felt a congruency with the seminars led by Carl F. H. Henry, R. C. Sproul, and James Packer, among others. In the following twelve years, Newport helped Southwestern to invite scholars to the campus for dialogue with faculty and students and to speak in chapel services. This group was a veritable cross-section of leaders from the evangelical world: Millard Erickson, Robert Johnston, Carl F. H. Henry, Gordon Fee, Richard Lovelace, David Hubbard, J. Edwin Orr, F. F. Bruce, Bernard Ramm, Donald G. Bloesch, and Walter Kaiser, to name only a representative sampling.[28] They echoed the same theme almost universally—that authentic theological education is threatened by liberal theology on one hand, but just as seriously by fundamentalist ideologues who go too far on the other hand.

In a similar vein, Dilday also saw the importance of the Baptist contribution to the concept of religious freedom and diversity within biblical guidelines. Baptist polity allowed for churches who could reach all types of people. This meant that there would be different styles of churches planted. The only hope in avoiding a threat to world evangelism, he believed, was to develop a strong and adequate doctrine of religious liberty. To this end, Dilday became more involved in the Baptist World Alliance, which championed religious liberty for all on a global scale, and encouraged his faculty and administration to participate as well. He was missional and visionary, seeking Baptists to be dialogical in the manner in which Newport and his biblical worldview had been received in even the most liberal denominations and secular institutions. John was a scholar who could serve as such a model of open-minded, biblically anchored, Christ-centered, theological engagement with all people.

John implemented this shared value of dialogue and open-minded learning and asked the faculty to avoid all unfair caricatures or cynicism

President and Cabinet, c. 1981: Bottom Row, John P. Newport (left), VP of Academic Affairs and Provost, and President Russell H. Dilday (right). Top Row, Huber R. Martin Jr., VP of Business Affairs; Lawrence R. Klempnauer, VP of Student Services; John E. Seelig, VP of Public Affairs; and Jeter Basden, Registrar and Director of Admissions

about diverse groups within the SBC. If discussed, both sides of any controversy should be presented fairly in spoken and written word. The faculty agreed; what followed was constructive work that resulted in amiable discourse. In fact, when the Peace Committee came to Southwestern in 1986 to interview students and faculty, both Jerry Vines and Jim Henry commented that "Southwestern Seminary was at the very heart of what Southern Baptists wanted in theological education."[29]

As the question concerning the inerrancy of the Bible grew to a fever pitch in Southern Baptist circles, John had the privilege of helping to assemble two more "inerrancy" conferences between 1987 and 1989. These conferences brought to Southern Baptist audiences some of the best evangelical scholars to discuss the matter of the nature of the Bible and its

Newport in academic regalia, 1981

interpretation. During this period, in a variety of lecture series before academic groups and the Southwestern faculty, John tried to position himself in relation to the evangelical perspective.

Newport's Constructive Evangelical Identity, 1980s and 1990s

During this period, John wrote almost incessantly in the early mornings and evenings. He served as editor of the volume *Nineteenth Century Devotional Thought* in the Christian Classic series published by Broadman in 1981. He also tried to express his evolving evangelicalism in another semi-popular book called *What Is Christian Doctrine?*, published in 1984, about the same time he was asked to give a series of lectures on Paul Tillich at Wheaton College. The latter engagement eventuated in a book which took a dialectical approach (yes and no) to his subject, called *Paul Tillich*, in the Makers of the Modern Theological Mind series, published by Word in 1984. In John's commentary on Revelation entitled *The Lion and the Lamb*, published two years later, his evangelical approach was evident. This was John's decade of publishing and flourishing.[30]

In answer to those who were interested in and wanting a more precise definition of an "evangelical identity," John answered by explaining his perspective. In a broad sense, he said, he understood the term "evangelical" to refer to those who agree on salvation by faith in Jesus Christ in a conversion experience, the centrality and absolute authority of the divinely inspired Bible, and the centrality of evangelism and missions. In a narrower sense, he used the term "evangelical" to refer to those post-fundamentalists who had moved beyond the confrontational style of "revivalist fundamentalism" to a broader cultural, theological, and ecclesiastical engagement. For John, it would be "more historically correct to include much of the Holiness movement as evangelical, with its emphasis on the higher Christian life expressed in the baptism of the Holy Spirit or in the more moderate Keswick's infilling of the Holy Spirit."[31] Later, John contended in his 1989 book, *Life's Ultimate Questions*, that the biblical worldview can provide a unifying perspective for evangelicals.[32]

What was specifically inherently theological in the content of evangelicalism, John believed, lay in its *ultimate authority* for Christians—the triune God in self-revelation. The *practical authority* is the Bible confirmed by the Holy Spirit, or the Holy Spirit speaking through the Bible when it is properly interpreted in light of the centrality of Jesus Christ and in its historical and literary background.[33] For John, constructive evangelicals were those who maintained the delicate biblical balance between the divine and human in relation to the Bible and Christian theology. Upon this point of balance is a potential contribution distinctive to evangelical theology in contrast to other Christian traditions.

The Bible as the divine-human book parallels in many ways the incarnation of the eternal Son of God. As the divine and human are organically related in the person of Christ, so the inspiring Spirit of God associated himself with the conscious and unconscious processes of the human agents as he guided and inspired the Bible's writing. John believed both in theological unity and its situational "pluriformity," that is, its range and variety of theological emphases and perspectives that Scripture as a whole embodies. When hermeneutical impasses seem to become barriers, John observed that some evangelicals attempted to meet the perceived problems defensively rather than constructively. Evangelicals, he said, "should stress both the theological unity and situational pluriformity of the biblical writings. Since there are levels of meanings within the Bible, the meaning related to a specific historical context should be compared to the meaning of a text that has been re-contextualized within the total biblical canon."[34] Another way that evangelicals should seek to maintain the delicate biblical balance between the human and divine, John thought, was in relation to the image of God in humans and their sinfulness, free will and providence, human responsibility and Satan's power and temptation, and their acceptance of God's grace in Christ. Added to these was the human responsibility for Christian discipline and service. To make all of this applicable, John was convinced that the balance of the "already-not-yet" concept of eschatology could, and even should, be the unifying or organizing vision for Christians.

As John explained his thinking on the matter, according to the New Testament, the "age to come" is already coexisting with and penetrating this "present age." Briefly, this means that "already," in the first advent of Jesus Christ, his birth and ministry, and in the coming of the Holy Spirit, the spiritual blessing and power of God are made available. However, evil and Satan are still active, and so Christians look forward to the second advent of Christ, his second coming, when the fullness of the spiritual blessings of God will be given to his people.

Thus, biblical eschatology is not merely a set of beliefs that may be pushed aside when certain events, like the second coming, are delayed, or when similar events are thought to be near. Although the Bible does not specify when exactly the consummating events will occur, it insists that the last times are *already here* in a preliminary way. The eschatological atmosphere of the "already-not-yet" emphasis should pervade every action and thought.

In short, the eschatological expectation of the first Christians bestowed a unique vantage point from which to view every dimension of reality. It also gave them a unique impulsion to act in light of this hope. Their eschatology was not merely a set of beliefs concerning future events, but also the attitude, or atmosphere, aroused by these events. The eschatological framework is thus not one element of Christianity, but it is the medium of the Christian faith as such.[35]

The far-reaching implications of this mindset may be displayed in the evangelicals' balance between the personal and social aspects of the Christian faith. The evangelical insists that the church of God should not be seen in its fundamental mission as either a humanitarian agency or an ethical culture society. Its primary goal is to bring the glad tidings of reconciliation and redemption to all races and nations. However, the church is responsible for teaching people to be disciples of Christ in the very midst of the world's plight and dereliction. Admittedly, there is a secondary, but crucial, cultural and social mandate. The gospel has expansive social and political implications. The "already-not-yet" theme provides a strong motivation and dynamic context for Christian ethics and action.

Evangelical Theology Shifting Ground

When John reflected upon how evangelical theology had shifted since midcentury, compared with how Southern Baptist theology had also evolved, he saw some differences, and these, he felt, had contributed to the growing impasse among Southern Baptists in his day as the controversy gained momentum. He thought that Southern Baptists could be seen as both evangelicals and uniquely denominational. Prior to World War II, Southern Baptists had been somewhat semi-isolated from the Fundamentalist-Liberal battles taking place in the north.[36] Southern Baptist expansion in postwar years brought many Southern Baptists into contact with many fundamentalist, evangelical, and liberal ideas and influences. Southern Baptists of Newport's era embraced facets of all of these groups.

John had observed for many years the developing balance in the Wheaton, Trinity Evangelical, Gordon-Conwell, and Fuller Seminary associations. The earlier rationalistic dominance was mollified and qualified by the activities of renewal and the charismatic groups.[37] Especially in evangelical academic circles, John had noted the movement of leaders toward a more balanced and centrist emphasis instead of a concern with extremist positions. In many ways, this movement was reflected in the changing emphases of Billy Graham and the *Christianity Today* magazine. These changes and the more balanced approach were seen in the addresses of James I. Packer (Regent College), Mark Noll (Wheaton College), Walter Kaiser, Grant Osborne, Kenneth Kantzer (Trinity Evangelical Divinity School), and Robert Johnston (then at North Park University), who spoke at the two Southern Baptist Inerrancy Conferences. The earlier hallmarks of fundamentalism and evangelicalism, such as creation science and dispensational premillennialism, were now disallowed by this newer generation of evangelicals. Additionally, under certain conditions, this group affirmed that the Bible, properly interpreted, would support women in ministry. In and over all of these discussions, a reverent, believing, biblical criticism was affirmed. While the Inerrancy Conferences were helpful, they did not satisfy some strands of the Southern Baptist constituency.

Evangelical Challenges in the 1980s and 1990s

For John, these years were heavy. Like a medical specialist, he was observing his own denomination, of which his and Eddie Belle's families had been loyal supporters for generations, in the throes of divisive convulsions. He attempted both to diagnose and offer a remedy. John thought that Baptists and evangelicals, for him synonymous terms, all believed the Bible as the sole rule of faith and practice for the individual and the church together. Despite and beneath this broad affirmation, however, were the complex questions concerning the nature of the Bible and its interpretation. Could there be fellowship, mission, and cooperation between those inerrantists who were nuanced and those who were strict or blunt inerrantists? Could Baptists allow for diversity, even disagreement, for the sake of ministry and common witness? A positive answer to these questions, John thought, would require a return to theological definitions that were discernibly and unashamedly evangelical, but open enough to permit a confessional flexibility.

John had watched, for example, Carl F. H. Henry's struggle to recover "kingdom preaching" to support a renewal of the social vision lost in the earlier expressions of rigid dispensational suppression of such themes. He had observed George Eldon Ladd's career-long refutation of rigid dispensational categories in the interpretation of Scripture. John had also noted the transformation of the faculties of Wheaton, Trinity Evangelical, Gordon-Conwell, and Fuller, in their move to a more historical premillennialism, or post-tribulationalism, to retain a basic premillennialism orientation while at the same time engaging modern, believing biblical scholarship and Christian mission. For John, these examples displayed the need for evangelicals to acknowledge openly that some of their own views of the Bible and its interpretation were often influenced by cultural developments. This meant that a desire for an evangelical balance must include a healthy self-critical stance of one's own tendency to intrude an individual agenda into the exposition of the Scriptures.[38]

To aid this healthy posture, evangelicals should be open in every age to dialogue with other devout believers. When this happens, thinking Christians are often dismayed to learn that a commitment to biblical inerrancy does not guarantee agreement on how Christians are to apply biblical principles to today's social problems. Having said that, the process of looking at the Word with other believers, wrestling with their diverse interpretations, and supporting one another in Christian love nudges all believers nearer to what is truly right and just. For John, there was a difference between *meaning* and *significance* in any given biblical text. John pointed out that meaning is that which is intended by the author. It is what he called the "determinate entity." The original determinate meaning, however, may have various applications, or significance, in different cultural contexts today. The skill in knowing how to apply Scripture faithfully and precisely to current events is a learned and thoughtful craft.

John also saw a challenge in the ways evangelicals balance academic approaches to the Bible with practical and devotional approaches. Faculties and scholars should recognize that the intellectual study of the things of God constitutes only a part of a person's proper preparation for ministry. Another challenge, he thought, lay in the convergence of the Bible and science.[39] For John, evangelicals should emphasize the importance of the Christian doctrines of creation and humans made in the image of God. These doctrines underscore the prime importance of Christians' stewardship of the Creator's world, the need to preserve human freedom and dignity and sanctity as over against the hazards of research and the individual and social responsibilities of scientific knowledge. How were Christians to arrange such influence in the secular world in which they were living?

John believed that evangelicals should refrain from seeking to establish a self-consciously Christian nation in which Christian symbols are invoked to "justify social, political, or public policy, or to sanctify imperial ambition." Instead, John maintained, Christians should press for a just nation, one informed by a Christian life and worldview. There was a difference, he claimed, between a nation suffused with Judeo-Christian values and a nation that actively promotes the dogmatic beliefs and practices of a particular church. For Newport, evangelical "belonging" was not predicated upon a New Israel as a Christian America, but in the New Israel as a spiritual church, comprised of called out believers, the *ecclesia*.[40] John was expressing in these years his open-armed, generous, and reasonable scholarship, teaching this balanced evangelical approach in master classes and doctoral seminars and conversing with other scholars in the evangelical world.

During these years, at the height of his scholarship and mature thinking, John was constantly investing his enthusiasm and love of learning in the lives of students. Known as a master teacher, his masters-level classes were always full, and there was always a steady stream of doctoral students who studied with him and asked him to supervise their dissertations. John had even taught doctoral seminars for Southwestern while he was teaching at Rice in Houston, driving up weekly for the two-hour sessions. He guided dozens of philosophy Ph.D. students through the years. Students he supervised have gone on to serve on the faculties of the six SBC seminaries, twelve different universities, several convention agencies, and churches of all sizes. Many of them wrote dissertations in the field of apologetics. Rarely, a student would stay at Southwestern and teach in the philosophy department. He treated them all as colleagues, kept their papers in his memoirs, and corresponded with them until his death.[41] He was proud of their work and considered himself blessed to have learned with these bright minds.

Newport teaching a doctoral seminar, 1982

Faculty Relationships

John also enjoyed the collegiality with the professors of the three schools, both older and new faculty, and was still aiding the president, department heads, and trustees in the selection and recommendation of new faculty. During the 1980s and early 1990s, he was glad to see dozens of scholars join the seminary's faculties. He was a smiling presence in most of these interviews, leaning back in his chair and offering encouragement to newcomers.

In the School of Theology, Newport helped to bring on board Joel C. Gregory in Preaching (1982-1985), Daniel R. Sanchez in Missions (1983-present), Paul L. Gritz in Church History (1983-2015), Douglas M. Dickens in Pastoral Ministry (1985-2000), James L. Heflin in Preaching (1985-1996), Dan Crawford in Evangelism (1985-2016), Bob Ellis in Old Testament (1986-1996), James Denison in Philosophy of Religion (1987-1989), and Raymond Higgins in Ethics (1987-1994). He also recommended James Spivey in Church History (1987-2003), Henry Smith in Missions (1988-1994), Grant Lovejoy in Preaching (1988-2004), Paul Stevens as Director of Field Education and the D.Min. program (1988-2003), Marion G. "Bud" Fray in Missions (1989-1994), Steve Warner Lemke in Philosophy of Religion (1990-1997), B. Keith Putt in Philosophy of Religion (1990-1998), David K. Trimble in New Testament (1990-1993), Linzy Bill Hill in Old Testament (1991-1994), Calvin Miller in Preaching and Scholar in Residence (1991-1998), Alan Brehm in New Testament (1992-1998), Jeff Pool in Theology (1992-1997), Rick Johnson in Old Testament (1992-2002), Steve Lyon in Pastoral Ministry (1994-2001), Theodore J. Cabal in Philosophy of Religion (1995-1998), Karen O'Dell Bullock in Church History (1995-2004), Stephen M. Stookey in Church History (1995-2004), and Robert I. Garrett Jr., in Missions (1995-2004).

In the School of Religious Education, Newport welcomed the following faculty to campus: William R. Yount in Foundations of Education (1981-2012), Wesley Oneal Black in Youth Ministry (1983-2012), Lucian E. Coleman Jr. in Adult Education (1983-1993), Wynona Tipton Elder in Psychology and Counseling (1984-1998), Daryl Roger Eldridge in Foundations of Education (1984-2003), Gary W. Waller in Church Administration (1984-2006), Dan Earl Clement in Psychology and Counseling (1985-1990, 1996-2002), James Woodrow Walter Jr. in Church Administration (1986-2000), Dennis K. Parrish in Communication Ministry

(1987–2004), Terrell M. Peace in Foundations of Education (1987–1998), Royce Alan Rose in Church Administration (1987–1997), James Scott Floyd in Psychology and Counseling (1990–2010), Norma Sanders Hedin in Foundations of Education (1991–2006), Robert Horton Welch in Church Administration (1991–2008), Marcia McQuitty in Childhood Education (1994–2012), and John E. Babler in Christian Social Work (1995–2020).

The School of Church Music saw the addition of a cadre of scholars specializing in music ministries, vocal and instrumental performance, conducting, and music theory: Bruce H. Leafblad in Church Music and Worship (1983–2006), Elem H. Eley in Voice (1984–1987), James David Robinson in Voice (1985–2015), Cynthia Dobrinski in Instrumental Performance (1986–1999), R. Allen Lott in Music History (1986–present), James Stanley Moore in Church Music and Worship (1987–2004), Rhonda Jayne Edge Buescher in Church Music Education (1988–1997), Angela Faith Cofer in Voice (1989–2017), Michael Thomas Cox in Music Theory (1990–2009), Bill E. Green in Church Music and Age-Grade Choirs (1990–1991), David W. Music in Church Music History (1990–2002), Jill Trudgeon Sprenger in Piano (1993–2017), William Lyndel Vaught in Church Music Education (1993–2008), Benjamin Lee Harlan as Dean and Music Theory (1995–2005), and Howard Gerald Aultman in Music Theory and Organ (1995–2019).

Because of John's voracious appetite for books, and the fact that he tried to read every new acquisition, the library corps were delighted to see him come through the door. In each of their respective positions, Keith C. Wills, Robert Phillips, Barbara Russell, Kenette Harder, Carol Bastien, Benjamin Rogers, Robert Trimble, Steven Storie, Myrta Ann Garrett, and Phillip Sims labored to supply him, and the rest of the faculties, with much-needed classroom and scholarly resources.

In 1987, John turned seventy years old and was just completing his manuscript for *Life's Ultimate Questions*, to be published in 1989. His academic career had been lived at an almost frenetic pace. The decades of writing and speaking and teaching had begun to take their toll on his health.[42] That year, still vigorous, lithe, and strong, John began thinking of laying down some administrative responsibilities, giving himself more freedom to focus primarily on the things that he gauged to be essential in these latter years of ministry—traveling, speaking, guiding his Ph.D. students with their research, writing, and spending more time with Eddie Belle.

John and Eddie Belle,
c. 1990

John Newport's Retirement, 1990

The trustees elected John Newport as Distinguished Professor of Philosophy of Religion in 1989 in anticipation of his intended retirement at the end of the 1990 academic year. The seminary could not afford to lose such a valuable leader, however. John was then elected to serve as Distinguished Professor of Religion Emeritus and Special Consultant to the President, the role he served under presidents Russell Dilday and Kenneth S. Hemphill until the year 1997, when John celebrated eight decades of life.

By the year 1990, John Newport had earned a reputation in Baptist and broader evangelical circles as a constructive evangelical. Academicians viewed Newport as constructive because of his willingness to dialogue honestly with theologians of other beliefs and saw him as evangelical because of his unwavering stand for Jesus Christ. His counsel was sought on all matters concerning New Age, alternative religions, and the occult. He had also been one of the few in these academic contexts to use the term "worldview," particularly his "biblical worldview," and to explain its meaning.

John Newport stepped away from the vice presidency of academic affairs and provost roles, but he did not move from his office, his books, his students, or his legacy. His scholarship was still moving forward, like a powerful river in flood stage, dynamic and awe-inspiring in its strength. Dilday described Newport from a similar view: "He has helped his students put together the diverse strands of knowledge from various intellectual disciplines into a consistent worldview."[43] For more than thirty-five years, John Newport had expanded the religious worldview of students at Southwestern. He was going to continue to teach Ph.D. students, supervise dissertations, travel the world with Eddie Belle, and write.[44] In 1990 he wrote, "I've had a wonderful experience here at Southwestern. I found here a remarkable balance between scholarship and evangelism, between the theoretical and practical," he said. "Nobody could ask for a greater opportunity in terms of the fellowship on the faculty and working with the administration."[45]

John's work with Ph.D. students brought him great fulfillment as he settled in to focus on their research together. He tried to convey to his students a sense of the relevance, the excitement, and the urgency of the Christian gospel. "This is where true freedom is, where true joy is, where true fulfillment is," he said, never losing the childlike joy of reading the Bible and applying it to current culture.[46] That excitement of the Christian faith had been part of Newport's life since his childhood days in Buffalo, Missouri, where he had lived only three blocks from the Baptist church and next door to his pastor. From the moment Jesus Christ had captured his mind and heart at a revival meeting at age ten, and he was baptized in a nearby river, John was convinced that God had called him into Christian service. This core conviction had never wavered.

Now, ten books later and having served as an interim pastor in more than fifty congregations in Oklahoma, Kentucky, Mississippi, Louisiana, and Texas, John had deserved some time to arrange as he wished. One might have thought that these next few years would ease some of John's burden and tension. This was not to be the case. In fact, the most intense and challenging time of his life was just around the corner.

Dark Days

The days unfolded on Seminary Hill with the routine pattern of academic life; however, many began to feel a palpable strain. Students attended classes, meetings, chapels, and studied in the library. Professors lectured, graded exams, conducted committee work, and attended faculty meetings. Underneath, there was a pervasive concern for the president and for the seminary's future. Dilday now had other vice presidents, and Newport was serving as his special consultant. In this role, Newport continued to write reports and letters, sometimes every day, to the president, who had asked John to monitor the SBC controversy, offer his wisdom, and make recommendations for new faculty.

Dilday's Leadership

The importance of obtaining faculty members who conformed to the seminary's confessional approach was augmented by a new emphasis upon full-year sabbatical leave programs with additional financial help for those who would seek to obtain further degrees in non-Southern Baptist schools. This approach assured that faculty members would have a basic evangelical, conservative, confessional background but could also have opportunities for the highest levels of training available in the world. It was thought that Southwestern Seminary's faculty, engaged with faculties of other institutions, would spark creative and beneficial dialogue for both sides and further both understanding and scholarship in the evangelical world.

Dilday was sensitive to establishing departments and programs that were on the forefront of theological education: communications and drama, emphasis on geriatrics, and programs for church business managers, children's music, recreation, and church administration. An archaeology and an Oxford Study program were instituted. In these years, Betty Dilday, the president's vivacious and gracious wife, spent her focus on seminary wives and families. As a result, greater emphasis was given to student services and recruitment. The Dildays considered the plight of financial pressures on young families in school, and so night courses were added; summer intensives allowed students to move through the program as well as keep jobs to provide for family needs.

Continuing education became another focus for Dilday, as did a new diploma program. On the Houston and Oklahoma extension campuses, new buildings were raised and furnished for a growing student population, and another center was opened in Lubbock. The needs of older pastors were addressed as the pastors were afforded college credit for seminary programs. The community and mayor of Fort Worth showered Southwestern with accolades, commendations, and awards for its beautification of the grounds and for stabilizing the Southside of Fort Worth. Businesses readily employed family members of seminary students, who had gained a reputation for integrity in the workplace. The National Association of Music Schools Accrediting Commission designated Southwestern Seminary's Music School as the outstanding school of its type in the United States. Visitors came from far and wide to attend the performances each December of Handel's *Messiah*.

John kept a close eye on the seminary's reputation and kept detailed records, clippings, and statements from convention and trustee minutes, as well as denominational and society columns regarding the health of the institution. In the late 1980s and 1990s, it was evident that Southwestern was becoming the school of choice for students from all segments of the Southern Baptist Convention. The children of the conservative movement's leadership, such as John Bisagno, Adrian Rogers, and Edwin Young, were attending Southwestern. Leaders in all facets of SBC life were chosen from Southwestern's graduates, including leaders for Southern, Southeastern, Midwestern, and Golden Gate seminaries. At one time, the heads of the major SBC agencies, such as the Foreign Mission, Home Mission, and Sunday School boards, and the Executive Committee were all Southwestern graduates.[47]

Dilday made it a point to visit each new trustee in his or her hometown and home church, and many trustees were deeply appreciative of the president and his collegial leadership style. He favored a constructive, conservative approach, open to and inviting prominent conservative leaders to speak at campus chapels, revivals, and other special occasions.[48]

During August, September, and October 1989, however, Baptist newspapers had published notices about upcoming meetings that had been requested of Dilday by Southwestern's more antagonistic trustees. There were rumblings throughout the convention that Dilday was to be "censured," "silenced," or "fired." In the wake of these notices and articles, copies of most of them clipped and resting in Newport's many files on this subject, Southern Baptist leaders wrote hundreds of letters, which jammed the mailboxes of then-chairman of the trustees, Dr. Kenneth E. Lilly, and then-secretary John C. McNaughton. These letters from pastors of churches small and large, missionaries, lay businessmen and women, women's mission societies, and petitions from Baptist church members, pled with the trustees not to consider any action against Dilday, who had consistently been commended each trustee meeting since he took office for his exceptionally fine leadership. Almost to a letter, the writers sought an answer to the question of why the trustees would want to do such a thing.[49]

Inerrancy Controversy and Southwestern

The answer linked back to early 1979, when the question of the inerrancy of the Bible had become a focal point in the SBC. Dilday had been asked to write a book on the doctrine of the Bible that would be the doctrinal study book for the entire SBC.[50] Russell Dilday and other seminary presidents had also formulated the well-known "Glorieta Statement" on the Bible in 1987.[51] Dilday pointed out that Southwestern had long held a strong view of the Bible, which could be called functional, or nuanced, inerrancy. J. I. Packer, a recognized leader of the Chicago inerrancy statement, was brought to the campus to speak with trustees and faculty. He pointed out that a number of the fundamentalist-conservative leaders held a view that was an aberration of classical orthodoxy. Packer criticized those on the extreme right who were claiming that the Bible was a book of technical science, that it opposed a place for women in teaching, and that it clearly taught an extreme dispensational view of prophecy.[52]

The continuing conflict over biblical inerrancy led the SBC seminary presidents to propose a national Conference on Inerrancy to be held at Ridgecrest, North Carolina, in 1987. The conference was recognized as an outstanding success. Paige Patterson, who had promoted the rigid inerrancy doctrine, stated that he felt essentially positive about the conference. He said, "I honor the seminary presidents for the idea of bringing together scholars from outside the convention. The inerrancy position did receive a very clear hearing both in terms of the major papers and responders." Moderate conservative leaders, such as James Flamming, also said that the major sessions represented a good balance.[53] Dilday had been personally responsible for assembling the first Inerrancy Conference. The general agreement was that the great majority of Southern Baptists held a very strong view of the Bible. That was not in doubt. The conflict, then, was over the matter of its interpretation.

The seminary presidents thus projected another conference in 1988 on biblical interpretation. Most of the non-Southern Baptist inerrancy leaders who spoke at the 1988 Conference on Biblical Interpretation agreed that the Warfield-Hodge nineteenth-century semi-rationalistic pre-understanding of the nature of the Bible was the dominant fundamentalist-conservative view. Newport commented that this view is not necessarily the inductive view taught by the Bible itself.[54]

Following the two inerrancy conferences, Southwestern Seminary, under Dilday's leadership, designed a new interdisciplinary course on biblical interpretation, or hermeneutics, that would be required of all incoming Master of Divinity students during their first year. Russell Dilday co-taught one of the sections each of the next four years. He affirmed in his lectures and in his book on biblical authority that the Bible is God's divinely inspired word and the sole and infallible authority for faith and practice. His lectures pointed out the dangers of rationalistic higher criticism of the Bible and the weaknesses of neo-orthodoxy.[55] John Newport consulted with Dilday each week, considered the daily changes, charges, rumors, and incessant criticism, discerned the best responses, and weighed consequences. James Leo Garrett, John's dear friend and distinguished professor of systematic theology, said of these days that John had what he called "a premonition that unpreventable disaster would take place."[56]

By the time of Newport's retirement in 1990, Earle Ellis, perhaps one of the most respected conservative evangelical scholars in America, had joined Southwestern's faculty. He brought with him the International Institute for Biblical Research. Millard Erickson, a brilliant constructive conservative theologian, also joined the faculty, as did the creative, artistic, and beloved Calvin Miller. Bill Tolar had stepped into the role vacated by Newport's retirement. Bruce Corley became dean of the School of Theology. All of these scholars were recognized as leading conservatives. Dilday had been elected president of the American Association of Theological Schools, the first time in thirty years that a Southern Baptist had been chosen for this important position. His election had signaled both a confidence and recognition that evangelicals were providing excellence in theological education.

At Southwestern, the new music building renovation and music library were funded. The Advisory Council was enlarged and a spirit of enthusiasm among donors reached high proportions. Indeed, the seminary endowment under Dilday had grown from twelve to seventy million dollars and the prospects for even larger gifts were promised. An Institute for Contemporary Music was considered, suggested by Scotty Gray, longtime respected music faculty and newly appointed executive vice president. A new Scarborough Institute, focusing on church growth, was founded. The entire seminary was computerized in 1993 and 1994,[57] and a reorganization of the administrative staff resulted in greater efficiency, even as Huber Martin, vice president of financial affairs, secured a new health care program at a greatly reduced cost. Newport's files are full of these matters, as he served as a "sounding board" for President Dilday.[58]

In the decade between 1985 and 1994, top administrators and faculty at three of the four seminaries and most of the agencies of the SBC had been terminated or forcibly retired. Trustees favoring the ultra-conservative movement, called the "Conservative Resurgence," had been named in majority percentages to the governing boards of all SBC agencies. By using this new political methodology, ultra-conservative leaders replaced age-old Baptist patterns of inclusivity at local, associational, state, and national levels.[59]

In 1994, those actions came to Southwestern.

Dilday Fired, 7–9 March 1994

When the trustees arrived on the Southwestern Seminary's campus on Monday, 7 March 1994, for their semi-annual meeting, every knowledgeable person knew that the tensions felt were the result of personal criticisms that had been leveled against Dilday and the close scrutiny of his recommendations. Rumors of his dismissal were flying; however, following the executive committee meeting of the trustees after dinner on Tuesday evening, this rumor was dispelled. Dilday had been commended by the trustees for providing able administrative leadership. He had asked the trustees directly whether he were to be fired, and the trustees had assured him that they knew nothing of such plans, even though most of his recommendations had been deferred until the October meeting of the board. The budget for the fiscal year 1994–1995 had finally been approved, but without the reorganization plan proposed or schedule of student fees set.[60] Two faculty recommendations were also deferred, but one was approved.[61] Tenure considerations were deferred, but promotions were approved. Faculty was not invited to the trustee dinner, a traditional event. Further, the invitation to Keith Parks, former president of the Foreign Mission Board, to be the spring commencement speaker was withdrawn.

On Wednesday morning, the chapel speaker called for an end to denominational infighting and for a renewed emphasis on evangelism. Moments later, Ralph Pulley, T. Bob Davis, Damon Shook, Lee Weaver, and Gerald Dacus, the latter a Dilday supporter, waited at the front of the auditorium and asked if they could speak to Dilday in his office. They gathered around his small conference table and Pulley asked for Dilday's immediate resignation. Dilday was offered a generous retirement package if he would agree to resign. If not, he would be fired within the next hour with no compensation.[62] In that moment, Dilday thought about his calling from God, how the seminary had flourished, and his years of excellent commendations from the board of trustees. He replied that in this case, he would have to follow his conscience and do what he thought was right. He declined to retire but said that he would be glad to enter into a dialogue about a plan for future retirement.[63] With this reply, the next steps were carried out.

Chairman Damon Shook then called the late morning trustee session to order, and Ralph Pulley stood and moved that the meeting go into executive session. Miles Seaborn called for the public address system to be silenced. The room was cleared except for the trustees and Dilday. Pulley explained that Dilday had refused their "exit plan" and made a motion to relieve the president of his duties. Twenty-six trustees voted to fire Russell Dilday, with seven trustees voting against the action, Dacus among the few. Dilday was not allowed back into his office or access to his computer, personal files, or library. The locks were changed on his office door, and his computer access code to the seminary's system was deleted. All personnel were told to refrain from talking with Dilday. A person was appointed to monitor the press releases sent out from the seminary.

Russell Dilday went to his home across the street to tell his wife Betty what had just happened. Soon, faculty and students heard that a press conference was to be held at 2:30 Wednesday afternoon in the Truett Auditorium. The new chairman of the trustees, Ralph Pulley, attempted to explain that all of the decisions had been made with the students' welfare in mind, but the 1200 students and faculty in attendance were outraged that their president had been treated with such disrespect. He asked students to recommend names for a new president. They shouted Russell Dilday's name. After his comments, Pulley refused to entertain questions and left the building under an armed security escort hired by the trustees for the day.[64]

Immediately after the press conference, those from the auditorium joined hundreds of other students on the lawn of the president's home. Here they were met by a smiling and relaxed Russell and Betty. Dilday's composure reflected a man with a clear conscience and at peace with himself and God. He assured the students that God was still on his throne, encouraged them to get back to studying, and assured them of his love.[65]

On Thursday, the seminary community looked to the Lord. The chapel service, under the leadership of Bruce Leafblad of the School of Church Music and the five vice presidents, was one of the most deeply moving services ever experienced at Southwestern. It began with silent prayer, followed by a reading of Psalm 27 and a choral affirmation by the men's chorus with a rendering of Handel's "Know that the Lord is Good." The congregation joined in declaring its collective faith in the singing of Luther's immortal hymn, "A Mighty Fortress Is Our God." As the service came to a close, Fosdick's "God of Grace and God of Glory" never meant as much to the worshipers as it did in that hour. The third stanza was sung, with most eyes streaming with tears:

> Cure Thy children's warring madness. Bend our pride to Thy control:
> Shame our wanton, selfish gladness, rich in things and poor in soul.
> Grant us wisdom, grant us courage, lest we miss Thy Kingdom's goal,
> Lest we miss Thy Kingdom's goal.[66]

The irate voices of the day before were now given to prayer as the seminary family grieved.

After chapel, faculty and staff were asked to remain in the auditorium for a briefing regarding the next few weeks. Bill Tolar, vice president of academic affairs and provost, informed the group that he had been asked, along with the other vice presidents, to "govern" the seminary until a new interim president could be chosen. He was the designated chair of the group, an assignment he had accepted with great reluctance. With a tearful voice, he explained that he and the vice presidents had told the trustees that they did not support the actions that had been taken against Dilday, but that for the sake of the seminary they would serve. He opened the meeting for discussion.

A motion was made to commend Russell and Betty Dilday and assure them of the esteem, love, and prayers of the faculty and staff. C. W. Brister, chair of the pastoral ministry department, was asked to write an official letter of commendation on behalf of the seminary faculty and staff. The group then passed a motion to notify the trustees of their prayers, but also to rebuke them, not only for the firing, but for the way in which it was done. This was written by Thomas V. Brisco and sent to every member of the seminary's board of trustees. John Newport stepped to the platform from the side entrance. He was weeping.[67] John's trust was a great strength. It was also a weakness, for it made him vulnerable. His dignity, integrity, and grace in this moment was revealed for all to see, as was his broken heart. His spirit seemed to have been crushed. He was mourning deeply.

Meanwhile, as the faculty and staff met after chapel, 1,500 students made their way to the lawn of the president's home. Dilday came out and stood on his porch until they quieted. In the hush that followed, he told them, "We are doing fine. We have a great peace about things. We are quite at ease about the future." As he brought his remarks to a close, he thanked the students for their expressions of love. He encouraged the students to "Look to the Lord. This is the ultimate thing. Betty and I have thought and prayed about it. We answer to the Lord. He called us, brought us here, and has given us outstanding years of ministry in a strategic place. We have been accountable to Him and we can rest in a sense of confidence and fulfillment."[68] Unlike other seminary presidents, who were ousted, ostensibly, for their more moderate views, Dilday was considered a theological conservative. He was viewed as a mediator who, despite his conservative stance, was willing to work with Baptists who held more moderate opinions than his.

Following the Firing

In the weeks and months that followed, Newport's presence was a stabilizing encouragement to faculty and staff and students, even though he was not present on campus as much as previously. John was a mediating force, however, during the traumatic transition, retaining what relationships he could between the two groups. "My father's love of knowledge and ideas, I think, bred into him a perspective where he could see many sides of any issue," John's son, Frank Newport, said. "I think that trait put him in positions where he could bring people together."[69] The trustees asked Bill Tolar to serve as interim president until Kenneth Shell Hemphill was elected as the new president in October 1994.

When Hemphill arrived in the fall, even as he and Paula were moving into their new home, he invited John Newport to continue in his role as special consultant to the president. Newport represented continuity during the tumult, for he had served under the last four of the seminary's six presidents: E. D. Head, J. Howard Williams, Robert E. Naylor, and Russell H. Dilday. He had seen the campus transform from five buildings to a sprawling academic center.[70] He had participated in both internal administrative and academic decisions for more than four decades. His memory was keen, and his files were a trove of informational treasure, should the president need a briefing or documentation about nearly any event that had occurred in Southern Baptist or evangelical life in nearly half a century. John accepted this role, even in his retirement. He was still teaching, speaking, attending society meetings and lectures, traveling with Eddie Belle, and writing. He still loved the school and the faculty and students. He wanted to be there, to walk with his seminary family during the shadowed days. It was all he could do.

Although John was away from campus most days during the week, he was still a pivotal figure. He hoped that he could be of some service to the new president. John loved the institution where he had invested most of his career but knew that the SBC controversy would not lessen in intensity, even with the firing of John's dear friend Russell. Like the faculties and administrations of Southeastern and Southern seminaries and SBC agencies before her,[71] Southwestern was now to become the knot in the bitter tug-of-war of convention politics. In the final five years of his life, John Newport would work incessantly to negotiate peace between the parties. This final chapter of his life was, perhaps, his most intense.

7

The River Joins the Sea

1994–2000

> Ever to the last an intermediary between the continents
> and generations and divisions.
>
> **Diarmaid MacCulloch**[1]

Newport navigated the transition between presidents and his appointment as special consultant to Kenneth Hemphill in his inimitable style. Still grieving Dilday's departure and the betrayal he felt about the manner in which it happened, he plunged into his old patterns with a heavy spirit. He read everything he could find in theology, world religions, philosophy, psychology, the Old and New Testament, hermeneutics, and art. He made notes. He dictated and penned letters to specific people he had in mind for these articles. He then copied them and supplied his old and new faculty friends, along with the new president, stacks of ample reading material with his commentary. The packets were appreciated.

Newport Under Kenneth Shell Hemphill, 1994–1999

John wrote to Ken, like he had to Russell before him, letters and memoranda and notes, almost every day. He sent Ken suggestions about books to read, items of interest in the academic world, and research on matters that were circulating throughout the convention. This was who John Newport was. Insatiably curious about all things, he was one who dug deeply to find the philosophical approach behind any movement or idea

John Newport c. 1995

or dialogue. He also collected materials and documented the controversy as it was unfolding in the media and in the public square, and its impact upon local churches.[2]

Travel with Eddie Belle

Between 1995 and 1997, John and Eddie Belle continued to host their world travel tours each summer and to attend family reunions and functions in Springfield, Buffalo, Houston, Princeton, and New York. Family events continued to be a special focus. In 1996, John and Eddie Belle and four other couples traveled to Rome for a study tour in May. In July, Eddie Belle returned to Missouri for a Leavell family reunion while John flew away, back to Edinburgh, Scotland, for his own reunion with the students and faculty with whom he had studied fifty years before.

In June 1997, they hosted another tour of the Mediterranean, something John and Eddie Belle had done thirty-seven times before. This year they visited Athens, Rhodes, Halicarnassus (Bodrum), Kusadasi and Ephesus, Mykonos, near Patmos, Delos, and Skiathos, all in Greece. They studied Greek culture and the ancient philosophers and visited sites associated with the preaching tours of Paul. These were golden days together.

Since his retirement in 1990, John and Eddie Belle had grown closer in their relationship than they had ever been before. Their adult children remember these days as a sweet period of life for them.[3] John grew gentle and solicitous of Eddie Belle, whose health was at times precarious. In March 1997, John wrote to a friend who had just lost a spouse. He related that Eddie Belle had been going through surgery and that was why they had been out of contact during her initial recovery period. Later, to another friend whose husband had died in January 2000, John said, "Please be assured of my sympathy and prayers. I have had some deep empathy since Eddie Belle continues to undergo illnesses and health problems of various types. She has had two heart operations, cancer, bone deterioration of the knees and feet."[4] These days, he doted on Eddie Belle.

They were still a strong couple that supported each other, a team that was much better working together than each could have been alone. For more than half a century, Eddie Belle had managed all aspects of the family life, including the rearing of the children, their involvement in church life, the family's health and finances, the cooking and cleaning, the maintenance of the house and the car, and the buying, selling, packing up, unpacking, and settling into homes each time they moved. She even clipped John's news and magazine articles and filed them in John's voluminous documentation boxes.

Eddie Belle had managed the world tours each year, and still did so at almost eighty years of age. She handled the logistics for travel, booking ship passage and air flights and managing accommodations, meals, entertainments, museum tours, and the finances, leaving John to deliver lectures and engage the participants in learning. Eddie Belle provided for John the space and world in which he was free to read, think, write, speak, and teach. John could not have been who he was without her. In turn, John supported Eddie Belle, encouraged her in her Bible study teaching, participation in societies, social and book clubs, academic endeavors, speaking engagements, and her social responsibilities. Together, they enjoyed fine music, dramatic performances, exploring new places, and the arts. Their

John teaching c. 1998

curiosity, still at this age, was undimmed. From the beginning they had been friends, sharing similar interests and intellectual pursuits. They still enjoyed each other as they spent these years together.[5]

New Writing Projects

While Eddie Belle was actively involved in her projects, John was finishing his latest book, *New Age Movement and the Biblical Worldview: Conflict and Dialogue*, which was the last book he was to publish.[6] He was in much demand after its distribution. Invitations poured in from churches and student conferences for him to speak and teach about this critical topic. John traveled to Sedona, Arizona, in March 1998 to speak at the New Age Conference. Mars Hill was taping a series on the book for a release in January 1999, and Bill and Phyllis Nichols, dear friends, former students, and now television executives, had arranged a Kaleidoscope television wellness interview program promoting the book that would air once a month for a year.[7]

John and Eddie Belle also attended the Gallup International Institute Program on Religion and the Inner-City Crisis in Princeton in June. They flew to the American Academy of Religion and the Evangelical

Theological Society meetings in Florida, where more than ten thousand professors gathered to exchange ideas that fall. They also enjoyed attending the Wheaton College Philosophical Conference in Illinois, which helped them to renew academic friendships and keep John involved in the technical academic world.[8] As a special consultant to the president, he was also called upon to answer sometimes complex and lengthy letters from Baptists across the nation, a task on which he spent much time researching and writing.[9]

John was also collecting materials for his own autobiography, which began to take more of his time and focus. He had written to his brother, Russell, as early as 1989, "I am projecting a new book. Part of it will involve digging into our roots. I know that you have a great deal of materials, for which I am grateful. While I am in Springfield, I would at least like to look over your materials and later, with your permission, I may like to have some of it copied."[10] This project absorbed his energies in his last years of life.

John designed dozens of outlines for his own life's story, scribbled on all sizes and scraps of paper in his scarcely legible handwriting and filed without regard for alphabet or dating. Stacks of John's jotted notes, revised lists, biographical information, bibliography records, themes for sections, and newspaper, magazine, and journal articles of interest, exist.[11] John sensed that his odyssey, as a lad called by God into ministry from the dark Missouri soil, to become a voice in constructive conservative evangelicalism for his denomination, was worth the telling. His sense of his own destiny in God's redemptive plan was unwavering. He knew his place. He hoped his story could be helpful to someone who might be asking the same questions he had pursued. His assurance that a thoughtful and biblical worldview could speak to all aspects of life and answer all of life's most challenging questions was rooted deeply in his conviction of the uniqueness of Jesus Christ in an increasingly pluralistic world.

"Eighty Plus One Celebration" in 1998

On 1 June 1998, Southwestern friends and faculty hosted a beautiful evening of celebration for John's eighty-first birthday in the Williamsburg Room. An elegant reception and dinner were held. So many dear friends were there to pay him honor for a life well lived. There were Scripture readings, congregational hymns sung, special music performed by his brother Russell, testimonials from students and colleagues, recollections from friends, and life sketches from all three of the adult Newport children. There were prayers of gratitude and remembrance, *Festschrift* highlights, personal tributes from Kenneth Hemphill and Russell Dilday, who returned for the evening's celebration, a special presentation of gifts and art, and a video of greetings from friends across the globe who could not attend.

When the evening's program was almost finished and it came to his turn for unrehearsed remarks, John stood and in his gracious way thanked the assembly. Humbly and with a broken voice, he acknowledged that his dream of twenty years before had been greatly realized. The Southwestern family had been home to him. They had journeyed together toward embracing a constructive, positive evangelical scholarship while retaining their love of Christ and his word. Individually and collectively, this family was joined in an unmatched bond of love and respect. John's gratitude overflowed with his tears.[12] At the end of the year, John was writing, "This has been a realization year, a time when we realize how much we cherish our faith, our immediate family, and our wider circle of friends."[13]

Last Things of 1999

John and Eddie Belle's schedule did not slow down in the last year of the decade. They traveled in July to participate in the Leavell family reunion in Oxford, Mississippi, where Eddie Belle's father and eight brothers had been born and reared. The whole extended clan met at the Alumni House at the University of Mississippi, where the brothers had studied and where the Leavell family archives are now housed. Eddie Belle had finished the papers of the Leavell and Boone families for inclusion in the collection. In June, she visited the families of Frank and John in Princeton and Nyack and, in November, she visited them all again, including Martha, now in New York. John called Eddie Belle "the family center, past and present."[14]

John's *New Age* book was now in its second printing. He had a busy travel schedule this year as well. In June, he attended the International Tillich Conference at the New Harmony Conference Center in Indiana and was quite impressed with the restoration work of Mary Owen of Houston, particularly the "Roofless Church" built on the Center's grounds.[15] He also attended the Princeton Gallup Institute. In the fall, he taught two courses on the New Age movement, one at Southwestern Seminary and the other at Dallas Baptist University. He attended the Evangelical Theological Society Conference and American Academy of Religion meetings in Boston, Massachusetts. He gave the inaugural address at the newly constituted Institute of Religion and Health at the Medical University of South Carolina, where his former student and friend Don Berry was appointed its first director. John also gave the address at Mark Brister's inauguration ceremony as president of Oklahoma Baptist University.[16]

John Newport closed the year of 1999 looking forward to the new millennium. Always the optimist, John in his Christmas letter related the news of the family, his pride evident. Martha had accepted the position of chairman of the math department of the well-known private Brearley Girls School in Manhattan, located at East 83rd Street and East River. She had made the transition to New York City with the help of her son Nicholas, nephew Mark, and brother John Paul. Nicholas, the Newports' eldest grandson, was completing his last year at Houston Law School.

Frank's demands at the Gallup Poll had mounted as the election year of 2000 advanced. He often appeared in interviews on CNN, after which many of John and Eddie Belle's friends would call to tell them how wonderful Frank was. Kim, Frank's wife, served on the school board in the Hopewell Valley Regional School District in Mercer County, New Jersey. Their sons, Christopher and Cal, were leaders in their own spheres. Christopher was on the U.S. Naval cycling team at the Naval Academy in Annapolis. Cal was taking a course at Princeton in computer science. Sarah, at fifteen, played the clarinet in the Princeton Area Youth Orchestra, and Emily, at thirteen, was a violinist enrolled in Princeton's Westminster Music School's Young Artists' Certificate Program. John Paul's book was in the printing stage, and he had just accepted a writer's position with *Golf* magazine to begin in the upcoming year. His wife Polly's paintings had been displayed in four shows in New York, Massachusetts, Virginia, and Nantucket, and she was devoting her time to John, Anna Belle (their daughter who was now in kindergarten), and her canvases.

None of the Newports and Leavells who gathered at the Newport home in Fort Worth for Christmas in 1999 realized that this would be their last time together with John. Their love as a family, ever strong and loyal, was binding and secure. It was enough at that moment that God had given them another year together, and for that they were thankful.

The Year 2000

In January and February, John was working hard at his writing desk. He had agreed to pen two new articles on the New Age movement and was researching a new book on futurology. He had also been requested to revise his *Life's Ultimate Questions*, a project he wanted to undertake with colleagues who had been former students.[17] All along, he was still collecting materials and arranging them for his autobiography.

Newport's last conference, on New Age, just weeks before his death in 2000

In February, he and Eddie Belle attended the William Jewell College Celebration of Achievement that honored John's brother Russell Newport. It was also the occasion upon which Carolyn Newport, Russell's wife, received an honorary doctorate. In March 2000, John prepared for his upcoming addresses for the SBC North American Mission Board's Interfaith Evangelism Team's National Seminary Workshop from 7-9 June in Orlando, Florida. The convener of the conference, N. S. R. K. Ravi, was excited about John's coming to speak to the students on the "New Age Movement in the World View Crisis" and "New Age Movement: Radical Transformation."[18] John's commitment to the spiritual growth of college students had never lessened through the years.

On 9 March, John delivered the Founder's Day Address at Southwestern Seminary. He said in a letter to a friend that he "recently struggled with our denominational seminary heritage as I prepared the Founder's Day speech week before last. I am sending you a copy of the outline and a copy of the speech and materials about the speech. I think you will appreciate what I tried to do."[19] The title was "On Preserving Southwestern Seminary's Denominational-Evangelical Balanced Biblical Foundation in a Rapidly Changing World." Newport focused on the uniqueness of Jesus Christ as the world's only savior in an increasingly pluralistic religious world. His basic presupposition was that "this missionary and evangelistic confession of the uniqueness of Jesus Christ has been and is at the heart of the foundation and history of Southwestern Seminary."[20]

In this address, John related that he had served under five of the seven seminary presidents and had known another personally.[21] Newport spoke of the new movements in theology that attempted to undercut both the uniqueness of Jesus Christ and the exclusivity of the Christian gospel. He then mentioned the contemporary developments that were helping to undergird the renewal of a balanced denominational-evangelical foundation, especially the work of Hendrik Kraemer, James Leo Garrett Jr., Mark Noll, N. T. Wright, and Alister McGrath. He reminded the audience that the Christian proclamation has always taken place in a pluralistic world, in competition with rival religions and intellectual and philosophical convictions. He noted that Earl Ellis in particular was using the premises of history and faith to refute the Jesus Seminar findings.

Further, Newport championed evangelical exclusiveness, humility, and appropriate tolerance in the face of critics like W. Cantwell Smith and Arnold Toynbee, who were proclaiming that exclusivity was "immoral," and that the only way to purge Christianity of its "sinful state of mind" of exclusive-mindedness and its accompanying spirit of intolerance was to "shed the traditional belief that Christianity is unique and Christ is the only Savior." Instead, Newport countered by affirming the conviction of Southwestern Seminary and most evangelicals and Baptists in their historic position that they can fully hold to the nonnegotiable teachings of biblical faith in Christ as the only Savior in their relations with other religions, and yet still have a proper kind of tolerance. He cited Southwestern professors William R. Estep and Leon McBeth as leaders in this emphasis.[22]

Newport closed with these stirring words, the last spoken to the Seminary family:

> The context of our world has radically changed since the foundation of Southwestern Seminary. As we have noted, we now live in a post-modern and pluralistic theological, philosophical, cultural, and

technological world. Nevertheless, the human situation is still chaotic and sinister. Satan and the demonic are active. Human selfishness and greed are still evident. The wrath of God is being revealed as humans rebel against the revelation of the cosmic and historical Christ. There are antichrists and there will be a final antichrist. History is moving toward its climax in the Second Coming of Christ. For me and the administration and faculty of Southwestern Seminary, the balanced denominational-evangelical good news of the Christian gospel is even more needed and relevant than in the days of Southwestern's foundation.[23]

As Newport concluded and stepped away from the pulpit, the packed audience in Truett Auditorium stood and applauded. This had been a masterful retelling of the historical emphases of Southwestern Seminary. She and her faculty were still under attack, and the days would grow darker in the near future. Yet this was a moment to remember and give God glory for the faithful stewardship of God's Kingdom message delivered by men and women of integrity across the years. It was also a tribute to their beloved statesman, John Newport, who had helped to guide Southwestern's course for more than half a century.

John spoke at Park Cities Baptist Church on 17 April for the Holy Week services, where his former student and colleague, James Denison, was then serving as pastor. He also attended the International Biblical Theology Conference at Wheaton, Illinois. In early May, he spoke at the Rotary Club in Fort Worth, a group with which John had been associated since 1969. He had written to Kenneth Hemphill that he felt it was important for Southwestern to be represented in the community's societies and clubs.[24]

After their return from Orlando on 10 June from the Interfaith Conference, John and Eddie Belle readied to take an extended family trip. They were to go to Princeton for the Gallup Institute from 14–16 June, and then spend the next couple of days with Martha in New York City. Then they were planning to visit with John Paul's family in Nyack and travel on to Pennington for Cal's graduation on Tuesday, 20 June. They anticipated with excitement their last leg of the trip to Williamsburg for the family reunion, which would last until the 25th.[25] In the middle of their preparations, however, John and Eddie Belle took time to celebrate her eighty-first birthday on 12 June.

Death of John Newport, 18 August 2000

When you get to the end of all of the light you know
and it is time to step into the darkness of the unknown,
faith is knowing that one of two things will happen:
either you will be given something solid to stand on,
or you will be taught how to fly.

Patrick Overton[26]

Three days later, John and Eddie Belle were packing the car at 6:15 a.m. on Saturday, 15 June. Their suitcases had been loaded and Eddie Belle was already seated in the passenger side. John sat down in the driver's seat but found he could not close the door. He could not feel his feet. John was rushed to Harris Hospital in downtown Fort Worth where it was determined he was suffering from a cerebral hemorrhage that had caused a stroke.[27] At first, he was conscious and communicating, moving fingers and toes on his right side, but soon he could no longer do so. Nicholas, their grandson, arrived quickly to give aid to Eddie Belle while Martha flew in from the East Coast. At 5:30 on Sunday morning, John was taken to neurosurgery, where doctors attempted to stem the blood loss. C. W. and Gloria Brister sat with Eddie Belle all day as other friends and colleagues also came by to lend comfort.

On Tuesday, 18 July, Eddie Belle, Martha, and Nicholas met with the surgeons and specialists, all of whom were holding out very little hope for recovery. Early in the wee hours of Friday morning, John underwent a second surgery, like the first one, to try to stop the bleeding. John Paul and Frank arrived soon after to keep watch with their mother and sister.[28] On Sunday, 23 July, John began responding faintly to commands. He had not yet spoken but had shown signs of communication and responsiveness and no longer required a respirator. The next day, however, his condition worsened, and he was returned to intensive care.[29] John was moved to hospice care on 12 August, where family and friends kept watch at his bedside. What he had written was their comfort: "Christians are called to have the last look, the last touch, and the last word with those who are dying—to minister to them and uphold them."[30] On 18 August 2000, John breathed his last and entered into the fullness of life with God. He was eighty-three years old.

John Newport's Funeral

John's funeral, "A Celebration of a Life Well Lived," was held at 2:00 in the afternoon of 22 August 2000 at the Newports' church, Broadway Baptist, in Fort Worth. Hundreds of family members, colleagues, community leaders, students, and friends filled the beautiful sanctuary as Al Travis played the magnificent organ.[31] The service was led by John's closest friends. Doug Dickens, former colleague in pastoral ministry, gave the call to worship, followed by a reading of the Scriptures by Ken Hemphill.[32] William Tolar offered a prayer, and David Crutchley, James Leo Garrett Jr., Bruce Corley, and C. W. Brister reflected on John's life and contributions. William Hendricks read Psalm 23. The congregation stood as one to sing "Amazing Grace," led by Jack Coldiron, and Russell Dilday brought the message. Russell Newport, John's beloved brother, with whom John had conducted hundreds of revivals and meetings since they were young men, filled the room with his beautiful voice. After a reception, John's remains were buried at Greenwood Memorial Park, accompanied by Newport pallbearers: sons, grandsons, nephews, and Linda Leavell.[33]

Reflections from Closest Colleagues and Friends

As the news of his illness and death became known, there was an immediate outpouring of sympathy to Eddie Belle, Martha, Frank, and John Paul. Hundreds of letters and cards came from friends and colleagues and students and scholars in the broader evangelical world. Newspapers across the nation included his obituary in which colleagues and seminary presidents spoke of his influence with deep love and appreciation.

Distinguished professor of systematic theology emeritus James Leo Garrett said of him, "He put his whole effort in the framework of, 'How can Christians be led to see the truth and viability of the Christian faith?' and 'What is necessary to represent the gospel to unbelievers?' Salvation history was strongly fixed as the key beginning point for his approach."[34] Noting John's abiding faith and his strong sense of purpose and destiny, Garrett shared that John's overall life's emphasis was centered upon an evangelical Christian apologetic and that this focus was probably his most important contribution to Southwestern.

President Kenneth S. Hemphill said that the evangelical world and the Southern Baptist Convention had lost a giant. For Kenneth, John Newport was a scholar, a gentleman, a churchman, and a friend. Few men combined academic excellence and pastoral passion like Dr. Newport did. "I will miss him, for he was a confidant and friend to me," Hemphill said.[35] The death of John Newport was like losing one's own father.

Russell Dilday's relationship with John had been particularly close. As one of Newport's students and former president of Southwestern Seminary, Dilday had hand-selected John for his vice presidential team because of his wisdom and vision as a constructive evangelical. At Baylor and Southwestern, many a future minister had the same rewarding experience that Dilday had in Newport's classes, of moving from foggy confusion into a new level of insight. Dilday said, "There were frequent 'now I see!' intellectual breakthroughs for which we were all grateful. He is a great hero for me and many others."[36]

Curtis Vaughan, distinguished professor emeritus of New Testament at Southwestern, said, "John Newport was one of the most remarkable persons I have ever known. He had a vast range of knowledge and moved comfortably among intellectual giants. Yet, the thing that impressed me most about John was his childlike faith and his warm devotion to Christ. Through his life and his teaching, John Newport made a huge contribution to Southwestern Seminary, to Baptist people generally, and to all those who knew and loved him. I will miss him."[37] The entire Southwestern family joined these and so many others in expressing deepest sympathy and grief to Eddie Belle and the Newport family.

Eddie Belle's Last Years

> In a good book, the best is between the lines.
>
> **Swedish Proverb**

For the beloved of John Newport, Martha, Frank, and John Paul, Eddie Belle's next weeks were difficult. Because her children had to return after a brief time to their jobs and families on the East Coast, many of her closest friends stayed nearby. These joined her family in constant communication and encouragement as she made the transition to living without John's daily presence and companionship. She was a courageous and stalwart woman. She also missed John sorely.

For all of their married life, Eddie Belle had been a devoted wife and mother, keeping the family together through the years as John was away from home. Since he was preaching almost every Sunday somewhere in the world, Eddie Belle was the parent who encouraged their children in the Lord, took them to church, enrolled them in camps, and attended their athletic and academic functions. As the daughter of the famous Frank Hartwell and Martha Maria Boone, she was accustomed to the sacrifices made by children of ministers. No doubt remembering her own years as a child, growing up with a father away for much of the time, she was conscious of her own children's needs and provided stability for them. During those years of child-rearing, John's parents and brothers and sister, together with Eddie Belle's parents and siblings, also kept the extended family closely connected.

Eddie Belle was a mother, a grandmother of six, and recently a great-grandmother.[38] With four generations of Newports now on her mind and heart, she was busy. She was also a member of Broadway Baptist Church in Fort Worth, where she had taught an adult Sunday School class. She had also taught the independent Ray Reimer's Bible Class and was known as a marvelous teacher in her own right. She taught at the Edna Gladney Home, now the Edna Gladney Center for Adoption, in Fort Worth. While she and John lived in Houston in the 1970s, she taught at River Oaks Baptist School in Houston.[39]

Eddie Belle was equally known as a hostess of annual travel groups, which she conducted with John and, when he could not go, without him. If he could not lecture, Eddie Belle did so, and Martha sometimes accompanied her. Eddie Belle had earned a master's degree in history from Texas Christian University in the 1970s, writing her thesis on the urban designs of Frenchman Pierre Charles L'Enfant for the city of Washington, D.C. This knowledge brought a depth and richness to her tours of that famous city and its monuments. She was a fine administrator, handling the details and logistics of travel with ease and caring for each individual member of the party. Her favorite destinations, spanning five continents, were the Holy Land, India, and New Zealand. In 1979 she had led one of the first tourist groups from the United States into mainland China, where she returned numerous times afterwards.

Eddie Belle was also a member of the Fort Worth Women's Club, and loved to square dance with John and explore the world with him. She made certain that her children also had opportunities to experience other cultures, sometimes spending her precious inheritance funds to finance the trips.[40] She was full of grace and humor, a woman who could dissolve into peals of laughter with her brother and sister at reunions each summer.

She was, most of all, a dedicated servant of Christ, a woman of the utmost integrity and honesty. One of her most outstanding characteristics was her goodness, the way she continually found ways to serve other people and taught her children to do the same. Eddie Belle lived another dozen years after John's death, missing him in each of them.

Eddie Belle's Homegoing

> Have courage for the great sorrows of life, and patience for the small ones.
> And when you have finished your daily task,
> go to sleep in peace. God is awake.
>
> **Victor Hugo**[41]

In her later years, Eddie Belle downsized her home and moved to the Broadway Plaza in Fort Worth for several years, where she lived with other friends who retired to live in community together. As she approached ninety years old, she then moved to Holly Hall Retirement Community in Houston, Texas, to spend her later years. In Houston, Eddie had a large circle of friends that she had made while they lived there years before. Nicholas lived nearby, visited her often, and looked after her for the family. She and Nicholas had been especially close since his childhood, partially because he and his mother had lived so close in Texas and could visit John and Eddie Belle more regularly.

Eddie Belle died on 29 September 2012 at Holly Hall Retirement Home in Houston. The caregivers there had attended to Eddie Belle with both scrupulous professionalism and friendship. Even in her last years, Martha remembers Eddie Belle asking what she could do to help someone there in her own community. To the last, Eddie Belle was thinking of others.

On that bright and warm October day, 6 Saturday, hundreds of people assembled at Broadway Baptist Church for a celebration of the life of Eddie Belle Leavell Newport. Magnificent music filled the grand sanctuary, and longtime friends of the Newports paid tribute to her faithful life. Special moments occurred as the children of John and Eddie Belle stood to speak about their mother. The dignity and beauty of the celebration reflected not only her life in relation to John, but her accomplishments in her own right.[42] A lovely reception followed the service, and the body of Eddie Belle made its last trip, to lie at her husband's side. Eddie Belle, however, was not dead. She is alive in Christ and with John now in the presence of the Lord.

John's legacy, and Eddie Belle's intertwined with his, continues to impact the lives of students, Christians, former friends, and pupils, as well as devotees of other religions. John's investment of thinking carefully, and the time he spent writing his thoughts in books to share, texts still widely read and consulted today, have continued to reap benefits. The hours spent with his doctoral students, in particular, have left a lasting imprint of his philosophical approach in the generation of professors who were trained by him.

8
Nourishing Waters

The Thought of John Paul Newport

> Though I am free and belong to no one,
> I have made myself a slave to everyone, to win as many as possible . . .
> I have become all things to all people so that by all possible
> means I might save some.
> I do all this for the sake of the gospel, that I may share in its blessings.
> **1 Corinthians 9:19–22, 23**

John Newport spent the last few years of his life thinking through his half-century-long teaching career and what it had meant to him. He was in the process of writing his autobiography when he died. At some point, he penned a number of closely linked paragraphs situating both his own position and purpose in the writing of such a volume. He said, "It is generally accepted that most of us are born into a particular cultural and religious heritage. It has also been established that it is important for us to bring this heritage out of the unconscious to the critical consciousness. We must not allow culture or our religious heritage to dominate us without examining it in the light."[1]

Self-aware and historically savvy, he demonstrated generational wisdom in reflecting that his life was somewhat symbolic, mirroring the transformation that had occurred in much of Protestant life during the twentieth century. He knew that he had been transformed as a person. Newport was born, as he claimed of himself, into a somewhat closed, "limited, midwestern, fundamentalist cultural religious and psychological background."[2] At the end of his days, he had become instead an open, dialogical, constructive evangelical, conversing with the noted intellectual minds of his day in philosophy, theology, biblical studies, world religions and Christianity, Baptist studies, art, and culture. The previous chapters have shown the progression of his metamorphosis, one in which he never lost his biblical roots. This chapter will briefly summarize his mature biblical worldview and present a succinct review of his philosophical approach.

Biblical Worldview

> So we must realize this: the suicidal framing story that
> dominates our world today
> has no power except the power we give it by believing it.
> Similarly, believing an alternative and transforming framing story
> may turn out to be the most radical thing any of us can ever do.
>
> **Brian McLaren**[3]

Respected globally for his intellectual teaching, speaking, and writing, John nonetheless nourished throughout his life a simple but profound biblical foundation. This did not happen by accident. Deliberate, thoughtful, compelling, methodical, sometimes complex, yet practical, John derived his philosophical orientation from Scripture and, as he matured and grew in his own knowledge, continued to find it sustainable in the face of all arguments.

For Newport, a biblical worldview, or biblical philosophy, is informed by "key categories" derived from biblical material. The biblical materials themselves are not a metaphysical system; however, they contain an "implicit metaphysic" or comprehensive view of reality. The biblical worldview is built upon the events recorded and interpreted in the biblical materials, including such crucial categories as incarnation, personalism, singular history, freedom, and purpose.[4] This foundation gave rise to all else. In a clear statement of his vocational focus, in light of this understanding, John said:

> My personal struggle has been to help evangelicals allow their faith to shape their understanding of the world. I have sought to show evangelicals the coherence and viability of their beliefs. To construct an edifice, one must first be assured of the reliability of its

foundation. My teaching and writing has aimed to secure the public acceptance of the intellectual adequacy and sufficiency of evangelicalism, in terms both of its own internal criteria and in terms of the alternatives in the modern Western world. We must continue to help shape and renew the life of the Christian mind and heart.[5]

Russell Dilday noted that Newport saw himself in the lineage of Paul, Augustine, Anselm, Calvin, and others who "have tried to interpret biblical faith in the context of current worldviews rather than in the family of those who have tried to frame *a priori* philosophical systems."[6] He described Newport as a philosopher who "synthesized" different strands of knowledge into a consistent worldview,[7] one that was foundationally biblical. Frank Louis Mauldin, a cogent summarizer of Newport's biblical worldview, asserted like so many others that "all knowledge beckoned him" and centered Newport's thoughts in the "essential core," the "deep down bone marrow" of his biblical worldview as seen in his organizational concepts.[8]

Newport sought to integrate knowledge, from his earliest days of teaching philosophy, into what was then a new term, a worldview, or a comprehensive vision of reality that reveals who one is and why one is here. He believed that a worldview originates from a "key category," or a faith principle selected from one's experience. Although this key category stems from a subjective, convictional basis, "A worldview says something about the ways in which objective reality transcends experience."[9] A worldview explains this "transcending" in terms of models or analogies found within experience. His key category and metaphysic unfolded from a faith commitment, from the interaction of revelation, redemption, personal realism, and history found in the Christian Scriptures, which contain a common set of presuppositions. Mauldin, like Newport, calls this an "implicit metaphysic."[10]

Newport's key category was his "already-not-yet" theme of redemptive history "centered in Jesus Christ," "the history-centered nature of the biblical worldview," the "revelation that came through particulars," the "durational history-centered and narrative nature of the biblical worldview," "God voluntarily revealed himself in mighty deeds and words through particular historical events and people," "eschatological-holy history," "the personal," "incarnation and reconciliation," "the revelation model that finds the center, norm, and power for existence in Jesus Christ," "a breaking into the historic order from beyond its bounds; from Being, the personal God, who created not only man and his history, but all of the world."¹¹ Newport was convinced that particularity and history merge as common components in a biblical worldview. Mauldin suggests that the essence of Newport's very being rested in the knowledge that when he sought for God, he himself was found. When he looked for God, Newport himself was grasped. When he spoke to God, he himself was addressed. This relationship with his Creator God gave Newport the confidence to respond concretely on the boundary of this metaphysic.¹²

The term "metaphysics," Newport explained, was almost synonymous with the original meaning of "philosophy," as opposed to "physical science."¹³ In this sense, then, metaphysics seeks to interpret, organize, and relate the diversity of human experience into a comprehensive worldview. This worldview is a concept that encompasses all dimensions of reality, from the existing individual to the universe itself. "The worldview of a person or an individual," Newport wrote, "is that which brings integration, a comprehensive interpretation, to life. Worldview includes a sense of meaning and value and principles of action."¹⁴ For Newport, the biblical worldview "is the systematic development of one alternative in the philosophical, metaphysical, and religious quest."¹⁵ Mauldin says, "Newport sought God, as religious people do; however, he finds himself called, as biblical persons do, by a God who searches for persons within the concreteness of the life-world and the historical drama."¹⁶

Newport discovered that personal revelation through personal circumstances of time and space is the only way to become acquainted with the sovereign, free, and personal God and his purposes. "Particularity," Newport claimed, "far from being a scandal, has the highest metaphysical credentials, for God himself is a particular, a Person. Thus, for the biblical worldview, the starting point is in revelation, which comes through particulars, not through philosophical reasoning, religious intuition, divination, or human religious consciousness."¹⁷

Drawing heavily upon the thought of G. Ernest Wright, with whom he had studied at Harvard, and who was one of the leading voices of the biblical theology movement,¹⁸ Newport began not with the premises of philosophy, but with scriptural tenets of historical faith. Though he did employ the traditional philosophical categories of epistemology, metaphysics, and axiology, he based his biblical worldview upon categories as found in Scripture, the "centrality of history and covenant." That is, he "began with history, plus existence, then proceeded to revelation and to reason, and from reason to dialogue with world religions, art, science, etc."[19] Such an approach helps the believer, he thought, to view the world not according to Greek categories of thinking, which are immersed in the abstract, but through the lens of Hebraic thinking as found in the Bible, a much more concrete framework.[20] Newport's philosophical system was based upon this linchpin.

Philosophical Approach

> Wherever you encounter truth, look upon it as Christianity.
>
> **Desiderius Erasmus**[21]

Newport came to identify philosophy with worldview, that "very general perspective on things" which affects one's outlook, attitude, and their conduct, although he believed a worldview was much more.[22] Newport's philosophy was a Christian philosophy. He believed that, at the most basic level, Christian philosophy can explore every philosophical question of life and its meaning. It can also develop a metaphysical worldview that reflects and is made philosophically persuasive by key concepts of the Christian faith.[23] To call this approach biblical philosophy is in line with the identification of other individual philosophies by the commonalities they share in a general philosophical method. These approaches, called empirical, analytical, naturalistic, and idealistic, are qualifiers that clearly indicate that such philosophies work within distinctive methodological parameters.[24] Biblical philosophy is one of these approaches.

Probing Questions of Life

For more than two thousand years, the aim of philosophy has been understood to seek to answer the vexing questions of humanity, what Newport called those "ultimate questions" of living as humans. Philosophers have struggled over the "problem of suffering and evil; the meaning of life and the goal of happiness; the nature of truth and the problem of subjectivity; the meaning and purpose of history; the role of reason in religious belief; and morals, obligation, and freedom of the will."[25] After Darwin published his *Origin of the Species*, and scientific methodology came into its own, modern scientists began to question whether philosophy was indeed a knowledge-producing discipline after all, a role philosophy had assumed for centuries. By the mid-twentieth century, the philosophical trend was to abandon the notion that philosophy's task was to include the broader questions of life and their meanings. Instead of this quest, Newport's own peers in wider circles, the ones he read, interacted with at conferences, and knew as friends, were limiting much of their work to the analysis of language, like Ludwig Wittgenstein (1889–1951), G. E. Moore (1873–1958), and Gottlob Frege (1848–1925), or to the investigations of scientific propositions, like Bertrand Russell (1872–1970) and A. J. Ayer (1910–1989).[26]

From Newport's perspective, this was neither acceptable nor efficacious. He knew that such views of philosophy were "too shallow for humanity's concerns with ultimate questions," those queries that were "too deeply true to our nature to be permanently displaced."[27] He was unwilling to surrender the discussion of the broad questions of humanity or their meanings. His stance, then, had implications for the wider academic community. Newport felt he must adopt a philosophical method that both clarified and analyzed questions and then answered them for the common man.

He explained that both clarification and analysis fall under the traditional critical task of philosophical investigation, which involves the emphasis of a "range of questions concerning the relationship of our thought and language to reality, truth, and fact."[28] This task also requires the critical analysis of one's intellectual tools and the process of thinking itself. The constructive task is another traditional task of philosophy that seeks to "integrate all of our knowledge in an inclusive and comprehensive understanding of reality."[29] This latter constructive task had to do with meaning.

Since much modern philosophy had ignored or minimized the constructive task and confined itself to a critical role, such as analytical philosophy's preoccupation with the critical analysis of language, Newport urged biblical philosophy to challenge Christians "to think constructively as well as critically, to consider the inclusive dimensions of existence and being, including life's ultimate questions."[30] For Newport, this kind of constructive investigation necessitated the study of science, culture, world religions, and other areas of human experience that may be of interest to all of humanity, including philosophers. It explains why Newport was ever exploring subject areas seemingly at a distance from his own academic field. John Newport simply felt that all knowledge was related and that every discipline could shed light on the quest for truth. His philosophy investigated all dimensions of reality, ranging from the individual to the universe, and brought integration to life, including "a sense of meaning and value and principle of action."[31]

Dialogical and Reasoned Approach

Newport's approach was dialogical. Posing meaningful questions and answering with all known possibilities, he then tested these answers. This method of "doing" philosophy not only included the critical task involving the analysis of one's thought and the constructive task that integrated one's thought into a coherent worldview. He also compared various worldviews for "adequacy and normativity," analyzing and clarifying their ideas, and critiquing them for strengths and weaknesses.[32] In these tasks, the use of reason was important to the process.

Early Christians, like Tertullian (155–254), had separated philosophy from theology, or reason from faith, while medieval Christians, like Thomas Aquinas (1224–1274), had developed a two-storied approach to the use of reason. The bottom floor was human reason, not totally defaced by the fall, as Newport states it, and the foundation of humanity's knowledge of God. Divine revelation, however, was necessary to complete the structure of the knowledge of God.[33] Since the Enlightenment, Christian scholars attempted to show "how one can still believe in Jesus Christ and not violate an ideal of intellectual integrity."[34] Later in the eighteenth and nineteenth centuries, revivalists emphasized emotions and the will over reason in matters of faith, further removing reason from the practice of Christian living.

Newport stood in the lineage of an integrative approach to the use of reason that avoids both extremes, or "either-or," and embraces a "both-and." On this subject, he concurred with aspects of the thoughts of Augustine (354–430), Anselm (1034–1109), Abraham Kuyper (1837–1920), Karl Barth (1886–1968), Carl F. H. Henry (1913–2003), George Lindbeck (1923–2018), and Millard J. Erickson (1932-present) in that there is a biblical basis for an "intertwined, mutually dependent, simultaneously progressing faith and historically-reasoned approach." In this view, the two factors are held in conjunction: not the Jesus of history alone nor the Christ of faith alone, but the proclaimed Christ of the *kerygma* as the key that unlocks the historical Jesus, and the facts of Jesus' life as support for the message that he is the Son of God. "Faith in the Christ will lead us to an understanding of the Jesus of history. It is a matter of 'faith *and* reason.'"[35]

To Christians who claimed that reason was of no value, Newport countered that it is actually Christianity alone that leads reason to its proper end. Therefore, the approach that best presents the relationship between faith and reason is that which begins with faith and is followed by the use of reason, what Newport called "faith seeking understanding."[36] McDonald states that, although one may argue that Newport is "guilty of begging the question; that is, he argues for the 'faith seeking understanding' approach because he already presumes its truthfulness, Newport claims that everyone operates from a faith principle."[37] Appealing to philosopher John Hutchison, Newport claimed that to have faith in something, whether in God or a substitute god, is "universally human, and that to act is to have faith in the assumptions upon which one acts."[38]

Newport went on to explain that all philosophies or worldviews, then, operate upon a faith principle that one assumes. There are, therefore, no atheists per se, for "each person has a source of meaning (consciously or unconsciously) for his or her day-by-day decisions and life purposes . . . Deep in the structure of your personality is an absolute or final value, a faith principle, or your god. A crisis will reveal the key category of your belief system."[39] The key category frames all of one's being, much like a lens through which one views all of life.

Complementarity

Because Newport was always seeking to gain a richer, deeper, and wider perspective and to understand those of others, he appealed to the principle of complementarity. As Mauldin explains, this interplay in tension between themes pervades his work: event and word; ultimate and mediating influences and authority; and Scripture's persons, values, and purpose against science and the natural phenomena. According to Newport, Christians may be open to dialogue with modern science, philosophy, or any other discipline, even to those that elevate reason to the exclusion of religious faith and experience. Science (reason) and Scripture (faith) "occupy different domains and use distinct methods to answer distinct kinds of questions." Nevertheless, they are "separate maps for the same terrain"; they complement one another.[40] All truth is God's truth; therefore, the various disciplines all deal with aspects of God's truth. When these disciplines do present something that is true, then the Christian may, and even should, embrace that truth. If something is not true, Christians do well to engage in dialogue to clarify the non-truth and offer a cogent, reasoned truth-counter.

In his apologetics, a field in which Newport had earned distinction, he challenged Christians to address the hard questions, to think and live their faith fully in the twenty-first century. He reminded Christians that the "main emphasis of Christianity is on the availability of God's power and love in Jesus Christ and the Spirit." The Christian is to take on a "new way of thinking . . . and pursue a life of redemptive love."[41] The evangelical Christian must be prepared not only to draw the distinction between contrasting worldviews, but also to give positive witness to the Christian gospel. The evangelical Christian cannot embrace an alien worldview. Newport knew that, this side of history's consummation and the Second Coming of Christ, the conflict of worldviews appeared to be inevitable. Nevertheless, he was not without hope, nor did he give way to divisive polemics. Instead, he offered a model for Christian conservative evangelical response that was both winsome and substantial.

His apologetic of complementarity suggests that a dialogical engagement with the cults and the cosmic power of the demonic is at least one approach that the evangelical church can take in addressing its great commission. Undergirded by the gospel itself and the empowering presence of the Holy Spirit, Newport believed that the evangelical Christian must engage the growing expressions that brush the boundary of the Christian worldview.[42] Many sectors of evangelical life, even Baptists, ignored, refused to engage, or denied the existence of these influences. In contrast, Newport's integration of scholarship and faith in addressing the phenomena of distinctly different worldviews stands as a monument of devoted commitment to the Christian world mission. It also reverberates with the apologetic challenge of the Christian gospel.

Mauldin notes that, more than any other Southwesterner, Newport called for a new encounter of the world's philosophies and religions, an engagement with science, the arts, and the humanities, and a continual interaction with the postmodern world.[43] He restated Newport's complementary approach best when he said, "Nothing short of the free exposure to the truths in all viewpoints and the incorporation of compatible truths in a biblical worldview will suffice, for truth, all of it, is God's truth."[44]

Newport's Application

The value of Newport's philosophical system may be best found in its application to human flourishing. His work serves as a guide to living well holistically. Newport invites Christians to embrace philosophy. Indeed, since the Christian faith illumines reason, leading reason to its proper end, one may benefit from its employment. Together with the heart, where emotions reside, one's mind may be transformed by the Holy Spirit through the living God in Christ, and life may then be lived according to God's teachings. Only this path can bring meaning to humanity.

Newport was a champion of a biblical worldview, which he believed to be the only worldview that may be tested to address life's ultimate questions adequately. This biblical worldview is valid and reliable because its faith principle is founded upon God's self-revelation and man's encounter with God through faith in Jesus Christ. Reason, then, is neither avoided nor denigrated, but is instead employed to good effect in one's faith-walk. The Christian who reflects deeply on biblical truths in order to develop a cohesive, comprehensive worldview is better equipped to witness in a world in need of answers.[45] This was Newport's gift to Christians, evangelicals, and to Baptists in particular.

The final chapter of this volume turns now to Newport's legacy through his own work and the remembrances of his colleagues, students, and family, concluding with some reflections that may be made upon his extraordinary life.

9
Enduring Legacy
1949–2000 and Beyond

> You're here to be light, bringing out the God-colors in the world.
> **Matthew 5:14**[1]

John Newport's calling and career were to spend his days in relationship: with God, his family, students, and churches, and within the larger Christian and secular spheres of his influence. John Newport did this well. Testimonies from those who knew him over time demonstrate how he impacted others in significant ways.

Faculty Colleagues

In his half-century of teaching, Newport served with dozens of academic colleagues, including the faculties of Baylor, New Orleans and Southwestern seminaries, Rice, and at the many other institutions where he either studied or taught for short-term assignments. Those friends with whom he served the longest were his Southwestern colleagues. In the many roles he filled while the years unfolded there, his closest friends were among the administration, the theology and philosophy departments, and those with whom he and Eddie Belle traveled on tours.[2] These colleagues remembered Newport's legacy of scholarship as being significant and powerful and enduring. They also remembered laughter and deep joy. As they served the Lord together in that special place, their days were intertwined in a mutual calling and service that were beautiful and endearing, full of comradery and ministry. Some of their best times were spent around the table in the faculty lounge. Here are some of the remembrances in the words of John's friends.

Russell Dilday Memories

Russell Dilday recalled that John was famous for the fact that he was always reading, even when he walked on the treadmill at the aerobic center.[3] From time to time, in the faculty lounge, John would appear with the latest academic book that scholars were anticipating. He would say to the professors, "Haven't you read this yet? It's been out three days!"

Russell's first opportunity to be with John personally was his first semester at Southwestern in 1952. He was pastor of the Antelope Baptist Church in Jack County, and Dr. John Newport was scheduled to speak at a "Worker's Conference" in his association at First Baptist Church, Jacksboro, Texas. Russell was asked to drive Dr. Newport from Fort Worth to the meeting and then back home again that night. Russell was so excited to have this one-on-one time with the famous philosopher! When he picked John up at his house, however, Newport greeted Russell and, with the famous briefcase in hand, then opened the back door of the car and said, "You won't mind if I catch up on some reading on the way."

Sure enough, says Russell, that was about the end of the conversation, but he knew that on the way back to Fort Worth that night, they would be able to talk. However, when they got ready to leave for the return trip, John again opened the back door of the car, flipped on the ceiling light, and said, "This light won't bother you, will it? I need to catch up on some reading on the way home!" Russell says that later, when he became John's grader and got to know him, they had lots of great conversation. His admiration for John was the reason why he invited him to be his vice president of academic affairs and provost. Dilday's wonderful tribute to his teacher, colleague, and friend, was spoken eloquently at John Newport's memorial service on 22 August 2000.[4]

William B. Tolar Memories

William (Bill) Tolar and John were colleagues for more than fifty years. As an earlier chapter has explained, he and John had planned Southwestern's first "around the world tours" to the Holy Land. Bill gave the Old Testament site lectures, and John gave the rest. In 1970, they visited fourteen countries in less than six weeks between 10 June and 19 July. In the days before spacious terminals, rolling suitcases, and moving sidewalks, this was a major feat. Bill remembers how sick John was when he reached India and that he was bedridden for a time under a doctor's care.

Bill said that John's humor was infectious. These two, along with dozens of others, spent countless hours across the years in the faculty lounge at lunch telling tall tales and hooting with laughter. Both Bill Tolar and John Newport were known for their keen wit and droll senses of humor. Bill followed John as vice president of academic affairs and provost following John's retirement, learning this role from one who had carried the responsibility with such grace and strength. Always polished and calm, Newport had tried during the Dilday years to be a peacemaker between divisive groups among Southwestern Seminary's constituencies. When Hemphill became president, Newport's presence was a wise and beneficial addition to his presidency as well, consistently demonstrating his gentlemanly character to the end of his days.

Bill said that he was away on a study tour in Israel with students when John died. As soon as he returned, Eddie Belle called him and Scotty Gray to ask for their help with John's office. His books and files had not been moved after his retirement, and John had made no plans for his office's removal, so there was a lifetime of work there to be sorted, packed, and transported. This poignant time for Bill was full of memories.[5]

James Leo Garrett Jr. Memories

James Leo and John were dear friends, going back to their experiences as young professors. They had both taught elsewhere and then returned to Southwestern to invest the mature years of their scholarship in the lives of students. They shared a love of theology. James Leo respected John's deep roots in Baptist life, his college campus speaking, his interim pastorates, and what those continued ministry roles brought to John's scholarship.

James Leo spoke of John's expanding mind, his gifts of scholarship, and masterful teaching and preaching. He spoke of the effective way that John synthesized various viewpoints. John was open-minded but anchored to Scripture and a biblical worldview. John was "very conservative," he said, and "an evangelical Christian of the Baptist variety."

James Leo said that he and John often spoke about the growing conflict within the SBC, especially in the 1980s. John was loyal to Southwestern Seminary, but he was apprehensive about the future unless there could be a resolution.[6] His preferred approach was rapprochement, negotiation, respectful discourse, but he said John had "sort of a premonition that an unpreventable disaster" would take place. These two old friends had many conversations between 1990–1994, between John's retirement and Dilday's firing. James Leo noted that John was worried about Russell and feared that he would not be able to continue a negotiation posture, and that matters were becoming confrontational. John supported Russell but had grave reservations about where the situation at Southwestern was leading. James Leo said that they would often seek each other out and kneel in one or the other's office and pray.

One of the joys of John and James Leo's relationship was the common bond they shared concerning their sons. The son of James and Myrta Ann, Robert Garrett, was a college roommate at Harvard of John Paul Newport, son of John and Eddie Belle. These two sons of noted Baptist professors became great friends, and Bob Garrett was often in the home of John and Eddie Belle Newport. Bob Garrett and John Paul are still friends. James Leo said with pride, "It was a two-father plan that worked out well."

Scotty Wayne Gray Memories

Scotty Gray joined the music faculty at Southwestern upon his graduation from the doctoral program in music in 1966 and taught for the next thirty-five years there. President Dilday asked Scotty to become vice president of academic administration in 1989, and Scotty faithfully served in this role until 2001, when he retired. Scotty and John Newport worked together closely as vice presidents.

Scotty remembers that John Newport was his professor in the seminar "Christian Faith and the Arts," which gave impetus to his doctoral dissertation, "The Musical Treatment of Implied Theological Concepts of Man in Contemporary Operas." John was significant in guiding that dissertation and served on the committee before which Scotty made the defense of his dissertation. Newport twice referred to Scotty's writing in his book, *Life's Ultimate Questions*.[7]

Scotty said that John continued to be his mentor when he became executive vice president of Southwestern. Without exception, John was insightful, gracious, and encouraging. Scotty remembers that during many of the difficult days at Southwestern and the tensions with the board of trustees, John offered sound counsel. Often, his profound insights into the issues were coupled with that little chuckle that frequently reflected both his delight in wrestling with challenging problems and his confidence that his approach was based on sound biblical teachings. He would greet Scotty in the hallway with a twinkle in his eye and say, "How goes the battle?" indicating his encouragement and understanding that they "were both trying to do what was right."

The academy was the major sphere for most of Newport's life, and he possessed an unusual skill in wedding faith and reason. John's primary interests, even in daily life, were focused on substantive matters and he seemed to find more joy in those than some other people find in entertainment. He and Dr. Arthur L. Mallory, a member of Southwestern Seminary's board of trustees at the time, were in the Grays' home for a meal one evening, and June and Scotty remarked afterward about the real delight of meaningful conversation and how it always revolved around significant matters.

When John Newport spoke to large groups, Scotty recalls, his common posture and gesture was to lean forward and stretch both arms widely to reflect his desire to be understood as he invited people into his broad and comprehensive thinking. John enjoyed humor and laughed often but was not a regular jokester. Scotty remembers John's delight in once telling a story of a public speaker who turned to a person on the platform saying, "The major problems of our time are ignorance and apathy! Don't you agree?" to which the person replied, "I don't know and I don't care." Even his humor was about the human experience.

Finally, Scotty recalls John's rare ability to integrate his deep Christian commitment, his profound thinking about a vast range of issues, and his skill to articulate these with clarity and force in speaking and writing. He was able to call to mind the writings of a vast number of scholars and compare and contrast their thinking. Scotty's associations with John always challenged him to seek to understand the world more broadly and deeply, to integrate what he understood, and to express that understanding in clear and convincing ways. A few days before John's death, Scotty visited him in the hospice center where John lay in a coma. The physician explained that John might be able to hear him, so Scotty sat with John for some time talking to him, expressing his deep appreciation for John's friendship and mentorship.

William Morris Tillman Memories

Bill Tillman, Christian ethicist, came to Southwestern in 1981 from the SBC Christian Life Commission. He served for seventeen years alongside John Newport and the rest of the faculty. Bill took a Ph.D. seminar on hermeneutics with John Newport, which was quite helpful for a Christian ethics major. The class work with him remains some of the most memorable that Bill experienced at Southwestern.

Bill recalls that when his family returned to Fort Worth from Nashville, John was one of the most welcoming of all of the Southwestern faculty. Their families were also members together at Broadway Baptist Church. Bill still remembers some of the conversations around the Wednesday night prayer meeting supper tables with John. Always down to earth, John was a Christian gentleman.

Bill says that John was very encouraging, supporting his classroom work and beyond. John demonstrated the practical side of philosophy of religion and more than once related to Bill how important the emphasis on Christian ethics was. John was a good example of one who was in the best sense a seeker, a disciple of Jesus, a devotee of the way of Christ. He was not put off by but rather gravitated toward the challenging biblical passages and those controversial facets of congregational and ministerial life. He was one who was seeking the truth of God wherever it might be found. He was one of the best examples of Southwestern Seminary's "world class" faculty. Though he had two doctorates, he never flaunted the credentials.

In the turmoil that surrounded Southwestern Seminary in the late 1980s and 1990s, John consistently tried to be a peacemaker, a negotiator with the contentious trustees who came to populate and characterize the board. He did not compromise his basic convictions, but rather demonstrated the essential challenge to all, that is to love one's enemies.

If anything could be stated as a weakness about his daily life, it would be that John *was his work*, and *his work was John*. He would forget to go home sometimes because of a book or presentation he was working on. Bill did not know if John had any hobbies. After his cardiac scares, John became a regular at the Aerobic Center and an evangelist to the faculty to be more involved and concerned with their own health.

Bill remembers John as being a very funny person, recalling a memorable incident that still makes him laugh. Bill says that there were three or four lecture series that happened through the academic year at Southwestern. One of those had an evening lecture as part of the format, preceded by a nice formal dinner. Bill and his wife, Leta, sat at a table with George and Susan Gaston just a few feet from the dais, where John and Eddie Belle sat, with John on the very end. Bill noticed during the evening that John's chair was fairly close to the edge of the platform but assumed that John would be careful. Sometime during the lecture, the two right legs of John's chair slipped off the edge of the dais. There was quite a bit of noise and kerfuffle, he recalled, enough to disrupt the proceedings. John landed on his back, and for a moment his arms and legs were extended straight up in the air. The image was that of an armadillo just passed over on the highway. But John tucked and rolled up on his feet, and with that unique smile of his, stood up and waved to the crowd that he was fine. This was "classic Newport."[8]

Bill also remembers Newport's most noticeable shoulder roll, usually the right shoulder. The shoulder roll sometimes happened as he was making a serious point. Ordinarily, though, the shoulder roll was the giveaway that a punch line was coming. John used puns, irony, anything that could demonstrate the incongruities of life, the essence of humor.

Yandall Clark Woodfin III Memories

Yandall Woodfin joined the faculty of Southwestern Seminary and its philosophy department in 1967 during the year John Newport was away. Upon John's return, they served together in the same department for almost thirty years. Their backgrounds had been somewhat similar. Yandall had studied at Baylor University, Princeton Theological Seminary, Southwestern Baptist Theological Seminary with Newport, earned a second doctor of philosophy from the University of Edinburgh in Scotland, and did additional graduate study at Cambridge University in England. He taught at Baylor University and the International Baptist Theological Seminary in Rüschlikon, above Lake Zurich in Switzerland, before coming to Southwestern. As the years unfolded, and as Yandall and John became larger than life in the same department, their relationship became more complex. Impeccably cordial, and effective teachers and supervisors, both of them were popular with the students.

By the time this biography of John Newport was underway and interviews were scheduled, Yandall Woodfin was eighty-five years old and in ill health. He sent along a brief note and two funny memories through his wife, Leta. He said that John was an outstanding communicator with an ebullient personality.[9] A funny quirk about John Newport was, in Yandall's words, "John's almost bizarre penchant for reading with a book balanced on the dash board as he drove!" The Woodfins said that they were "always fearful that John would kill himself and others, but thank God he never did."[10]

The other tale involved John and the great Baptist historian and humorist, H. Leon McBeth.[11] At the seminary there had been at least three retirement dinners for John: one when he left to teach at Rice in 1976; another when he retired to become vice president of academic affairs in 1990; and still another when he retired from that position in 1994. There was also a seventieth birthday celebration dinner in 1987, and one marking his eighty-first birthday in 1998, complete with great pomp, programs, speeches, and ceremony. Yandall remembers that Leon leaned over one time in a faculty meeting to murmur to John in *sotto voce*: "You haven't had a retirement dinner in some time now, have you John?" Yandall never forgot McBeth's mischievous barb. It was often repeated in the faculty lounge, accompanied by much knee-slapping. John Newport thought it was as funny as everyone else did, answering that it was "about time for another."

This sampling of colleagues' memories represents a much larger group that taught, researched and wrote their volumes, served on committees, listened to each other's opinions in faculty meetings, shared laughter around the faculty lunch tables, and prayed for students, the seminary, and the convention. As one of many fine minds, Newport earned the respect of them all and carried his share of the faculty load of theological education, marked by effective leadership, diplomacy, and grace.

Philosophy of Religion Doctoral Students

By the time of his death in 2000, John Newport had supervised fifty-six doctor of philosophy of religion students in the research and writing of their dissertations. Some of these graduates went on to serve as faculty members in all six Southern Baptist Convention seminaries and several of the newer theological schools across the Baptist world. Some served in the religion faculties of twelve different universities. Others served as leaders of SBC agencies, pastors of churches large and small, and still others as foreign missionaries.

Like Newport before them, the students had traveled to study with the best minds they could find. These sought to be guided by John Newport. Several of his graduates reflected upon Newport's influence on their lives and ministries. In so doing, these brief recollections give witness to John's vast reach and enduring legacy that continue to extend to second and third generations today.

John Newport's well-used leather briefcases and shelves of his students' doctoral dissertations

B. Keith Putt Memories

Keith Putt was both John Newport and Yandall Woodfin's student in doctoral study. When he graduated in 1985, Keith began teaching at Houston Baptist University and earned another Ph.D. at Rice. He joined the faculty at Southwestern in the philosophy department from 1991 until 1998. He later joined the faculty at Samford University in 2002, where he still serves on faculty.

Keith spoke of Newport's incessant reading habit and, assuming that everyone had read what he had read, his launching into discussions of widely diverse subjects. His was a "shotgun" rather than a "rifle" approach. Newport was deeply conversant, never became bored, and chose not to linger long. There was too much to learn. Yet Newport learned and thought deeply. He was not a shallow man. Newport never lost his "child-like exuberance about existence," Keith recalls, "his insatiable wonder of life."[12]

Keith says that when his own father died in 1991, both John Newport and David Kirkpatrick became like fathers to him. With great fondness,

Newport added depth to Keith's spiritual and psychological life. He recalls that one day, later in his life, Newport called Keith at home to talk about deconstructionism. John was excited, like a child on Christmas morning. He and John Newport and Russell Dilday then attended a Derrida conference in 1997 at Villanova University in Pennsylvania when Newport was eighty years old and analyzing his own biblical worldview against this new approach. In the spring of 1999, Newport taught a doctoral hermeneutics seminar on the scholars Paul Ricoeur, Jacques Derrida, and John Caputo, something Keith admired in his aging mentor with the agile mind.

Keith said that Newport favored the Continental approach to philosophy rather than the analytical, but that Newport always held to the existential certitude of his biblical worldview. Newport kept a deep humility, knew that he was not always right on every point, wanted to encounter "alterity," "the other," and was certain that he could learn from "the other." John's drive, he said, was to write a "Summa," because all knowledge connects back to God, an element that Keith said was quite modern. John's fascination with hermeneutics was due to its nature as the science of trying to understand. This is what made Newport love Tillich. He did not have to agree with Tillich to converse with him.

Keith relates that John Newport was someone who loved much. He loved God, his family, his students, and the intellectual pursuit. He was a lover of godly wisdom. After Putt had gone to Houston, he saw Newport and Kirkpatrick often. He considered them his chief mentors. One time he took the opportunity to thank John Newport again for his influence upon him. John simply looked him in the eye and said, "Don't thank me anymore. Do for your students in the future what I have done for you." Newport made an indelible imprint upon Keith. He says that every day he walks into his classrooms "with Newport on my shoulder."

Steve W. Lemke Memories

Steve Lemke studied with Newport at the same time as Keith Putt and graduated in 1985 with his Ph.D. in philosophy of religion. Steve did further philosophical study at Texas Christian University, the University of Texas at Dallas, and Texas A&M. While a doctoral student, Steve taught at Weatherford Junior College, Blinn College, and Williams Baptist College, where he continued to teach after graduation. He then joined the faculty of Southwestern Seminary from 1990 until 1997, when he became the provost and vice president for institutional assessment and professor of philosophy and ethics at New Orleans Baptist Theological Seminary, where he still serves.

Steve loves what Curtis Vaughan used to say about John Newport: "He maintained a simple, child-like faith even though he was acquainted with the great intellects of his day."[13] He never stepped far from the influence of his parents' devout love for Christ. Steve says he never saw Newport discouraged. He was a positive soul who never said a negative word about anyone, even writers with whom he disagreed.

Steve credits Newport with teaching him how to teach philosophy, learning from him how to think, write, and express himself. Newport taught him how to condense information into "bullet" form, address issues in a concise fashion, and put difficult material into smaller packages, an approach Newport had mastered and modeled.

As far as Newport's impact on churches, Steve says that Newport was always powerful and popular in the pulpit, helping laypeople and university students to understand complex issues. Newport would stand on objective truth, but would be kind and gracious, dialogical when discussing strengths and weaknesses, curious about all viewpoints. Steve recalls Newport's intensity at work. One night, he stayed in the library into the wee hours of the night. Eddie Belle had to call Russell Dilday to go find him and send him home.

John was a peacemaker. Steve remembered that when an SBC leader, Bailey Smith, remarked that God would not hear the prayer of a Jew, Baylor University invited John to come to Waco for a dialogue session with many Jewish leaders. John was able to diffuse the statement by explaining the worldview that had occasioned such a remark. Newport always had two hands outstretched—one to the more moderate side of the SBC and one to the more conservative—in trying to understand both viewpoints. Yet John was not confined to the SBC, Steve said. He and William Hendricks engaged the world of ideas better than any other scholars of their day. Steve spoke of Newport's ability to be open-minded and fair, friends with everyone.

Theodore (Ted) J. Cabal Memories

Ted Cabal was another of John Newport's students. He graduated and taught philosophy at Dallas Baptist University before joining Southwestern Seminary's faculty in 1995. Three years later, Ted moved to Southern Baptist Theological Seminary in Louisville, Kentucky, where he has taught apologetics and philosophy for more than two decades. Ted wrote his dissertation, "Problems and Promise in a Biblical Worldview with Special Reference to John Paul Newport," on Newport's worldview.

Cabal said that Newport was ahead of his time in SBC life, where not much attention was given to either philosophy of religion or "worldview" in the 1960s and 1970s. He was an amazing thinker and humble, but he also frustrated some philosophers, who felt that John was inconsistent in his approach. Of the two primary paths, continental and analytical, John was dialogical between the two, and leaned toward the continental.[14] He was not, however, clearly parallel with either. John was open to both approaches and wanted to find a way to make both fit into the same conversation. Because of this search for synthesis that never truly resolved, there was dissonance for the graduates of John Newport as they left his seminar rooms for teaching in faculties that expected a strong approach from one or the other method. Newport, says Cabal, put all of philosophy together to present a metanarrative to "Everyman," and this was effective for his purposes, although it was not fully aligned with either approach.

Ted considered John a true friend and Christian brother. From their first moment of meeting, Ted was extremely impressed with his kind heart, warm and gentle spirit, and remarkably keen mind. John was a great teacher because he made students think. He did not accept pat answers; instead, he made students see the other side of issues they might not have been willing to consider otherwise. What made the experience so enjoyable was John's ability to inject his unique wit into an otherwise serious discussion. And nothing, but nothing could compare with his amazing ability to call upon a ready understanding of so many thinkers and often share stories of his personal encounters with them. He never took the easy road in seminars when a difficult issue presented itself to the group. When in deep thought he would "bend over the seminar table and continue talking while rubbing his temples with his large hands, as if he were massaging out every last bit of his genius for our profit," Ted said.

Newport led evangelicals with his emphasis upon the notion of worldview that has blossomed in recent decades. He began writing on the topic regularly as early as the 1970s. For him, the idea of a biblical worldview became a powerful analytic tool for compassionately comparing and defending the Christian faith with its competitors. Ted said he would never forget how passionately Newport felt about the importance of his personal responsibility to share this message with anyone anywhere.

Being Newport's student opened doors for Ted to teach in the several SBC institutions where he has served. No matter the administration's theological leanings, every administrator Ted has known has greatly respected John Newport, who exemplified the honored terms of scholar and gentleman. Ted did eventually perceive that the style of philosophy of religion that has dominated in SBC colleges and seminaries for decades was not always interested in or in tune with dramatic developments in the analytic tradition since the 1970s. Very often, he said, Baptist philosophers have been trained in a continental and/or anti-analytic model. But John happily encouraged his students to engage such leading Christian analytic thinkers as Plantinga and Wolterstorff. Ted has increasingly come to appreciate the emphasis upon the practical, biblical, and even eclectic approach Newport imparted. Ted says he is a better teacher and person when he employs the lessons learned from his great teacher.

Dennis L. Sansom Memories

John Newport directed Dennis' dissertation from 1979 through 1981. Dennis served as his graduate student, accompanied John on day trips, and traveled to San Francisco for an AAR meeting and to Chicago for a philosophy conference at Wheaton. Dennis joined the faculty at Samford in the fall of 1988 and, since 2000, has been chair of the department of philosophy there.

Newport had a large impact on Dennis' life. His seminars were interesting, filled with good analysis and stories of his experiences and acquaintances. Dennis was always impressed with John's knowledge of many, many books and authors. This inspired him to read more and try to incorporate differing vantage points into his own thinking. Newport also modeled gentleness, respect for others, and humor in the classroom. Dennis will never forget his tall, angular walk across campus with his two leather briefcases full of books, one in each hand. He had the look of a bookish scholar with his thick glasses and often disheveled suits. He was always respectful, never dogmatic or condescending in any way.[15]

Dennis loves the way John presented a Christian worldview as a viable alternative to other worldviews, helping him to know that Christianity is as intellectually cogent and legitimate as any other intellectual system. John knew that a biblical worldview is not a settled set of doctrines but a conversation within often inconsistent perspectives. This last point had a large impact on Dennis, and to this day he gives it as the way to present a Christian worldview; that is, Christianity is grounded on a fundamental experience with God in Christ, defined by broad views of creation, salvation, human nature and destiny, eschatology, etc., but that within these views are multiple and competing explanations, which should be acknowledged and learned from. John had a humorous way of laughing, Dennis recalled, kind of under his breath, which was often funnier than what made him laugh in the first place. He would shrug his shoulders sometimes and smile. He had a contagious manner that made people lower their defenses and feel relaxed.

John influenced Dennis in several ways, not only educationally and personally, but also professionally. It was through his strong recommendation that Dennis was invited to join the faculty at Samford University, where Dennis has made his career since. John had a love for life and the world. He was not afraid of differences and novelty. He found interest in each culture and its art. He cultivated friendships with people of other societies and religion, and Dennis was most impressed with his deep friendship with a rabbi.

John had an almost unlimited amount of energy, both intellectually and physically. Through everything, Dennis always knew that John was at his core a Christian, and that prayer, church life, and Christian communion were important to him. In addition to all the others, this aspect has greatly shaped who Dennis is to this day.

W. Reagan White Memories

Reagan White was another student of Newport. He served as a patient representative at Cook Children's Hospital and chaplain with Texas Health Harris Methodist Hospital. Since 2013, he has taught philosophy at B. H. Carroll Theological Institute in Irving, Texas.[16] Reagan remembers John Newport as genial, tall and lean in his gray suits, with a quick smile and a relaxed demeanor. He recalls going into John's office and not being able to see him at his desk from the doorway. He had to navigate a maze of columns and shelves of books standing in the way before he could find John.

Reagan says that "we all were Southern Baptists back then, and I remember so well his deep sense of personal betrayal at having been told that Dr. Dilday would not be fired shortly before he actually was." Reagan was impressed at how John soldiered on at the seminary afterward, when it suddenly became so much less appealing there, but he never found him out of sorts about it afterward. Back behind the stacks of books, John told

Reagan that he considered it a ministry of his in later years to write letters of recommendation on behalf of his students.

Reagan remembers attending John Newport's funeral in 2000 and, like Keith Putt, it was the first time Reagan had visited Broadway. Afterward, as Reagan and Keith spoke of the passing of John Newport, and all that had been lost at Southwestern, they both wept. As the twenty years since have gone by, Reagan has grown to celebrate what he learned from Dr. Newport more than he grieves for the losses of the school. He said he supposed that many early Christians grieved the "loss" of Jerusalem, even as they fulfilled the great commission by going out and spreading the faith. John would have liked that analogy.

James Denison Memories

Jim Denison was also John's student, graduating in 1987 and teaching at Southwestern from 1987 to 1989. He then pastored at the First Baptist Church in Midland from 1988 to 1994, the Second-Ponce de Leon Baptist Church in Atlanta from 1994 to 1998, and the Park Cities Baptist Church of Dallas, Texas, from 1998 to 2008. Jim then launched the Denison Forum in February 2009, which had formerly been the Center for Informed Faith of the Baptist General Convention of Texas and is now a nonprofit media organization that comments on cultural issues through biblical and apologetic lenses. Jim claims John Newport as his spiritual and personal mentor.[17]

Dr. Newport was one of the most brilliant men Jim has ever met. His ability to understand and synthesize ideas was remarkable. His intellect was clearly a gift from God; yet, at the same time, he was engaging with students, seeking to draw them into conversation with the great ideas and issues of the day. He never imposed his thoughts or worldview but sought to include students in what John called the "great conversation." He was amazingly current, reading all the latest works across the spectrum of theological inquiry. Specialists in various fields seldom knew of journal articles or books that he had not read. He carried home two large satchels every night, and often returned them the next day with their contents read and synthesized.

John consistently sought to demonstrate the relevance of academic inquiry to the Kingdom. Jim thinks that John's mother taught him the importance of evangelism and the work of the Spirit so much so that Jim thought of him as an evangelist as much as a scholar. John never forgot that he was teaching students in preparation for ministry and so related his students' academic work to the life of the church. His background as a pastor, evangelist, and preacher made him an outstanding role model for such integration and synthesis.

John preached a revival at Jim's rural church one week and related the material to each person in the small sanctuary so masterfully that many in the congregation told Jim that those days were the greatest "revival" the church had ever experienced. A prayer ministry came directly from those services and continued in the church for two decades afterward. When Jim thinks of John Newport, those four days come quickly to mind.

Newport constantly emphasized the "biblical worldview," the argument that the Bible contains and teaches a consistent way of looking at all of reality, something that Jim had never thought of in such a holistic way before he took John's seminars. Due to his influence, Jim seeks to understand and apply biblical thinking to every dimension of life and ministry each day.

Jim's father died when he was in college, and Jim says John became a genuine spiritual father to him. He constantly challenged and encouraged Jim to think as effectively and broadly as possible, recommending books and articles, movies and TV shows, and becoming his mentor in personal and professional life. He was a true man of God, a minister in every sense of the word. He cared about each person he met and truly wanted the best for them. John Newport's synthesis of Spirit, Scripture, and philosophical investigation have been a model for Jim across three decades.

Richard W. Harmon Memories

Richard graduated from Hardin-Simmons University and earned his M.Div. and Th.D. (1975) degrees at Southwestern Baptist Theological Seminary. John Newport was his major professor. While completing his graduate studies, Richard became an editor of young adult Bible studies for the SBC Baptist Sunday School Board and eventually became the curriculum development coordinator for all Sunday School materials. In 1981, he joined the Interfaith Witness Department of the Baptist Home Mission Board as a specialist in American Christian studies, participating on the Faith and Order Commission of the National Council of Churches and coordinating the national scholars' dialogue between Southern Baptists and Roman Catholics. He wrote *Baptists and Other Denominations* (1984), which summarized the views and polities of six different Christian groups in America. Since 1987, Harmon has been an Episcopalian and served on the faculty at the Anglican School of Theology in Dallas from 1989 until 2005. He was an inaugural member of The Newport Foundation, serving as secretary/treasurer for twenty years.

Richard's relationship with Newport was primarily one of student and professor. John asked Richard to be his teaching assistant and grader when he entered doctoral studies. John expected much from that position, but he also supported Richard in that role with the students. Newport taught by example that the mind is to be exercised to the fullest in the practice of faith; he taught his students to ask questions and to be bold when facing uncertainty. Those who worked with him were amazed at the breadth and retention of his reading. Richard says, "He didn't have to tell you to read. His lectures made you want to read more."[18]

One funny incident Richard recalls had to do with one of Newport's habits in class. When discussion became prolonged, he had an unconscious habit of lifting his right shoulder, clearing his throat, and declaring, "Well, we've got to move on." Once, when Richard was presenting a paper in one of his seminars, Newport stopped Richard and asked a question about the content. Richard answered and then on a whim, lifted his right shoulder, cleared his throat, and said to the group, "Well, we've got to move on." Newport laughed as much as the other students at this gentle tease. Working with John and being his student gave Richard a love for reading that has never been quenched. He says he shall always be in Newport's debt for that, and for the gift of his life and friendship.

These students represent only a slice of John Newport's preaching and teaching ministry. Across the years, many thousands of participants and students filled his audiences: laymen and laywomen in sanctuaries, Sunday School classes; undergraduate, masters, and doctoral students in courses and seminars, intensives, semester-long, extension, and weekend courses; and scholars in conference sessions. Transformative learning and life experiences happened in all of these places with John standing to facilitate learning. This was one of many sides of his person. Perhaps the most intimate portrait, however, may be found as one looks in the window of his home, where he lived as "Daddy."

Family Memories

If anyone has ever wondered what it might be like to grow up in the home of John Newport, to sit across the supper table each evening, or watch him open his Christmas presents each year, or walk through the room when his favorite basketball team was on the television, or hear him roar with the crowd when his son scored a touchdown at a high school football game, then this chapter's close will answer some of those musings.

John Newport loved his family deeply, and his pride, reflected in hundreds of letters through the years, testifies to the fact that Eddie Belle, Martha, Frank, and John Paul were ever on his heart and mind. Each of Eddie Belle and John's children contributed their recollections to help readers understand John as the human being he was and the legacy he left to his own family.

Martha Ellen Newport Family Memories

Martha Ellen Newport Shimkus was born on 24 January 1946, just nine months before her father went to Scotland to study.[19] Her nuclear family was comprised of her father, mother, brothers Frank and Johnny, and herself. As the eldest child and a girl, she helped her mother take care of their home, her father, and her brothers, particularly as she grew. Like her mother before her, she experienced a childhood where her father was gone most of the time as he traveled to be an interim pastor at various churches on the weekend. Martha remembers attending church every Sunday, but almost always without her father. He was there during most weekdays at supper almost every evening, and attended Wednesday nights at church with the family, but Martha credits her mother as bearing most of the responsibility of child-rearing in the early days.

During the summers and on academic study leaves, however, the family traveled extensively to places across the country and the world. These were important, special times for the family as they explored the nation from coast to coast. She particularly loved the 1958–1959 sabbatical to Harvard for her father to study with Paul Tillich and others. This trip opened up a new world to Martha as a young teen, as her family traveled throughout New England for her father's job with Boston University. She remembers going to an island off the coast of Maine, to New Hampshire, Vermont, Rhode Island, and Massachusetts. She loved the exposure to different cultural and intellectual elements in Boston. She recalls how happy her father was with the new experiences.

Martha loved the road trips the family took every year. One summer was particularly special because they traveled with her paternal grandmother to California. Martha roomed with her while her brothers and parents took the other room. One day, the family went to Disneyland. John and Eddie Belle left Martha and her grandmother for a while and were amazed when they returned to see them both riding "Dumbo the Flying Elephant" together. That was a warm, loving trip. Another day on that trip, the family attended a live filming of the Art Linkletter Show. The topic of the day was teenagers and how they would change their parents if they could. John told Martha to tell Art Linkletter that her father was a Baptist preacher and that she wished he would practice what he preached on Sunday every day of the week. Sure enough, Martha was chosen and was briefly interviewed by Linkletter on television. This funny moment shows that her father was able to laugh at himself. He taught them the value of family and standing by each other no matter what.

Martha recalls that her father took each of the children on major trips during which he lectured. When she was seventeen years old, in 1963, she went to Russia, Egypt, the Middle East, and Europe with him on a tour he was leading. Her parents together took her brothers on trips around the world. Also, in 1978, her parents took the whole family on a Mediterranean cruise on which her father lectured every night, and her mother handled the business details. Her mother subsequently took many trips around the world by herself, taking Martha on one, and another later with Martha's son, Nicholas.

Although Martha does not consider their family to have been wealthy, she realized early that they all had opportunities to travel, exposure to other cultures, and intellectual influences that were unusual and fine. Her father arranged for Martha and three friends to spend the summer of 1966 serving at Rüschlikon Seminary, and another in 1971 with a friend at the Arusha International School in Tanzania. To this day she is very grateful for all of these opportunities. Since John was completely committed to and almost obsessed with learning, whether from books, from art, or from people, when the family traveled, "he usually made a beeline to the nearest bookstore and ALWAYS toured whatever college or university was in the area."

Martha confirms that the Newport-Leavell extended family was very important to them. She remembers her maternal grandfather and grandmother Leavell and their important Baptist contributions. She loved her uncle and aunt, Frank and Mary Martha Leavell, and all of the cousins. This family enjoyed extended Leavell reunions where descendants of the nine Leavell brothers came together regularly.

For Martha, however, her notion of family came from her father's side, and she also loved the reunions in Missouri. As a girl, her two favorite people were her paternal grandmother, Mildred Morrow Newport, and her father's sister, Mary Ellen Newport Zorbaugh. Martha received from these two women an abundance of warm, unconditional love that she carried with her for life. Martha spent two weeks at a time in Springfield with this grandmother and loved playing hymns with her on the organ and piano in her living room by the hour. Martha was special to her grandmother because she was the only girl and the eldest grandchild. Her father's youngest sister, Mary Ellen, was only a dozen years older than Martha, seventeen years younger than John Newport.

By the time the Newports moved to Fort Worth in 1954, it was Martha's seventh place to live. She recalls that it was somewhat difficult for her to be uprooted continually. By way of comparison, Frank had lived in four places by that time, and John Paul was born in Fort Worth and grew up in that area. The three children, then, had different perspectives. As a girl and young woman, Martha was also expected to help in the kitchen with her mother and aunt at holiday meals while her father, her Uncle Frank, and her brothers were in the living room having interesting discussions. As a teenager, she felt this to be less than fair. She did not mind the work, but felt removed from the intellectual, challenging discussions in the other room and wished she could have joined them. This changed as she became older.

She remembers her father being very driven in his work, both academically and spiritually, and that sometimes he could be preoccupied, his responses short. As an adult, her relationship with her father matured and they became quite close. They spent many hours talking, and he supported her dreams. She applied for a Klingstein scholarship at Columbia in the 1990s, for example, and he spent many hours helping her with the application. He was affectionate and kind, and Martha felt they had a special relationship. After college, Martha lived in Houston most of her career and visited her parents often. She treasured their time together and greatly respected her father both as a person and for the work he was doing. She still believes in his ideals and tries to live her life according to those biblical patterns each day. She loves the faith and mind approach to life.

Martha says that, although she and Eddie Belle had different personalities, she respected her mother for raising the children almost alone in the early years. Eddie Belle handled the house and the financial affairs and conducted trips around the world by herself. She was an amazing person who often lived in the shadow of her husband, but was a unique individual in her own right, writing book reviews and serving as president of several clubs and societies. Martha realizes that much of who she is today is a result of the morals and ethics her mother taught her and the social graces and manners she instilled in her. Eddie Belle encouraged them all to be active in church, and Martha was in discipleship groups, choir, and Girls in Action, the mission group for teens.

The children were taught Christian morals, to value education, to serve others, and to try to make a difference in the world. Whether one had wealth or not was not emphasized. Eddie Belle always had a high moral ethic and taught the children to be honest at all times. They could never tell even a white lie. Martha says Eddie Belle was so honest that if someone called Martha on the telephone and Martha did not want to talk to the person, her mother would not tell them Martha was not home unless Martha actually walked outside into the neighbor's yard! She would never lie. She also told them that the greatest thing they could do in life was to serve others and to make a difference to the world through helping others. Martha holds all of these values to this day.

Martha recalled how funny her father was when he was with the family. One time the family was on an outing, touring an animal park near Glen Rose, Texas. The object was to drive slowly to see the animals in their natural habitat. Sometimes animals would come to be fed or to be seen up close. After a while, her father grew impatient and then started honking at the car in front of them, as if to hurry them along. The children were mortified, but later he was able to laugh at the memory. He often made fun of himself and certainly recognized his own foibles; he had a good sense of humor.

Another funny family remembrance concerned their father's deep interest in people at all levels and at all times. When they went to a restaurant, for example, he would ask their waitress all kind of questions about herself and get to know her. By the time they left, she was their new best friend. As they would drive down the street, he would wave randomly to people and they would wave back, smiling. He had a kind innocence about him that made people trust him and not take offense at these overtures.

When Martha moved to New York City in 1999, the year before her father's death, both of her parents encouraged her to go, despite the fact that it would take her further away from them. After she had acquired her job and apartment, her father came to New York for a conference before she had moved. He went to her new school, the Brearley School in

Manhattan, which was conducting a fire drill when he arrived. Everyone was on the street. John approached a person who was the math department head. He told her who he was and talked to her. She gave him a tour of the building and introduced him to people. Once again, his demeanor made people trust him and like him. The school administration later told Martha how endearing he was. He then went to Martha's apartment and looked it over, approvingly.

He called Martha when he got home and told her that he had "scoped out" her situation and thought it was good. Everyone that he met loved him, and that made Martha feel very special. During her first year in New York, she would always call him after she had gone to a special event to share it with him. He loved to know what she was doing and was very knowledgeable about the speakers she had heard or knew of the musical pieces she had heard performed. He was an amazing support.

Finally, Martha reflected that her father's weaknesses were perhaps connected to his strengths. At times he did not spend enough time with his family as the children were growing up. Sometimes he seemed overly absorbed in his work and his mission. He was unable to attend many of the children's activities, leaving it to their mother. It was at times difficult on all of them, she said. On the other hand, his strengths were his curiosity, his love of learning, his interest in all aspects of life from reading, to people's lives, to literature, to art, to music, to travel. He was an insatiable learner and shared that love with others. As a scholar, he was able to take myriads of difficult concepts and synthesize them into a clear summary that the average person could understand. He was a committed Christian and loved combining his faith with the intellectual world. He always knew what he believed and never hesitated to express it but did so in the context of the bigger "Christian worldview." Martha says she will be eternally grateful for her parents and family.

Frank M. Newport Family Memories

Frank Marvin Newport was born on 1 November 1948 in Tulsa almost a year after his parents moved back from Scotland to pastor. His maternal grandfather, for whom he was named and who was a well-known Baptist figure in his own right (Frank H. Leavell), died when Frank was only a year old, so he never knew him. His maternal grandmother, Martha Boone Leavell, however, was a strong presence in their lives. Although she lived in Nashville, they saw her frequently. Frank loved her because she would take time to play games and chess with him, giving him her undivided attention.[20]

Frank also remembers how important his paternal grandfather and grandmother were to the family, and visits to Springfield, Missouri, were special times of joy. John's brother Russell and his wife Carolyn also lived in Springfield, so Frank loved spending time with them and the cousins, especially Mark, a year or so younger than himself. Frank remembers with fondness how his grandfather would take him on trips to his businesses, to all of his five and dime stores in the Ozarks.

The uncle with whom Frank most closely related was Frank H. Leavell Jr., his mother's brother, who was a professor of English at Baylor for thirty years. Frank saw him fairly frequently, particularly when he was a student at Baylor, and later when his family lived in Houston for eleven years. He was one of the finest people Frank has ever known because he cared about other people and focused on them when he was in their presence. In the years when Frank's own father was traveling so much, Uncle Frank became to some degree a surrogate father to Frank. He taught him about guns and fishing and, after Frank and Kim had their own children in Houston, they would regularly go camping with Uncle Frank and the cousins, Linda and Neal, at various lakes and campgrounds in Texas. Although he had a Ph.D. in English, he was a man grounded in Southern traditions and the earth and soil. He was funny, caring, and had a deep underlying insight into human behavior, no doubt honed by both his years of studying characterizations of humans in literature and, like his sister Eddie Belle, spending his childhood with his own father away from home on ministry assignments.

Frank's childhood was spent helping his mother, who was in practical terms a single mother much of the time. Since he was the first son, even as the middle child, he helped to take care of John Paul. As a child, Frank missed knowing his father well, often wishing that his dad could be home on the weekends. John was gone on sabbatical to Union Seminary in New York City during Frank's senior year in high school. His memories of parental presence, then, are mostly of his mother, whom he admired greatly. He says that he respects her more each year as he reflects back on their upbringing. His mother emphasized and communicated integrity, spirituality, honesty, and kindness. Since she came from a very prominent Baptist family herself, she emphasized faith and her Christian heritage and was a saintly Christian woman herself.

Frank's main awareness of being a Newport was twofold: he remembers his father's extraordinary emphasis on scholarship and love of knowledge, and the family heritage as owners of a string of retail stores in the Ozarks. He also was aware that his uncle Russell was a well-known Baptist singer who sang around the country and appeared on the Ed Sullivan Show when Frank was in high school.

Frank was more aware of being a Newport on occasions when he was in a religious setting, such as visiting other churches or during summers at Glorieta Baptist Encampment in New Mexico, places where his father was well-known as a prominent seminary professor. He was also aware of being a Newport when he arrived at Baylor as a freshman and throughout his years there, since his father was acquainted with many faculty. He had taught there briefly about fifteen years before Frank arrived, but he was a household name among some of Frank's fellow students who also came from devout Baptist families. Of course, Frank's uncle was also a professor there.

Frank describes his father's greatest interest as his love of knowledge. He spent his life acquiring knowledge of all sorts in all arenas and never stopped in this pursuit until the day he died. Nothing thrilled him like new knowledge, new scholarship, new ways of looking at things he discovered. His father loved history, and when the family took their annual trips together, his father enjoyed learning about the background and history of places they went. He loved bookstores and books. His idea of heaven on earth would be to discover new books on new topics, or to be able to listen to lectures or speeches by well-known or controversial theologians or philosophers or other thinkers. His daily life was consumed by the pursuit of knowledge. In fact, later in his life, people in Frank's hometown of Pennington, New Jersey, remember his father's visits and how John would walk around town reading as he went.

Frank recalls the wonderful travel, both domestically and internationally, that his father and mother provided for them. Frank was able to go on the "around the world tour" in 1968, and Frank and his wife Kim, along with his brother John Paul and sister Martha, went on the "Holy Land Tour" of the Mediterranean in 1978. Frank was impressed that his mother essentially took over the business end of those tours later in her life and ended up hosting tours on her own. They also took long trips in the summer, and he remembers well the year when, in the fifth grade, they lived in Cambridge when his father took the sabbatical at Harvard.

Frank also acquired a strong respect for and love of knowledge, together with a deep understanding of theology and religion. He said he also acquired from his home a worldview that valued accomplishments and work, but which looked with some disdain on seeking pleasure for its own sake. Nevertheless, Frank did not perceive himself as any different from other children as he was growing up. He and his siblings rarely socialized with or even knew other children of seminary professors. He recalls that they were not allowed to take dance lessons and that there was no use of alcohol, but they did have a very church-centered life at Broadway Baptist, which meant that Frank had a lot of friends in that circle. He does not remember feeling different than any of the other kids who went to the same church and whose parents had secular occupations.

Frank recalls with appreciation his father's habit of writing regular and frequent letters. Once Frank left home to go to college, his father would write letters very often that were personal and encouraging. Frank remarked that his father died before the advent of email, before social media created the new ways of communicating that Frank uses today with his own children.

John Paul Jr. Family Memories

John Paul Jr. was born on 2 April 1954 in Fort Worth, Texas, about a year after John's first tenure on faculty at Southwestern.[21] John Paul remembers that family life was anchored around dinner almost every night at home, at 6:30 p.m. with his father, mother, big brother Frank, and oldest sibling Martha. He remembers his growing-up years revolving around attendance at Broadway Baptist on Sunday mornings, Sunday evenings, Wednesday evenings, and the church's Friday night family night. His father was usually there on Wednesdays, since he traveled to preach on weekends. Outside of this family unit, his uncle Frank Leavell was a favorite of his. John Paul remembers that he was a great raconteur and joke-teller who took a personal interest in the kids. He was also a bit eccentric in his opinions about things, and that endeared him to them all.

John Paul was also particularly fond of his Uncle Russell and Aunt Carolyn Newport. John Paul thought Uncle Russell had charisma and was a more practical man of the world than his own father because of all of his stores and various business interests. One Sunday night in the early 1960s, the Newport children were allowed to stay home from Sunday evening church to watch Uncle Russell sing two songs on the Ed Sullivan Show.

Russell had great stories, too, especially about his service in WWII in the Pacific. He and Aunt Carolyn had a beautiful modern home in Springfield, out from town up on a bluff. They all loved visiting Springfield for Christmas and also often in the summer.

As the youngest of three kids, six school grades behind his brother, John Paul was essentially an only child from seventh grade onwards. This was probably an advantage, John Paul thinks, because his parents seemed a bit less strict with him than with Frank and Martha, not that they needed to be reined in much. Later in life, John Paul had a closer relationship with his father, partly because John's life became slower with the lessening of his responsibilities. He seemed to mellow a bit too as he aged.

John Paul also remembers his mother as by far the more active parent. His father came home for dinner but on most nights would work after dinner in his study near the front of the house and sometimes go back to the seminary. He was rarely home on weekends since he usually held down interim pastorates, often far away, to which he would drive on Saturdays and return on Sunday nights or Monday. John Paul remembers two especially long interim periods, one in Beaumont and the other in Midland.

John says he cannot recall ever playing catch or ball with his father or doing much of anything else with him, just the two of them. John Paul credits Frank with doing all of the yard work until he went to college; after that, John Paul took over the responsibility. His father did, however, attend his high school football games when John Paul was the starting quarterback at Paschal High School, and John served as master of ceremonies at the sports banquet during his son's senior year. Once, during Newport's interim pastorate in Beaumont, when John Paul was an early teen, a group of members of that church organized a deer hunt, and his father invited John Paul to go. Years later, when John Paul was in college, he and Frank went with their father on a duck hunt in Louisiana, organized by Harry Chavanne, the man who had endowed the chair John filled at Rice University.

John Paul's international trip abroad was during the summer of 1970, after his sophomore year of high school. It was a forty-two-day trip around the world to fourteen countries in almost six weeks. His mother was eager for him to come along. Eddie Belle and John had a close relationship during his high school years, as both of his older siblings were gone from home. John described his mother as sensitive, energetic, highly ethical, and moral. She also had a great sense of humor. He remembers her and her brother Frank and sister Mary Martha, and sometimes all of the kids, getting into such laughing fits that she could not stop. She was warm and sweet, but not much of a "hugger." She was brilliant in her own right, and a keen organizer and businesswoman. Eddie Belle's world tours occupied much of her time and were quite successful. John notes that she even made a fair amount of money from these tours, which she and John were able to save, helping to secure their retirement. John Paul admired his mother's speaking ability, her keen intellect, her book reviews, and popular Bible classes, which women from across the city and different denominations attended.

John Paul remembers an eccentricity about his father. Whenever John would go visit his own mother in her final years, which he did often, they would always go on a drive together and end up visiting the School of the Ozarks. The family always chuckled about it, because they always seemed to make the same trip, but it was a beautiful drive and both he and his mother found comfort in it.

Another outlet for John was his exercise schedule at the YMCA, and later at the Fort Worth Club, where he visited the gym many days a week. John Paul thinks his father enjoyed the exercise, but also being in the company of men who were not clergy, but instead men of commerce. He also loved to watch college basketball on television as well as other shows, including "Police Woman," starring Angie Dickinson.

John Paul also remembers his father's humor. He would sing "O Little Town of Bethlehem" during annual Christmas programs at home. While he was not necessarily a poor singer, he would sing this carol lamentably off key, perhaps deliberately so, to make everyone laugh. John always said he was proud of John Paul when he got good grades and paid him a quarter or fifty cents for straight As. John Paul said, "That was good money for the 1960s!" When he reached his full height of 6'4", his father took to calling him "Big Man," which used to make John Paul laugh. When John Paul was studying at Harvard, he served as an usher in Memorial Church on the campus and came to know the minister, Peter Gomes. In 1977, Reverend Gomes invited the elder John Newport to deliver the main Sunday sermon one week. John Paul believes his father considered this to be quite an honor.[22]

John Paul says his father really adored his mother. It was sweet, he said, that when she came to visit John Paul's family when he was an adult, his dad would call every night, and Eddie Belle would smile afterwards at how helpless he sounded on the phone, how much he missed her. But she liked that he did so. They enjoyed traveling together in their later years. Sometimes they met his father's brothers and their wives someplace. In one case, it was a week in St. Andrews in Scotland, for some kind of elder classes there.

His father used to say that Eddie Belle's heart was bigger than her body. This was later in life when she started to have heart troubles. He said that she had the "Leavell curse," that is, always wanting to do more than she had the time or energy to do. John Paul says the same could be said, of course, for his father.

For John Paul, the intellectual atmosphere at his house was the biggest difference he recognized from other children and their families. From his childhood perspective, his father's greatest weakness was being so absorbed in his work that he spent very little time with his family. John Paul says he understands it better now, of course, and knows that those days were another era in which expectations for parental roles were different. His father was a product of the Depression years, and warmth and affection and attendance at every childhood event were rarely modeled or found. Yet he admires his father for his mind, his energy, his discipline, and his sincere and devout Christian convictions. He remembers his father as curious, intellectual, and sweet. He had a fine sense of humor and could see both sides of things. He understood other people well and was unwaveringly friendly to strangers, waiters, salespeople, and to everyone he met.

Reflections upon Legacies

This section has been a poignant look into the personal life of a famous man. John Newport belonged to the world in many ways. Thousands of people have purchased his books, read his work, and heard him speak at conferences and academic guild meetings across the fifty years. These people gleaned some aspects of his mind, his ideas, his reflections, and his work. These are valid glimpses of him.

Church members who prayed with him after supper on Wednesday evenings or students and laypersons who heard his biblical proclamation or teaching from pulpits briefly brushed against the man he was. Yet in these encounters they discovered depth, conviction of faith and calling, soul care, and a gentle nudging challenge to become more than they were in Christ. The Spirit of God uses contacts like these to whisper deeply into the heart.

Friends who met him exercising next to them in the gym, or sitting around the dining table at the club, or tapping a toe at a square-dancing event, or servicing his car at a gas station, found in John an open, generous spirit. Even brief moments can be powerful exchanges of kindness.

Others knew him as a colleague, walked the hallways and sat around the lunch table in the faculty lounge with him, heard his advice in board rooms and presidential offices and faculty meetings. These are longer examinations. Here he was known as gracious, intellectual, wise, warm, and collegial. And these, too, are clear portraits.

Students saw yet another aspect of John's life. Passing in the Rotunda, watching his tall frame enter the classroom with stacks of books in his arm, eager to discuss, ready to probe the boundaries, John was found to be captivating, a giver of knowledge, a facilitator of thought and understanding, a transformative agent, a model and mentor. These recollections are long-lasting, positive, and consistent across generations.

His own children, however, saw him when he was not "professor" or "vice president" or "friend." John Newport to them was simply "Daddy." And it was the sound of "Daddy" that he loved to hear best. His files are filled with hundreds of letters addressed to Eddie Belle, Martha, Frank, and Johnny, or to friends with references to his children, or notes to his parents about them, pride-swelling stories about their accomplishments.

It is hoped that these memories from those who loved John Newport, standing to speak from the many concentric circles of his life, have detailed a fuller, richer portrait of this enigmatic and unique man of God. John Newport left a legacy, indeed, which is still ongoing. This is a legacy of faith in Christ. At its core is the simple gospel story he learned at his mother's knee. Beneath it all, John was a human being who both shared and needed the grace of God. And he would be the first, in all humility, to acknowledge this need, and to thank God for such a priceless, boundless gift.

Epilogue

> A good book has no ending.
>
> **R. D. Cumming**[1]

The story of John Paul Newport is indeed complex. Like a mighty river, coursing his way through life until he joined the sea, his journey was reminiscent of a cosmic, eschatological metaphor. He was part of the river of the water of life, clear and crystal.[2] He was an enigma, a man who balanced between the varied sets of tensions that encompassed his days.

From his rural roots, he became urbane, conversing with some of the greatest minds of his day. Brilliant in his academic prowess, he never lost his common touch. Flitting among the theological disciplines like a Hercules moth, he nonetheless dove deeply and with keen comprehension. The breadth *and* depth of his knowledge was legendary. More continental than analytical, he appreciated and was conversant with both philosophical approaches. Originally Western in his thinking, he explored and understood Eastern constructs. Born a classical fundamentalist, he became a constructive conservative evangelical statesman. As a Southern Baptist, he networked with larger circles of Baptists, evangelicals, Catholics, and those from non-Christian religions. As a Christian, he engaged secular science, philosophy, and culture with perceptivity. Seeming at times larger than life, he never left his humility. He remained childlike in heart and delighted with life's beauty.

Questions Answered

This volume has explored the question of whether John Newport's life and legacy contributed anything of singular and lasting significance to Baptist life in the twentieth and twenty-first centuries. The first eight chapters of his life's story unfolded to demonstrate the nature of his contributions and their singularity. The ninth chapter demonstrated his biblical worldview and nuanced philosophical approach. The last chapter treated John's personal legacy from comments made by representative faculty, friends, and students. His family also remembered and shared their most intimate memories. The John Newport portrait revealed here is one of consistency.

From strong Missouri stock, Newport was endowed with natural gifts of intellect and curiosity, two most distinguishing characteristics that never left him. He learned his conservative Christianity at his mother's knee, encouraged to trust in the God who is self-revealing, creative, and personal. His conversion in 1927 at the age of ten was transformative, adding to his knowledge base the experiential, relational faith of an evangelical.

His models were a father and mother devoted to Christ, to sharing the good news of Jesus with others. His grandfathers and grandmothers were equally attentive to spiritual growth and discipleship that resulted in hearts and minds that loved God and resulted in Christlike action. His early family connections taught him, then, that the plan of God is to reconcile the world. The grace of God covers the redemption of mankind. The Son of God and his claims are essential, unique, authentic, and trustworthy. The Kingdom of God is both now and future. Upon this holy, eschatological basis, his early years laid the foundation on which John was later to found his biblical worldview. This background provided a significant contribution. It produced in John a consistent model of conservative Christianity that never wavered throughout his long and scholarly career.

As a young man in high school and college, Newport made the most of opportunities that opened to him: education, recognized leadership roles, travel, and the debating skills of research, rhetoric, and the drive to present a convincing argument. Called by God to the gospel ministry, he was confident that God had a reason for drawing him away from law for this higher purpose. While in seminary, John was trained to study the Scriptures carefully, to ask questions, to broaden his midwestern cultural understandings of the world and how the Bible spoke into culture. He continued to love people and found them fascinating. He learned to listen. He served as pastor of congregations where people asked questions and each query drove him to study further. He read unceasingly.

John married Eddie Belle, who was his equal in almost every area of life, and loved her heart, her Baptist people, her culture, and her thinking.

He realized that he must learn more, for he was beginning to glimpse the edges of his own understanding. He was convinced that there was infinitely more to explore, investigate, consider, analyze, as he considered his own theological and doctrinal positions and experiences. Scholars from Scotland, Germany, Switzerland, and New England opened the world of ideas to him. He learned from the greatest theological minds of his era. He began to formulate his own worldview in the crucible of these conversations, some of which challenged his belief system. This is a second contribution of Newport: a passion for knowledge that was consuming and enduring until his last breath. A unique lifelong learner, Newport interpreted and translated his vast reading and knowledge for the average layperson to comprehend.

As Newport began to teach graduate students and supervise the research of Ph.D. students, his biblical worldview crystallized. At mid-career, John had come into his own as a philosopher of religion, finally systematizing all that he had learned into a synthesis of philosophical understanding. He became known as a constructive, conservative evangelical, aligned with those who were positive and open to dialogue. He engaged in the larger conversations with theology, biblical studies, ethics, world religions, art, science, and culture. He developed his now famous dialectical approach, which laid out questions, presented all variations of responses, tested each of the alternatives, and settled on the best of all possible answers.

Newport believed that all knowledge was connected and that a search for truth was always productive, for when found, all truth was God's truth. With students and faculty friends, in conferences, symposiums, church meetings, and study sessions, academic societies, in Southern Baptist, larger Baptist, and beyond Baptist circles, John became known as a voice of reason, of authenticity, of faith seeking understanding in ways that were constructive and wholesome, scholarly, biblical, and non-threatening. His contribution to Baptists in the development of the concept of "biblical worldview" was cutting-edge. His apologetic work, especially regarding the occult and demonology, also set him apart. Like few others of his generation, he addressed the emerging New Age movement, explored its philosophical and theological roots, and interpreted it to both church laypersons and the evangelical world. He showed people how to engage with those who believed in these new ways. He was an academic adventurer, a delightful influencer, and a winsome apologist, all of which were distinct contributions to Baptist scholarship.

In the second half of the twentieth century, while vast changes were taking place within the world, across America, and in the churches of her land, Newport became known as a peacemaker, a statesman who advocated for space in which differences of opinion and approaches to theology could come together safely and dialogue constructively, even while he championed conservative Christianity's doctrinal tenets. He was one of the few Southern Baptists in his day who earned a respected place among the new evangelicals that arose from mid-century to its end.[3]

When considering the impact of Newport's life and work, one cannot ignore the great tensions that grew within the Protestant denominations, in which Baptists, Northern and Southern, played a part. As John began his teaching career, modernism and theological liberalism were already entrenched in mainline denominational structures and their seminaries. Those trying to hold to conservative theology and doctrinal stances in the face of such inroads had already split into "fundamentalist" and "evangelical" factions, each founding new seminaries to conserve their most basic and valued tenets. Newport aligned early with those who were intentionally taking a middle path between the extremes of the modern liberals and militant fundamentalists, inviting the Southern Baptist Convention leadership to join the positive work being accomplished across the world in theology, missions, and evangelism.

Newport was convinced that Christians must *engage* culture to be effective change-agents *of* culture. He delighted to encounter culture in non-threatening and conversational ways. He feared that, without an intentional directional change, Southern Baptists could become militant separatists, using politics and its rhetoric to remove themselves and their churches further from the work of God's Kingdom as they consumed their own institutions and denominational structures. He worked tirelessly to present evangelicalism as a more positive alternative for engagement with the world. He believed strongly that conservative Christian doctrine could be held and extended in a fresh, appealing, and non-polemical light, without sacrificing either original scholarship or the causes of the world's injustices. In his day, as a Baptist from the southland, he was a voice both to and for Southern Baptists. Not only a peacemaker and a statesman, bringing to his denomination a measure of respectability, Newport was prophetic. This was yet another profound contribution.

Finally, Newport's academic legacy lives through the scholarly work of his doctoral students, noted in their lengthy lists of publications and contributions to the academic guilds. One thinks of the postmodernism of Keith Putt, the ecumenical focus of Steven Harmon, the apologetics of Ted Cabal, the hermeneutics and New Testament studies of Steve Lemke, the popular-level Christian cultural commentaries of Jim Denison, all of which call to mind the inquisitive and wide-ranging interests and emphases of their professor. These students pushed further John Newport's scholarship into deeper and wider philosophical and ecclesial and cultural circles. Perhaps it is this legacy that is most significant for him as a scholar.

Closing Observations

As one views Newport's life, several observations surface, like water depth gauges along a river's length. First, Newport was a man of supreme curiosity. This trait is essential for good scholarship. Next, he was a master teacher. His classes covered epistemology, religious authority, religious language, religion and contemporary art forms, religion and American thought, including literature, pragmatism, process philosophy, and contemporary European philosophies of religion, like existentialism and phenomenology. He taught primitive, Middle Eastern, and Far Eastern religions, mysticism, East and West occult studies, religion and science, dealing with faith and nature, theology and the philosophies of history and eschatology, evil and suffering, Jewish theologies and philosophies, and biblical history and interpretation. He said in 1990, "I try to convey to my students a sense of the relevance, the excitement, and the urgency of the Christian gospel. This is where true freedom is, where true joy is, where true fulfillment is."[4] His students for fifty years raved about his classes, claiming that Newport was the professor who taught them to think.

Next, Newport was a gentleman. Copies of hundreds of gracious thank you and appreciation letters exist to testify to the time and energy he expended throughout his long life to express his appreciation and gratitude to people who had helped him. Similarly, he was an encourager, one whose life brought joy to so many. Students and faculty and family speak of his consistent habit of saying only good things about other people, perhaps one of the most amazing of his personality traits. When he entered a room with his broad smile, excitement and energy accompanied him.

Newport was also known as a churchman who preached from pulpits from one end of the United States to the other and in many missionary settings around the world. The gospel of Jesus Christ was precious to him, and he never lost the desire to see men and women come to know his

Jesus. He related to others easily, equally at home in the local church and in the scholar's world. Not only did he serve as interim pastor of fifty-two churches in five states, but he taught at numerous seminaries, universities, and colleges. He was known for his excitement to converse with theologians of other beliefs while still holding firm to his belief in Jesus Christ.

Some might question why John, in his last years, stayed at a seminary and with a denomination that had disappointed him deeply. Why did he not leave? Although one cannot say for certain, the answer likely lies in the character of the "builder generation," who were themselves the World War I and Spanish Influenza babes, the children of the Roaring Twenties and the Great Depression. They were the teens and young adults of the Soviet buildup, fascism, Nazism, and World War II. In the devastation of the postwar years, men like John Newport turned their faces toward the future and built institutions that were stable, indestructible. These institutions were expressions of their hope that the world could be better for their children. They remained, like sentinels, with the institutions into which they had poured their lives.[5] To this end, they sought to build security and unity. They sought to forge peace. Newport was one of these.

Yet, while all of the above is true, one cannot miss the poignant statements of John's own children, who simply voiced, in their different ways, that they deeply missed their father in many of their childhood days. They grew up in a world before phone cards or cell phones, when letters and a collect call from a public booth were the ways to connect when traveling. John had no personal computer, no email, no ready text, no Facetime, no any instant means of communication. John's ministerial calling was costly for him, traveling as he did by car, train, ship, plane, taxi, constantly on the road to church interims, conferences, revivals, and teaching assignments. Yet his ministry was also costly for his family, as it was, and still is, for ministry families across the world. John's greatest strengths, his insatiable search for knowledge and his call to minister with the people of God, were perhaps also the point of his greatest frailty. It took him, like it did Billy Graham and dozens of others in that generation, away from those he loved best, his own family. In retrospect, one wishes at times that one could go back in life to redress these moments of loss.

Eddie Belle knew what living with a minister would cost her family and children, having been acquainted with this kind of "life without father" as a girl, but the Newport children had no experience by which to gauge their own father's absence. It is this matter of remembered longing by his children that remains a sobering and challenging vulnerability of his legacy.

Having said that, the Newport children not only survived but became remarkably successful in their own lives, marriages, and families. They became parents who love their children and spend time at home. They fostered strong families of their own. In turn, their children, John and Eddie Belle's grandchildren, are walking confidently in the successful footsteps of their own parents and grandparents. In this respect, then, the Newport home's training in the ways of God and in the appreciation of family and shared values bore good and lasting and bountiful fruit. Martha, Frank, John Paul, their spouses, children, and the newest generation now coming along are indeed the blessing and enduring legacy of which John and Eddie Belle were most proud.

In the final analysis, John Newport was a New Testament Paul to the end of his days. Paul was an apologist in a religiously fractured culture. He presented Christ clearly and powerfully to the philosophically minded. Neither a seeker of fame nor fortune nor freedom apart from Christ Jesus, Paul simply wanted Christ to be made known. Newport was the same. For all that his life accomplished, the thread that runs through his life, like the great current beneath the river's surface, was his faith in and commitment to the God who called him and redeemed him. John was from his earliest years on his way to Jesus, the one he loved with every fiber of his being, the author and perfecter of his faith. He could say with great joy at the end of his race, "And this is my prayer: that your love may abound more and more in knowledge and depth of insight, so that you may be able to discern what is best and may be pure and blameless for the day of Christ, filled with the fruit of righteousness that comes through Jesus Christ—to the glory and praise of God. . . . For me to live is Christ, and to die is gain."[6]

And so it was that an imaginative, insatiably curious boy, son of a merchant, sitting alone in his backyard with the *Encyclopedia Britannica* open upon his lap, became the one to ask mankind's ultimate questions and to find their answers in the God of the universe.

Appendix A
The Bibliography of John Paul Newport
(primary works are listed chronologically)

Primary Works

Dissertations and Theses

"The Jewish Messiah of the Apocrypha and Pseudepigrapha." Th.D. diss., Southern Baptist Theological Seminary, 1944.
"An Investigation of Factors Influencing John Calvin's Use of Linguistic and Historic Principles of Biblical Exegesis." Ph.D. diss., University of Edinburgh, 1953.
"Representative Contemporary Attempts to Establish the Meaningfulness and Uniqueness of Religious and Biblical Language." M.A. thesis, Texas Christian University, 1968.

Unpublished Manuscripts

A Guide to a Christian Philosophy of Religion. 4 vols. Fort Worth, Tex.: Southwestern Baptist Theological Seminary, 1957.
Questions People Ask about a Christian Philosophy of Religion. 2 vols. Fort Worth, Tex.: Baptist Book Store, 1975.

Books

Theology and Contemporary Art Forms. Waco, Tex.: Word Books, 1971.
Coauthored with William Cannon. *Why Christians Fight Over the Bible.* Nashville: Thomas Nelson, 1974.
Cristianismo y Ocultismo: Un Enfrentamiento. Translated by Guillermo Kratzig. Buenos Aires: Junta Bautista de Publicaciones, 1974.

Christ and the New Consciousness. Nashville: Broadman, 1978.

Editor. *Nineteenth Century Devotional Thought. Christian Classics*. Nashville: Broadman, 1981.

Paul Tillich. Edited by Bob E. Patterson. Makers of the Modern Theological Mind. Waco, Tex.: Word Books, 1984.

The Lion and the Lamb. Nashville: Broadman, 1986.

Demons, Demons, Demons: A Christian Guide through the Murky Maze of the Occult. Nashville: Broadman, 1972. *Demonios, Demonios, Demonios*. Translated by Talleres Graficos. AR: Argen-Press, 1973. *Demonios, Demonios, Demonios: Una Guia Cristiana para la Baraunda del Ocultismo*. Translated by Arnoldo Canclini. Buenos Aires: Junta Bautista de Publicaciones, 1973. Rev. ed. El Paso: Casa Bautista de Publicaciones, 1987.

What Is Christian Doctrine? Layman's Library of Christian Doctrine. Nashville: Broadman, 1984. *Qué es la Doctrina Cristiana? Su Valor, Necesidad y Base*. Translated by Roberto Gama. Biblioteca de Doctrina Cristiana. El Paso: Casa Bautista de Publicaciones, 1985; 2nd ed. 1988.

Life's Ultimate Questions: A Contemporary Philosophy of Religion. Dallas: Word Publishing, 1989.

The New Age Movement and the Biblical Worldview: Conflict and Dialogue. Grand Rapids: Eerdmans, 1998.

Chapters Contributed to Books

"The Church Member." In *J. Howard Williams: Prophet of God and Friend of Man*, edited by H. C. Brown Jr. and Charles P. Johnson, 121–29. San Antonio, Tex.: Naylor, 1963.

"Interpreting the Bible." In *Broadman Bible Commentary*, edited by Clifton J. Allen, 25–33. Vol. 1. Nashville: Broadman, 1969.

"Understanding, Evaluating, and Learning from the Contemporary Glossolalia Movement." In *Tongues*, edited by Luther B. Dyer, 105–27. Jefferson City, Mo.: Le Roi Publishers, 1971.

Preface to *Introduction to Solzhenitsyn's Religion* by Niels Nielsen Jr. Nashville: Thomas Nelson, 1975.

"The Arts from a Conservative Perspective." In *Arts in Society*, edited by Edward Kamarck, 56–57. Madison: University of Wisconsin Extension Division, 1976.

"Response." In *Demon Possession: A Medical, Historical, Anthropological and Theological Symposium*, edited by John Warwick Montgomery, 58–61. Minneapolis, Minn.: Bethany Fellowship, 1976.

"Satan and Demons: A Theological Perspective." In *Demon Possession: A Medical, Historical, Anthropological and Theological Symposium*, edited by John Warwick Montgomery, 325–45. Minneapolis, Minn.: Bethany Fellowship, 1976.

"Christianity and the Arts." In *At the Edge of Hope: Christian Laity in Paradox*, edited by Howard E. Butt Jr., 102–16. New York: Seabury, 1978.

"The World: A Tangled Web and a Scarlet Thread." In *Waiting in the Wings*, edited by Porter W. Routh, 117–24. Nashville: Broadman, 1978.

"The Future Church Faces Radical New Religions." In *Future Church*, edited by Ralph W. Neighbor Jr., 187–205. Nashville: Broadman, 1980.

"The Mystery of Immortality and the Life Beyond." In *The Miracle of Easter*, edited by Floyd Thatcher, 115–23. Waco, Tex.: Word, 1980.

"Holy Spirit: Empowering for the Living of the Witnessing-Giving Life." In *Witnessing-Giving Life*, 84–101. Nashville: SBC Stewardship Commission, 1988.

"The Purpose of the Church." In *The People of God. Essays on the Believers' Church*, edited by Paul Basden and David S. Dockery, 19–40. Nashville: Broadman, 1990.

"The Challenge of Recent Literary Approaches to the Bible." In *Beyond the Impasse? Scripture, Interpretation, and Theology in Baptist Life*, edited by Robison B. James and David S. Dockery, 64–90. Nashville: Broadman, 1992.

Journal Articles

"Who Is a Faithful Teacher?" *The Baptist Training Union Magazine* (June 1949): 4.

"New Developments in New Testament Theology." *Review and Expositor* 49 (1952): 41–56.

"Philosophy of History." *Southwestern News* (June 1954): 6.

"Skeptic and Apologist." *The Baptist Student* 36 (1956): 36–37, 52.

"Religion and Morals." *The Baptist Student* 39 (1959): 21–33.

"Man Seeking God: Religion." *The Baptist Student* (1960): 7–9.

"Biblical Interpretation and Eschatological-Holy History." *Southwestern Journal of Theology* 4 (1961): 83–110.

"Called to Life Commitment." *Young People's Teacher* (April 1962): 4–5.

"Communicating the Gospel through Contemporary Art Forms." *The Journal of the Southern Baptist Church Music Conference* (1962–1963): 18–25.

"The Arts and Their Worth." *The Baptist Student* 42 (1963): 4–8, 33.

"Biblical Philosophy and the Modern Mind." *Baptist Faculty Paper* 6 (1963): 1–2, 4.

"Christianity and Contemporary Art Forms." *Baptist Program* (August 1963): 10–11.

"Is the Theory of Evolution in Conflict with the Christian Faith?" *The Baptist Student* 42 (1963): 5–7.

"The Unique Nature of the Bible in the Light of Recent Attacks." *Southwestern Journal of Theology* 6 (1963): 93–106.

"God, Man, and Redemption in Modern Art." *Review and Expositor* 61 (1964): 142–55.

"Falando em Languas." *Home Missions* (May 1965).

"Some Thoughts about Miracles." *The Baptist Student* 44 (1965): 2–4, 39.

"Environment of Religion." *The Adult Teacher* 3 (1967): 10–13.

"Student Shapers." *The Baptist Student* 47 (1967): 14–20.

"Questions Ministers Ask about Contemporary Literature and Drama." *Southwestern Journal of Theology* 10 (1968): 31–47.

"Secularization, Secularism, and Christianity." *Review and Expositor* 68 (1971): 81–93.

"Sexuality in the Contemporary Arts." *Review and Expositor* 68 (1971): 203–15.

"Should Christians Be Interested in Contemporary Art Forms?" *The Baptist Student* 50 (1971): 8–13.

"Biblical Language and Religious Authority." *Foundations* 17 (1974): 58–67.

"The Occult World and Youth Culture." *Council News*. Fort Worth City Council, 4 December 1974.

"Why Christians Argue over Biblical Interpretation." *Southwestern Journal of Theology* 16 (1974): 15–29.

"Satan, the Bible, and the Modern Mind." *Biblical Illustrator* (Winter 1975).

"Presenting an Authentic Christian Witness in a World of Secularism and Religious Obsession." *Southern Baptist Educator* 41 (1976): 11–17.

"Religious Communities and the Arts." *Arts and Society* (1976).

"The Theology and Experience of Salvation." *Greek Orthodox Theological Review* 22 (1977): 393–404.

"Christianity and Contemporary Arts: Competitive? Antagonistic?" *New Orleans Religion and the Arts Conference* (8 June 1978).

"God's Representative in Troubled Times." *Young Adult Bible Study* 9 (1979): 24–79.

"Religion, Architecture and the Arts in the 1980s." *Faith and Form* 13 (1979): 10–11, 19–21.

"Living in Two Worlds." *The Baptist Student* 60 (1980): 4–6.

"The Baptist Journey." *Christianity Today*, 7 August 1981.

"America's Continuing Controversy over Humanism." *Liberal and Fine Arts Review* 3 (1983): 87–98.

"The Arts in Worship." *Review and Expositor* 80 (1983): 71–83.

"Satanism and Demonism." *Baptist Standard* (July 1983): 10–11.

"Guest Editorial: The Musical Heritage of Baptists." *Baptist History and Heritage* 19 (1984): 2–3.

"Humanism and the Future: A Tentative Proposal for an American Solution." *Liberal and Fine Arts Review* 4 (1984): 53–61.

"The Pastor and the Local Church." *Baptist Standard* (10 October 1984): 12–13.

"The American Dream: Religion, Religious Liberty and the Public Schools." *Missouri Schools* 51 (1985): 22–26.

"Representative Contemporary Approaches to the Use of Philosophy in Christian Thought." *Review and Expositor* 82 (1985): 507–19.

"Contemporary Approaches to Biblical Interpretation." *Faith and Mission* 3 (1986): 37–48.

"Representative Historical and Contemporary Approaches to Biblical Interpretation." *Faith and Mission* 3 (1986): 32–48.

"Updating the American Dream." *Report from the Capital* 41 (1986).

"The Problem of Demonic Power and the Nature of the Christian Response." *Ogbomoso Journal of Theology* 3 (1988): 27–31.

"The Biblical Worldview and Church-Related Colleges." *Southern Baptist Educator* 53 (August 1989): 3–20.

"Southern Baptists and the Bible: Seeking a Balanced Perspective." *Southwestern Journal of Theology* 34 (1992): 31–42.

"Facing toward the Millennial Year 2000 under Biblical Guidance with a Focus on the Resurrection." *Ex Auditu* 9 (1993): 109–121.

"Lessons From the Odyssey of an Evolving Baptist Theologian." *Southwestern Journal of Theology* 37 (1995): 38–42.

Encyclopedia and Dictionary Articles

"Bible, The Authority of the Bible." *Encyclopedia of Southern Baptists*. 4 vols. Nashville: Broadman, 1958–82.

"Athens," "Inheritance in the New Testament," and "Savior in the New Testament." *Mercer Dictionary of the Bible*. Macon, Ga.: Mercer University Press, 1990.

Festschriften in Honor of John Paul Newport

Perspectives in Religious Studies. Journal of the National Association of Baptist Professors of Religion, edited by Bob E. Patterson. Spring 2005.

Berry, Don. "John Newport and His Books." *Perspectives in Religious Studies* 32, no. 1 (2005): 77–83.

Dilday, Russell H., Jr. "John Newport and Revelation." *Perspectives in Religious Studies* 32, no. 1 (2005): 11–24.

Dominy, Bert B. "John Newport and Eschatology: A Hopeful Future." *Perspectives in Religious Studies* 32, no. 1 (2005): 43–50.

Ferguson, Milton. "John Newport and *Life's Ultimate Questions*." *Perspectives in Religious Studies* 32, no. 1 (2005): 33–42.

Garrett, James Leo, Jr. "John Newport and Systematic Theology." *Perspectives in Religious Studies* 32, no. 1 (2005): 25–32.

Kirkpatrick, David. "John Newport's Apologetic of Complementarity: Cults, Consciousness, and Cosmic Evil." *Perspectives in Religious Studies* 32, no. 1 (2005): 51–58.

Patterson, Bob E. "Editorial Introduction." *Perspectives in Religious Studies* 32, no. 1 (2005): 3–9.

Sands, Paul. "Paul Tillich's Theology of Religions." *Perspectives in Religious Studies* 32, no. 1 (2005): 59–75.

Secondary Works

Bush, L. Russ, III. "John Paul Newport: A Man for All Seasons." *Southwestern Journal of Theology* 29 (1987): 5–11.

Bush, L. Russ, III, Joe M. Cooper, Frank Louis Mauldin, Warren McWilliams, Samuel Mikolaski, and John P. Newport. "Forum: Reflections on John Newport's *Life's Ultimate Questions*." *Theological Educator* 41 (1990): 35–61.

Cabal, Ted. "Problems and Promise in a Biblical Worldview with Special Reference to John Paul Newport." Ph.D. diss., Southwestern Baptist Theological Seminary, 1995.

Dilday, Russell H., Jr. "Practical Apologist: Faith Seeking Understanding." *Southwestern Journal of Theology* 29 (1987): 12–18.

Ferguson, Milton U. "Revelation, Religious Authority and Biblical Interpretation." *Southwestern Journal of Theology* 29 (1987): 29–32.

Mauldin, Frank Louis. "John Newport and a Biblical Worldview." *Southwestern Journal of Theology* 29 (1987): 33–45.

———. "John Paul Newport: Philosophy of Religion." In *The Legacy of Southwestern: Writings that Shaped a Tradition*, edited by James Leo Garrett Jr., 208–10. North Richland Hills: Smithfield Press, 2002.

Appendix B
Philosophy of Religion Doctoral Students Supervised by John Paul Newport

This list of students was printed in John Paul Newport's funeral order of service, 22 August 2000.

Arnold Grayum Ashburn
Joseph Pearson Hester
Clinton Matthew Ashley
C. A. Johnson Jr.
Woodrow Behannon
Steve Warner Lemke
Donald Clarke Berry
William Randall Lolley
Wayne Alton Blankenship
Sanders Truman Lyles
James Walker Bryant
Roy Lenere Lyon
Luther Russell Bush III
Billy H. McGee
Theodore James Cabal
Clyde Rolston Majors
Pat Harold Carter
Gerald E. Mann

John David Cave
Frank Louis Mauldin
Kenneth Leon Chafin
Jerald Robert McBride
Robert Earl Clarke
Frank Lee Moore
Harold Gordon Clinard
Isaac Mwase
Dan Wray Cochran
Alan Preston Neely
Samuel Alexander DeBord
George William Nichols
James Clarence Denison
Joseph Drury Patteson
Allen A. Denton
Julius Eugene Petty
Russell Hooper Dilday
Harold Gordon Potts
William J. Fritts
B. Keith Putt
R. Page Fulgham
William Wallace Road
David Charles George
Dennis Lee Sansom
Billy Burke Glover
William Graydon Tanner
Joseph Franklin Green
Daniel Glenn Vestal
William Purdy Greenlee
Larry D. Williams
Karl L. Harman
Forrest Edward Wood
William Lorenzo Hardee II
Alfred Vernon Woodard
David M. Haynie
Yandall Clark Woodfin III
James Roy Heath

Appendix C
John Paul Newport (1917–2000) Memorial Service

*Broadway Baptist Church,
Fort Worth, Texas, August 22, 2000*

Russell H. Dilday

Introduction

How does one assess the greatness of a noteworthy man? I've known John Newport most of my life. We first met in 1949 when I was an 18-year-old freshman at Baylor University. Even though upperclassmen warned me he was an "unknown entity," I signed up for young Professor Newport's required New Testament 111.

So for over half a century, my friendship and admiration for John Newport have grown through stages of different relationships: I a student—he the teacher, I as a pastor—he a denominational leader, I the president—he the faculty member, and finally, both of us colleagues in theological education.

So how do you measure the greatness of such a man? I've thought of words like genius, astute, studious, extraordinary, and exceptional. They all fit in one way or another. I know that John Newport's death is an irreplaceable loss, but these assessments of greatness fall short.

The Bible, which was so central to the life and work of John Newport, says: *Whoever would be great among you must be your servant* (Matt 20:26), *He who . . . teaches these commandments shall be called great in the kingdom of heaven* (Matt 5:19). Since John Newport served others all his life, since he taught the words of God, therein must his greatness be found.

Where do you find greatness in a life? The Bible says: *Let him who glories glory in this, that he understands and knows me . . . says the Lord* (Jer 9:23–24). Since John Newport spent his life trying to understand and know the God he trusted, it must be in this that greatness is rooted.

In preparing these remarks it was also difficult to spotlight certain elements as more important than others in his life. John told me about being the last speaker on a program once when everyone before him had taken too much time. It was getting late, so the moderator said, "Dr. Newport, since we're running a little late can you just give us the gist of your paper?" John answered, "Not really. It's ALL gist." The life of John Newport is ALL gist.

1. We Remember Him in Relation to His Family

He was a family man, not in the traditional sense, because like other young, underpaid seminary teachers, he was often away, traveling to innumerable interim pastorates, pulpit supplies, revivals, lectures, and student retreats. We all know Eddie Belle faithfully bore the greater responsibility for their growing family.

But he loved his family—particularly Eddie Belle. He always gave her credit for their home. He bragged on her church and community involvement. He was proud of her family heritage. Eddie Belle kept John grounded.

Louisa May Alcott said: "My definition of a philosopher is of a man up in a balloon, with his family holding the ropes which confine him to earth, trying to haul him down."

It was Eddie Belle who kept John's philosophical feet on the ground, kept him humble and focused on the real world.

2. We Remember Him in Relation to His Church

John Newport was a churchman. And it's rare to find a scholarly academic who is also a devoted, practicing church member. But this academic always served his Lord in the context of the churches.

Before beginning his remarkable educational career, John held significant pastorates:

—a conservative rural church,

—a college church in Clinton, Mississippi,

—a growing congregation in Tulsa, Oklahoma.

That explains why, as a professional philosopher, he always maintained a practical, congregational perspective. John never forgot that he was teaching in order to train leaders in the church. He wanted to be sure our teaching did not unintentionally drift into the theoretical realm of purely academic philosophy.

John and Eddie Belle were active at Broadway Baptist Church in Fort Worth, but John also played a big role in the denomination. He was at home in Ridgecrest and Glorieta assemblies, Convention sessions, and Baptist World Alliance meetings.

Like all of us, the recent denominational power struggles broke his heart. He worked hard to expose the real issues, and to enlighten the seminary's critics about biblical truths and authentic Baptist ideals. As he worked on his autobiography detailing his experiences at Southwestern, he hoped it would help Baptists move into the next century better informed and more united.

John called himself a "constructive conservative," believing you could be biblically conservative without being cranky. Theological nitpicking was useless, he was convinced, and Christians should not waste their energies putting down other believers with whom they disagreed.

He said, "There is no competition between lighthouses. The world is lost in darkness. We need all the light we can get."

So, a part of the greatness of the life we honor today is found in his constructive relationship to the church. And that's biblical. The Bible says Jesus loved the church and gave Himself for it, and in spite of its human failures, John Newport loved the church too. Therein is found his greatness.

3. We Remember Him in Relation to the Community

John was a convictional Baptist, but he enthusiastically participated in the broader life of the community—honoring and respecting those of other denominational loyalties as well as those with no faith commitments.

He participated in the Cattle Country Clerics, an ecumenical group of local pastors and church leaders. He was active in the Fort Worth Rotary Club. He and Eddie Belle were at every Kimbell Art Museum opening and were involved in other cultural events.

So John Newport was a productive citizen of the broader community. And that's biblical. The Bible says we should conduct ourselves with wisdom toward outsiders (Col 4:5). A part of John's greatness was in his work outside the gate—in the broader community.

4. We Remember Him Most in Relation to His Work

John Newport was first of all a philosopher, a teacher, and our professor. In 1978, when I came back to Southwestern as president, my first accomplishment was to persuade him to come back from Rice University to Southwestern as Vice President for Academic Affairs and Provost.

John was a skilled administrator, but he never lost his primary identity as a teacher. We were always amazed at his voracious appetite for reading—usually out in front of his fellow teachers in assessing the latest publications. He would read at every spare moment in the daily schedule, sometimes long into the night (and sometimes even while driving!).

How often in the last 20 years he sent me copies of articles or chapters with sections bracketed in pencil on the margins, with the comments "good, important, excellent summary." The problem: nearly **every** sentence was bracketed!

We students liked Professor Newport because he was:

—erudite without being pedantic,

—fresh without being trendy,

—humorous without resorting to comic silliness,

—creative without an obvious straining to be novel,

—practical without being simply functionary.

As a teacher, John Newport was to us a compiler, a synthesizer, and a reconciler. As a philosopher, he helped us put together diverse strands of knowledge from other intellectual disciplines into a consistent worldview.

At Baylor and Southwestern, many a future minister had the same rewarding experience I had of emerging from foggy confusion into a new level of insight. He taught us the importance of saying "yes" and "no" to great writers, identifying their strengths and weaknesses from a Christian viewpoint.

It was that practical, balanced, common sense approach in the classroom that influenced me (and scores of others) to pursue the Ph.D. in Philosophy of Religion under his supervision at Southwestern Seminary. Nearly sixty young seminarians completed Ph.D. degrees with John Newport as their major professor. They serve in all six Southern Baptist Convention seminaries, plus several of the new theological schools across the Baptist world. They serve in twelve different universities, convention agencies, and major churches, foreign missions.

His name suggests his greatness as a teacher:

New = fresh, current, vigorous, up-to-date
Port = a haven, where ships can unload and load cargo safe from injury by storms.

Newport was to us a fresh, vigorous, up-to-date haven where we could load and unload our cargos of intellectual questions safe from storms and injury. In reaching for a measure of life's greatness, we remember that Jesus was called a teacher more than any other designation, and John Newport was a teacher.

5. Ultimately, We Remember Him as a Believer Saved by Grace

Family, church, community, and profession are all important, but the ultimate measure of greatness is found in a person's relationship to God, in their personal faith in Christ.

Influenced by godly parents and dedicated grandparents, John Newport confessed his faith in Christ at an early age in Missouri. In obedience to his Lord, he was baptized and took his place in the family of faith. And that's why we are confident today that even though he died last Friday, he is alive and in the presence of the Lord Jesus today.

I don't know that I've ever participated in a memorial service for one who had studied, specialized, and even written extensively on the subject of death. It occurred to me we could let John Newport speak at his own memorial service. So listen to some of his own convictions about death and the life beyond:

> *For Christians, death can be a blessing, not only because it means the end of suffering, but also because it is a way home . . . to the Father's house.*

> *Heaven is not just an endless time of dull amnesia. It will surely involve some memory. There will be recognition. In fact, we will know each other more thoroughly than now, for there will be no possibility of camouflage.*

> *Eternity will be no haven of inactivity where inhabitants draw unemployment benefits. The spiritual rest that heaven offers the redeemed is not a life of indolence. There will be purposeful activity in heaven.*

The experiences of heaven will far surpass anything experienced here. "No eye has seen, nor ear heard, nor the heart of man conceived, what God has prepared for those who love him."

Throughout his lifelong pursuit for understanding, John remembered Paul's words: *"Now we see in a mirror dimly, but then face to face; Now I know in part, but then I shall understand fully."* So, John Newport, the man who wrote about **Life's Ultimate Questions** is now experiencing firsthand **Life's Ultimate Answers!**

Notes

Preface

1 Aurelius Augustine, *The Confessions of St. Augustine*, Harvard Classics, trans. Edward Pusey (New York: P. F. Collier & Son, 1909–1914), vol. 7, part 1, book 8, chap. 12, paras. 27–28.
2 Frances Ridley Havergal, "Perfect Peace," published originally in *Hymns of Consecration and Faith* (public domain, 1876).

Prologue

1 In this section, the writer is indebted to John Fea, whose article outlines both the gradual changes and widening differences within Protestants who became "evangelicals" and "fundamentalists" during Newport's lifetime; see John Fea, "Understanding the Changing Façade of Twentieth-Century American Protestant Fundamentalism: Toward a Historical Definition," *Trinity Journal* 15, no. 2 (1994): 181–99. Fea masterfully summarizes the early and subtle differences within Protestants, noting that the story of conservative Protestants is neither static nor monolithic. While a certain amount of continuity existed between the four phases of its development, it was marked by gradual, consistent change. The terms "evangelicals," "fundamentalists," and "neo-evangelicals" arose from within what was originally an open, irenic body of Christians that generally agreed about doctrine in a time when modernist thinking was on the rise in mainline denominations. Other helpful summaries are T. P. Weber's "Fundamentalism," 461–65; George Marsden and B. J. Longfield's "Fundamentalist-Modernist Controversy," 466–68; and George Marsden's "The Fundamentals," 468–69, in *Dictionary of Christianity in America*, ed. D. G. Reid et al. (Downers Grove, Ill.: InterVarsity Press, 1990).

2 See the work of premier University of Chicago historian and noted interpreter of religion in America Martin Marty and the multimillion-dollar project funded by the Academy of Arts and Sciences, called the "Fundamentalist Project," which he codirected. George M. Marsden, a leading scholar of Protestantism of the twentieth century, is also known as a primary chronicler of movements and their impact upon America. See Marsden, *Fundamentalism and the American Culture: The Shaping of Twentieth-Century Evangelicalism* (New York: Oxford University Press, 1980, 2006); *Evangelicalism and Modern America* (Grand Rapids: Eerdmans, 1984); *Reforming Fundamentalism: Fuller Seminary and the New Evangelicalism* (Grand Rapids: Eerdmans, 1987, 1995); and *Understanding Fundamentalism and Evangelicalism* (Grand Rapids: Eerdmans, 1990). See also Mark A. Noll, David W. Bebbington, and George M. Marsden, *Evangelicals: Who They Have Been, Are Now, and Could Have Been* (Grand Rapids: Eerdmans, 2019); Ernest R. Sandeen, *Roots of Fundamentalism* (Chicago: University of Chicago Press, 1970); W. R. Hutchison, *The Modernist Impulse in American Protestantism* (Cambridge, Mass.: Harvard University Press, 1976); and Ferrenc Morton Szasz, *The Divided Mind of American Protestantism, 1880–1930* (Montgomery: University of Alabama Press, 1982).
3 Martin Marty, *Modern American Religion: The Irony of it All, 1893–1919* (Chicago: University of Chicago Press, 1986), 17–24.
4 A. C. Dixon and R. A. Torrey, eds., *The Fundamentals* (Chicago: Testimony Publishing, 1910–1915). This was a set of ninety essays, originally in twelve volumes, published from 1910 to 1915. Universally considered to be the founding document of the Fundamentalist movement, contributors included B. B. Warfield, G. Campbell Morgan, Philip Mauro, R. A. Torrey, A. T. Pierson, E. Y. Mullins, James Orr, C. I. Scofield, and W. H. Griffith Thomas. Fea notes that *The Fundamentals* set forth evangelical doctrine in a nonconfrontational manner. Contributors to the project came from many denominational affiliations, but all were moderate in their tones. In fact, there were no specific attacks on modernist views, and no article encouraged ecclesiastical separation, what Fea refers to as "the view that Scripture demands true believers to 'separate' from a denomination influenced by modernism or modernist leadership." Indeed, several essays painted higher criticism in a positive light, while others supported some form of biological evolution. See Fea, "Understanding the Changing Façade," 185.
5 Marsden, *Fundamentalism*, 4.
6 Curtis Lee Laws, editor of the Baptist periodical, *The Watchman Examiner*, was the first to propose the term "fundamentalist" in 1920 and use it of those like himself who "still cling to the great fundamentals and who mean to do battle royal for the great fundamentals." See William H. Brackney, "Curtis Lee Laws (1868–1946)," in *Dictionary of Christianity in America*, ed. D. G.

Reid et al. (Downers Grove, Ill.: InterVarsity Press, 1990), 634; and Hutchison, *Modernist Impulse*.

7 Fea makes the strong point that "militancy or anti-modernism distinguished fundamentalists as a subset of a broader evangelicalism. Several denominations were evangelical in doctrine (Methodists, Southern Baptists, Missouri Synod Lutherans) but did not possess the militancy associated with fundamentalists. While the label 'evangelicalism' can be applied to a broad cross section of American religion that upholds the authority of Scripture, justification by faith, the deity of Christ, and evangelistic zeal, it can also be used to describe a unique subset of former fundamentalists that emerged in the 1940s as 'new evangelicals.'" Fea, "Understanding the Changing Façade," 20, 187.

8 The ACCC was led by Carl McIntire (1906–2002) and Harvey Springer (1907–1966), coleaders of the new Orthodox Presbyterian Church, founded in 1936 along with J. Gresham Machen (1881–1937), who had been tried at a modernist-dominated Presbyterian ecclesiastical court in 1935–1936 and whose ordination had been withdrawn over his conservative opposition. Robert Thomas Ketcham (1889–1978) was the Northern Baptist leader of the group, fresh from founding the new General Association of Regular Baptist (GARB) churches in 1932 in opposition to the Northern Baptist Convention's leanings toward modernism, as well as modernism's perceived threats to the convention's seminaries.

9 The NAE's founding president was Harold J. Ockenga (1905–1985), one of the leaders of evangelicalism and cofounder of Fuller Seminary, Gordon-Conwell Seminary, and *Christianity Today*. Others in this movement were Carl F. H. Henry (1913–2003), Harold Lindsell (1913–1998), Wilbur M. Smith (1894–1976), and Edward John Carnell (1919–1967).

10 Fea, "Understanding the Changing Façade," 195–98.

11 Carl F. H. Henry, "What Is This Fundamentalism?" *United Evangelical Action*, 15 July 1955.

12 Fea, "Understanding the Changing Façade," 192–93.

13 Fea, "Understanding the Changing Façade," 197.

14 Historically, deeply conservative Southern Baptists had not been bound to the term "inerrancy" to describe either the authenticity of the Bible and its message or its truthfulness "without any mixture of error." However, the new conservative resurgent group, which others who disagreed with their political methodology called "insurgents," insisted upon its use, making this term a litmus test for theological orthodoxy while ostensibly rejecting Princetonian scholasticism. See Jerry Sutton, *The Baptist Reformation: The Conservative Resurgence in the Southern Baptist Convention* (Nashville: Broadman and Holman, 2000). Sutton rejected the term "fundamentalist" in favor of "conservatives," as opposed to those he called "moderates," and outlined what this group saw as encroaching theological compromise. See Sutton, *Baptist Reformation*, 1–4. Other volumes that cover this period in Southern Baptist

life are David S. Dockery, *Southern Baptists and American Evangelicals: The Conversation Continues* (Nashville: Broadman and Holman, 1993), David S. Dockery, *Southern Baptist Identity: An Evangelical Denomination Faces the Future* (Wheaton, Ill.: Crossway Books, 2009), Joe Edward Barnhart, *The Southern Baptist Holy War* (Austin, Tex.: Texas Monthly Press, 1986), Russell H. Dilday, *The Doctrine of Biblical Authority* (Nashville: Sunday School Board, 1982), Russell H. Dilday, *Columns: Glimpses of a Seminary Under Assault* (Macon, Ga.: Smyth and Helwys, 2004), Bill Leonard, *God's Last and Only Hope: The Fragmentation of the Southern Baptist Convention* (Grand Rapids: Eerdmans, 1990), Nancy Tatom Ammerman, *Baptist Battles: Social Change and Religious Conflict in the Southern Baptist Convention* (New Brunswick, N.J.: Rutgers University Press, 1990), and John F. Baugh, *The Battle for Baptist Integrity* (Austin, Tex.: Battle for Baptist Integrity, 1995).

15 See J. D. Douglas, *Let the Earth Hear His Voice: International Congress on World Evangelization, Lausanne, Switzerland* (Internet Archive: World Wide Publications, 1975), Leonard I. Sweet, *The Evangelical Tradition in America* (Macon, Ga.: Mercer, 1984), William H. McLoughlin, *American Evangelicals, 1800–1900* (Gloucester, Mass.: Peter Smith Publishers, 1968), and Bruce L. Shelly, *The Gospel and the American Dream* (Sisters, Ore.: Multnomah Books, 1989).

16 The aim of this biography is not to dwell in detail upon, or provide an analysis of, the convulsive nature of Southern Baptist life in the late twentieth century, nor is it to serve as an exhaustive treatment of particular events, such as the removal of Russell Dilday as president of Southwestern Seminary. These matters will necessarily be addressed in part, however, as they intersect the life of John Newport, who served during his mature years on the faculty of Southwestern Seminary and as a special consultant to both presidents Russell Dilday and Kenneth Hemphill during the last decade of the twentieth century. These were key days, and Newport served a vital role in many of these events.

17 At the date of this writing, July 2021, the term "evangelical" no longer means what it did when John Paul Newport lived and wrote. The term "evangelicalism" has undergone a significant shift in definition. Once an easily understood moniker, representing a wide swath of Christianity in America, it was relatively free from political entanglements, polarization, and right-wing agendas. Today, and for these reasons, many "former evangelicals" have stepped away from the term itself, choosing no longer to be included within its parameters. John Newport obviously never saw this shift that no longer describes his beloved community. In fact, John Newport may not have chosen to describe himself as an "evangelical" were he alive today. The story of this book, then, describes a different era, a more gentle, open, dialogical, and engaging expression of the term's history.

1 Headwaters Deep in Missouri Soil

1. Anne Frank, *Tales from the Secret Annex: A Collection of Her Short Stories, Fables, and Lesser-Known Writings*, ed. Gerrold Van der Stooms, trans. Susan Massoty (Basel, Switzerland: Anne Frank-Fonds, 2003), 87.
2. The Native American name for the river, "Niangua," meant "I will not go away." The county was first organized on 29 January 1842 with this name; however, it was so difficult to pronounce and spell that it was changed to Dallas County on 10 December 1844, to honor George M. Dallas, then Vice President to President James Knox Polk. See *A Reminiscent History of the Ozark Region: Comprising a Condensed General History, A Brief Descriptive History of Each County, and Numerous Biographical Sketches of Prominent Citizens of Such Counties* (Chicago: Goodspeed Brothers, 1894), 23.

    Some two hundred miles away in the Mississippi Valley, near St. Louis, between the years 1050 and 1250, the Indians had built one of the largest centers in North America, part of a culture that extended from that valley far into what would later become the states of Alabama, Georgia, and Florida. The Spanish, who controlled this territory during the latter part of the eighteenth century, allowed European settlers to occupy the Missouri territory after 1795 in exchange for military help in defending the land against the British.

    After the British prevailed, however, twenty-nine tribes came to St. Louis in 1816 to sign treaties formalizing the reconciliation between the new settlers and the Indians in Missouri. The St. Louis Treaty, which was actually a series of agreements struck between 1804 and 1816, was signed by Ninian Edwards, William Clark, and Auguste Chouteau for the United States and by representatives from the Council of Three Fires, which was composed of the united tribes of Ottawa, Ojibwa, and Potawatomi who lived on the Illinois and Milwaukee rivers. It was signed on 24 August 1816. The tribes, chiefs, and warriors relinquished all lands previously ceded to the United States by Fox and Sac tribes in the 1804 St. Louis Treaty. In addition, they gave title to a twenty-mile strip of land that connected Chicago and Lake Michigan with the Illinois River. Subsequent canals were built on this land in 1848 and 1900. In exchange, the tribes were to be paid $1,000 in merchandise across the next twelve years. See Francis Paul Prucha, *American Indian Treaties* (Berkeley: University of California Press, 1997), 120.
3. Buffalo was founded in 1839 as a pioneer village promising new beginnings for western settlers. See Ron W. Marr, *Explorer's Guide, Ozarks: Includes Branson, Springfield, & Northwest Arkansas*, Explorer's Complete Guide Series, 2nd ed. (Taftsville, Vt.: Countryman Press, 2012), 18.
4. It was this ancestor that John Newport most closely identified with his own birthplace of Buffalo, primarily because of the Morrow family mercantile

business that was passed down from this pioneer to John's own generation. William Lockhart Morrow was the eldest of the fourteen children born to Robert Morrow II (1795–c.1849) and Julia Simpson (m. 1816–1830). Robert then married his second wife, Elizabeth Shaw Joiner (1796–1849), who reared all of these children together, including five more of their own. Originally from Warren County, Tennessee, this family immigrated to Ozark, near Springfield, Missouri, in 1842. See Bullock's Newport Biography Reference Box, The Texas Collection and University Archives, Baylor University, Waco, Texas.

5   A seventh-generation American, born in Americus, Georgia, Sarah Lydia Brown (1823–1911) was a tiny, gentle, educated, and refined Southern belle whose Huguenot relatives, the Guerry and Van der Voort (Vanderford) families, had emigrated from Holland to the new world a hundred years before the Revolutionary War. John Newport spent a great deal of time with his maternal grandmother, from whom he learned rich and detailed family stories; see Newport Papers, "Autobiographical Materials," Bullock's Newport Biography Reference Box, The Texas Collection.

6   Missouri was the twenty-fourth state to achieve statehood on 10 August 1821. Tennessee had been a state since 1798, and Mississippi since 1817. Arkansas, which lies between Mississippi and Missouri, did not become a state until 1836.

7   Sarah would sew money into the lining of William's clothes, and he would ride the 220 miles by horse to St. Louis, stay several days, and purchase goods. He would have them shipped down the Mississippi River to the Osage River, and then transported via Lin Creek. Here they would be off-loaded and taken by wagon to Buffalo. In this manner, William prospered and became a wealthy merchant in the region. See Newport Papers, "Sarah Brown Morrow Genealogy," in "Autobiographical Materials," Bullock's Newport Biography Reference Box, The Texas Collection.

8   The children born to William and Sarah were William L. Jr., Robert, George (who would become John Newport's grandfather), Julia, Harriet, and Tabitha.

9   The family reported that Union soldiers treated with contempt the citizens of Missouri, whom they derided as slave-supporters, whether that assumption was accurate or not. William Morrow sympathized with the Union, but his wife's family had deep roots in the South, even owning slaves at one point. Sarah's family had sent six family slaves with William and Sarah to help them settle in their new home. When they arrived, however, William freed them. Most of them chose to stay with the family. Union soldiers targeted Sarah for harassment, while Confederate soldiers threatened William. One family story told of an episode in the early 1860s when drunken "Bushwhackers"— Confederate radical partisans who attacked Union forces—met in Buffalo and hatched a plan to lynch William. He escaped with his life by "sleeping on quilts in the orchard, where the grass was as high as his head," and then

fled to St. Louis. A Methodist pastor friend conveyed the rest of the Morrow family that night to Jefferson City, and then on to Collinsville, Illinois, where they rejoined William and lived in hiding to escape the marauding rebels from both sides. See Newport Papers, "Autobiographical Materials," Bullock's Newport Biography Reference Box, The Texas Collection, Frank M. Newport written notes to the writer between 2012 and 2020.

10 On one of his farms, on Section 22, Township 37, Range 19, a valuable lead mine was discovered by a Mr. Hatfield, and was explored about 1883. A shaft was sunk to a depth of sixty feet, and the mineral was found in abundance. About eighty thousand pounds of lead were removed and sold. See "William L. Morrow," *The History of Dallas County, Missouri* (Chicago: Goodspeed, 1889), 956, http://www.mygenealogyhound.com/missouri-biographies/mo-dallas-county-biographies/w-l-morrow-genealogy-dallas-county-missouri-buffalo-mo.html.

11 John Newport shared that in about 1870, the citizens of Buffalo were so sure that their town would become the center of the region that they supported a railroad line to be built from Lebanon, Missouri, to Fort Scott, Kansas. In good faith, they issued $235,000 in railroad bonds and built the roadbed. At the last minute, however, because of "fraud, intrigue, and misrepresentation," the railroad project failed. It was ultimately built thirty miles to the north and ensured the growth of Springfield as the economic center instead.

The Dallas County Commissioners refused to repay the bondholders, and the Morrows and other citizens fought for repayment in the courts. Finally, the bond debt was settled on 4 July 1940 for $300,000, seventy years later. John remembers the unfinished roadbeds lying unused in various parts of the county for many years afterward. He credits this debacle for the conservative skepticism of Dallas County citizens and their general, anti-progressive stance. Primarily for this reason, he recounted, his father decided to move to Springfield to open his business there in 1939.

12 John wrote fondly of Grandmother Vanderford Morrow, who instilled in him a sense of her heritage from both Europe and Britain. Grandmother Mary Ann was fascinated with Dutch and German culture. She had visited the World's Fair in St. Louis in 1904 and regaled him with tales of these cultures that were developing in that great city. In large part, her influence and knowledge intrigued John and motivated him later to study in the very places where his family had lived before migrating to the United States.

The family celebrated Mary Ann's long life of 104 years. A remarkable woman with an iron constitution and equally strong intellect and memory, she gardened on her hands and knees until well after she turned one hundred years old and left recorded remembrances comparing the assassinations of Presidents James Garfield (1881) when she was fourteen; William McKinley (1901) when she was thirty-four; John F. Kennedy (1963) when she was ninety-six; and of Dr. Martin Luther King Jr. and Robert Kennedy, both of whom were assassinated in 1968 when she was 101. After George and Mary Ann retired, they moved to Springfield around 1940 and lived in a craftsman cottage located at 730 S. McCann Street. This little house, with the charming porch, still stands today, and was the home where John Newport and his siblings visited their maternal grandparents.

13 Reverend Richard was married twice. With his first wife, Sarah Conner Newport (1751–1800), they had four children: Ezekiel Newport, Cavanaugh Newport, Sarah Claypool Newport, and Elizabeth Boydston Newport. After Sarah died, Pastor Richard married Hannah Hines, and they reared the four children along with two more she and Richard had together: Asa Wright (1802–1876), born in Knox County, and Calvin (1806–1840), born in Bull Run, both in Tennessee.

14 Much information exists in genealogical records to verify the families of John Newport's heritage. Margaret Abel (1808–1893) married Calvin Newport, Baptist pastor, in 1828. Together, they had six children before her husband died in 1840. Their children were: Richard Calvin Newport (1830–1904); John David Newport (1932–1907); Sarah Elizabeth Newport Powell (1834–1922); Mary Jane Newport Lindsey (1835–1899); Phebe Ann Newport (1838–1839); and Asa Monroe Newport (1840–1922). When her husband died, she married Nathaniel Wollard, also a Baptist minister, who died in 1863, and with whom she had four more children: Rachel Louisa (1842–1847); Nathaniel Jackson (1844–1914); Silas Benton (1846–1912); and James Moses (1849–1907) Wollard. When Nathaniel died, Margaret married a third time in 1872. Her third husband, Joseph Cavin, with whom she had no children, died in 1877. She then returned to Dallas County, Missouri, and was buried in the Wofford Cemetery there. See "United States Census, 1850," database with images, and MyHeritage.com FamilySearch, https://familysearch.org/ark:/61903/1:1:MDZ4-7RC, 9 November 2014, Margaret Wollard in household of Nathaniel Wollard, Dallas County, Dallas, Missouri, United States, citing family 384, NARA microfilm publication M432 (Washington, D.C.: National Archives and Records Administration, n.d.) (accessed 28 June 2020).

15 Roane County was formed in 1801 and is about forty-six miles west-southwest from Knoxville in East Tennessee. Its county seat is Kingston, and its largest town is Harriman.

16 These Newport children were Moses Calvin, Richard Jackson, Margaret Charlotte, Sarah Jane, Nathaniel Monroe, Mary D., John Benjamin, Louisa H., J. Lee, James Benton, and Phebe Ann Newport. See MyHeritage.com, https://www.myheritage.com/research/record-1-392943-3-2465/harriet-narcisses-newport-born-burnett-in-myheritage-family-trees?s=763394271 (accessed 27 June 2020).

17 John William Barrick reared Sarah Ellen as his own child and, together with Mary, had six more children, all half-siblings to Sarah: Nancy, Charles, John

William, Hiram Phillip, Mary Barrick Highfill, and Amelia Barrick Austin. See MyHeritage.com at https://www.myheritage.com/research/record-40001-781206975/john-barrick-in-familysearch-family-tree?s=763394271 (accessed 27 June 2020).

18 The oldest children, Lloyd Brooks (1880–1966) and Roy Acker (1881–1969) Newport, were born in Clatsop County, now Oregon, a region named for the Native American tribes who inhabited this land before the Europeans came to settle. It is located in the farthest northwestern corner of the United States. Lewis and Clark had wintered there in 1805–1806 and established Fort Clatsop, one of the oldest structures in what is now Oregon. The last three of the five children, all born in Buffalo, were Ola (Oly) Earl (1886–1970), Marvin Jackson (1890–1959), and Achsa Harriet (1897–1979) Newport. Marvin Jackson, called "Jack," was John's father.

19 John Newport spoke tenderly of this grandmother. She may have been the more stable parent of the two, since her husband and his brothers were often away from home, gone out west. John tells of how his own father, Marvin Jackson ("Jack"), would go with them as a teenager, staying and sleeping in the livestock cars to care for the cattle and horses. As a result of these western migrations, three uncles moved to the West Coast permanently—two to Oregon, and one to California. Sarah Ellen died in 1941, a year before her husband Moses. Both of them are buried in the Oak Lawn cemetery in Buffalo, Missouri, near the town square. They were known in the family as "Ma" and "Pa" Morrow. See Newport Papers, "Autobiographical Materials," Bullock's Newport Biography Reference Box, The Texas Collection; and information from Mark Newport, son of Russell Newport, John's brother, dated 27 June 2020.

20 The families were large and industrious. All of the Newport and Morrow siblings from John Newport's family have been traced through the generations and listed in the notes above, except for the siblings of John Newport's mother, Mildred Dupont Morrow. She and her brothers and sister all married and lived most of their adult lives in Buffalo as well. Mildred had a sister, Grace Cromwell, who married Harlie Roswell Gleason. Her brothers were Harold Michau Morrow, married to Helen Turner, and Cecil Guerry Morrow, married to Miriam Lois Keeler. These were the maternal aunts and uncles of John Newport and his siblings.

21 Jack Newport was born in 1890 and was Sam Walton's senior by twenty-eight years. Sam Walton (1918–1992) was actually more a peer of Russell Newport, John's brother, who was born in 1921. After Russell returned from his service in the navy during WWII and earned a master's degree at Harvard's business school, he returned to Springfield and began helping Jack run his chain of Ben Franklin stores in the Ozarks region. At one point, Russell and Sam Walton roomed together at a merchandising buyer's convention in Chicago, continuing the "friendly rivalry." When Jack Newport died in 1959,

the Newport and Walton dime store chains were about the same size and slightly overlapped: the Newport stores were mostly in southwest Missouri, but there were a few in northwest Arkansas; the Walton stores were mostly in northwest Arkansas, with a few in southwest Missouri around Branson.

Sam Walton invited Russell to partner with him to create a vast merchandising enterprise, which Russell prayed about and ultimately refused. He had a lovely tenor voice and felt called to use that gift in spiritual service, just as his brother, John, felt called to do through his ministry of preaching, teaching, and writing. Sam Walton went on to open his first Walmart store in 1962, three years after Jack died, and the two families diverged as Sam Walton began to focus his attention on building what would become superstores.

Later, in 1964, Ed Sullivan asked Russell to sing on television on his *Ed Sullivan Show*, the same year the Beatles debuted in the United States. Russell accepted on the condition that he would be allowed to sing a religious song. Sullivan agreed. The show happened to air on a Sunday evening and, of course, First Baptist Church of Springfield was having the evening service during that hour. However, a television was set up so that everyone could watch and hear Russell sing The Lord's Prayer.

2 An Ozark Boy and His Cumberland Girl

1. Jorge Francisco Isidoro Luis Borges, *Twenty-Four Conversations with Jorge Luis Borges: Interviews by Roberto Alifano, 1981–1983*, Altamira Inter-American Series, ed. Roberto Alifano, trans. Willis Barnstone and Noemi Escandell (Housatonic, Mass.: Lascaux Publishers, 1984), 15.
2. John Newport, Newport Papers, "Testimony," Bullock's Newport Biography Reference Box, The Texas Collection.
3. John was not the only child in his family. His two younger brothers were Russell E., born in 1921, and Jack Winston, who arrived in 1923. Mary Ellen, much younger than her brothers, was welcomed into the family in 1933. After World War II, Russell met Carolyn Davis at Cabool, Missouri, during the time when he and John were leading youth revivals together. John would preach and Russell would lead in musical worship. Russell and Carolyn married in 1948 and had three sons together: Mark Davis, Russell Stephen, and Timothy Grant. Russell Newport served as minister of music at the First Baptist Church of Springfield as a noted vocalist. As a businessman, he carried on the family tradition and owned a dozen retail stores. Their youngest brother, Jack, married Patsy in the early 1950s, and they had sons Mike and David Newport together. Jack spent his career as an orthopedic surgeon in Tulsa, Oklahoma. Their sister Mary Ellen Newport and Harvey W. Zorbaugh were married 24 June 1958. They had two children: Charles Louis and Russell Warren Zorbaugh. Harvey was a superb teacher and organizer, working for the National Education Association in Columbia, Maryland. Mary Ellen

followed her great passion for music as a vocal instructor, music teacher, and editor. At the time of this writing, Russell, Mary Ellen, and her husband Harvey are living in retirement and have furnished much information about the years of their youth for this volume.

4   As Russ Bush put it, "Formative years form the years," and this was certainly true of John Newport. See the brief biographical introduction found in L. Russ Bush, "John Paul Newport: A Man for All Seasons," *Southwestern Journal of Theology* 29, no. 3 (1987): 5.

5   Jack and Mildred's grandchildren remember going the rounds with their grandfather to the stores and his jovial generosity. He would give them a gift of anything in the store, which delighted the children and made their visits seem magical. In his older years, Jack would attend the opening day of hunting season, standing by the car with gun ready, enjoying the special outing with family and friends. Even after their move to Springfield in 1939, this frugal yet enthusiastic man always seemed to be obtaining the "latest and newest" invention, gadget, or technology. He purchased a television for the John Newport family when they were still a rare commodity, for example, and owned the most efficient refrigerator, and drove the latest style of automobile. He was quite an entrepreneur. These vignettes of Jack's vibrant personality were summarized from the longer narrative from "Jack Newport Eulogy, 1959," and from grandchildren's recollections, in Newport Papers, "Autobiographical Materials," Bullock's Newport Biography Reference Box, The Texas Collection.

6   John P. Newport, "The Theology and Experience of Salvation," *Greek Orthodox Theological Review* 22, no. 4 (1977): 393–404.

7   Newport, "Theology and Experience of Salvation," 401.

8   Lee Rutland Scarborough (1870–1945) was an American Baptist pastor, evangelist, denominational leader, and professor at the Southwestern Baptist Theological Seminary. There, in 1901, he founded and chaired the first seminary "department of evangelism." He then served as president of the seminary from 1914–1945 upon the death of its founder and first president, Dr. B. H. Carroll. Scarborough led in a program of evangelism for the Southern Baptist Convention and the Baptist World Alliance and made an evangelistic tour of South America for the Foreign Mission Board in 1936. He had an intense spirit of cooperation regarding denominational work. Today, Baptist Hill is still located thirty miles west of Springfield, Missouri, on State Highway V. Baptist Hill had been an older campground used for the Lawrence County Assembly. It was purchased and dedicated for Missouri Baptist purposes in 1918. Camping was a rustic and adventurous experience for John and his brother when they attended these special weeks. Newport Papers, "Autobiographical Materials," Bullock's Newport Biography Reference Box, The Texas Collection.

9 John's mother often spoke of his spending the afternoon in the backyard as a child, reading anything he could get his hands on—including the *Encyclopedia Britannica*. See Martha Newport Shimkus, notes to the writer, "Newport Family Memories," 20 June 2013,
10 It was here in Baptist Young People's Union that John learned the rudiments of apologetics. Newport Papers, "Autobiographical Materials," Bullock's Newport Biography Reference Box, The Texas Collection.
11 John credited W. O. Vaught, who served as Missouri State Baptist Student Director from 1928–1940, with aiding his admission to Southern Seminary at the last minute, a few years later, when his room had already been secured and the preliminary down payment on his tuition had been paid to Harvard Law School in 1942. Newport Papers, "Autobiographical Materials," Bullock's Newport Biography Reference Box, The Texas Collection.
12 See the prologue, which spoke to the modernism that had been creeping across the northeast in the 1920s and 1930s.
13 Newport, "Testimony," Bullock's Newport Biography Reference Box, The Texas Collection, 1.
14 In March 1925, the state of Tennessee passed into law the Butler Act, named for Tennessee state representative, farmer, and head of the World Christian Fundamentals Association, John W. Butler. This bill, signed into law by Governor Austin Peay, forbade the teaching of evolutionary theory as a hypothesis in any state-funded school. John Scopes, a high school biology teacher in Dayton, Tennessee, had been accused of violating the Butler Act. The formidable agnostic lawyer, Clarence Darrow, took up the side of Scopes, and the equally famous lawyer and three-time presidential candidate, William Jennings Bryan, argued for the prosecution. The case became a national sensation from April to July that year until the decision was read on 21 July 1925. Scopes was found guilty and was fined $100; however, the verdict was overturned on a technicality. This decision catapulted fundamentalism into the spotlight, where it seemed to lose ground with public opinion as narrow and militant in its approach. See Charles Alan Israel, *Before Scopes: Evangelicalism, Education, and Evolution in Tennessee, 1870–1925* (Athens: University of Georgia Press, 2004), 161.
15 The World Unity Headquarters was then and still is home to Unity School of Christianity, founded by Charles and Myrtle Fillmore in 1890. The rolling campus is located fifteen miles south-southwest of Kansas City, Missouri. William Jewell College in Liberty, where Newport was a student, was located the same distance just northeast of Kansas City. Myrtle Fillmore died on 6 October 1931 while John was in college. The publication, *Modern Thought*, was well-known in the region at the time. Newport wrote of his interest in New Age thought as early as his young manhood. See Newport Papers, "Autobiographical Materials," Bullock's Newport Biography Reference Box, The Texas Collection.

16 John Newport spoke of some of the tensions, or the divides, that bracketed his life: Methodist and Baptist traditions, Conservative and Progressive politics and viewpoints, cultures of East, West, North, and South, European and American, cultured and primitive, existential and rational, American Baptist and Southern Baptist; see Newport Papers, "Autobiographical Materials," Bullock's Newport Biography Reference Box, The Texas Collection.
17 Franklin Delano Roosevelt, born 30 January 1882 in Hyde Park, New York, was elected president in November 1932 and served to the beginning of his fourth term when he died on 12 April 1945.
18 See Roger Daniels, *Franklin D. Roosevelt: Road to the New Deal, 1882-1939* (Champaign: University of Illinois Press, 2016), chapters 7-8.
19 John Newport, Newport Papers, "Autobiographical Materials," Bullock's Newport Biography Reference Box, The Texas Collection.
20 John Newport, Newport Papers, "Autobiographical Materials," Bullock's Newport Biography Reference Box, The Texas Collection. John later wrote an honors thesis on Roosevelt's New Deal. George Washington University began as Columbian College, started from a desire of President George Washington, but was opened after his death in 1821 by Baptist pastor, Luther Rice, several other friends, and James Madison. It was then located between 14th and 15th Streets. It later moved to a location at 15th and L Streets and changed its name to Columbian University in 1873. The third change reclaimed the founder's intent, renaming the school George Washington University in 1904 and moving it for its final time to its present location at Foggy Bottom in the center of Washington, D.C., just four blocks from the White House and within walking distance to museums and monuments.
21 John Newport, Newport Papers, "Autobiographical Materials," Bullock's Newport Biography Reference Box, The Texas Collection; see Newport, "Testimony," Bullock's Newport Biography Reference Box, The Texas Collection, 1.
22 George Washington Truett (1867-1944) became pastor of the First Baptist Church in Dallas in September 1897 and remained in that role until his death in July 1944. During his forty-seven-year pastorate, membership increased from 715 to 7,804. He was a noted denominational leader and statesman, president of the Southern Baptist Convention from 1927 to 1929, and of the Baptist World Alliance from 1934 to 1939. Constantly in demand for evangelistic, academic, and denominational sermons and addresses, Truett, in addition to his pastorate, was for thirty-seven summers preacher to the "Cowboy Camp Meetings" in West Texas. He also preached to Allied forces for six months in World War I, by appointment by President Woodrow Wilson. He also gave the famous address on religious freedom on the Capitol steps in Washington, D.C., on 16 May 1920, and toured South America, England, and world mission fields, to preach from 1930-1936.
23 John Newport, Newport Papers, "Autobiographical Materials," Bullock's Newport Biography Reference Box, The Texas Collection.

24 John Newport, Newport Papers, "Autobiographical Materials," Bullock's Newport Biography Reference Box, The Texas Collection. John was twenty-two when he enrolled in seminary. Just months later, in 1939, John Newport's parents sold some business concerns and moved to Springfield, Missouri. The lack of railway transportation was restricting the growth of Jack's businesses. Also, the Buffalo city leadership was finally settling the old railroad dispute of seventy years' duration and had paid back on the financial bonds just pennies on the dollar. Jack was seeking a more progressive community in which to start a new chapter. Jack, Mildred, their son Jack, and daughter Mary Ellen moved to a smaller house at 701 W. Monroe Street for a few months. They then moved around the corner to 683 S. Kickapoo Avenue, where the two youngest children finished grade school, which was just a short walk down the street.

At this time, Mildred's parents also moved to Springfield from Buffalo. They lived in a craftsman cottage at 807 McCann, around the corner from Jack and Mildred. When John came home from seminary, and Russell from college, they stayed in this house on Kickapoo until Jack and Mildred built a lovely home at 920 Brookside Drive, which still stands today. This is a spacious brick home with a long front drive and expansive lawns. Across the street was Fassnight Creek, and the beautiful Phelps Park. In this home, the family met to celebrate birthdays, anniversaries, and special events for the rest of his parents' lives. Mary Ellen finished high school here, where she was president of the class. Russell returned from WWII and graduated from Harvard Business School. He then stepped in to help his father, Jack, run the family businesses. They added two new stores in Springfield, one each in Branson, Cabool, Willow Springs, and Bolivar in Missouri, and one in Harrison, Arkansas. Ever adventurers, Jack even purchased a large orange farm in Edinburgh, Texas, where Jack and his father, Moses Calvin, would travel each winter to check on the produce.

Jack and Mildred became active members of the First Baptist Church of Springfield, where Jack served on the finance committee, and they were as active here as they had been in Buffalo. He was also a member of the Kiwanis Club and continued his work as a Gideon. Jack lived until heart illness took his life in 1959. Mildred lived until 1987.

25 The Leavells are a multigenerational Baptist family. George Washington and Corry Alice Berry Leavell had nine sons. Frank Hartwell (1884–1949) was the fourth of these. He graduated from the University of Mississippi, earned an M.A. at Columbia University, and attended Harvard Law School. From 1913 to 1922, Frank served as secretary of the Baptist Training Union in Georgia. He then pioneered organized student work in 1922 across the SBC and served as secretary of the Department of Student Work of the Sunday School Board from 1928 until his death. He served in other roles as treasurer of the Education Commission (1928–1929) and a member of the promotional agency of the SBC (1928–1930). He also served as lecturer of the Baptist Bible Institute in New Orleans (now New Orleans Baptist Theological Seminary, 1930) and as a member of the Executive Committee (1934–1949) and secretary of the

Youth Committee (1931–1949) of the Baptist World Alliance. He initiated the annual student retreat at Ridgecrest Baptist Assembly in 1926, promoted youth conferences in 1926, 1930, 1934, and 1938, and was a prolific writer. He took research tours to Europe, Asia, China, Japan, Hawaii, the Near East, and South America. See William Hall Preston, "Frank Hartwell Leavell," in *Encyclopedia of Southern Baptists*, vol. 2 (Nashville: Broadman, 1958), 781–82.

26 The fascinating story of Eddie Belle's father's family, and its nine famous brothers from Oxford, Mississippi, may be found in Charlotte Henry Leavell's family account, *Genealogy of Nine Leavell Brothers of Oxford, Mississippi* (Charlottesville, Va.: Private printing, 1957), 123. Her father was the fifth of these brothers. Eddie Belle was also descended on her mother's side from George Washington and from the Boones of Kentucky. Her fifth-generation grandfather, Samuel Boone (born 1728), was the brother of the famous Daniel (1734–1820). She brought this sterling lineage to her marriage with John Newport.

27 Eddie Belle's mother, Martha Maria Boone (1894–1960) married Frank Hartwell Leavell on 5 April 1917 in Memphis, Tennessee, and they had three children, Eddie Belle, Mary Martha, and Frank Hartwell Leavell Jr. Eddie Belle's sister, Mary Martha Leavell (1923–1986) lived many years in White Settlement, Texas, a suburb of Fort Worth, Texas. Her brother, Frank Hartwell Leavell Jr. (1928–2005), taught English on the faculty at Baylor University from 1965–1995 and retired in Waco, Texas. Eddie Belle lived until 29 September 2012. Eddie Belle's maternal grandparents (parents of her mother, Martha Maria Boone) were Arthur Upshaw Boone (1860–1956) and Eddie Belle Cooke Boone (1866–1924), who were married in 1891. Her grandfather served for more than thirty-five years as pastor of the First Baptist Church of Memphis, Tennessee.

28 Martha Newport Shimkus, Eddie Belle's daughter, handwritten notes to the writer, 20 June 2013.

29 In 1913, Ward Seminary, a prestigious finishing school, merged with Belmont College for Young Women to become the Ward-Belmont College, which operated as such until 1951. By 1920, Belmont numbered 1,200 young women as students. See its 1938 yearbook, "Milestones," digitized by Internet Archive, https://archive.org/stream/milestones1938ward#page/n135/mode/2up/search/Eddie+Belle+Leavell (accessed 4 December 2014).

30 See Meredith College's 1940 yearbook, "Oak Leaves," digitized by the North Carolina Digital Heritage Center, a statewide digitization and digital publishing program housed in the North Carolina Collection at the University of North Carolina at Chapel Hill, https://lib.digitalnc.org/record/27416#?c=0&m=0&s=0&cv=3&r=0&xywh=-189%2C0%2C4464%2C2898 (accessed 9 February 2022).

31 Eddie Belle had just returned from touring Europe with a group that included George Hale, John's college friend and former roommate. George told John of Eddie Belle's beauty, intelligence, and dynamic personality, so John was eager to meet her when they both arrived at Ridgecrest. See

Newport Papers, Bullock's Newport Biography Reference Box, The Texas Collection, "Autobiography Notes," 12. Eddie Belle was a lovely young woman, as was her mother before her, and later, her daughter Martha. In fact, all three of them were beauty queens.

32 Frank Louis Mauldin, from his interview with John Newport, quoted in "John Paul Newport: Philosophy of Religion," in *The Legacy of Southwestern: Writings that Shaped a Tradition*, ed. James Leo Garrett Jr. (North Richland Hills, Tex.: Smithfield Press, 2002), 208. This was the inscription John wrote for the dedication page to his book, *Life's Ultimate Questions: A Contemporary Philosophy of Religion* (Galena Park, Tex.: Galena Institute, 1989).

33 John Newport, "Skeptic and Apologist," *Baptist Student* (December 1956): 36.

34 John came back to the United States in 1948 and did not finish his degree until 1953. At that time, he attended his graduation in Edinburgh, Scotland, and visited London before he returned home. By his own account, he was a face in the crowds that witnessed the coronation of Queen Elizabeth II on 2 June of that year.

35 Immanuel Baptist Church was once a thriving church in a complex of buildings at 1915 E. Third St., just east of downtown Tulsa, with more than 100,000 square feet of space and weekly attendance of about one thousand. It was one of Tulsa's largest and most prosperous congregations from the 1950s through the 1970s. The original building was completed in 1926, and the new sanctuary, where the church still meets, was added in 1968, with a seating capacity of 1,750. The church began to decline in the 1980s, however, when the construction of Interstate 244 bisected the area and many young families moved away. In early 2014, however, the declining church became by adoption one of the four satellite congregations of the Church at Battle Creek. In 2020, now called The Church at Downtown, the church family there has begun afresh with new families moving back into the neighborhood and revitalized growth under the leadership of Battle Creek Pastor Alex Himaya, who preaches by video each week.

36 John and Eddie Belle had a houseful with these three children. Even more, there were lots of cousins: ten grandchildren on John's paternal side of the family, among them nine boys and a single granddaughter—John's and Eddie Belle's daughter, Martha, named after her maternal grandmother. The Newport children, Martha, Frank, and John, remember the wonderful family reunions in Springfield, Missouri, where grandparents Jack and Mildred Newport and their son, Russell, and his wife, Carolyn, lived. When the extended family gathered, the children would play with cousins in the large backyard, where Grandfather Jack had built a high swing for them, eat cold watermelon, and play Ping Pong in the basement. They remember producing programs with skits, and the poetry readings and carol sings each Christmas, when their father, John, would sing Christmas carols off-key on purpose. On summer nights, when the sun went down, the cousins would listen to their parents tell

ghost stories and laugh together. This was a warm and loving family. See notes from Martha, Frank, and John Paul Jr., to the writer, in the Newport Papers, Bullock's Newport Biography Reference Box, The Texas Collection.

37 In John's own words, he considered his biblical heritage, with all of its converging tributaries, to contribute to the strong river that rolled onward through his life, propelling him toward the ultimate destination that would be found in God's very being and presence. See "Columbus, Cultural and Religious Self-Understanding, and the Caribbean," in "Autobiographical Materials," Bullock's Newport Biography Reference Box, The Texas Collection.

3 Streams of Knowledge

1 Austin Phelps, *The Theory of Preaching: Lectures on Homiletics* (New York: C. Scribner's Sons, 1882), 76; a reproduction is published by Wentworth Press, 2019, 218.
2 Goerner, author of *America Must Be Christian* (1947) and *Thus It Is Written* (1958), was from Mart, Texas, earned his Ph.D. from SBTS in 1935, and accepted a teaching position in the department of comparative religion and missions at his alma mater. In 1957, he became the Foreign Mission Board's (FMB) Area Secretary for Baptist Missions in Africa, Europe, and the Near East and, as the work of the Foreign Mission Board expanded, oversaw work in Africa until his retirement in 1977. During his lifetime, he was also pastor of several churches. See "Henry Cornell Goerner Historical Collection," Southern Baptist Historical Library and Archives, Nashville, Tennessee, 2006, at http://www.sbhla.org/downloads/805.pdf (accessed 6 December 2014).
3 Calling Norfolk County, Virginia, his home, in 1913, Davis earned his Th.D. from SBTS and in 1920 began teaching New Testament hermeneutics, the role in which he served for the rest of his life. Over the next sixteen years, he authored *A Beginner's Grammar of the Greek New Testament* (1923) and coauthored with professor E. A. McDowell *A Source Book of Interbiblical History* (1948). See J. Estill Jones, "William Hersey Davis," in *Encyclopedia of Southern Baptists*, vol. 1 (Nashville: Broadman, 1958), 350–51, and The Southern Baptist Theological Seminary Archives and Special Collection at http://archives.sbts.edu/the-history-of-the-sbts/our-professors/w-hersey-davis/ (accessed 6 December 2014).
4 John graduated from Southern Seminary with his M.Th. in 1942 and then stayed to earn his Th.D. in New Testament, with special research in apocalypticism. Davis served as the supervisor for John's dissertation, "The Jewish Messiah of the Apocrypha and the Pseudepigrapha," which was completed in 1944.
5 From Raleigh, North Carolina, Adams was still a seminary student when his president, E. Y. Mullins, appointed him as a Fellow in systematic theology. He became a lecturer in 1925 and, after earning his Th.D. in 1929 from SBTS, taught biblical introduction for more than twenty years. He became

famous for his eleven trips to Europe and the Near East for archaeological study and research, often taking students with him. His works include *Syllabus for Biblical Introduction Studies* (1926); *Biblical Backgrounds* (1934); *The Heart of the Levant: Palestine and Syria* (1937); and *Ancient Records and the Bible* (1946). See J. Morris Ashcraft, "James McKee Adams," in *Encyclopedia of Southern Baptists*, vol. 1 (Nashville: Broadman, 1958), 2–3.

6 Originally from Tennessee, W. O. Carver was beloved among Southern Baptists. Carver graduated with an M.A. from Richmond College (now Richmond University) in 1891. He earned a Th.D. in New Testament from SBTS in 1896 and began teaching missions two years later. He was a prolific writer, publishing twenty-one books, including *Missions in the Plan of the Ages* (1909); *Missions and Modern Thought* (1910); *The Course of Christian Missions* (1932); and *The Glory of God in the Christian Calling* (1949); see Alan Neely, "Carver, William Owen," in *Biographical Dictionary of Christian Missions*, ed. Gerald H. Anderson (New York: Macmillan Reference USA, 1998), 118.

7 Gaines Stanley Dobbins was born in Langsdale, Mississippi. He authored thirty-two volumes and more than five thousand articles on church life and growth. As a former newspaper editor, Dobbins earned his Th.D. from SBTS in 1914. He then joined the Southern Seminary faculty in 1920 in the areas of church efficiency and Sunday School pedagogy, which he taught until his first retirement in 1956 at seventy years old. He then taught at Golden Gate Theological Seminary in Mill Valley, California, for a decade, then in Switzerland and Nigeria, back at SBTS for a few years, and finally, served as a chaplain of a retirement center. His work included *The Efficient Church* (1923); *A Winning Witness* (1938); and *Evangelism According to Christ* (1949); see the digitized finding guide for the "Gaines Stanley Dobbins Papers," Southern Baptist Historical Library and Archives, http://www.sbhla.org/downloads/795-281.pdf (accessed 11 December 2014).

8 Edgar Young Mullins was born in Franklin County, Mississippi, and earned a Ph.D. from Texas A&M University in 1879 in anticipation of pursuing a law degree. Following conversion, however, he was called into the gospel ministry. In 1899 Mullins was elected, without his knowledge or consent, to be president of SBTS, a role he served until his death. Professor of theology, author, administrator, and denominational leader, Mullins was an extraordinary and significant influence upon succeeding generations. His works included: *Why Is Christianity True?* (1905); *The Axioms of Religion* (1908); *Baptist Beliefs* (1912); *Freedom and Authority in Religion* (1913); *Commentary on Ephesians and Colossians* (1913); *Spiritualism, A Delusion* (1920); and *Christianity at the Crossroads* (1924); see "Edgar Young Mullins," Southern Baptist Historical Library and Archives, http://www.sbhla.org/bio_eymullins.htm (accessed 6 December 2014).

9 John Newport, *The New Age Movement and the Biblical World View: Conflict and Dialogue* (Grand Rapids: Eerdmans, 1998), xii. Briefly, secular humanism, as John Newport encountered it in 1944, was a philosophy or worldview that embraced human reason above supernatural revelation, secular ethics, and philosophical naturalism. It rejected religious doctrines and superstitions as the basis of morality and decision-making. Along with this, an essential part of secular humanism is a continually adapting search for truth, primarily through science and philosophy. The first Humanism Manifesto appeared in 1933, with fifteen descriptive statements outlining its positions, signed by thirty influential academics, ministers, newspaper editors, and other leaders. See Edwin H. Wilson's *Genius of a Humanist Manifesto* (Washington, D.C.: Humanist Press, 1995). Since then, two more manifestos have been written as the movement continues to evolve.

  The New Age Movement was also emerging, partly from what John called the "futurology movement, which had roots in occultism, UFO, and counter-culture elements." See Newport, *Life's Ultimate Questions*, 73–77. In the next twenty years, Newport observed the movement's unfolding into what was called "New Age" in the 1960s and 1970s. Religion scholar Daren Kemp's description is helpful: "One of the few things on which all scholars agree concerning New Age is that it is difficult to define. Often, the definition given actually reflects the background of the scholar giving the definition. Thus, the New Ager views New Age as a revolutionary period of history dictated by the stars; the Christian apologist has often defined New Age as a cult; the historian of ideas understands it as a manifestation of the perennial tradition; the philosopher sees New Age as a monistic or holistic worldview; the sociologist describes New Age as a new religious movement (NRM); while the psychologist describes it as a form of narcissism." See Daren Kemp, *New Age: A Guide* (Edinburgh: Edinburgh University Press, 2004), 1.

10 This church was founded in 1768 by the famous Scotch Baptist minister Archibald McLean and was led by bi-vocational laymen until its first full-time pastor, William Grant, was called in 1870 and served until his death in 1902. See the brief history of this congregation at https://www.bristobaptist.org/history-of-bristo (accessed 9 February 2022).

11 See John Newport, Letter to his mother, 20 September 1946, Newport Papers, Bullock's Newport Biography Reference Box, The Texas Collection. John sent his mother a list of items that would be of help to the Pattersons: cans of Spam, peaches, pears, pineapples, chocolate bars, Crisco, Eagle Brand Milk, nylon hosiery—size 9.5, and a little dress for a girl of three. There were no automobiles more recent than 1939 models, and none were promised for the foreseeable future. The coal strikes darkened the country for extended hours during the day and every evening. Clothing was of poor quality and the women, particularly, seemed ragged. Food supplies were rationed and sundry items in Woolworth's store were astronomical in price.

Upon arrival, John reported that he had purchased a necessary umbrella at the cost of more than six pounds, which would be fifty-one pounds today, or sixty-eight dollars.

12 In Edinburgh, John visited Edinburgh and Holyrood castles, the hereditary residences of Scotland's monarchs, and then made his way to Culzean Castle. Culzean Castle Country Park had been for decades the former seat of the Kennedy Clan of Scotland, having originally been built atop a cliff along the Ayrshire coast by Robert Adams between 1777 and 1792 for the 10th Earl of Cassilis. When the war ended in 1945, the Kennedy Clan gave the castle and its grounds to the National Trust for Scotland with the stipulation that the apartment at the top of the castle be given to then-general of the army Dwight D. Eisenhower in recognition of his role as supreme commander of the Allied forces in Europe during World War II. Eisenhower stayed at the castle for the first time in 1946 and in future years returned three other times, including once while he was President of the United States. Today the National Trust has opened the castle to the public, and an Eisenhower Exhibit occupies one of the rooms of the top floor. Culzean Castle's picture is featured on the reverse of the Royal Bank of Scotland's five-pound note.

13 The Georgian Duff House, in Banff, Scotland, was designed by William Adam and built between 1735 and 1740 for William Duff of Braco, Earl of Fife. Duff never lived there, but in the twentieth century, the estate was an elegant hotel and a sanatorium before the government commandeered its use as a military base during World War II. From 1939 to 1946, surrounded by an eight-foot wire fence, and patrolled by Scots from the Scottish Regiments, it was used as an internment camp, followed by a brief period as a prisoner of war camp, and then as an Allied headquarters for various English and Scots regiments. In 1942 it became the headquarters for Norway's Norwegian Brigade and, after the war, a base for Polish soldiers waiting for resettlement in Scotland.

After extensive refurbishing, Duff House was reopened in 1995 by the Aberdeen Council, Historic Scotland, and the National Gallery of Scotland as an historic country house and gallery. It was during its Prisoner of War days, in 1940, that Dr. Galzen ministered to prisoners there. See Aberdeenshire Council's online museum at https://online.aberdeenshire.gov.uk/smrpub/master/detail.aspx?Authority=ASH&refno=NJ66SE0007 (accessed 9 February 2022). See also John Newport's small notebook in Newport Papers, "Autobiographical Materials," Bullock's Newport Biography Reference Box, The Texas Collection, detailing his journey to Scotland, his day trips, and his earliest professors there.

14 When New College opened its doors in 1846, it was to train ministers of the gospel for the Free Church of Scotland, known later as United Free Church of Scotland. Candidates for ministry in the old Church of Scotland studied with the faculty of divinity at Edinburgh University in Old College. In 1929,

a merger took place between the two bodies, approved by an act of Parliament in 1935. In 1937, the now-merged faculty moved to the New College site in renovated buildings on "The Mound," the ancient location of the University near the city center.

New College continues to have an official relationship with the Church of Scotland, and its "Hall" is home to its Assembly, which meets there annually. This Hall was also used by the Scottish Parliament as a debating chamber from its establishment in 1999 until its removal to the new Parliament Building at Holyrood in 2004. The principal of New College is still appointed by the General Assembly of the Church of Scotland and is responsible for all ministry candidates within that body. As a school of divinity, however, it is also under the umbrella of Edinburgh University and is led by the Head, who is appointed by the university and oversees larger academic and financial stewardship.

15 David Hume (1711–1776) was a Scottish Enlightenment philosopher, historian, economist, and essayist who is best known today for his highly influential system of philosophical empiricism, skepticism, and naturalism. John Knox (c.1514–1572) was a Scottish minister, theologian, and writer who was a leader of the country's Reform that culminated in 1560 in the founding of the state-supported Presbyterian Church of Scotland.

As the fall weather turned chilly, John asked his mother to send a black overcoat, two to three pairs of long underwear, sweaters, and four pairs of thick, ribbed, maroon socks. He also asked for "a new pair of rubbers, size 12–13, please," to cover his shoes and keep his feet dry in the pouring rain. His mother sent him boxes of supplies, along with gum, candy, prunes, and canned beef, for which he was most grateful. His first box arrived on 11 November and the second the next day. John was so cold that he wore his sweater and overcoat from the moment he arose until he went to bed, "including during meals"; see John Newport's letter to his mother dated 20 September 1946 in Newport Papers, Bullock's Newport Biography Reference Box, The Texas Collection.

16 John Baillie was born in Gairloch, Scotland, the son of a Free Church minister, and educated in Edinburgh, Marburg, and Jena. He taught at Auburn Theological Seminary in New York (1920–27), Emmanuel College, Toronto (1927–30), and Union Seminary in New York (1930–34) before returning to New College, Edinburgh, to teach theology (1934–56). He was brother to two other famous Baillies: Donald Macpherson Baillie, who taught theology at St. Mary's in St. Andrews; and Peter, who died by accidental drowning while training to become a medical missionary in India. John Baillie's works include *The Interpretation of Religion* (1928); *A Diary of Private Prayer* (1937); *Our Knowledge of God* (1939); *Invitation to Pilgrimage* (1942); *The Belief in Progress* (1950); *The Idea of Revelation in Recent Thought* (1956); and his Gifford Lectures, *The Sense of the Presence of God* (1962), published

posthumously. Additional material about Baillie can also be found in Donald S. Klinefelter, "The Theology of John Baillie: A Biographical Introduction," *Scottish Journal of Theology* (December 1969): 419–36; and in John A. MacKay, "John Baillie, a Lyrical Tribute and Appraisal," *Scottish Journal of Theology* (June 1956): 226–27. John Baillie was made Companion of Honour to Queen Elizabeth II in 1957.

17 Torrance was born to Church of Scotland missionary parents in Chengdu, China, and was educated in Edinburgh, Oxford, and Basel universities. As part of the famous Torrance family of theologians, he was regarded as one of the most significant of twentieth-century thinkers. He was awarded the Templeton Foundation Prize for Progress in Religion in 1978. Torrance retired from the University of Edinburgh in 1979 but continued to lecture and publish, completing more than sixty-one major works in his lifetime. Several influential books on the Trinity were published after his retirement, including: *The Trinitarian Faith: The Evangelical Theology of the Ancient Catholic Church* (1988); *Trinitarian Perspectives: Toward Doctrinal Agreement* (1994); and *The Christian Doctrine of God, One Being Three Persons* (1996). His later doctrinal focus helped to forge an historic doctrinal agreement on the Trinity between the World Alliance of Reformed Churches and the Orthodox Church in 1991. See Alister E. McGrath's *Thomas F. Torrance: An Intellectual Biography* (Edinburgh: T&T Clark, 1999).

18 Born in Dundee, Scotland, Stewart had earned degrees at the universities of St. Andrews, Edinburgh, and Bonn. From 1952–1966 he served as chaplain to the Queen of Scotland. So popular was his preaching that he attracted crowds of Americans that came both to hear him preach and to study under his influence. He mediated the tensions between Baillie's moderate liberalism and G. T. Thomson's aggressive Barthianism during the fourth chapter of New College's history, 1935–1955; see A. C. Cheyne, *The Spirit of New College: New College, Edinburgh, 1846–1996* (New College, Edinburgh, July 1996), 11, http://www.docs.hss.ed.ac.uk/divinity/About%20the%20school/History/The%20sprit%20of%20New%20College.pdf (accessed 12 December 2014). Stewart's books include: *A Man in Christ* (1935); *The Strong Name* (1941); *Heralds of God* (1946); and, coedited with H. R. Mackintosh, the English translation of Friedrich Schleiermacher's work, *The Christian Faith* (1928). The first edition was published in Germany as *Der christliche Glaube nach den Grundsätzen der evangelischen Kirche im Zusammenhange dargestellt* in 1820–1821, and the second edition, greatly revised, in 1830–1831 (reprinted Berlin: G. Reimer, 1884).

He and John Newport arrived at New College about the same time. Stewart commenced full-time teaching on 1 January 1947. See Stewart's obituary, "The Very Rev James Stewart," in *The Times* (London), 10 July 1990.

19 William Manson was born on 14 April 1882. He studied at Glasgow University, Oriel College in Oxford, and at the United Free College (later Trinity

College), Glasgow. He served as pastor in Oban from 1911 to 1914 and at Pollockshields East in Glasgow. He spent a brief time in Canada as chair of New Testament language and literature at Knox College in Toronto from 1919 to 1924 and returned to Scotland to occupy the chair of New Testament at New College, Edinburgh University, from 1925 to 1946 and chair of biblical criticism from 1946 to 1952. Between 1950 and 1952 he was vice president of the British Council of Churches. His publications included *Jesus the Messiah* (1943); *The Epistle to the Hebrews* (1951); and *The Way of the Cross* (1958). William Manson died on 4 April 1958; see Obituary, *Glasgow Herald*, 5 April 1958.

20 Norman Porteous, living just six days shy of his 105th birthday, was Britain's oldest living army officer of World War I when he died on 3 September 2003. Born, reared, and schooled in Haddington, where his father served as the rector of Knox Memorial Institute, he left Edinburgh University as a student in 1916 for war service in France (1917–1919), where he was commissioned as a second lieutenant with the Royal Scots. Upon returning to the university, he earned first-class degrees in classics (1922) and the *Literae Humaniores* from Trinity in Oxford (1924), returning to Edinburgh to earn a divinity degree in Old Testament at New College (1928), which was at the time one of the three colleges of the United Free Church of Scotland, where he studied with H. R. Macintosh. He then won scholarships that funded his postgraduate studies at Berlin, Tubingen, and finally Munster (1927–1929), where he was Karl Barth's first English-speaking student.

Porteous served as a minister in Fife before being called to the Regius Chair of Hebrew and Semitic Languages at the University of St. Andrews. He then moved to succeed A. R. S. Kennedy at New College, Edinburgh, in 1937, and served as the Ancient Chair of Hebrew and Semitic Languages until his retirement in 1968, together with his roles as dean of the faculty and principal of New College. As Senior Professor Emeritus, Porteous was for twenty-one years a member of the panel of translators for the *New English Bible*, a project initiated at the 1946 General Assembly of the Church of Scotland. Organizer of international symposia, societies, and essays in *festschriften* for Barth, Eichrodt, von Rad, and Weiser, Porteous was perhaps most famous as the author of *Daniel* (1965) and *Living the Mystery* (1967), both collections of his papers; see Graeme Auld, Obituary, *The Scotsman*, on 9 September 2003.

21 Born and reared in Scotland, Rankin was one of two brothers who had excelled in their day. His younger brother, Sir George Claus Rankin, became Chief Justice of Bengal. Rankin was educated at George Watson's College, Edinburgh University, and at Berlin University. He held the Vans Dunlop Scholarship in Hebrew, Arabic, and Syriac in 1908. Rankin was ordained and became the parish minister in Sorbie, Wigtownshire, in 1912. His publications include: *The Origins of the Festival of Hanukah* (1930); *Israel's Wisdom*

Literature: Its Bearing on Theology and the History of Religion (1936); and Jewish Religious Polemic: A Study of Documents Here Rendered in English, the latter volume published posthumously in 1956.

For an understanding of generational and theological transitions made by faculty through the years, see Cheyne, *Spirit of New College*.

22 Macmurray was born in Maxwelltown in Kirkcudbrightshire, to the son of an excise officer of Scotland's Inland Revenue Department. Moving to Aberdeen at age ten with his family, Macmurray was educated at Aberdeen, Glasgow University, and Balliol College, Oxford. He enlisted in the medical corps in 1914 when World War I broke out, served in France in the 58th Field Ambulance of the 19th Division of the British Expeditionary Force, was severely wounded in the Battle of Somme near Arras in 1918 as second lieutenant in the Queen's Own Cameron Highlanders, and was awarded the Military Cross for gallantry. Following the war and completion of his *Literae Humaniores* in 1919, he became well-known for his BBC radio broadcasts on philosophy and taught with distinction at the universities of Manchester, Witwatersrand in South Africa, Balliol in Oxford, and the University College London, where he served as Grote Professor of Mind and Logic from 1928 to 1944. He joined the Edinburgh University faculty in 1944 and taught there until his retirement in 1958.

His major works are: *Freedom in the Modern World* (1932); *Interpreting the Universe* (1933); *The Philosophy of Communism* (1933); *Creative Society: A Study of the Relation of Christianity to Communism* (1935); *Reason and Emotion* (1935); *The Structure of Religious Experience* (1936); *The Boundaries of Science: A Study in the Philosophy of Psychology* (1939); *The Conditions of Freedom* (1949); and his two Gifford Lectures, *The Self as Agent* (given in 1952 and published in 1957) and *Persons in Relation* (given in 1957 and published in 1961). See Brannon Hancock's biographical sketch, "John Macmurray," at The Gifford Lectures Online, at http://www.giffordlectures.org/lecturers/john-macmurray (accessed 16 December 2014).

23 Brannon Hancock, University of Glasgow, "The Self as Agent," at https://www.giffordlectures.org/books/persons-relation (accessed 9 February 2022).

24 *British Weekly: A Journal of Social and Christian Progress*, 7 November 1946.

25 "Arts Festival Launch," *The Scotsman*, 25 August 1947, 1. The Kirk's new openness to the arts reflected a widespread ecclesiastical surge in the interest in the arts that had developed during the war years.

26 Each year the Festival officially opened with a ceremony in the "Mother Kirk of Presbyterianism," St. Giles Cathedral in Edinburgh. The attempts by the Kirk to engage the arts were to prove significant in the 1960s when, against the contexts of decreasing religiosity and increasing secularization, representatives of the Kirk made efforts to maintain contact with the Scottish people, particularly the youth, through arts and media. Today the festival is called "The Fringe."

27 When the writer became a new faculty member at SWBTS in 1994, John Newport appeared in her doorway one afternoon bearing a large envelope containing his memoirs of travel. He thought they might be of interest and even useful someday. He was correct, particularly as this writer also became a lecturer on many trips to Great Britain and Europe in the years following. This collection of notes, numbering almost one hundred pages of text, is the source of many details contained in this chapter. See John Newport, "Memoirs," a copy in the hand of the writer and also in the Newport Papers, "Autobiographical Materials."
28 He wrote, "It is impossible for me to describe how much this work here and the experiences are meaning to me. My entire ministry and life will be enriched from now on out. It is a rare privilege and I do appreciate all you have done to help make it possible." See John Newport's handwritten letter to his parents dated 15 December 1946, "Family Letters," Newport Papers, Bullock's Newport Biography Reference Box, The Texas Collection.
29 See Newport's letter to Eddie Belle and his parents, dated 28 December 1946, Newport Papers, Bullock's Newport Biography Reference Box, The Texas Collection.
30 See Newport's letter to his parents dated 5 January 1947, Newport Papers, Bullock's Newport Biography Reference Box, The Texas Collection. Professors W. J. Martin, Oliver Barclay, Donald Wiseman, and others founded Tyndale House in 1946 as a research and training center for biblical studies with the overarching aim of providing Bible scholars and Bible scholarship for the building up of the global church. Sir Norman Anderson (1908–1994), a Cambridge Trinity College law graduate, had served as a missionary to Egypt before serving with distinction in the British military during World War II. He returned to Cambridge at the end of the war and served from 1946 to 1949 as the first warden of Tyndale House. He was immediately recruited to lecture on Islamic law at the universities of Cambridge and London and, in 1949, accepted the position of full-time lecturer at the School of Oriental and African Studies (SOAS) in London. He became the head of the law department there from 1953 to 1971 and, simultaneously, professor of Oriental Laws and director of Advanced Legal Studies until his retirement in 1973.
31 Although John had taken German in preparation for his Th.D. and had finished an intensive course on theological German at the University of Edinburgh, Thomas Torrance had recommended further study with Frau Dr. Dück-Tobler. The people in the region of Basel spoke Swiss-German, but the lectures at the university, newspapers, and radio programs were in High German. Frau Dück-Tobler took John into her home, on the edge of the Black Forest, for two weeks. John had five lessons in German and one in French each day. Hers was an immersion program of travel and study. She took him to churches, where he would listen to and then report on the

content of the sermons, to restaurants at noon, where he would order his food, and to cities, such as Bern, where she made him translate to her in English what the tour guides said in German about the historical sites they visited. He said of her, "I believe Frau Dück-Tobler was the best teacher that I ever had on any subject." Even after he moved into the Theological *Alumneum*, John continued to take German lessons from her on the weekends; see John Newport's personal letters to Eddie Belle and his parents from this period, "Family Letters," Newport Papers, Bullock's Newport Biography Reference Box, The Texas Collection.

32 Cullman was born in Strasbourg when that city was part of Germany and studied classical philology and theology at the seminary there. Upon graduation in 1926, he accepted the assistant professorship post, one that Albert Schweitzer had once held. In 1930, he became a full professor of New Testament and began to teach early church studies as well. In 1938, he began to teach at Basel Reformed Seminary and, a decade later, added teaching theology at the Sorbonne in Paris to his academic schedule. Cullman established a theological dialogue between Lutherans and Roman Catholics and was so well respected that he was invited to observe the Second Vatican Council (1962–1965). In 1999, following his death, Cullman was honored by the World Council of Churches for his ecumenical work. Among his most important works are: *Baptism in the New Testament* (1954); *Immortality of the Soul or Resurrection of the Dead? The Witness of the New Testament* (1958); *Christ and Time* (1964); *The Christology of the New Testament* (1967); and *Salvation in History* (1967).

33 Martin Nieden, Newport's roommate at the theological hostel where he lodged, had been involved in the Hitler Youth Corps before his dramatic conversion and call to ministry in the Lutheran tradition. From Nieden, who had immersed himself in every form of occult and Satanism in his early years in Hitler's army, Newport was introduced in their many dialogue sessions to the subjects of black magic and the darker side of the occult. See Newport, *New Age Movement*, xii–xiii; see also John Newport's letter to his parents dated 28 April 1947, Newport Papers, Bullock's Newport Biography Reference Box, The Texas Collection.

34 Karl Barth was born in Basel to Johann Friedrich "Fritz" and Anna Barth. His scholar-pastor father was also a theology professor who was greatly interested in philosophy and influenced his son greatly. Reared in Bern, Barth was trained in theology, absorbing classical nineteenth-century liberalism from 1904 to 1909 at the universities of Berne, Berlin, Tübingen, and Marburg under Adolf von Harnack and others. He became a pastor in 1909 in Geneva and, in 1911, in Switzerland in Safenwil. He then became a professor and taught in Göttingen (1921–1925), Munster (1925–1930), and Bonn (1930–1935) in Germany. As a young scholar, he was influenced by Søren Kierkegaard's writings and began to change his own thinking in

response. He joined Emil Brunner, Eberhard Grisebach, and Rudolf Bultmann in a new movement called "Dialectical Theology," which rejected the doctrines of nineteenth-century liberalism and reevaluated the teachings of the Reformation.

Barth left Germany in 1935 after he had written his Barmen Declaration, voicing his conviction that the German churches should resist allegiance to any power other than God. After mailing this document directly to Adolf Hitler, Barth refused to swear allegiance to *Der Führer*, resigned his post at the University of Bonn, and returned home to Basel, where he taught theology at the university from 1935 to 1962. During World War II, Barth became, with his student, Dietrich Bonhöeffer, the leader of the "Confessing Church" that resisted Hitler's aims.

Barth is famous for his *Der Römerbrief* or *Epistle to the Romans* (1919–1921), in which he breaks from his former theological stances, and his magnum opus, the thirteen-volume, six-million-word, nine-hundred-page *Kirchliche Dogmatik* or *Church Dogmatics* (1932–1967), which addresses the four major doctrines of Revelation, God, Creation, and Atonement or Reconciliation. In his later years, Barth taught at Princeton Theological Seminary, Union Theological Seminary, the University of Chicago, and San Francisco Theological Seminary. His students, Thomas Torrance, Reinhold Niebuhr, and others became the premier theologians of Europe in the rest of the twentieth century. See Eberhard Busch, *Karl Barth: His Life from Letters and Autobiographical Texts* (Eugene, Ore.: Wipf & Stock, 2005). John wrote home that Barth and Cullman did not get along well at the time.

35 Emil Brunner was born and reared in Winterthur, near Zurich, and was educated at the universities of Zurich and Berlin, earning his doctorate in theology from the University of Zurich in the year 1913. He pastored from 1916 to 1924 in the mountainous Swiss Canton of Glarus, near where the Swiss Reformer Ulrich Zwingli (1481–1531) had also served as minister. Brunner had also spent a year in New York, studying at Union Theological Seminary. He then published a second, postgraduate dissertation, and in 1924 won the faculty position of professor of systematic and practical theology at Zurich, which he held until his retirement in 1953. Among Brunner's most important works include: his renunciation of the nineteenth-century liberal theology of Friedrich Schleiermacher, *Mysticism and the Word* (1924); *The Mediator* (1927); *God and Man* (1930); *The Divine Imperative* (1932); *Man in Revolt* and *Truth as Encounter* (1937); *Philosophy of Religion from the Standpoint of Protestant Theology* (1937); *Revelation and Reason: The Christian Doctrine of Faith and Knowledge* (1946); *Scandal of Christianity* (1951); and his life's work, *Dogmatics*, in three volumes (1946–1960).

36 See Newport, *Life's Ultimate Questions*, vii–xi.

37 Carl Jung was born in Kasswil, Switzerland, to a Swiss Reformed pastor and his wife, Paul and Emilie Preiswerk. Paul later lost his faith, and

Emilie became a follower of the occult. Carl read philosophy as a youth and attended the universities of Basel (1895–1900) and Zurich (1900–1902) in order to earn his medical degree to become a psychiatrist. He was appointed to the staff of Burgholzli Asylum, attached to the University of Zurich, under the directorship of Eugen Bleuler, a founder of the study of mental illness. Jung then met Sigmund Freud, with whom he collaborated between 1907 and 1912, before the break in their relationship that stemmed, in part, from disagreements over their divergent views concerning the bases of neurosis. Jung went on to differentiate attitude types of people into introverts and extroverts, upon which the later Myers-Briggs Type Indicator (MBTI), a psychometric instrument, was developed. He published *Psychologische Typen* (1921), outlining his theory of psychological types. Perhaps the best-known and accepted collection of Jung's published writings in English is found in Herbert Read, Michael Fordham, and Gerhard Adler, eds., *The Collected Works of C. G. Jung*, trans. R. F. C. Hull, 20 vols., 2nd ed. (Princeton: Princeton University Press, 1966–1979).

38 See Aniela Jaffe's foreword in Carl Jung, *Memories, Dreams, Reflections*, ed. Aniela Jaffe, trans. Clara Winston (New York: Vintage Books by Knopf-Doubleday, 1961), x. This is the personal memoir that Jung began in 1957 at age eighty-one. Some chapters of this book were written in his own hand and others by Jaffe following conversations they had. Jaffe continued writing this volume until Jung died in 1961, after which it was published in the same year.

39 In John's Diary Letters home to his parents, written in his spidery hand on onionskin paper, John bragged about little Martha Ellen's progress as a baby. In almost every letter he would remark about her. On Saturday, 13 September 1947, for example, he wrote, "E. B. went tonight [to hear the Vienna Philharmonic Orchestra] and I watched the baby and studied." The next day, he said after preaching the evening service, "M. E. is grand and developing rapidly. You will hardly recognize her. We were anxious to get back home to see her. She has stolen all hearts here." See John Newport, letter to his parents, 13–14 September 1947, in Newport Papers, "Autobiographical Materials," Bullock's Newport Biography Reference Box, The Texas Collection.

40 As a teenager, the writer toured this ship and had dinner aboard. Queen Mary sailed on her maiden voyage on 27 May 1936 and ferried Allied troops during World War II. She was officially retired from service in 1967 and moored at Long Beach in Southern California. Even in her aging years, this ship was beautifully appointed and elegant, giving a glimpse of its glory days of passenger and military service.

41 For the next three years, John wrote his dissertation while pastoring and teaching, finishing his degree while living in the United States. He then returned to Scotland in April through May 1953 to defend his research and attend his graduation at New College. This was the occasion upon which, as

he passed through London on his way home, he stood in the crowd, catching a view of the coronation procession of Queen Elizabeth II, on 2 June 1953, from Westminster Abbey to Buckingham Palace.

42 John Newport's note to his parents dated 29 October 1948 included the news that the due date for Frank's birth had come and gone. "I will call when the great event takes place," he said. He also gave a good report of the church's vitality, citing the annual budget of $104,000; see Newport Papers, Bullock's Newport Biography Reference Box, The Texas Collection.

43 John spent many hours studying both texts in the library of the University of Tulsa and the artifacts and displays in the halls and archives of the Gilcrease Museum in Tulsa, one of the finest museums dedicated to Native American Indian culture in the nation.

44 Oral Roberts was born in abject poverty in Pontotoc County, Oklahoma, to Ellis and Claudius Priscilla Irwin Roberts. His mother claimed to have been of Cherokee descent, and Oral grew up as a member of the Choctaw Nation. Roberts attended the universities of Oklahoma Baptist and then Phillips for two years each, but without earning a degree from either. He preached part-time in churches and from a large tent with folding chairs for many years until 1947, when his ministry changed. At twenty-nine years of age, Roberts read verse 2 in the book of 3 John that, he said, meant that Christians were to be rich. The next day he bought a Buick, started a radio ministry, and reported that God appeared to him, telling him to heal the sick. Roberts continued his tent revivals and attracted millions of followers worldwide when he launched his television ministry in 1954 and began to conduct crusades of healing.

During his lifetime, Roberts claimed to have personally laid hands of healing on two million people. He founded Oral Roberts University in 1963 on 500 acres, located south of Tulsa, to which he eventually attached a medical school and hospital as well. Its prayer tower opened in 1967. Roberts published three volumes: *Oral Roberts' Life Story, as Told by Himself* (1952); *The Call: An Autobiography* (1972); and *Expect a Miracle: My Life and Ministry* (1995). See the more objective biography by David Edwin Harrell Jr., *Oral Roberts: An American Life* (Bloomington: Indiana University Press, 1985).

4 Widening Currents

1 The above events were sampled from Frank Wallis, ed., *Ribbons of Time: World History Year by Year Since 1492* (New York: Weidenfeld and Nicolson, 1988), 113–14; and *Readers' Digest Book of Facts* (Pleasantville, N.Y.: Readers' Digest Association, 1987), 32–57.

2 While this statement is true, it is not altogether complete. The Texas Baptist Education Society petitioned the congress of the Republic of Texas to

charter a Baptist university in the fall of 1844. Republic President Anson Jones signed the act of Congress on 1 February 1845, officially establishing Baylor University. In 1844, the United States Congress agreed to annex the territory of Texas; thus, on 29 December 1845, Texas entered the United States as its twenty-eighth state. Baylor was indeed the first educational institution in Texas, but it was actually almost eleven months older than the state of Texas.

3   John P. Newport, "Who Is a Faithful Teacher?" *Baptist Training Union Magazine*, June 1949. He sent this manuscript to be published just about the time he and Eddie Belle made their move to Texas.

4   Russell Dilday, "Practical Apologist: Faith Seeking Understanding," *Southwestern Journal of Theology* 29, no. 3 (1987): 12. In his lifetime, Dilday would come to know Newport in many relational roles: student to teacher; pastor to denominational leader; president to professor; and colleague to colleague in theological education administration. Three decades later, Dilday invited Newport to return to the faculty of Southwestern Baptist Theological Seminary in January 1979 to become vice president of academic affairs and provost in August of the same year.

5   New Orleans Baptist Theological Seminary had originally been founded by the SBC in 1917 as "Baptist Bible Institute," an undergraduate training school modeled after the Moody Bible Institute. In 1946, it had been renamed "New Orleans Baptist Theological Seminary" and was now offering graduate-level training. Baylor had offered to raise Newport's annual salary of $6,000 by fifty dollars per month if he would stay, but John and Eddie Belle were praying through the decision as late as April 1951. John longed to concentrate on a single academic discipline instead of "so many fields," and the New Orleans position offered John an eight-month contract so that he could preach revivals, write, and travel during the summers. Large apartments were also available for faculty near the campus. The faculty addition of John Newport, still fresh from his study in Scotland and the Continent and on the cusp of finishing his dissertation, was an indication that the seminary was deepening its faculty scholarship. See John Newport's letter to his parents dated 12 April 1951 in Newport Papers, Bullock's Newport Biography Reference Box, The Texas Collection.

6   The Evangeline tradition, which fascinated Newport, has its seeds in the Acadian expulsion from their homeland in Nova Scotia by the British between 1755 and 1763. Some of the Acadians made their way to New Orleans, bringing their culture intact. Nathaniel Hawthorne and a friend told this tale over supper to Henry Wadsworth Longfellow in May 1844, after which Longfellow wrote his famous 1847 poem, "Evangeline: A Tale of Acadie," which became an overnight sensation and sold five thousand copies in the same year. The tale is told of Evangeline Bellefontaine and Gabriel Lajeunesse, two young Acadian people torn apart on their wedding day by

the British deportation. Evangeline travels with a group of the Acadians to Louisiana. After a lifetime of fruitless searching, she later finds Gabriel on his deathbed in Philadelphia, where they are united with a last kiss before he dies. See Carl A. Brasseaux, *In Search of Evangeline: Birth and Evolution of the Evangeline Myth* (Thibodaux, La.: Blue Heron Press, 1988).

7   See John Newport's letter to his parents dated 18 December 1951 in Newport Papers, Bullock's Newport Biography Reference Box, The Texas Collection. See also his "New Developments in New Testament Theology," *Review and Expositor* 49 (1952): 41–56.

8   Dewey had lived on Fifth Avenue for many years. His funeral was held on Wednesday, 4 June 1952, at 1:00 p.m. at the Community Church of New York on East Thirty-fifth Street. At his death at ninety-two years of age, Dewey had published more than one thousand books and articles in journals, hundreds of them after he retired in 1930. Of his forty books are the influential *Democracy and Education* (1916); *Human Nature and Conduct* (1922); *Experience and Nature* (1925); *The Public and its Problems* (1927); *Arts as Experience* (1934); *A Common Faith* (1934); and *Knowing and the Known* (1949). In 1991, Southern Illinois University Press published his collected writings in three multiple-volume sets. See his obituary from the *New York Times*, 2 June 1952, http://www.nytimes.com/learning/general/onthisday/bday/1020.html (accessed 30 June 2015).

9   Robert A. Baker, *Tell the Generations Following: A History of Southwestern Baptist Theological Seminary, 1908–1983* (Nashville: Broadman, 1983), 306. Southeastern Baptist Theological Seminary (SEBTS) was the fourth of the six SBC seminaries to be founded by the denomination. The Southern Baptist Theological Seminary (1859), Southwestern Baptist Theological Seminary (1908), and New Orleans Baptist Theological Seminary (1917) preceded it, and the establishment of Midwestern Baptist Theological Seminary (1956) and Golden Gate Baptist Theological Seminary (1963) followed it.

10 The first president of Southwestern Baptist Theological Seminary was its founder, Benajah Harvey Carroll (1843–1914), who served from its inception in 1908 to his death. He was a pastor and professor of the English Bible. Lee Rutland Scarborough (1870–1945), hand-selected by Carroll to follow him, was the second president and professor of evangelism and served from 1915 to 1942. Eldred Douglas Head (1892–1964) served as professor of evangelism and the third president from 1942 to 1953. During his tenure, the beautiful, central columned B. H. Carroll Memorial Building, housing the rotunda, new chapel, library, and School of Theology, was erected in 1949. The next year, the J. M. Price Hall was finished to house the School of Christian Education. The faculty was already legendary, having toiled together in extreme circumstances as the seminary weathered its move to Fort Worth and the construction of its first two campus buildings, Fort Worth Hall and the Women's Missionary Training Center, despite dire financial, physical,

housing, and transportation needs. For campus improvements in this period, see Baker, *Tell the Generations Following*, 290–94. Dr. Head retired because of his health. J. Howard Williams (1894–1958) became the fourth president, taking office in 1953 until his unexpected death five years later.

11   The accessions and tenures of faculty members from this section were taken from Baker, *Tell the Generations Following*, 191–94 and 282–84.

12   The writer heard many fascinating stories about this era in the School of Theology faculty lounge of SWBTS between 1995 and 2005, when a dozen or more professors from this period, at that time distinguished professors with decades of experience, would sit at a lunch table and reminisce. The Southwestern Seminary campus sat atop a hill beneath which bubbled a spring. The limestone aquifer was a boon to the seminary, which drilled a well to capture the water, but a nemesis in other ways. For example, during the 1950s, the perimeter sycamore trees were planted on campus, along with many oaks. It was necessary to use dynamite to blow deep holes in the limestone just below the soil's surface in preparation for planting. Tan, roll-down window shades hung limply across the windows of the school's unairconditioned offices and classrooms. Each time the dynamite blast exploded, professors ceased to lecture, the window shades swayed inward, and debris and dust would rattle against the shades and settle on the students' paper notepads. William B. Tolar remembers well the blasting operations that occurred during his first semester at seminary. See *Proceedings*, Baptist General Convention of Texas (BGCT), 1913, 23; see also the recollections of Kevin Walker, director of landscaping and later of support services, between the years 1982 and 2005 in Newport Papers, Bullock's Newport Biography Reference Box, The Texas Collection. Walker's vision and team transformed the campus into a lush and beautiful garden park. During his tenure across two decades, Kevin employed more than one thousand student workers and landscapers, who took pride in making the seminary campus one of the attractions of the Fort Worth-Dallas area, winning garden club awards and special recognition from the City of Fort Worth.

13   Baker, *Tell the Generations Following*, 312. This number includes sixty-seven students who took classes in two schools at the same time.

14   Southern Baptist Convention, *Annual*, 1952, 368–69. President Head's Seminary Report to the Convention, the last before his death, pled for resources to meet the "imperative, clamant, and inescapable needs" of the seminary, perhaps the greatest of which was student housing. No new provision had been made in more than twenty-five years, and 64 percent of students were living off-campus.

15   Stewart A. Newman, *W. T. Conner: Theologian of the Southwest* (Nashville: Broadman, 1964), 75; see also Baker, *Tell the Generations Following*, 333. In his inaugural address, Head deplored the fact that the seminary was using a "packhorse method of teaching, where professors had as many as 180 students

in each class, and more than 900 wives were unable to attend class and receive training because there was no place for them to leave their children."
16 During this time, John also published a brief article, "Philosophy of History," *Southwestern News* (June 1954): 6.
17 Newport, "Skeptic and Apologist," 36–37, 52; and Norman Wade Cox, ed., "Authority and the Bible," in *Encyclopedia of Southern Baptists*, vol. 1 (Nashville: Broadman, 1958), 161–62. The SBC controversy concerning biblical authority would break open in 1961 following the publication of Ralph Elliott's *The Message of Genesis* (Nashville: Broadman, 1961). Some leaders criticized the doctrinal interpretations of the book as being liberal and subverting Southern Baptist views on the inspiration of the Scriptures. See Leon McBeth's brief summary of this period in *Baptist Heritage: Four Centuries of Baptist Witness* (Nashville: Broadman, 1987), 674–75, 679–80.
18 See the "Memorial Resolution," passed by the SBC, https://www.sbc.net/resource-library/resolutions/resolution-on-memorial-resolution/ (accessed 9 February 2022).
19 Robert Slater was born in England, served in the military during World War II in Burma, and survived the long retreating march from Burma to Assam. He taught at Huron College, London, Ontario, and McGill universities before coming to Harvard and breaking new ground in the study of world religions. He became known as a Buddhist scholar, writing many books among which are: *Letters to a Non-Christian* (1950); *Paradox and Nirvana: A Study of Religious Ultimates, with Special Reference to Burmese Buddhism* (1951); and *World Religions* (1966). He retired to the province of Quebec and then taught at Benares Hindu University of Ceylon, the Hebrew University in Jerusalem, and in Australia, Uganda, and New Zealand. He later helped to facilitate one of John Newport's sabbatical leaves at Benares Hindu University, in Benares, India, in the summer of 1965.
20 Stendahl was born in Stockholm, was educated at Uppsala University in Sweden, and wrote his dissertation on the Dead Sea Scrolls. He joined the faculty at Harvard Divinity School in 1954, and in 1961, at a meeting of the American Psychological Association, turned then-current New Testament studies on its head by asserting that the idea of an angst-ridden Paul would have been foreign to the first three centuries of the church. Instead of being paralyzed by inner wrestling with his conscience, Paul dealt with profound theological problems concerning Jewish law and the meaning of sin, he claimed. Stendahl was, perhaps, most famous for his article, "The Apostle Paul and the Introspective Conscience of the West," and subsequent book, *Paul among Jews and Gentiles* (1977), which changed the way many theologians viewed Paul. After serving as director of the Shalom Hartman Center of Religious Studies in Jerusalem, he retired and returned to Harvard as the Mellon Professor of Divinity Emeritus and also taught at Brandeis University. He wrote *Scrolls and the New Testament* (1958); *The Bible and the Role of*

Women (1966); *What the Spirit is Saying to the Churches: Essays* (1975); and *Meanings, the Bible as Document and Guide* (1984). See Stendahl's obituary, *New York Times*, 16 April 2008.

21 George Buttrick was born on the Northumberland coast of Seaham Harbour in the United Kingdom and graduated in 1915 from Victoria University in Manchester with a degree in philosophy. He immigrated to the United States and pastored Congregationalist churches in Quincy, Illinois, and Rutland, Vermont, before accepting the pulpit of First Presbyterian Church in Buffalo. In 1927, Buttrick took the pulpit of the Madison Avenue Presbyterian Church in New York City until 1955. From 1955 to 1965, he was the Plummer Professor of Christian Morals and Preacher to the University at Harvard. In his later years, he taught homiletics on the faculties of Garrett Seminary, Davidson College, Vanderbilt University, and the Southern Baptist Seminary in Louisville. Author of twelve books, he was a model preacher, the synthesis of his pastor's heart, scholar's mind, and preacher's passion. When he died in the year 1980, he still had his latest sermon on the desk and a stack of theological books on his bedside table. See George A. Buttrick's obituary, "George Arthur Buttrick, 87, Dies; Presbyterian Pastor and Scholar," *New York Times*, 24 January 1980.

22 Samuel Howard Miller was a student at the Massachusetts Institute of Technology from 1917 to 1918, graduated from Colgate University with a B.Th. in 1923 and a D.D. in 1953, and received honorary doctorates from seven colleges and universities. He was ordained to the Baptist ministry in 1923. He served churches in New Jersey from 1923 to 1935, after which he became pastor of Old Cambridge Baptist Church in Massachusetts until 1959. He served as adjunct professor of philosophy of religion at the Andover Newton Theological School from 1951 to 1958, was a lecturer at Harvard Divinity School from 1954 to 1958, professor of pastoral theology from 1958 to 1959, and the dean of Harvard's Divinity School from 1959 to 1968. He served as the secretary to the Commission on Worship and the Arts for the National Council of Churches and was a fellow of the Academy of Arts and Sciences. During his career, he wrote *The Life of the Soul* (1951); *The Life of the Church* (1953); *The Great Realities* (1955); *Prayers for Daily Use* (1957); *The Dilemma of Modern Belief* (1963); and *Man the Believer in an Age of Unbelief* (1968). His final work, *Religion in a Technical Age*, was published on 20 March 1968, the day of his death. Under his leadership, the Divinity School sponsored the first major conference of Roman Catholic and Protestant scholars in 1963 in the spirit of the Second Vatican Council. A similar conference of Jewish and Christian scholars was held in 1967.

23 John Adams, perhaps the most famous Unitarian Universalist theologian of the twentieth century, was born the son of a Plymouth Brethren preacher in Ritzville, Washington, and graduated from the University of Minnesota (1924) and Harvard Divinity School (1927). He then earned his Ph.D. from

the University of Chicago in 1946. He became a Unitarian minister in Salem (1927–1934) and Wellesley Hills (1934–1935), both in Massachusetts. He spent much time in Germany during the 1930s, befriending Karl Barth and Albert Schweitzer, before joining the faculty of the Meadville Lombard Theological School in Chicago (1937–1956). In 1956, he was elected as professor of Christian ethics at Harvard, a post he held until his retirement in 1968, after which time he taught again at Andover and at Meadville Lombard until his death in 1994. Adams was elected to the American Academy of Arts and Sciences in 1958 and, in 1962, helped to found the Society for the Arts, Religion, and Culture. His books include: *Being Human Religiously: Selected Essays in Religion and Society* (1976); *The Prophethood of All Believers* (1986); *An Examined Faith: Social Context and Religious Commitment* (1991); and Adams' autobiography, *Not Without Dust and Heat: A Memoir* (1995).

24 Harvey Gallagher Cox Jr. was born in Malvern, Pennsylvania and earned degrees at the University of Pennsylvania (1951), Yale University Divinity School (1957), and a Ph.D. in philosophy of religion from Harvard Divinity School (1963). A Baptist minister, Cox served on the faculties of Andover Newton Theological School (1957–1965) and Harvard Divinity School from 1965 until his retirement in 2009. Included among his fourteen books are: *Secular City* (1965); *Religion in the Secular City: Toward a Postmodern Theology* (1985); *When Jesus Came to Harvard: Making Moral Choices Today* (2004); and *The Future of Faith* (2009), the latter published the year he retired.

25 Joseph Fletcher was born in New Jersey and earned degrees at West Virginia University (1929) and Berkeley Divinity School the same year. As a fiery social activist, he was arrested as a young man in the coalfields of West Virginia for working toward union organization and was beaten unconscious twice for speaking for this cause at union rallies. Senator Joseph McCarthy even accused Fletcher of being a communist, calling him the "Red Churchman." Fletcher taught Christian ethics at the Episcopal Divinity School at Harvard in Cambridge between 1944 and 1970. After renouncing Christianity in the late 1960s and becoming a self-proclaimed atheist, he then became the first professor of medical ethics and cofounded and directed the program in Biology and Society at the University of Virginia Medical School from 1970 until he retired in 1977. He was one of the signers of the *Humanist Manifesto II* (1973) and served as president of the Euthanasia Society of America (now Society for the Right to Die) from 1974 to 1976. Among his eleven books are: *Morals and Medicine* (advocating euthanasia, 1954); *Situation Ethics* (1966); *The Situation Ethics Debate* (with Harvey Cox in 1968); *The Ethics of Genetic Control: Ending Reproductive Roulette* (1974); and *Humanhood: Essays in Biomedical Ethics* (advocating eugenic cloning, 1979). See his obituary by Peter Steinfels in *New York Times*, 30 October 1991 at http://www.nytimes.com/1991/10/30/us/dr-joseph-f-fletcher-86-dies-pioneer-in-field-of-medical-ethics.html (accessed 18 February 2015).

26 Paul L. Lehman was born in Baltimore, son of a German Protestant pastor, Timothy Lehman, who migrated from Ukraine and became president of Elmhurst College in Illinois. Paul was educated at Ohio State University and Union Theological Seminary, where he earned his doctorate in 1936. Lehman taught first at Elmhurst and Wellesley colleges before joining the faculty of Princeton Theological Seminary where he taught ethics from 1947 to 1956. He was appointed Florence Corliss Lamont Professor of Divinity at Harvard Divinity School in 1956, where he served until 1963. He returned to Union Theological Seminary to teach systematic theology until his retirement in 1974. Having studied with Reinhold Niebuhr and Karl Barth in Germany, Lehman focused on the Christian-Marxist dialogue, war and peace, and human sexuality, steering a middle road between "situation ethics" and Kant's absolute rules, categorical imperatives, and moral law. Lehman also opposed McCarthyism and became the founding chairman of the Emergency Civil Liberties Committee in 1951, formed by 150 clergymen, educators, and professionals to advocate for the safeguarding of constitutional rights. Among his several books are *Ethics in a Christian Context* (1963) and *The Decalogue and a Human Future* (2009).

27 Following the publication of *The Cost of Discipleship* in 1937, Bonhoeffer had been invited by Union Theological Seminary in June 1939 to lecture in the United States. Almost immediately after he arrived, however, he felt that leaving his homeland had been the wrong decision. He wrote to Reinhold Niebuhr that he did not believe it would be right for him to participate in the restoration of Christian Germany following the war if he were not willing to endure the suffering of his people with them during the difficult years. He determined to return home and continued to lead the resistance movement, which went underground upon his return. Bonhoeffer was arrested in April 1943 and was allegedly charged with participating in a plot to take the life of Adolf Hitler. He was held at Tegel prison near Berlin for nearly eighteen months and then, in October 1944, was taken to the Gestapo prison in Prinz-Albrecht-Strasse, Berlin, and then to Regensburg on 3 April 1945. Finally, he was transferred to the Flossenbürg concentration camp, where he was hanged in a cell on 9 April 1945. This was just two weeks before Allied forces liberated the camp, three weeks before Hitler committed suicide on 30 April, and one month before the Germans surrendered on 7 May 1945. See Eric Metaxas, *Bonhoeffer: Prophet, Pastor, Martyr, Spy* (Danvers, Mass.: Thomas Nelson, 2011).

28 G. Ernest Wright, son of a Presbyterian minister, was born in Ohio, where he earned his undergraduate degree at Wooster and his theology degree from McCormick Theological Seminary in 1934. He did further study with William Foxwell Albright, a founder of the American Schools of Oriental Research (ASOR) at Johns Hopkins University, earning M.A. (1936) and Ph.D. (1937) degrees. He taught at McCormick University from 1939 to 1958

before joining the faculty of Harvard Divinity School in 1958. Here he taught Old Testament and was also curator of the Semitic Museum from 1961 until his death of a heart attack in 1974. Wright led three significant digs: The Drew-McCormick Archaeological Expedition to Shechem (1956–1974); the Hebrew Union College Expedition to Tell Gezer (1964–1965); and the Joint American Expedition to Idalion, Cyprus (1971–1974). He also founded the periodical *The Biblical Archaeologist* (1938–1997), now called *Near Eastern Archaeology Magazine*, published by ASOR.

29 Harvard Divinity School claims that the Hancock Professorship is the third oldest university chair in the United States. Like Wright before him, Frank Cross was also the son of a Presbyterian minister, but was born and reared in Birmingham, Alabama. He earned degrees from Maryville College (1942) and McCormick Theological Seminary (1946). He studied with William Albright at Johns Hopkins University, earned his Ph.D. in 1950, and attended Harvard for a M.A. degree in 1958. In his later years, he was awarded a D.Phil. from the Hebrew University in Jerusalem in 1984 and a D.Sc. from the University of Lethbridge, Alberta, Canada, in 1990. He served as professor at Johns Hopkins University (1949–1950), Wellesley College (1950–1951), McCormick University (1951–1957), and served on the faculty at Harvard Divinity School from 1957–1992, after which he held the title Emeritus. He served as curator of the Semitic Museum before Wright, from 1958–1961, and director after Wright's death, from 1974–87.

He supervised more than 100 dissertations, including those of Emanuel Tov, John J. Collins, William G. Dever, Lawrence Stager, Richard Elliott Friedman, Hector Avalos, and Mark S. Smith. His lifetime work, however, from June 1953 onward, was in translating the Dead Sea Scrolls, particularly the manuscripts of Qumran's Cave 4. He was one of only two Americans to do so and published many books arising from this work, among them *The Ancient Library of Qumran* (third edition published in 1995).

30 John Wild was educated at Chicago and Harvard universities, earning his Ph.D. in 1926 from Chicago University. He taught for a year at the University of Michigan before joining the faculty of Harvard Divinity School in 1927, where he served until 1961. He then moved to Northwest University, where he served as chair of the philosophy department and where, at that time, phenomenology and existentialist scholarship were exploring the leading edges of the discipline. After just two years, Wild moved on to Yale University from 1963 to 1969 and then to the University of Florida, where he taught until his death. He authored nine volumes, including *Plato's Theory of Man: An Introduction to the Realistic Philosophy of Culture* (1946); *Introduction to Realistic Philosophy* (1948); *The Challenge of Existentialism* (1955); and *Christianity and Existentialism* (1963).

31 Paul Tillich, the German American theologian considered one of the most influential theologians of the twentieth century, was born in Stazeddel, in

Brandenburg. His father was a Prussian Lutheran pastor, and when Paul was only a child, the family moved to Poland, and then to Berlin, where Paul grew up and attended school. He attended the universities of Berlin (1904), Tübingen (1905), and Halle-Wittenberg (1905–1907), and then earned his Ph.D. from the University of Breslau (1911) and a Licentiate of Theology degree at Halle-Wittenberg (1912). He was licensed as a Lutheran minister in 1912 and served as a chaplain in the German Imperial Army during WWI. He taught theology at the universities of Berlin, Marburg, Dresden, Leipzig, and Frankfurt between 1919 and 1933, when he came under the scrutiny of Hitler's Nazi regime. Tillich was fired in 1933 from his teaching post and, due to the influence of Reinhold Niebuhr, was invited to teach at Union Theological Seminary in New York. He taught theology at Union from 1933 to 1955, at which time he was appointed to the faculty of Harvard Divinity School and was internationally acclaimed for his philosophical theology courses and writing. He moved to the University of Chicago faculty in 1962 and remained there until his death in 1965. He is perhaps most noted for his three-volume *Systematic Theology* (1951–1963); *The Courage to Be* (1952); and *Dynamics of Faith* (1957). See John Paul Newport, *Paul Tillich*, ed. Bob Patterson, Makers of the Modern Theological Mind Series (Waco, Tex.: Word Books, 1984). Newport was a constant friend of Tillich and found his work to be significant to evangelicals. He categorically denied the rumors of Tillich's infidelity, possessing in his papers proof of Tillich's uprightness.

32 Huston Smith was born to missionary Methodist parents in Soochow, China, where he lived the first seventeen years of his life. Upon returning to America, he earned degrees from Central Methodist University and University of Chicago. He taught from 1944 to 1945 at the Denver University, and from 1947 to 1957 at Washington University in St. Louis, Missouri. In 1958, he was appointed as professor and chair of the philosophy department at Massachusetts Institute of Technology (MIT), where he served until 1973. He then moved to Syracuse University, where he served as the Thomas J. Watson Professor of Religion and Distinguished Professor of Philosophy until his retirement in 1983, after which he moved to Los Angeles and served as visiting professor of religious studies at University of California at Berkeley.

In 1962, he participated in the Harvard Center for Personality Research's "Harvard Project" and "March Chapel Experience" on Good Friday, directed by a student of Dr. Timothy Leary and Dr. Richard Alpert, just after arriving at MIT. This project's goal was to document the raising of spiritual awareness through the effect of entheogenic plants, most notably psilocybin mushrooms, and later mescaline and LSD—all of which were considered research chemicals at the time but were not illegal drugs. While Leary and Alpert (known later as Ram Dass) were eventually dismissed from Harvard in 1963 in the wake of these experiments, Smith continued exploring the religions and mystic traditions of the world, spending a decade each in the practice of

Vedanta, Zen Buddhism, and Sufi Islam. A lifelong Christian, he gave credit in later life to his parents, who "instilled in me a Christianity that was able to withstand the dominating secular culture of modernity." See Dana Sawyer, *Huston Smith: Wisdom-keeper, Living the World's Religions, the Authorized Biography of a 21st Century Spiritual Giant* (Louisville, Ky.: Fons Vitae, 2014). He is author of thirteen books, among them *The World's Religions*, first published as *The Religions of Man* (1958); *Why Religion Matters* (2001); *Cleansing the Doors of Perception: The Religious Significance of Entheogenic Plants and Chemicals* (2003); *The Soul of Christianity: Restoring the Great Tradition* (2005); and *Tales of Wonder: Adventures Chasing the Divine, An Autobiography* (2010).

33 Frank, John's firstborn son, remembers vividly this sabbatical. He was ten years old when he first saw New England. The family enjoyed car trips, museums, visits to the most famous ivy league campuses, and northeastern cultural events. Sometimes Frank accompanied his father to his academic appointments, days that meant a great deal to both Frank and his father.

5 The Long Rolling River

1 Virginia Woolf, *The Letters of Virginia Woolf, 1923–1928*, vol. 3, ed. Nigel Nicolson and Joanne Trautmann (Boston: Mariner Books, 1980), 516.
2 Frank Louis Mauldin, "John Paul Newport," in *Legacy of Southwestern*, 209–10. Two other Christian philosophy scholars would later join them in the work at Southwestern: Yandall Woodfin (1973–1994) and L. Russ Bush (1975–1989).
3 Mauldin, "John Paul Newport," in *Legacy of Southwestern*, 210.
4 John P. Newport, "Religion and Morals," *Baptist Student* 39 (1959): 21–33.
5 J. Howard Williams had served as president from 1953 to 1958 and died from a heart attack on 28 April, just weeks before John began his study year in Cambridge.
6 In 1959, by vote of the SBC, an enlargement was made to what was then Bylaw Seven, which called for both ordained and laypersons to make up the board of trustees of the seminaries, with not more than two-thirds to come from either category. During this time, many fine and faithful lay men and women trustees came to serve Southwestern and helped to achieve unprecedented growth, including Howard E. Butt Jr., William Fleming, Jenkins Garrett (who later served as seminary attorney), Gladys Luther (the first woman to serve on the board), and F. Howard Walsh. In fact, so many trustees also secured or gave private gifts and bequests that visible improvements were seen across the campus at almost every level.
7 Baker, *Tell the Generations Following*, 387.
8 New colleagues from the School of Religious Education, with whom John interacted less frequently in his early days at Southwestern, were Harvey

B. Hatcher, Communication Arts (1958); Harold T. Dill, Youth Education (1959); A. Donald Bell, Psychology and Human Relations (1951–1960, and after 1963); James D. Williams, Adult Education (1964); Jeroline Baker, Childhood Education (1964); Charles A. Tidwell, Church Administration (1965); LeRoy Ford, Foundations of Education (1966); Jack D. Terry Jr., Philosophy and History of Education (1969); Hazel M. Morris, Childhood Education (1971); Clark Dean, Social Work (1973); Theodore H. Dowell, Psychology and Human Relations (1973); Alva G. Parks, Educational Administration (1973); George R. Wilson Jr., Educational Administration (1973); Derrel R. Watkins, Social Work (1974); William G. Caldwell, Educational Administration (1976); Tommy L. Bridges, Educational Administration (1977); and Charles W. Ashby, Foundations of Education (1978).

The School of Church Music faculty added the following faculty members during this period: David P. Appleby, Piano (1960); Cecil M. Roper, Church Music (1960); David L. Conley, Music Theory (1961); Jack H. Coldiron, Voice (1963); T. W. Hunt, Piano and Organ (1963); Scotty W. Gray, Church Music (1966); Evelyn Phillips, Church Music Education (1948–1952, and after 1967); Phillip W. Sims, Music Bibliography and Librarian (1967); Virginia Seelig, Voice (1958–1968 teacher, faculty in 1969); William W. Colson, Music Theory and Composition (1971); A. Joseph King, Church Music Education (1976); Claude L. Bass, Music Theory and Composition (1977); and Albert L. Travis, Organ (1977). Newport attended seminary functions and served on institution-wide committees with these faculty members of the other schools as the years unfolded. Later, he would interact more frequently when he became vice president of academic affairs and provost. See Baker, *Tell the Generations Following*, for these faculty accession listings: Theology, 397; Religious Education, 400–401; and Church Music, 402.

9 Newport later added courses on Jewish theologies and philosophies after studying with the world's leading Jewish philosopher and theologian, Abraham Joshua Heschel, at Union Theological Seminary in New York City in 1965.

10 John Paul Newport, "Biblical Philosophy and the Modern Mind," *Baptist Faculty Paper* 6 (1963): 1–2, 4.

11 Discussion concerning Wright's "realism" follows. See also James K. Hoffmeier and Dennis R. Magary, eds., *Do Historical Matters Matter to Faith?* (Wheaton, Ill.: Crossway, 2012), 100–104, from which much of the above material on Albright and his influence upon Wright is derived.

12 The movement was first named by Brevard Childs, *Biblical Theology in Crisis* (Philadelphia: Westminster, 1970), cited in Hoffmeier, *Do Historical Matters Matter to Faith?* 100.

13 G. Ernest Wright, *The God Who Acts: Biblical Theology as Recital* (Naperville, Ill.: Alec R. Allenson, 1952), 38.

14 Those who agreed with Wright were Roland de Vaux (1903–1971), Dominican archaeologist, historian, and theologian, and Gordon Wenhem (1943–present). As director of the *Ecole Biblique*, a French Catholic theological school in east Jerusalem, de Vaux led the team that initially worked to discover the Dead Sea Scrolls. He was charged with overseeing research on the five subsequent seasons of excavations of the Scrolls, even as his team also excavated the ancient site of Khirbet Qumran (1951–1956) as well as several caves near Qumran, northwest of the Dead Sea. He also worked with Kathleen Kenyon (1906–1978), the famous archaeologist from Oxford who worked on unearthing Jericho. From 1961 to 1963, she and de Vaux worked together in Jerusalem. See Jacques Briend, "Roland de Vaux," in *Encyclopedia of the Dead Sea Scrolls*, vol. 1, ed. Lawrence H. Schiffman and James C. VanderKam (Oxford: Oxford University Press, 2000), 202–3. See also de Vaux's "Method in the Study of Early Hebrew History," in *The Bible in Modern Scholarship*, ed. J. P. Hyatt (Nashville: Abingdon Press, 1965), 16.

As of 2020, Wenham still teaches as senior professor of Old Testament at the University of Gloucestershire, England. He served on the translation oversight committee for the English Standard Version Bible. Of his writings, Tremper Longman said that Wenham was "one of the finest evangelical commentators today." See Tremper Longman, *Old Testament Commentary Survey*, 2nd ed. (Grand Rapids: Baker, 1999), 64. See also Gordon Wenham, *History, Criticism, and Faith: Four Explanatory Studies*, ed. Colin Brown (Leicester: InterVarsity Press, 1976). One who took exception with the work of Wright was Childs, *Biblical Theology in Crisis*.

15 Mauldin, "John Paul Newport," in *Legacy of Southwestern*, 210.
16 These statements were made to Frank Mauldin, in John's later life, as Frank interviewed him for the chapter he wrote, "John Paul Newport," in *Legacy of Southwestern*, 210.
17 See John Newport's recollections in the preface to his *Life's Ultimate Questions*, xvi.
18 John Newport's articles aimed at university students were: "Man Seeking God: Religion," *Baptist Student* (November 1960): 7–9; "Called to Life Commitment," *Young People's Teacher* (April 1962): 4–5; "Is the Theory of Human Evolution in Conflict with the Christian Faith?" *Baptist Student* 42 (1963): 5–7; "The Arts and Their Worth," *Baptist Student* 42 (1963): 4–8, 33; "Some Thoughts about Miracles," *Baptist Student* (May 1965): 2–4, 39; and "Student Shapers," *Baptist Student* (December 1967): 14–20. For the general audience, he wrote, "Christianity and Contemporary Art Forms," *Baptist Program* (August 1963): 10–11; and "Speaking with Tongues," *Home Missions* (May 1965): 7–9, 21–26, published in Portuguese as "*Falando em Linguas*," *Home Missions* (May 1965).

Newport's scholarly articles were: "Biblical Interpretation and Eschatological-Holy History," *Southwestern Journal of Theology* 4 (1961):

83–110; "Communicating the Gospel through Contemporary Art Forms," *Journal of the Southern Baptist Church Music Conference* (1962–1963): 18–25; "The Unique Nature of the Bible in Light of Recent Attacks," *Southwestern Journal of Theology* 6 (1963): 93–106; "Biblical Philosophy and the Modern Mind," *Baptist Faculty Paper* 6 (1963): 1–2, 4; and "God, Man, and Redemption in Modern Art," *Review and Expositor* 61 (1964): 142–55. His remembrance of Williams, "The Church Member," was published in *J. Howard Williams: Prophet of God and Friend of Man*, ed. H. C. Brown Jr. and Charles P. Johnson (San Antonio, Tex.: Naylor, 1963), 121–29.

19 Martha recalls this trip fondly and is grateful for this aspect of her family's life together. Three years later, her father helped to arrange a summer work tour for Martha and three of her friends at Ruschlikon Baptist Theological Seminary, near Zurich in Switzerland. In 1971, he did the same for Martha and one other friend at the Arusha International School, now Arusha Meru, in Arusha, Tanzania, which first opened in 1964. The opportunity for domestic and international travel is one of the shared values of all three of the Newport adult children. With their father's heavy schedule of writing in the evenings after supper, teaching at the seminary, and interim pastoring and speaking on weekends, their family road trips across America, and to international sites, were some of the few times the five of them could spend together each year. In the childhood years of Martha, Frank, and John, Eddie Belle's responsibilities, to handle all of the details of house and home and the raising of the children almost single-handedly, were heavy.

20 John was especially grateful to Professor Slater, who had just joined the faculty in Benares, India, and with whom he spent considerable time at Benares Hindu University there. He was grateful as well to the many missionaries in Thailand, Hong Kong, Taiwan, Korea, and Japan who hosted him. Tucker N. Calloway (1919–1987), missionary in Japan, and expert on the overlapping borders of Christian and Zen Buddhist thought, would later author *Zen Way, Jesus Way* (Clarendon, Vt.: Tuttle Publishing, 1976). He was then professor of world religions and philosophy of religion at *Seinan Gakuin* University in Fukuoka and had already practiced *zazen* in Buddhist temples for more than a decade in order to understand the heart of the religious system. He would later serve in the same role for fifteen years at the Liberia Baptist Theological Seminary. See "Retired Missionary Tucker Calloway Dies," in *Foreign Mission News*, 27 January 1987, SBC Archives, Nashville, Tennessee.

Robert Harrell Culpepper (1924–2012) was for thirty years a professor of theology at the same seminary in Japan. He wrote *Interpreting the Atonement* (1966); *Evaluating the Charismatic Movement* (1977); and *God's Calling* (1981), his missionary autobiography. After he and his wife left Japan, Culpepper taught at the Southeastern Baptist Theological Seminary in Wake Forest, North Carolina. These two were especially helpful in hosting John's study at the *Seinan Gakuin* University in Japan. See Newport, "Preface," in *Life's Ultimate Questions*, xvi. The family did not join John in this year of study. Martha was nineteen, Frank was seventeen and a senior in high school, and John Paul Jr. was eleven years old.

21 John Bennett was born in Kingston, Ontario, Canada, son of a Presbyterian minister, and was educated at Williams College (B.A. 1924), Mansfield College, Oxford University (M.A. 1926), and Union Theological Seminary (B.D. 1927, S.T.M. 1929). He taught at Union from 1927 to 1930, at Auburn Theological Seminary from 1930 to 1938, at Pacific School of Religion from 1938 to 1942, became a Congregational minister in 1939, and then returned to serve at Union until his retirement. He taught Christian theology and ethics, was dean of faculty from 1955 to 1963, and then became the president from 1963 to 1970. As a social activist, Bennett was an early supporter of feminism, an ardent champion of the civil rights movement, an eloquent critic of the United States' involvement in Vietnam, and a prophetic supporter of economic rights for minorities. He and Abraham Heschel cofounded the group "Clergy and Laity Concerned about Vietnam," and with Reinhold Niebuhr, the magazine *Christianity and Crisis*. He was active in both the National and World Council of Churches. Bennett was arrested in several anti-war demonstrations, the most notable of which caused him to miss his own retirement party the year he stepped down as Union's president in 1970. Among his many writings were *Christian Realism* (1941); *Christian Ethics and Social Policy* (1950); *Christians and the State* (1958); *Nuclear Weapons and the Conflict of Conscience* (1962); *Christian Faith and Political Choice* (1963); *Foreign Policy in Christian Perspective* (1966); *Christianity and Communism Today* (1970); and *Radical Imperative: From Theology to Social Ethics* (1975). See David Stout's Obituary of Bennett in *New York Times*, 2 May 1995, http://www.nytimes.com/1995/05/02/obituaries/john-c-bennett-a-theologian-of-outspoken-views-dies-at-92.html (accessed 17 February 2015).

22 Reinhold Niebuhr was born in Wright City, Missouri, the son of a pastor of an Evangelical Synod German Lutheran congregation. When Reinhold was ten years old, he expressed his desire to become a pastor like his father, who, he said, was the most interesting person in town. Reinhold and Richard both attended Elmhurst College in Elmhurst, Illinois, and Eden Theological Seminary in St. Louis, Missouri. Following a thirteen-year pastorate at the Bethel Evangelical Church in Detroit, Reinhold was invited to join the faculty at Union Theological Seminary and served successively as associate professor of philosophy of religion (1928–1930), William E. Dodge Jr. Professor of Applied Christianity (1930–1955), Charles A. Briggs Graduate Professor of Philosophy and Theology (1955 until his death), and as vice president of the seminary concurrently from 1955 forward.

He fought Henry Ford on labor inequality, encouraged Christians to enter the war against Hitler, was an ardent anti-Communist and, following WWII, had impact upon U.S. State Department policies. Among his most important writings are: *Leaves from the Notebook of a Tamed Cynic* (1930); *Moral Man and Immoral Society: A Study of Ethics and Politics* (1932); *Interpretation of Christian Ethics* (1935); *Beyond Tragedy: Essays on the Christian Interpretation of History* (1937); *Christianity and Power Politics* (1940); *The Nature and Destiny of Man* (1943); *The Children of Light and the Children of Darkness* (1944); *Faith and History* (1949); *The Irony of American History* (1952); *Christian Realism and Political Problems* (1953); and *The Self and the Dramas of History* (1955). Reinhold died of a heart attack at his summer home on 1 June 1971 in Stockbridge, Massachusetts. See Arthur Schlesinger Jr.'s centennial memorial of Reinhold Niebuhr's birth in *New York Times*, 22 June 1992, http://www.nytimes.com/1992/06/22/opinion/reinhold-niebuhr-s-long-shadow.html (accessed 23 February 2015); and Alden Whitman's astute obituary following Reinhold's death in *New York Times*, 2 June 1971, http://www.nytimes.com/packages/html/books/niebuhr.pdf (accessed 23 February 2015).

His brother, fellow Missourian and theological ethicist, Helmut Richard Niebuhr (1894–1962), Sterling Professor of Theology and Christian Ethics at Yale Divinity School from 1931 to 1962, was author of *The Kingdom of God in America* (1937); *The Meaning of Revelation* (1941); *Christ and Culture* (1951); and *The Purpose of the Church and Its Ministry* (1954). Widely regarded as a leader in American Protestant neo-orthodox circles along with his brother Reinhold, the thinking of Richard and his Yale colleague, Hans Wilhelm Frei, founded the "Yale School" of post-liberal theology, which influenced other scholars like James Gustafson, Stanley Hauerwas, and Gordon Kaufman. Richard Niebuhr died in 1962 of a heart attack at his summer home in Rowe, Massachusetts, and was buried in Hamden, Connecticut. From Richard Niebuhr, Newport had absorbed the relational focus of Niebuhr and the notion that in every age, the static and fluid nature of humankind, as opposed to God's transcendence and absolute nature, resulted in the many different ways in which mankind has apprehended the knowledge of God.

23 Tom Driver earned his undergraduate degree at Duke University in 1950 before attending Union Theological Seminary (1950–1953), after which he joined the faculty. He served as Paul Tillich Professor of Theology and Culture from 1955 to 1991. In the 1980s, Tom Driver and his wife, Anne, became leaders of a nonviolent peace movement in Latin America. In retirement since the early 1990s, they now work with Witness for Peace, an ecumenical, faith-and-conscience-based organization committed to nonviolence and correcting the injustices of U.S. policies toward Latin American countries. They also support the Presbyterian Peace Fellowship. The Drivers have made two documentary films and continue to write and speak on behalf of those who have no voice. They received the Presbyterian Peace-seeker Award in 2006 for creating a program that sends volunteers to Colombia to walk

alongside churches and refugees undergoing persecution, and the Andrew Mellon Award from the Witherspoon Society in 2006 for similar work in Nicaragua, Haiti, and Colombia. They have been arrested for their activism multiple times. Driver is the author of many books, including: *The Sense of History in Greek and Shakespearean Drama* (1960); *Romantic Quest and Modern Query: A History of the Modern Theatre* (1970); *Patterns of Grace: Human Experience as Word of God* (1977); *Christ in a Changing World: Toward an Ethical Christology* (1981); and *Liberating Rites: Understanding the Transformative Power of Ritual* (1997). See "Tom Driver on Paul Tillich," a fascinating recollection of his student days at Union, http://theological-geography.net/?p=4183 (accessed 23 February 2015).

24 One curiosity that perhaps cannot be answered, except that John was not an ethicist, was why John Newport's interactions with these activist-ethicists did not engender more activism in his own life concerning the injustices he observed in America. For example, the Civil Rights Movement was taking place between 1954 and 1968, even as he was studying in New York, as were the disparities of the economic and educational systems that fractured America at the time.

25 John Macquarrie was born into a devout Presbyterian home at the end of WWI and attended the University of Glasgow, where he read philosophy under Charles Arthur Campbell and earned a B.D. in theology in 1943. He enlisted in the British army (1943–1948) and served as a chaplain (1945–1948). Following his military term, he served St. Ninian's Church in Brechin (1948–1953) as a parish minister of the Church of Scotland while earning a Ph.D. from Glasgow University (1954) and lecturing at Trinity College nearby. He was elected to the faculty of Union Theological Seminary, where he taught systematic theology (1962–1970). He was then appointed to the Lady Margaret Professor of Divinity Chair at Oxford in 1970 and served as Canon Residentiary of Christ Church from 1970 until his retirement in 1986, when he was appointed Professor Emeritus and Canon Emeritus. From 1996 until his death in 2007, he lived in Oxford. He also served from 1996 as the Martin Heidegger Professor of Philosophical Theology at the Graduate Theological Foundation in Mishawaka, Indiana, and traveled there to meet his obligations. He was a renowned Heidegger scholar, having co-translated with Edward Robinson Heidegger's *Being and Time* into English (1962). Among Macquarrie's other works are *Principles of Christian Theology* (1966); *Existentialism* (1972); *Jesus Christ in Modern Thought* (1991); and *Mediators Between Human and Divine: From Moses to Muhammad* (1996).

26 John Macquarrie, "Christianity and Other Faiths," *Union Seminary Quarterly Review* 20, no. 1 (1964): 39–48.

27 Newport, "New Developments in New Testament Theology," 41–56. John's next article, published soon after his return to Southwestern, was stimulated

by these conversations. See Newport's "Interpreting the Bible," in *Broadman Bible Commentary*, vol. 1, ed. Clifton J. Allen (Nashville: Broadman Publishers, 1969), 25–33.

28 Frederick Clifton Grant was born in Beloit, Wisconsin, studied at General Theological Seminary in New York City (B.D. 1913), and served parishes in Michigan and Illinois before becoming professor of systematic theology at Berkeley Divinity School in 1926. He was president of Seabury-Western Theological Seminary between 1927 and 1938 and facilitated the merger of the two institutions in 1933. He was appointed to the faculty of Union Theological Seminary in 1938, where he served until his retirement in 1959. As editor-in-chief of *Anglican Review* from 1924 to 1955 and an invited observer at Vatican II, Grant wrote thirty-one books, among them *The Growth of the Gospels* (1933); *The Earliest Gospel* (1943); *An Introduction to New Testament Thought* (1950); the *Mark* commentary in the *Interpreter's Bible* Series (1951); and *Ancient Judaism and the New Testament* (1959). One of Grant's most treasured friends was his major professor, Charles Harold Dodd (1884–1973), who taught at Oxford, Manchester, and became professor of divinity at Cambridge University in 1935 until he was named Emeritus in 1949. Dodd directed the team that translated and published the *New English Bible* in 1950 and is noted for his more than thirty books, "realized eschatology," and his many students who ushered in a new era in Pauline studies.

29 W. D. Davies (also called W. D. David), born in Carmarthenshire, Wales, into a Congregationalist family, was educated at the University of Wales (B.A. 1934, B.D., 1938) and Cambridge (B.A. 1940, M.A. 1942). He was an ordained Congregationalist minister who pastored churches in Cambridgeshire while he was studying under C. H. Dodd (see above) and David Daube, a rabbinic scholar who later became Regius Professor of Civil Law at Oxford. He received his doctorate (D. *operis causa* 1948) from the University of Wales. He served as professor of New Testament at Yorkshire (1946–1950) and then became professor of biblical theology at Duke Divinity School (1950–1955), professor of divinity at Princeton University (1955–1959), and then Edward Robinson Professor of Biblical Theology at Union Theological Seminary (1959–1966). He then rejoined Duke's faculty as the George Washington Ivey Professor of Advanced Studies and Research in Christian Origins (1966–1981). After retirement, he taught at Texas Christian University in Fort Worth, Texas, the University of California at Berkeley, at the University of Strasbourg, France, and was a Fellow of Clare Hall, Cambridge (1986–1987). His major works include: *Paul and Rabbinic Judaism: Some Rabbinic Elements in Pauline Theology* (1948); *The Background of the New Testament and Its Eschatology* (1956), coauthored with Daube; *Church Origins and Judaism* (1962); *The Setting of the Sermon on the Mount* (1964); editor of the three-volume *Cambridge History of Judaism* (1999); and coauthor of the three-volume *International Critical Commentary* on Matthew (with

Dale C. Allison Jr., 1991, and posthumously in 2004). His best-known student was E. P. Sanders, leader of the "New Perspective on Paul" group.

30 Polish-born American rabbi Abraham Joshua Heschel was the descendent of several generations of Jewish rabbis and received a traditional Jewish education and rabbinical ordination. He earned his doctorate at the University of Berlin and studied further at the *Hochschule für die Wissenschaft des Judentums* (Higher Institute for Jewish Studies, closed by the Nazis in 1942). In 1938, Abraham was arrested in Frankfurt by the Gestapo and deported to Poland, where he taught at Warsaw's Institute for Jewish Studies until he escaped to London and then to New York with the help of Julian Morgenstern, president of Hebrew Union College. His mother and three sisters all died at the hands of the Nazis, by bombing, murder, or in concentration camps. Heschel taught at Hebrew Union in Cincinnati from 1940 to 1945, after which he joined the faculty of the Jewish Theological Seminary of America, where he taught until his death in 1972. His work includes: *The Sabbath: Its Meaning for Modern Man* (1951); *Theology of Ancient Judaism*, 2 vols. (1962); *Who is Man?* (1965); *Israel, an Echo of Eternity* (1969); and *A Passion for Truth* (1972). See Edward K. Kaplan, *Prophetic Witness & Spiritual Radical: Abraham Joshua Heschel in America, 1940–1972* (New Haven: Yale University Press, 2009).

31 Daniel Day Williams was born in Denver, Colorado, to Methodist parents. His father was a friend and biographer of William Jennings Bryan and reared his son to value scholarship. Daniel earned degrees from the University of Denver (B.A. 1931), University of Chicago (M.A. 1933), and Chicago Theological Seminary (B.D. 1934). He studied with Wilhelm Pauck, Charles Hartshorne, Alfred North Whitehead, and Reinhold Niebuhr. Williams' principal books include: *The Advancement of Theological Education* (with Reinhold Niebuhr, 1955); *The Minister and the Care of Souls* (1961); *The New Life in Christ: The Meaning and Experience of Continuing Redemption* (1965); *Spirit and the Forms of Love* (1968); and *The Andover Liberals: A Study in American Theology* (1970).

32 It is interesting to note that beginning in 1959, student numbers at the SBC seminaries were at an all-time high, but in the next fourteen years, these numbers declined in each annual report. Baptist colleges and universities also reported a regular decline in numbers of students preparing for full-time vocational Christian service. Doubtlessly social and economic factors were in part responsible for this; however, the trend did not reverse until the academic year of 1972–1973, when the student count again reached the 1959 number of 2,395. See Baker, *Tell the Generations Following*, 417.

33 Theodore Klein (1934–present) taught philosophy at TCU for thirty-eight years, from 1963–2001, when he retired as Emeritus Professor of Philosophy. During that time, he became the director of the Honors program from 1968 to 1972 and chaired the faculty senate several times. He won the

distinguished John V. Roach Honors College award, "Honors Professor of the Year," in 1973. He still lives in Fort Worth with his wife, Winifred, and is an associate pastor of the First Christian Church, his boyhood congregation, where he has served faithfully for many years.

Alvin Fredolph Nelson (1917–1973) won his faculty tenure at TCU in 1964 and served notably. Sadly, he died of a heart attack in 1973 at the age of fifty-five, the year he chaired the philosophy faculty. Nelson authored many books on logic and basic philosophical issues, the most important of which are probably his *Primary Questions, Historical Answers: Problems of Philosophy* (Boston: Christopher Press, 1968) and *Inquiry and Reality: Discourse in Pragmatic Synthesis* (Fort Worth: Texas Christian University Press, 1978), the latter published posthumously. See TCU's campus newsletter, "Professor's Death Mourned," *The Daily Skiff*, 28 April 1973. Newport was impressed with the structure of Nelson's 1968 volume, which gave him ideas for his own *Life's Ultimate Questions*, which he published later in 1989.

Arthur Campbell Garnett (1894–1971) was born in southern Australia, earned his philosophy degree at the University of Melbourne, and taught in Adelaide, Australia, Yunnanfu, China, and Butler University in Indiana. He then studied at the universities of London, Berlin, Yale, and Edinburgh, and spent the remainder of his teaching career at the University of Wisconsin from 1937 until his retirement in 1965. He was author of several books, the most important of which was *Reality and Value: An Introduction to Metaphysics and an Essay on the Theory of Value* (London: Taylor and Francis, 1937, 2020).

34 John kept scrupulous notes, diaries, and appointment books. He listed every sermon he ever preached and every address he gave, complete with topic, Scripture reference, place, and date. He even kept his appointment schedules and telephone records of calls he made and received. From these records, one could almost reconstruct the events of his daily life from the time he entered college until his retirement, a span of more than sixty years. These, along with the letter files including correspondence with hundreds of acquaintances and former church members, are remarkably detailed. See Newport Papers, "Autobiographical Materials," Bullock's Newport Biography Reference Box, The Texas Collection.

35 Typical of such letters is the one John addressed in 1965 to Eddie Belle from Damascus which said, "My Darling, I was beginning to be concerned when I had not heard from you in several days. Now that your letter has come, I am greatly relieved. I am very homesick." A sampling from a decade before included many to the children. To Martha Ellen, he had written on the back of a postcard with a picture of the Mount of Olives, "Dear Martha Ellen, This is a picture of the place where Jesus walked. I want you to see it someday. I miss you very much and love you and want to see you. Love, Daddy." To Frank he had sent a picture of a camel with the pyramids of Giza in the

background. "Dear Frank Marvin," he wrote, "Daddy rode a camel like this one by the pyramids. I wish you could have been here with me to see the camels. I miss you very, very much and I hope you are a good boy. Watch after Mother while I am gone. Is Johnny growing? Love, Daddy." See these letters in Newport's correspondence files, "Autobiographical Materials," Bullock's Newport Biography Reference Box, The Texas Collection.

36 In an era when letters and telegrams were still the normal form of affordable and reliable communication while traveling, John and Eddie Belle kept in frequent contact. Both his parents and Eddie Belle kept his letters, hundreds of them handwritten, which still survive.

37 In 1968, C. W. and Gloria Brister accompanied the Newports, strengthening their already strong friendship. On the trip in 1970, John became very ill with a stomach sickness in India and was bedridden for several days while he recovered. Bill Tolar shouldered much of the lecturing and hosting duties during John's recuperation.

38 See John Newport, *Theology and Contemporary Art Forms* (Waco, Tex.: Word, 1971), republished as *Christianity and Contemporary Art Forms* (Waco, Tex.: Word, 1979). John wrote in the preface to this volume, "Above all, I am grateful to my wife, Eddie Belle, who not only read and gave advice on the manuscript, but also encouraged me to stay with it when my 'practical temperament' would beckon toward something less rigorous," 8.

39 The events of this decade are recounted in several books and collections of the 1960s, including Wallis, *Ribbons of Time*, 116–17. For the counterculture's details, see Joe David Brown, ed., "The Hippies: Philosophy of a Sub-culture," *Time Magazine*, 7 July 1967; and Barry Miles, *Hippie* (New York: Sterling, 2004), 106–12.

40 Eddie Belle's father, Frank Hartwell Leavell, had launched the first Baptist Student Ministry in 1922, and Baptists had been developing campus ministries since that time.

41 Some "Jesus People" were understandably aligned with the mounting anti-war sentiment across the land, for their classmates, friends, and relatives had been drafted to serve, and die, in Vietnam. Many Americans opposed the war on moral grounds, appalled by the devastation and violence of the war. Others claimed the conflict was a war against Vietnamese independence, or an intervention in a foreign civil war; others opposed it because they felt it lacked clear objectives and appeared to be unwinnable. Drugs and alcohol use, however, were not typical of the "Jesus People," but bell-bottoms, sandals, beads, and flower-painted Volkswagen buses were popular identity statements and symbols. It was not unusual for the "Jesus People" to share their faith with and care for prostitutes, drug addicts, and the homeless who were victims in the underbelly of the hippie counterculture as pushers and criminals made their ways to places like Haight-Ashbury and preyed upon the vulnerable. See Larry Eskridge, "Jesus People," in *Encyclopedia of*

Christianity, vol. 3, ed. Erwin Fahlbusch, Geoffrey William Bromiley, and David B. Barrett (Grand Rapids: Eerdmans, 1999), 912; Stella Lau, *Popular Music in Evangelical Youth Culture* (Abingdon: Routledge, 2013), 33; and Robert Coleman, *One Divine Moment: The Account of the Asbury Revival of 1970*, 2nd ed. (Wilmore, Ky.: First Fruits Press, 2013).

42 Note the complete list of John Newport's writings in Appendix A.

43 Southwestern opened an extension center on the campus of Houston Baptist University in 1975, and the next year, another in classrooms of the Oklahoma Baptist University in Shawnee.

6 Navigating Rapids

1 John Locke, "Of the Conduct of the Understanding," in *The Posthumous Works of Mr. John Locke*, ed. Peter King (London: W. B., 1706); Amazon classic reprint by the same title (Saskatoon, Calif.: Hardpress, 2018), 60.

2 Newport's "Lessons from the Odyssey of an Evolving Baptist Theologian," an address presented to the North American Baptist Professors of Religion in 1992, 4–5. For Newbigin, W. Cantwell Smith was a prime leader in this division between public and private knowledge and had been for many years director of the Center for the Study of World Religions at Harvard. John knew Smith, with whom he had exchanges in academic settings across the years. Once, Peter Gomes, minister of the Memorial Church on Harvard University's campus, asked John to preach and have a dialogue with students and faculty afterward. Smith was there and challenged Newport's claim concerning the uniqueness of Christianity. Newport responded with his unruffled but confident assertion that it was true that the world was radically changing into a postmodern and pluralistic theological, philosophical, and cultural milieu. Nevertheless, the human situation was still chaotic and sinister. Human selfishness and greed were still evident. The wrath of God was being revealed as humans rebelled against the revelation of the cosmic and historical Christ. "For me," John concluded, "the good news of the gospel is even more needed and relevant than in the youth revivals of fifty years ago." See Newport, "Lessons," 7.

3 John's literary publications during the time he was associated with Rice were numerous. His books were *Demons, Demons, Demons: A Christian Guide through the Murky Maze of the Occult* (1972); *Demonios, Demonios, Demonios* (1973); *Christianismo y Ocultismo: Un Enfrentamiento* (1974); John Newport and William Cannon, *Why Christians Fight Over the Bible* (Nashville: Thomas Nelson, 1974); and *Christ and the New Consciousness* (1978). His journal articles and chapters were "Understanding, Evaluating, and Learning from the Contemporary Glossolalia Movement," in *Tongues*, ed. Luther B. Dyer (Jefferson City, Mo.: Le Roi Publishers, 1971), 105–27; "The Arts from a Conservative Perspective," in *Arts in Society*, ed. Edward Kamarck (Madison: University

of Wisconsin Extension Division, 1976), 56–57; "Response" and "Satan and Demons: A Theological Perspective," in *Demon Possession: A Medical, Historical, Anthropological and Theological Symposium*, ed. John Warwick Montgomery (Minneapolis, Minn.: Bethany Fellowship, 1976), 58–61, 325–345; "Christianity and the Arts," in *At the Edge of Hope: Christian Laity in Paradox*, ed. Howard E. Butt Jr. (New York: Seabury, 1978), 102–16; and "The World: A Tangled Web and a Scarlet Thread," in *Waiting in the Wings*, ed. Porter W. Routh (Nashville: Broadman, 1978), 117–24.

4 Niels C. Nielsen Jr. (1921–2018), Rayzor Professor of Philosophy, earned his undergraduate degree from George Pepperdine University in 1942 and a B.D. and Th.D. from Yale University two years later. Nielsen served as an ordained Methodist deacon and elder and then pastor of Woodbury Methodist Church in Connecticut from 1944 to 1946. He then taught religious studies as a junior instructor at Yale for two years before joining the Rice faculty in 1951. In 1965, Nielsen was awarded a Fulbright grant and conducted research in Madras, India, through 1966. He founded the department of religion at Rice in 1968 in order to provide students with the opportunity to study religions from objective, critical perspectives and served as chair until 1991. He was well-known for teaching the history and philosophy of religions. He authored nine books, including *The Rice Institution: Monograph in Philosophy* (1957); *Religion and Philosophy in Contemporary Japan* (1957); *The Crisis in Human Rights* (1978); *Solzhenitsyn's Religion* (1983); *Religions of the World* (1983); *Revolutions in Eastern Europe: The Religious Roots* (1991); *Fundamentalism, Mythos, and World Religions* (1993); and *God in the Obama Era: Presidents' Religion and Ethics from George Washington to Barack Obama* (2009).

5 This book in Newport's mind, which took him almost two decades to put into final form, was *Life's Ultimate Questions*, published in 1989. The friendship and admiration were reciprocal. Nielsen valued John's mind and heart, asking him to contribute to his new book. See Newport's preface in Niels Nielsen Jr., *Introduction to Solzhenitsyn's Religion* (Nashville: Thomas Nelson, 1975).

6 The six SBC theological seminaries were Southern, established in 1859 in Greenville, South Carolina, and moved to Louisville, Kentucky, in 1877 following the Civil War; Southwestern, established in 1908 in Waco, Texas, and moved to Fort Worth in 1910; New Orleans, established in the same city in 1917; Golden Gate (now Gateway), founded in 1944 in Mill Valley and moved to Ontario, California, in 2016; Southeastern, established in 1951 in Wake Forest, North Carolina; and Midwestern, founded in Kansas City, Missouri, in 1957.

7 They also arranged, each summer between 1973 and 1976, ship cruises to Europe and the Middle East. Eddie Belle would arrange the logistics, and John would lecture each evening and before and during each port of call.

8 John Newport, "The Odyssey of an Evangelical Mind," Newport Papers, "Autobiographical Materials," Bullock's Newport Biography Reference Box, The Texas Collection. This was later published as an article by the same name in the *Southwestern Journal of Theology* 37 (1995): 38–42.

9 During his presidency, and for many years afterward, Robert Naylor would welcome incoming first-year students in the inaugural chapel service with his famous greeting. After the sermon, Naylor would come quietly to the pulpit and, when everyone was quiet and all rustlings had ceased, would say, "I now pronounce you 'Southwesterners.' It is a worthy and honorable name; not by what you have done but by a long line that has preceded you. . . . it says something about what you believe about this Book—that it is the Word of God. . . . you will not wear a better name in life than Southwesterner." In later years, he would add, "It would be better for you to leave this earth than to be disloyal to God and to this institution." Quoted by Jason G. Deusing, "Luther Russ Bush III," *Southwestern Journal of Theology* 1, no. 50 (2007): 4. See Robert Naylor's document, "I Now Pronounce You Southwesterners," on file in the Office of the President, Southwestern Baptist Theological Seminary. This traditional pronouncement has been used by every succeeding president. The writer heard it as a student firsthand in the spring of 1985 when Dr. Naylor pronounced the latter version upon the first-year class, which was a sobering and memorable decree.

10 One example of the friends who wrote to John was a letter from Harry Hunt, Old Testament professor, with whom John shared a close friendship, along with those of Bill Tolar and C. W. Brister. Harry assured John of his prayers, writing on 19 November 1976, "Dr. Drumwright shared with us this week that you are searching for God's leadership concerning your future teaching at Rice. I know that I am very prejudiced in my desire to have you back as part of the faculty at Southwestern. . . . I know that we all must follow God's will, even though at times His will is hard to understand. It is my hope that one day you will return to the ministry of the seminary." See letter in Newport Papers, Bullock's Newport Biography Reference Box, The Texas Collection.

John also received surprising correspondence related to his publications, such as the letter he received on 4 February 1976 from a man in Tampa, Florida. John's book on the occult had been released, but this gentleman believed John to be a traveling exorcist. He wrote, "Dear Dr. Newport, I have heard of the work you do through the Tattler's special issue in exorcism which was published in the spring of 1974. I have been unsuccessful in trying to locate someone in this area who can perform exorcism on my aunt, who has been troubled by undesirable and unwanted spirits for the last four to five months. . . . I look forward to hearing from you." Ever the Christian gentleman, and genuinely concerned about people, John replied. He expressed his sorrow about the aunt's condition and said that he wished he knew of someone to help, but that he was unacquainted with the Tampa area. He offered his chapter in the *Demons* book on possession as a way to help. He closed with, "We will pray that God will bless you and [that] your aunt can be helped." See Robert F. Hanan letter, 1 February 1976, Newport Papers, Bullock's Newport Biography Reference Box, The Texas Collection.

11 During these years in Houston, it was John and Eddie Belle's joy to live closer to their daughter Martha and eldest grandson Nicholas, who also lived in the city. Part of the draw to stay for extended semesters at Rice was their deep value of family and John and Eddie Belle's longing to be close by their children, of whom they were very proud. In the early summer of 1977, John Paul Jr. graduated from Harvard University, and John and Eddie Belle traveled to Cambridge, Massachusetts, to participate in the week's activities. Never had they been part of such a dignified and tradition-enhanced experience. They wrote glowingly to their parents and family members about the trip and their pride in Johnny. In the summer of the same year, John also wrote to their son, Dr. Frank, and his wife, Kim, "You have always been a delight to me and your love and appreciation mean more than I can put into words. At this age and stage, one of the greatest of all of life's satisfactions is the life and interests of a child. You have always been such a constructive and exciting person." See the letter from John Newport to Frank Newport on 21 June 1977, Newport Papers, "Personal Correspondence," Bullock's Newport Biography Reference Box, The Texas Collection.

12 The 1962 controversy over biblical authority erupted a year after the publication of *The Message of Genesis*, written by the first Midwestern Seminary faculty appointment, Hebrew and Old Testament professor Ralph H. Elliott (1927–present). Elliott's volume sparked a firestorm when some readers felt that the book questioned the authority of Genesis 1–11. A Houston pastor, K. Owen White, published an article, "Death in the Pot," *Arkansas Baptist*, 1 February 1, 1962, which called the book "poison" and led to Elliott's dismissal by Midwestern trustees by year's end. Elliott has pastored and taught for the remainder of his life in American Baptist churches, pulpits, and seminary classrooms, widely recognized as a scholar. See Leon McBeth's *Texas Baptists: A Sesquicentennial History* (Dallas: BaptistWay Press, 1998), 323, and Robert Craft, "Help for the Man in the Pew and in the Pulpit," *Baptist Standard*, 10 January 1962, 7. This controversy prompted the rewriting of the 1963 *Baptist Faith and Message* and the withdrawal of Elliott's volume from Broadman publications.

The 1970s Broadman Bible controversy further fed the SBC's perceived threat to the Bible's authority. It centered upon the publication in 1969 of volume one of the twelve-part *Broadman Bible Commentary*, written by England's G. Henton Davies (1906–1998), Old Testament scholar and principal of the Baptists' Regent's Park College in Oxford. This first book on Genesis and Exodus in the long-awaited series was similarly denounced because of Davies' unqualified endorsement of source-theory Pentateuch scholarship, his negation of the universality of the Noahic Flood, and his postulation that Genesis 22 was not a testament to Abraham's obedience, as affirmed by Hebrews 11:17, but "the climax of the psychology of his life." See G. Henton Davies, *Genesis, Broadman Bible Commentary*, vol. 1, ed. Clifton J. Allen (Nashville: Broadman, 1969), 117, 198. During the 1970 SBC Denver Convention, messengers voted to withdraw the volume and have it rewritten from a more conservative point of view. Clyde T. Francisco (1916–1981), John R. Sampey Professor of Old Testament Interpretation at Southern Seminary, published its replacement in 1973. See McBeth, *Baptist Heritage*, 680–81. Naylor unified the seminary family during these upheavals and kept the focus on students when politicizing began to divide the convention.

13 Baker, *Tell the Generations Following*, 445.
14 The material from this section was taken from Baker's meticulous details concerning the transition period; see *Tell the Generations Following*, 445–48. Naylor and his wife, Goldia Geneva Dalton Naylor, had met and married in 1930 and enjoyed sixty-eight years of marriage. They served together for more than thirty years in the pastorate until he was elected the fifth president of Southwestern Seminary in 1958, and then twenty more years there. The Naylors stayed in Fort Worth after retirement, continuing to minister in churches and at the seminary until Robert's death in 1999 and Goldie's death in 2010, when she was 100 years of age. The Naylors had two sons, Robert Naylor Jr. and Richard Naylor, and a daughter, Rebekah, who has come to be revered as a faithful missionary in India. See Keith Collier, "Goldie Naylor, 100, Dies," *Baptist Press*, 2 February 2010.
15 See letter from John Newport to Dr. Russell Dilday, 23 March 1978, Newport Papers, "Personal Correspondence," Bullock's Newport Biography Reference Box, The Texas Collection.
16 See letter from John Newport to Dr. Russell Dilday, 23 March 1978, Newport Papers, "Personal Correspondence," Bullock's Newport Biography Reference Box, The Texas Collection.
17 See letter from John Newport to Dr. Russell Dilday, 23 March 1978, Newport Papers, "Personal Correspondence," Bullock's Newport Biography Reference Box, The Texas Collection.
18 See letter from John Newport to his mother, Mildred Newport, 19 July 1978, Newport Papers, "Personal Correspondence," Bullock's Newport Biography Reference Box, The Texas Collection. When John and Eddie Belle returned from one of their study cruises in July 1978, they found, to their dismay, that a water main had broken and flooded John's study at his home. His rugs and many of the books were waterlogged. Fortunately, their son John Paul was in Houston for a few months. He was handy, with practical carpentry skills that

John lacked. John Paul was able to repair furniture, help salvage the books, and paint their house.
19 Newport, "Recollections," in Newport Papers, "Autobiographical Materials," Bullock's Newport Biography Reference Box, The Texas Collection.
20 Letter from Robert Ernest Naylor to John Newport, 6 November 1978, in Newport Papers, "Personal Correspondence," Bullock's Newport Biography Reference Box, The Texas Collection. The Newport house in Houston took until the spring to sell. Johnny stayed in Houston to help his mother with readying the house for the market and John returned there on the weekends to help pack. It was March before they moved their belongings and purchased a house in Fort Worth. They settled in a lovely home near Texas Christian University.
21 Desiderius Erasmus, *Spongia Adversus Aspergines Hutteni*, in *Collected Works of Erasmus*, ed. Manfred Hoffman, vol. 78 (Toronto: University of Toronto Press, 2011). An original pamphlet, with an inscription to a friend in Erasmus' hand, is located in the Queen's College Collection, Cambridge, England.
22 For example, the faculty voted unanimously in 1981 to invite Justice Anderson to be the new director of the World Missions Center and Bill Tolar to be the new dean of the School of Theology. The development of the new program in Christian counseling and its new center was also accomplished by this collegial leadership style. In 1981, George Kelm led an archaeological expedition to the biblical town of Timnah, *Tel Batash*, in the Sorek Valley of Israel, which he and Israeli archaeologist Amihai Mazar had uncovered from 1977 to 1979. These expeditions were conducted each year until 1989, putting Southwestern on the map as one of the few seminaries across the world to have an active archaeology program. The Tandy Center was opened, by the same kind of vote, and housed in the A. Webb Roberts Library to introduce the city where Samson had died and to display the artifacts of the digs.
23 Baker, *Tell the Generations Following*, 456–57. The dates listed represent the years each professor served on faculty at Southwestern, many beyond Newport's own tenure.
24 Baker, *Tell the Generations Following*, 457. This volume, published in 1983, listed the "new faculty" accessed in Newport's first years as vice president of academic affairs. Now, almost forty years later, most of these faculty have retired, having lived through cataclysmic, and in many cases, painful, upheavals in the latter years of their teaching careers.
25 Baker, *Tell the Generations Following*, 460.
26 Despite its core conservative beliefs, the "Billy Graham" way was not believed by the more fundamentalist sector to be adequate to safeguard against a liberal convention drift in the SBC, as evidenced by the more than half of voting messengers who elected Adrian Rogers to the SBC presidency in 1979 in Houston. This was also the year that "infallibility,"

an older term used to describe the Bible's "truth without any mixture of error," and its nature, generally accepted by Baptists and used in both the 1925 and the 1963 versions of the *Baptist Faith and Message*, was replaced by the term "inerrancy," the new word brought to American theology through European reformed traditions. This new term ushered into SBC life the "inerrancy controversy."

27 John Newport, "Russell Dilday and Constructive Conservative Theological Education at Southwestern Baptist Theological Seminary, 1978-1995," in Newport Papers, "Autobiographical Materials," Bullock's Newport Biography Reference Box, The Texas Collection. One questions whether Mohler's phrase "revisionist compromise" meant "evangelicalism." Newport's sixteen-page, single-spaced document furnishes most of the material for this chapter's backdrop of convention controversy, except where noted. These are John Newport's own words, his mature reflections written in 1994, after having served at Southwestern during some of its most difficult days. The next decade after his retirement would prove to be even more disruptive there. It is interesting to note that Russell Dilday wrote his Th.D. thesis on E. Y. Mullins (1860-1928), who was the fourth president of Southern Seminary from 1899 until his death. Mullins shepherded his seminary through a similar crisis in a different context, leading the way for a constructive alternative to the extremes of that particular situation. See Russell Dilday, *E. Y. Mullins: Shaper of Theology*, Southern Baptist Heritage Series (Nashville: Southern Baptist Historical Commission, 1987).

28 Newport spoke of his role during the first few years of his tenure as vice president of academic affairs in "Odyssey of an Evangelical Mind," 6, in Newport Papers, "Autobiographical Materials," Bullock's Newport Biography Reference Box, The Texas Collection.

29 "Odyssey of an Evangelical Mind," 2, in Newport Papers, "Autobiographical Materials," Bullock's Newport Biography Reference Box, The Texas Collection. During the annual meeting of the Southern Baptist Convention in Dallas, 11-13 June 1985, a special committee was created to attempt to determine the sources of the current controversy in the SBC and to make findings and recommendations to resolve it. The committee met fourteen times. Following each meeting, a report was given to Southern Baptists by Charles G. Fuller, chairman of the committee, through the denominational news service, the Baptist Press. The committee made a preliminary report to the 1986 Convention and a final report that was adopted in 1987. The committee consisted of twenty-two members who were selected to represent equally the various factions within the SBC. See SBC Peace Committee 1985-1988 Collection, housed at the Southern Baptist Historical Library and Archives, Nashville, Texas.

30 In addition to these books, John also published chapters in books and journal articles during the 1980s, sometimes multiple entries in a single year.

His chapters were "The Mystery of Immortality and the Life Beyond," in *The Miracle of Easter*, ed. Floyd Thatcher. (Waco, Tex.: Word, 1980), 115–23; and "The Future Church Faces Radical New Religions," in *Future Church*, ed. Ralph Neighbor Jr. (Nashville: Broadman, 1980), 187–205.

His journal and newspaper articles were many: "Living in Two Worlds," *The Student* 60 (1980): 4–6; "The Baptist Journey," *Christianity Today*, 7 August 1981; "The Arts in Worship," *Review and Expositor* 80 (1983): 71–83; "Satanism and Demonism," *Baptist Standard* (6 July 1983): 10–11; "America's Continuing Controversy over Humanism," *Liberal and Fine Arts Review* 3 (1983): 87–98; "Guest Editorial: The Musical Heritage of Baptists," *Baptist History and Heritage* 19 (1984): 2–3; "Humanism and the Future: A Tentative Proposal for an American Solution," *Liberal and Fine Arts Review* 4 (1984): 53–61; "The Pastor and the Local Church," *Baptist Standard*, 10 October 1984; "The American Dream: Religion, Religious Liberty and the Public Schools," *Missouri Schools* 51 (1985): 22–26; "Representative Contemporary Approaches to the Use of Philosophy in Christian Thought," *Review and Expositor* 82 (1985): 507–19; "Representative Historical and Contemporary Approaches to Biblical Interpretation," *Faith and Mission* (Spring 1986): 32–48; "Updating the American Dream," *Report from the Capital* 41 (1986): 4–5, 7; "The Problem of Demonic Power and the Nature of the Christian Response," *Ogbomoso Journal of Theology* 3 (1988): 27–31; and "The Biblical Worldview and Church-Related Colleges," *Southern Baptist Educator* 53 (August 1989): 3–20.

31 Newport, "Odyssey of an Evangelical Mind," 6, in Newport Papers, "Autobiographical Materials," Bullock's Newport Biography Reference Box, The Texas Collection. Later in the SBC controversy, the Peace Committee in 1987 called for a cessation of the terms then deemed to be "pejorative," pointedly the appellations "(any kind of adjective) fundamentalists" and "flaming liberals." As John is using the term "reactionary conservative-fundamentalist," he is using it in its historical sense as the self-designation of those who were against the "Modernists" in the theological debates of the 1920s through the 1940s. A stickler for historical accuracy, John was being precise in his application of this and other terms he used in his "Odyssey" to set forth his evangelical identity. He was speaking to Baptists, but he was also speaking to a broader audience of evangelicals.

32 Newport, *Life's Ultimate Questions*. John dedicated this book "To Eddie Belle, Encourager, Enabler, and Companion of the Years." This volume, the fruit of his spiritual and scholarly maturity, and perhaps Newport's *magnum opus*, lays out his understanding of life, his biblical worldview, and the importance of applying this worldview to life's most difficult questions. Newport then selects eleven of the most complex questions that humans ask about life and applies his biblical worldview to answer them. This is the most celebrated

of his writings and continues to be used as a textbook in master-level and seminary philosophy classes to this day.
33 Newport, "Odyssey of an Evangelical Mind," 6, in Newport Papers, "Autobiographical Materials," Bullock's Newport Biography Reference Box, The Texas Collection.
34 Newport, "Odyssey of an Evangelical Mind," 6, in Newport Papers, "Autobiographical Materials," Bullock's Newport Biography Reference Box, The Texas Collection. Fundamentalists at the time could have been wary of Newport's explanation of his approach. However, John did not mean by this that he doubted the Bible's authenticity and truthfulness.
35 Newport, "Odyssey of an Evangelical Mind," 8-9, in Newport Papers, "Autobiographical Materials," Bullock's Newport Biography Reference Box, The Texas Collection.
36 See the brief overview of the developments within the conservative evangelical movement in the prologue. One of the ways that the SBC became more involved with Baptists in the north had to do with the cancellation of comity agreements in 1942. This situation began on 12–13 September 1894, when the Northern Baptists' Home Mission Society leaders met with Southern Baptists' Home Mission Board leaders in a joint conference at Fortress Monroe, Virginia. In a cordial meeting, the first of its kind since the Civil War, Baptists voted unanimously to partner in a new venture to dedicate substantial efforts and resources toward opening more schools for African Americans and to help establish and conduct joint mission efforts in the South. A third decision, which relates to this discussion, has to do with each side's pledge to restrict their mission work and church planting to mutually agreed-upon territories. Neither would open new work in territories where work was already in place by the other group. In 1942, however, in what came to be called the "California Decision," the SBC voted no longer to abide by the older comity agreement. Now the SBC actively began establishing dual conventions in areas formerly open or occupied by the Northern Baptists. As they began to interact more, SBC leaders witnessed what they saw as "liberal tendencies" among Northern Baptists. See McBeth, *Baptist Heritage*, 430–32, 626–28.
37 Newport, "Odyssey of an Evangelical Mind," 9, in Newport Papers, "Autobiographical Materials," Bullock's Newport Biography Reference Box, The Texas Collection.
38 Newport, "Odyssey of an Evangelical Mind," 10, in Newport Papers, "Autobiographical Materials," Bullock's Newport Biography Reference Box, The Texas Collection.
39 Bob E. Patterson wrote of this juxtaposition, "Newport and I were drawn to each other, and our mutual interest in faith and science was one lasting point of contact. I was probably more interested in science as science than he was, but we were both concerned that science and faith have a cordial

relationship." See Bob E. Patterson, "Editorial Introduction," *Perspectives in Religious Studies* 32, no. 1 (2005): 5.
40 Patterson, "Editorial Introduction," 12.
41 A complete list of the philosophers who studied with and wrote their dissertations under John Newport is in Appendix B: "Philosophy of Religion Doctoral Students Supervised by John Newport." John was a collaborative scholar, encouraging his students to write on cutting-edge questions critical to the diverse and expanding fields of Christian philosophy in particular and secular philosophy in general. His library contains an entire wall of master's theses, D.Min. projects, and Ph.D. dissertations. Newport's copies of most of these dissertations were moved from the B. H. Carroll Theological Seminary to the Lanier Theological Library, located in Houston, Texas, which now houses the Newport Library.
42 In Fort Worth John had held a membership at the YMCA, as did several other faculty members. He continued his fitness club routine while in Houston and then resumed it upon returning to Southwestern in 1979. He underwent heart bypass surgery in 1981, and upon recovery, continued to work out into his last months of life. Even after retirement, he walked the trail and kept active. Students reported the surprise of walking into the sauna at the Recreation and Aerobics Center and seeing him, well into his 80s, relaxing in the steam.
43 Chip Alford, "John Newport Leaving Legacy of Scholarship at Southwestern," *Baptist Press*, 30 July 1990. John was also given a sumptuous retirement banquet to which friends and colleagues came to honor his thirty-five years of teaching.
44 During the 1980s and 1990s, John took great pleasure in his membership in a smaller group that met monthly, called "The Cattle Country Clerics." This ecumenical, multiracial group was comprised of eighteen couples from church and denominational leadership in Fort Worth, including the pastors, priests, and rabbis of United Methodist, Presbyterian, Episcopal, Baptist, Lutheran, Apostolic, Christian, Catholic, and Jewish churches and synagogues. There were conservative and liberal couples, black, Hispanic, and white couples, all of whom enjoyed gracious and stimulating programs at one another's homes in monthly meetings. John and Eddie Belle also enjoyed the fellowship with the Walls family of Fort Worth and about one hundred other couples. The Walls group was invited once a year to gather at Christmastime for an evening with an elegant dinner and a play. John and Eddie Belle attended these events, even during the years John was teaching in Houston, and once, John Paul accompanied his father.
45 The Academic Council and the Staff of the Academic Affairs division held a reception honoring John Newport on Tuesday, 31 July 1990, in the Justin Conference Room. In October of that year, a "Roast and Toast" of John Newport took place to honor him. His students, representing decades, spoke of his many influences upon their lives: Yandall Woodfin (1950s), William

Tanner (1960s), Russ Bush (1970s), Jim Denison (1980s), and Ted Cabal (1990s). The master of ceremonies was President Russell Dilday, yet another former student of Newport's. See Program for Roast/Toast of Dr. John Newport, in file "Ephemera," in "Autobiographical Materials," Bullock's Newport Biography Reference Box, The Texas Collection.

46 Alford, "John Newport Leaving Legacy," 1–2.
47 Newport, "Russell Dilday and Constructive Conservative Theological Education," in "Autobiographical Materials," Bullock's Newport Biography Reference Box, The Texas Collection.
48 Newport, "Russell Dilday and Constructive Conservative Theological Education," in "Autobiographical Materials," Bullock's Newport Biography Reference Box, The Texas Collection.
49 Copies of more than 170 letters to Lilly and McNaughton reside in a single file, with many more files containing similar materials related to this controversy. The overwhelming tenor of the letters is dismay, shock, and initial anger, that the trustees would consider such an action. See Newport Papers, "Inerrancy," Bullock's Newport Biography Reference Box, The Texas Collection.
50 Dilday, *Doctrine of Biblical Authority*. The book was a strong statement of biblical authority and questioned whether the SBC needed to adopt either the word "inerrancy" or the theory of inerrancy (relying on the perfection of the original autographs) as the only way to state how biblical authority may be guaranteed. He was comfortable, since no original autographs exist, to rely instead upon the word and phrase "infallible," and "without any mixture of error," used historically in the two 1925 and 1963 *Baptist Faith and Message* documents. James Draper's *Authority: The Critical Issue for Southern Baptists* (Ada, Mich.: Revell, 1984) was similar in that it did not demand that Baptists all use the term "inerrancy" to describe biblical authority. This term was originally used by Scots-rationalistic Presbyterian theologians, B. B. Warfield and his circle, with a weight of accompanying doctrinal presuppositions that had been a part of reformed doctrinal statements.
51 The *Glorieta Statement*, made jointly by the six SBC presidents during a prayer retreat of executives of SBC agencies and the SBC's Peace Committee, between 20–22 October 1986, announced a plan aimed at bringing an end to the seven-year theological/political divide in the SBC. The seven-point theological commitment affirmed and promised to enforce seminary confessional statements; to foster balanced teaching; pledged respect for the convictions of all Southern Baptists; committed the presidents to pick teachers and speakers from across the SBC theological spectrum; promised to lead seminary communities in spiritual dimensions; pledged to support evangelism and missions while emphasizing Baptist doctrine and heritage; and announced three national conferences to be held on biblical inerrancy. It also affirmed belief in the supernatural origin and history of Christianity and biblical accounts of miracles, and belief in full inspiration of the

Scriptures, including a statement that the sixty-six books of the Bible are not errant in any area of reality. It held that while the seminaries were fulfilling the purposes assigned to them, they were not perfect, and that there were legitimate concerns regarding them which were being addressed. See Dan Martin, "*Glorieta Statement* Discussion," *Baptist Press*, 7 November 1987.

52 Newport, "Russell Dilday and Constructive Conservative Theological Education," in "Autobiographical Materials," Bullock's Newport Biography Reference Box, The Texas Collection.

53 Newport, "Russell Dilday and Constructive Conservative Theological Education," in "Autobiographical Materials," Bullock's Newport Biography Reference Box, The Texas Collection. Both quotations were from this document.

54 Newport, "Russell Dilday and Constructive Conservative Theological Education," in "Autobiographical Materials," Bullock's Newport Biography Reference Box, The Texas Collection. Newport noted, "It is ironic that Warfield interpreted the Bible as teaching Theistic Evolution and Amillennialism in contrast to Creation Science and Dispensationalism," which is what many of the inerrantists of the 1980s and 1990s believed.

55 For a detailed look at the events of these years from Dilday's monthly presidential reports, see Dilday, *Columns*, written a decade after his firing, and *Higher Ground: A Call for Christian Civility* (Macon, Ga.: Smyth and Helwys, 2019) written twenty-five years later. From the perspective of the fundamentalist-conservatives, as Newport called the group, or "Conservative Resurgence," as they preferred to be called, see Sutton, *Conservative Resurgence*; and Paul Pressler, *A Hill on Which to Die* (Nashville: Broadman and Holman, 1999). This movement was primarily aimed at reorienting the denomination away from what the "Resurgent" group perceived to be "a liberal trajectory." These are merely representative voices, however.

56 James Leo Garrett, notes from interview with the writer, 8 December 2014.

57 Dilday became knowledgeable about computers, even writing an early book on the use of computers and technology in theological education and ministry. See Russell Dilday, *Personal Computers: A New Tool for Ministers* (Nashville: Baptist Sunday School Board, 1986).

58 In a completely different area of interest, in 1993, Newport was also monitoring the "Waco Siege," the law enforcement siege of the compound that belonged to the religious sect called Branch Davidians. It was carried out by American federal and Texas state law enforcement agencies and the U.S. military between 28 February and 19 April 1993. Cult leader David Koresh had gathered his followers to a compound called Mt. Carmel, just thirteen miles east-northeast of Waco, Texas. An apocalyptic group, Koresh and his leadership were accused of misconduct, sexual abuse, and the stockpiling of illegal weapons. The standoff of almost eight weeks ended in a fire, which resulted in the deaths of seventy-six Branch Davidians, including twenty-five children, two pregnant women, and David Koresh. Seen as an expert

in cults and alternative religions, Newport was asked to write a brief overview of such groups for use by law-enforcement negotiators and personnel as they managed encounters like this in the future. His chapter-length article, "Cults, Religious Conflict, Religious Liberty, and Frameworks of Order," *Journal of Police Crisis Negotiations* 2, no. 1 (2002): 5–29, was submitted on 1 June 2000, likely Newport's last publication.

59 For a recitation of these events, see "A Firing at a Southern Baptist Seminary," *The Chronicle of Higher Education*, 30 March 1994, and the volumes cited above.

60 William R. Estep, "Three Days at Southwestern," in Newport Papers, "Autobiographical Materials," Bullock's Newport Biography Reference Box, The Texas Collection. Newport had kept this document and written across the top. He intended this account to be included in his autobiography. W. R. Estep (1920–2000) was one of two long-term and esteemed church historians at Southwestern and specialized in Baptist and Anabaptist studies. After teaching at Southwestern for forty years, he died on 14 July, just a month and four days before John Newport. Harry Leon McBeth (1931–2013) also taught at Southwestern for forty-five years and was considered one of the top Baptist historians in America.

61 The faculty member who was elected on this day, after a false accusation almost derailed his appointment, was C. Mack Roark, longtime pastor of First Baptist Church Ponca City, Oklahoma, and, since 1984, vice president at Oklahoma Baptist University in Shawnee. He was a noted Greek and New Testament scholar. The two recommendations that the trustees deferred, both in church history, were Stephen Stookey and Karen O'Dell Bullock, who were Dr. Dilday's last faculty recommendations. They were both in attendance and experienced the events of these days as well.

62 Dilday recites this firsthand account in his *Columns*, 252–78. Dilday asked Pulley for what reason would they fire the president. Pulley responded, "We're the board; we don't have to have a reason. We have the votes to do it and we will."

63 Dilday, *Columns*, 252–78.

64 Dilday, *Columns*, 271.

65 Later that day, towards evening, Stephen Stookey and the writer made their way to Dilday's door and knocked. He answered and in the next few moments expressed his deep sorrow at what had transpired and how it would impact their lives. His pastoral care and devotion to the Lord in those moments were evident, and his benediction over these two young faculty as they left meant more than he will ever know.

66 Harry Emerson Fosdick (1978–1969), against racism and injustice, was an American Baptist pastor called to the interdenominational Riverside Church in Morningside Heights, Manhattan. He wrote this hymn text in 1930, most often sung to the tune RHONNDA, published in more than 135 hymnals.

67 John said through his tears, "They told me last night that they would not do this. They lied." Keith Putt recalled this moment in an interview with the writer, 10 December 2014.
68 Estep, "Three Days at Southwestern," 7–8. C. Mack Roark turned down his appointment to faculty. He returned to OBU in Shawnee and taught Greek and New Testament until he retired in 2004. He still serves as interim pastor in 2020 as a faithful servant of Christ.
69 Frank Newport, quoted by Jim Jones and Bill Teeter, "Baptist Theological Newport, 83, Dies," *Fort Worth Star Telegram*, 19 August 2020.
70 There were only two presidents that John had not known as colleagues: B. H. Carroll, who founded the seminary in 1908 and served until his death in 1914, and Lee Rutland Scarborough, who served from 1915–1942. When Newport first arrived in 1952, only five buildings were standing on campus: Fort Worth Hall (1910–1913), Barnard Hall (1915), Cowden Hall (1926), the Carroll Memorial Building (1949), and J. M. Price Hall (1950), the latter two having been built under E. D. Head's tenure (1942–1953). Under the J. Howard Williams presidency (1953–1958), John had seen the Student Village begin its construction in 1958. Under Robert E. Naylor's tenure (1958–1978), the Naylor Student Center (1965), the Walsh Medical Center (1968), the President's Home (1971), the Goldia and Robert E. Naylor Children's Building (1973), and the Myra and J. Roy Slover Recreation and Aerobics Center (1979) were built. Under Russell Dilday's presidency, the A. Webb Roberts Library was built on the east side of campus, next to the Memorial Building, and opened in 1982.
71 Southeastern Baptist Theological Seminary in Wake Forest, North Carolina, went through a similar experience in 1987. Upon the retirement of Olin T. Binkley, W. Randall Lolley had become president of SEBTS in 1974. He served as SEBTS president until 1987, when he resigned alongside longtime professor and dean, Morris Ashcraft, in response to pressure by leaders of the Conservative Resurgence. In 1988, trustees elected Southern Seminary evangelism professor Lewis A. Drummond to lead SEBTS.

For twelve years the SBC had elected ultraconservative convention presidents, who then appointed like-minded educators and administrators. In 1990, Al Shackleford and Dan Martin of the Baptist Press, the official news service of the SBC, were fired by the SBC's Executive Committee. These two, along with a group of more moderate conservatives, went on to form their own newspaper, *Associated Baptist Press*, which is now *Baptist News Global*. This was the year that the Cooperative Baptist Fellowship formed. In 1991, the Foreign Mission Board trustees voted to defund the Baptist Seminary in Rüschlikon, Switzerland, the same year that Lloyd Elder, president of the SBC Sunday School Board, resigned under pressure and was replaced by James Draper, a Conservative Resurgence choice. By November of that year, 159 employees either took voluntary retirement or were retired involuntarily.

At the Southern Baptist Theological Seminary in Louisville, Kentucky, President Roy Honeycutt (1982–1993) was accused in 1990 by a new trustee of not believing the Bible. He resigned in 1993 under pressure, after which R. Albert Mohler became president. In 1992, Keith Parks, president of the Foreign Mission Board, retired. In his thirteen years as president, missionaries entered forty new countries with a total of 3,918 missionaries. Dilday was fired in 1994. It was during this period that John Paul Newport felt his greatest internal struggles and labored to effect peace. See Newport Papers, "Inerrancy," Bullock's Newport Biography Reference Box, The Texas Collection.

7 The River Joins the Sea

1   Diarmaid MacCulloch, *Silence: A Christian History* (New York: Penguin Random House, 2014).
2   During the decade of the 1990s, local churches were beginning to feel heavy pressure by leaders on both sides of the SBC controversy to choose between them, to define their loyalty, and to prove that loyalty by directing portions of their offerings to one or the other's mission agency or other denominational entities. Many SBC church pastors did choose to align themselves with one or the other side. Many more simply decided to direct monies to both sides or to neither. Among churches in the southland, the Lottie Moon Christmas Offering for Foreign Missions and the Annie Armstrong Easter Offering for Home Missions were priorities, no matter what else was happening in SBC life. The missionaries and their work were primary values churches supported.
3   At their fiftieth anniversary celebration in 1991, someone asked Eddie Belle which period of marriage had been their best. She looked at John and answered, "Right now." See Martha Newport Shimkus, notes on the Newport family, 20 June 2013 in the Newport Papers, "Family Notes and Photos," in "Autobiographical Materials," Bullock's Newport Biography Reference Box, The Texas Collection.
4   Eddie Belle had suffered a heart attack while hosting a tour to eastern Europe with John in May and June 1990. They were in in Krakow, Poland, at the time, and Eddie Belle was able to return home for her bypass surgery. She continued to suffer pain, however, and John's surgeon, Dr. Manucher Nazarian, was able to perform a successful triple bypass in November of the same year. Letter from John Newport to Mrs. Evelyn Hudson, 3 March 1997, in Newport Papers, "Personal Correspondence," Bullock's Newport Biography Reference Box, The Texas Collection; and John Newport to Dr. Gerald Mann, 10 January 2000, Newport Papers, "Personal Correspondence," Bullock's Newport Biography Reference Box, The Texas Collection.
5   In these years of retirement, John and Eddie Belle were focused daily upon their family: children, grandchildren, brothers and sisters, and their nieces

and nephews. They were naturally very proud of their brilliant and accomplished adult children. Martha was a celebrated calculus and math "masterteacher" at Episcopal High School in Bellaire, in the greater Houston area. Nicholas, the Newports' eldest grandson, was in his second year at the University of Houston Law School after graduating with an engineering degree from Northwestern University in Evanston, Illinois. Frank, as editor-in-chief of the Gallup Poll, lived in Princeton with his wife Kim, who was a civic and educational leader, and four children: Christopher, who had accepted an appointment to the Naval Academy; Cal, who was a junior in high school and already a co-owner of a computer web page design firm; and Sarah and Emily, who were just entering their teen years as smart, spirited, and athletic young women. John was a writer, living with his wife Polly, an artist, and their preschool daughter Anna Belle. After serving as a noted journalist for several years, John Paul had just published his first book, *The Fine Green Line* (New York: Random House, Broadway Books, 1999), documenting one year of his life on the PGA Tour from inside the organization. See John Newport, "Christmas Greetings from the John Newports [1998]," Newport Papers, "Personal Correspondence," Bullock's Newport Biography Reference Box, The Texas Collection.

6 Newport, *New Age Movement and Biblical Worldview*.
7 Newport files on "Mars Hill," Bill Nichols correspondence, and "New Age Conference," in Newport Papers, "Autobiographical Materials," Bullock's Newport Biography Reference Box, The Texas Collection.
8 See Newport, Newport Papers, "Christmas Greetings [1998]," Bullock's Newport Biography Reference Box, The Texas Collection. Not all travel had an academic focus. They joined their family in November 1998 for Frank's fiftieth birthday celebration at the Washington's Crossing Inn on the Delaware River, and John's brother, Russell, and sister-in-law Carolyn Newport's fiftieth wedding anniversary in Springfield, Missouri. They were even able to visit with Jack, the other brother of John and Russell, and his wife Patsy at their home in Branson, Missouri. This was a busy year.
9 One such letter, by way of example, was from a pastor in North Carolina who was navigating some division in his church over the subject of proper ordination. When John received the invitation from Hemphill to research and answer this letter, John sent out a memo to his Southwestern faculty colleagues, an excerpt of which follows: "It is my understanding that local churches recognize a member's call to the ministry by licensing him to preach. Then he will be ordained when another church recognizes and ratifies his call by calling him as a pastor or as a chaplain. Should the licensing step be omitted and a person be ordained as soon as he tells of a call? Should a person be ordained when he enrolls in the Seminary? Should he be ordained upon graduation even though he has not been called to a church? Or rather should ordination wait until he is called by a church to the pastorate or other full-time ministry

or enters the chaplaincy? What about licensing and ordination of educational ministers? Are there any handbooks on ministry that explain the usual pattern for licensing and ordaining? Are there books that discuss this issue? I would appreciate help as soon as possible." Newport's colleagues responded quickly, and John was able to write the reply. This shows how thorough John was in his work, but also how collegial the faculty was to help each other. See Memo to the Faculty, "Concerning Ordination and Baptist Polity," 2 October 1998, Newport Papers, "Personal Correspondence," Bullock's Newport Biography Reference Box, The Texas Collection.

10 John Newport to Russell Newport Letter, 25 September 1989, Newport Papers, "Personal Correspondence," Bullock's Newport Biography Reference Box, The Texas Collection.

11 The Newport Collection's non-book boxes number more than 100, of which eight are specifically designated "Autobiographical Materials." The remaining boxes supplement his life's story with correspondence, travel, subject-specific files, gradebooks, lecture and book research, personal diaries, phone and sermon records, and more. The Newport Collection also contains more than twenty thousand volumes of John's books, which are now housed at Lanier Theological Library in Houston, Texas.

12 Later that month, the Henry and Hazel Chavannes of Houston, supporters of Rice University, hosted John and Eddie Belle on a Caribbean birthday cruise.

13 See Newport, Newport Papers, "Christmas Greetings [1998]," Bullock's Newport Biography Reference Box, The Texas Collection.

14 Newport, Newport Papers, "Christmas Greetings [1998]," Bullock's Newport Biography Reference Box, The Texas Collection.

15 John wrote about this discovery in the Newport Christmas letter of 1999. In 1824, Welshman Robert Owen travelled to America and in the next year invested most of his fortune in an experimental socialistic community at New Harmony, Indiana, which he intended to become his model for a utopian society. It lasted about two years; however, his life's labor for justice for the working classes endured. He returned to the UK and helped to bring about eight-hour workdays, labor unions, child labor laws, and free coeducational schools there. All of this impacted America as well. Jane Blaffer Owen (1915–2010) was born in Houston, Texas, the daughter of Robert Lee Blaffer and Sarah Campbell Blaffer. She grew up traveling the world, and in 1933, graduated from the Ethel Walker School in Connecticut. She studied at Bryn Mawr, the Washington School of Diplomacy, and the Union Theological Seminary in New York. In 1941, she married Kenneth Dale Owen, a geologist and descendant of Robert Owen, the founder of the 1825 New Harmony Community.

Early in their marriage, Kenneth Owen introduced his bride to the town of his birth. Jane Owen adopted this little town on the Wabash as her home and channeled her philanthropic efforts to establish the Robert Lee Blaffer

Foundation to preserve and promote the town's historical and educational attributes. Among numerous other New Harmony initiatives, she commissioned Philip Johnson to design the Roofless Church and orchestrated the building of the visitors' center, the Atheneum, with architect Richard Meier. She envisioned a spiritual retreat center and created the MacLeod Barn Abbey, inspired and supported the restoration of the Rapp-Owen Granary, and encouraged spiritual awakening through the Cathedral Labyrinth, built for meditation and prayer. See Jane Owen, *New Harmony, Indiana: Like a River, Not a Lake: A Memoir*, ed. Nancy Mangum McCaslin (Bloomington: University of Indiana Press, 2015).

16 See Newport, Newport Papers, "Christmas Greetings [1999]," Bullock's Newport Biography Reference Box, The Texas Collection. Mark Brister was the son of the Newports' dear friends, C. W. and Gloria Brister Jr., distinguished professor emeritus of pastoral ministry at Southwestern Seminary for forty-five years. Each time John and Eddie Belle attended the Princeton Gallup Institute, it was a reunion with Frank and Kim and the grandchildren. Frank was Chief Editor for Gallup Poll.

17 See Newport, "Memorandum," to Doug Blount and Paul Sands regarding the Wheaton trip, dated 10 April 2000. John writes, "Three of the publishers who were present asked me again to submit a revision of *Life's Ultimate Questions*: Eerdmans, Baker, and InterVarsity. It needs some transformation. I hope we can get together and discuss these issues soon." See Newport Papers, "Personal Correspondence," Bullock's Newport Biography Reference Box, The Texas Collection.

18 Letter from N. S. R. K. Ravi to John Newport, dated 28 March 2000, in Newport Papers, "Personal Correspondence," Bullock's Newport Biography Reference Box, The Texas Collection. In typical John Newport fashion, he checked out a number of books from Southwestern Seminary's library with his card, Number 45062556, to read on the way. He chose Daniel J. Meckel and Robert L. Moore's *Jung and Christianity in Dialogue: Faith, Feminism, and Hermeneutics* (1990); John Wilkinson's *The Bible and Healing: A Medical and Theological Commentary* (1998); Nicholas Wolterstorff's *Art in Action: Toward a Christian Aesthetic* (1997); and T. F. Torrance's *Calvin's Doctrine of Man* (1997). John died, however, before he could return these volumes. In what may be one of the world's greatest twists of irony, the man who respected books perhaps more than any other living mortal ended his days owing a library fine of $105; see Newport Files, Southwestern Baptist Theological Seminary Archives, located by Jill Botticelli, archivist, on 13 July 2020. This fine was later removed.

19 John Newport to Jenkins and Virginia Garrett Letter, 17 April 2000, Newport Papers, "Personal Correspondence," Bullock's Newport Biography Reference Box, The Texas Collection.

20 Newport, Founder's Day Address manuscript, 9 March 2000, Newport Papers, "Autobiographical Materials," Bullock's Newport Biography Reference Box, The Texas Collection.
21 This sixth president was L. R. Scarborough. John related that, as a young man and a first-year student at Southern Seminary, Scarborough had been invited to preach a major evangelistic conference at the school. As the time came for his address, Scarborough had not arrived, although he had called the president, Dr. Sampey, from the railroad station. He was indeed in the city. The audience continued to sing, and soon Scarborough walked in with a taxi driver whom he had led to Christ en route to the service; this had caused his delay. The driver "bore his testimony before the entire conference. This experience was for me a dramatic reminder of Southwestern's leadership in its evangelistic emphasis." Newport's Founder's Day Address, 9 March 2000, 2.
22 Newport's Founder's Day Address, 9 March 2000, 7. John went on to say that the historic Baptist approach to religious liberty and separation of church and state properly confronts the new pluralism, but that pride and self-centeredness constitute the essence of sin. Baptists are to hold and witness to our deep convictions about Christ with a sufficient degree of humility to allow us to live peacefully with those who have other convictions. As history teaches us, John said, "Unless we can develop this humility and charity, there are dire consequences related to religious fanaticism." Founder's Day Address, 8.
23 Newport's Founder's Day Address, 9 March 2000, 11–12.
24 Memo from John Newport to President Ken Hemphill, dated 5 May 2000, in Newport Papers, "Personal Correspondence," Bullock's Newport Biography Reference Box, The Texas Collection.
25 This itinerary was written by John to Martha in a letter dated 22 March 2000. Although tentative, this was the plan for the June travel schedule. He signed the letter, "Love, Daddy." See Newport Papers, "Personal Correspondence," Bullock's Newport Biography Reference Box, The Texas Collection.
26 Patrick Miles Overton's poem, "Faith," in *The Leaning Tree* by Patrick Miles Overton (Bloomington, Minn.: Bethany, 1975), 91. Patrick Overton currently serves as director of the Front Porch Institute, located in Boonville, Missouri. The Institute was created in 1996 while he was an associate professor at Columbia College and served as director of the Columbia College Center for Community & Cultural Studies.
27 This recounting of the events of John's last days is taken from John Paul Newport Jr.'s personal diary entries for the period of his father's illness, sent to the writer on 30 July 2020.
28 John Paul Jr. called his mother as he was driving to the airport on his way to Fort Worth. She began to cry, saying, "I don't know how I can live without John. Everything that happened, whether good or bad, we talked about it together. I saved things to talk to him about and he brought home a list of

things to talk about, too." They had been married almost sixty years; John Paul Jr., diary entries, 3.
29 John Paul Jr., diary entries, 5. John Paul wrote that on 7 August, he met personally with the two neurosurgeons who assured him that everything in their power had been done to help John Newport. The doctors said that John was being kept alive by modern medical technology, something that he himself had written about in *Life's Ultimate Questions*. John Paul returned home, and he and Eddie Belle read aloud the passages, pages 318–21 in John's book. There they gained a sense of peace and direction. John Paul wrote, "Everything Daddy says in that book tells us that he would not want to be kept alive when there is no chance of returning to a meaningful life," diary entries, 5.
30 Newport, *Life's Ultimate Questions*, 321.
31 This famous organ, donated in part by Van Cliburn in honor of his mother, is the largest pipe organ in the state of Texas. Installed in the 1990s to replace the older organ used since 1952, the Rildia Bee O'Bryan Cliburn Organ has 191 ranks with five keyboards on each of the two consoles and 10,615 speaking pipes. One of the world's leading pipe organ builders, Casavant Frères Limitée, built the Cliburn Organ in French-speaking Quebec. The organ was designed to provide exceptional support for worship, to play all classical music, and to be an extraordinary concert organ. John and Eddie Belle had enjoyed Al Travis' expertise on the organ for decades.
32 The passage was 1 Corinthians 15:50–58: "I declare to you, brothers and sisters, that flesh and blood cannot inherit the kingdom of God, nor does the perishable inherit the imperishable. Listen, I tell you a mystery: We will not all sleep, but we will all be changed—in a flash, in the twinkling of an eye, at the last trumpet. For the trumpet will sound, the dead will be raised imperishable, and we will be changed. For the perishable must clothe itself with the imperishable, and the mortal with immortality. When the perishable has been clothed with the imperishable, and the mortal with immortality, then the saying that is written will come true: 'Death has been swallowed up in victory.' 'Where, O death, is your victory? Where, O death, is your sting?' The sting of death is sin, and the power of sin is the law. But thanks be to God! He gives us the victory through our Lord Jesus Christ. Therefore, my dear brothers and sisters, stand firm. Let nothing move you. Always give yourselves fully to the work of the Lord, because you know that your labor in the Lord is not in vain" (NIV).
33 See Order of Service for John Paul Newport's funeral in Newport Papers, "Autobiographical Materials," Bullock's Newport Biography Reference Box, The Texas Collection. One of the pages in this lovely order of service contains the names of the fifty-six philosophy of religion doctoral students supervised by John Newport over the course of his career. More than a dozen other D.Min. students had also been his students.

34 See Cory J. Hailey, "John Newport, Longtime Professor and Religion Expert, Dies at 82," *Baptist Press*, 21 August 2000.
35 Hailey, "John Newport."
36 Hailey, "John Newport."
37 Hailey, "John Newport."
38 Eddie Belle became a grandmother when Nicholas was born in 1974, and a great-grandmother when Emerson Bailey, Nicholas and Miranda's oldest child, was born on 10 February 2010.
39 The details of these years of Eddie Belle's life were taken from her obituary in the Fort Worth newspaper, *Star Telegram*, 3 October 2012.
40 Martha shares that her mother made sure that the entire family could take a Mediterranean cruise tour together in 1978. Eddie Belle also gifted Martha, as a fifteen-year-old, with the experience of attending Camp Crestridge in Ridgecrest, North Carolina, paid for from Eddie Belle's inheritance. The next year, Martha earned her money and paid her own way. From notes to the writer, dated 20 June 2013.
41 Victor Hugo, *Œuvres complètes*, Edition chronologique publiée sous la direction de Jean Massin, vol. 4 (Paris: Club Français du Livre, 1968), 1205. Taken from Psalm 121:4: "He will not let your foot slip—he who watches over you will not slumber; indeed, he who watches over Israel will neither slumber nor sleep" (NIV).
42 See Order of Service for the funeral of Eddie Belle Leavell Newport in Newport Papers, "Autobiographical Materials," Bullock's Newport Biography Reference Box, The Texas Collection.

8 Nourishing Waters

1 John Newport, "The Forging of an Evangelical Mind and Heart in the Twentieth Century Cultural and Religious Cauldron," in Newport Papers, "Autobiographical Materials," Bullock's Newport Biography Reference Box, The Texas Collection.
2 Newport, "Forging of an Evangelical Mind and Heart."
3 Brian McLaren, *Everything Must Change: When the World's Biggest Problems and Jesus' Good News Collide* (Nashville: Thomas Nelson, 2009), 269.
4 Newport, *Life's Ultimate Questions*, 5.
5 Newport, "Forging of an Evangelical Mind and Heart," 2.
6 Russell Dilday, "John Newport and Revelation," *Perspectives in Religious Studies* 32, no. 1 (2005): 13.
7 Dilday, "Practical Apologist," 12.
8 Mauldin, "John Paul Newport," in *Legacy of Southwestern*, 211. See also Mauldin's excellent and more lengthy treatment of Newport's thought in "John Newport and a Biblical Worldview," *Southwestern Journal of Theology* 29, no. 3 (1987): 33–45.

9   Frank Louis Mauldin, "John Paul Newport," in *Tell the Generations Following: A History of Southwestern Baptist Theological Seminary, 1908–1983* (Nashville: Broadman, 1983), 211.
10 Mauldin, *Tell the Generations Following*, 211. Metaphysics is the branch of philosophy that deals with the first principles of things, including abstract concepts such as being, knowing, identity, time, and space. It has two primary strands: that which holds that what exists lies beyond experience (as argued by Plato), and that which holds that objects of experience constitute the only reality (as argued by Kant, the logical positivists, and Hume); see *Oxford Dictionary of English*, ed. Angus Stevenson, 3rd ed., s.v. "Metaphysics" (Oxford: Oxford University Press, 2010, online version 2015).
11 This section is informed by and in part taken from Mauldin, "John Newport and a Biblical Worldview," 33. Mauldin cites Newport's varied works that point to his framing of this foundational tenet: *What Is Christian Doctrine?* Layman's Library of Christian Doctrine (Nashville: Broadman, 1984), 42; "Biblical Philosophy and the Modern Mind," 1; *Life's Ultimate Questions*, 10; *A Guide to a Christian Philosophy of Religion* (Fort Worth, Tex.: Southwestern Seminary Press, n.d.), 30–34 and 193–244; "Why Christians Argue Over Biblical Interpretation," in *Southwestern Journal of Theology* 16 (1974): 15; and Newport and Cannon, *Why Christians Fight Over the Bible*, 33–50.
12 Mauldin, "John Newport and a Biblical Worldview," 33.
13 Newport, *Life's Ultimate Questions*, 2.
14 Newport, *Life's Ultimate Questions*, 2. Newport taught that everyone has a worldview whether they know it or not; see Newport, *The New Age Movement*, 40.
15 Newport, *Life's Ultimate Questions*, 10.
16 Mauldin, "John Newport and a Biblical Worldview," 33.
17 Newport, *Life's Ultimate Questions*, 10.
18 The biblical theology movement arose from the 1940s to the 1960s, primarily in America, among Protestant evangelicals who were trying to steer a path between the polarizing extremes of liberal theology on the one hand and Christian fundamentalism on the other. Other scholars of this movement included Floyd V. Filson, Otto Piper, and James D. Smart. See D. A. Carson, "Systematic Theology and Biblical Theology," in *New Dictionary of Biblical Theology*, ed. T. Desmond Alexander and Brian S. Rosner (Downers Grove, Ill.: InterVarsity, 2000), 89.
19 Mauldin, "John Paul Newport," in *Legacy of Southwestern*, 210.
20 See John Daniel McDonald's helpful analysis in "Toward a Baptist View of Metaphilosophy: An Analysis of E. Y. Mullins, John Newport, Richard Cunningham, and L. Russ Bush" (Ph.D. diss., Southern Baptist Theological Seminary, 2014), 85. Also, in *Life's Ultimate Questions*, 10, Newport describes Wright's approach: the historical grounding of the biblical worldview is

"unique among religions; that the Bible is the witness to the only religious movement in history that centers its case squarely in history and its inspired interpretation . . . Nature in itself does not contain ultimate meaning, although it can point to that meaning. Human beings cannot find authentic meaning through their elaborate attempts to get beyond or out of history. Rather, certain key events have been selected that are unique, remarkable, and unrepeatable and which, when interpreted under divine inspiration, hold the clues to meaning."

Newport's contrast between Greek and Hebrew thought is characteristic of the biblical theology movement. D. L. Baker cites B. S. Childs' summary of the movement's five emphases: 1) rediscovery of the theological dimension; 2) unity of the whole Bible; 3) revelation of God in history; 4) distinctiveness of the biblical mentality (Greek vs. Hebrew thought); and 5) the contrast of the Bible to its environment. See D. L. Baker, "Biblical Theology," in *New Dictionary of Theology: A Concise and Authoritative Resource*, ed. Sinclair B. Ferguson, David F. Wright, and J. I. Packer (Downers Grove, Ill.: InterVarsity Press, 1988).

21 Stefan Zweig, Eden Paul, and Cedar Paul, *Erasmus of Rotterdam* (New York: Plunkett Lake Press, 1934), 91.
22 Newport, *Life's Ultimate Questions*, 3-4. See also McDonald, "Toward a Baptist View of Metaphilosophy," 73-103. Instructive for this section is also the work of Ted Cabal, "Problems and Promise in a Biblical Worldview with Special Reference to John Paul Newport" (Ph.D. diss., Southwestern Baptist Theological Seminary, 1995). According to Cabal, Newport follows Dilthey in his understanding of the term worldview, which is "the means of obtaining an extensive comprehension of life," but he does not do so uncritically. Newport maintains that one should analyze worldviews for weaknesses and strengths, and compare for "adequacy and normativity," 54-55.
23 McDonald, "Toward a Baptist View of Metaphilosophy," 73-103.
24 John Newport, "Baptist Thought and Philosophy," paper presented at the Conference on Teaching Philosophy in Southern Baptist Colleges and Universities, Ouachita Baptist University, Arkadelphia, Arkansas, April 1986, Newport Papers, Bullock's Newport Biography Reference Box, The Texas Collection, 14-15. See also *Life's Ultimate Questions*, 21.
25 Newport, *Life's Ultimate Questions*, 1-2.
26 Newport, *Life's Ultimate Questions*, 2; see also Newport's "Baptist Thought and Philosophy," 3. These scholars are considered the major proponents of this shift in philosophical approach: P. Geach, ed., and M. Black, trans., *Translations from the Philosophical Writings of Gottlob Frege*, 3rd ed. (Oxford: Blackwell, 1980), Ludwig Wittgenstein, *Philosophical Investigations: The English Text of the Third Edition*, trans. G. E. M. Anscombe (New York: Prentice Hall, 1958); G. E. Moore, *Some Main Problems of Philosophy* (New York: Humanities Press, 1953); Bertrand Russell, *The Art of Philosophizing*

(New York: Philosophical Library, 1968); and A. J. Ayer, *Language, Truth, and Logic* (New York: Dover Publications, 1952).
27 Newport, *Life's Ultimate Questions*, 2.
28 Newport, *Life's Ultimate Questions*, 20.
29 Newport, *Life's Ultimate Questions*, 20.
30 Newport, *Life's Ultimate Questions*, 20.
31 Newport, *Life's Ultimate Questions*, 4.
32 Cabal, "Problems and Promise," 54–55.
33 Newport, *Life's Ultimate Questions*, 10. Newport also discusses the relationship between faith and reason in chapter 10, "The Question of Faith and Reason and the Knowledge of God," in *Life's Ultimate Questions*, 414–456.
34 Newport, *Life's Ultimate Questions*, 414. Karl Rahner (1904–1984) and the Princeton Theologians furthered this thought by bringing reason to the aid of faith. Princeton Theology was a tradition of conservative, Christian, Reformed, and Presbyterian theology at Princeton that lasted for a century from the institution's founding in 1812 until 1929, embodied by Archibald Alexander (1772–1851), Charles Hodge (1797–1878), and B. B. Warfield (1851–1921). Due to the increasing influence of theological liberalism at the school, the last of the Princeton Theologians left to establish Westminster Theological Seminary in 1929 under J. Gresham Machen (1881–1937), John Murray (1898–1975), and Cornelius Van Til (1895–1987). Others who believed that reason had little value and that faith was of utmost importance were Tertullian (160–c. 240), Martin Luther (1483–1546), Blaise Pascal (1623–1662), and Søren Abbey Kierkegaard (1813–1855).
35 Newport, *Life's Ultimate Questions*, 436.
36 Newport, *Life's Ultimate Questions*, 428.
37 McDonald, "Toward a Baptist View of Metaphilosophy," 96, footnote 118.
38 Newport, *Life's Ultimate Questions*, 6.
39 Newport, *What Is Christian Doctrine?* 7.
40 Mauldin, "John Paul Newport," in *Legacy of Southwestern*, 214.
41 David Kirkpatrick, "John's Newport's Apologetic of Complementarity: Cults, Consciousness, and Cosmic Evil," *Perspectives on Christian Apologetics* 32, no. 1 (2005): 50.
42 Kirkpatrick, "John Newport's Apologetic," 58.
43 Mauldin, "John Paul Newport," in *Legacy of Southwestern*, 215.
44 Mauldin, "John Paul Newport," in *Legacy of Southwestern*, 215.
45 McDonald, "Toward a Baptist View of Metaphilosophy," 102.

9 Enduring Legacy

1 *The Message.*
2 Among the initial steps in the writing of this biography were the interviews the writer conducted with colleagues, students, family, friends, and

acquaintances. Surveys were sent to those who knew Newport best and who served with him the longest, some during difficult days at Southwestern. Those colleagues and students who responded are included in this chapter, although by the time the book was begun in 2012, many of his close friends had already passed away. The responses were recorded in written form by the writer. Follow-up phone calls and personal visits were also conducted to obtain details that Newport's colleagues hoped would be remembered. The information received from these surveys is used here to address the legacy of Newport's life and work.

3   Russell Dilday's written notes to the writer, 12 June 2013. John Newport was self-disciplined throughout his career about his health, eating well and working out at the gym in both Fort Worth and Houston. He also frequented the sauna at the Recreation Aerobics Center at Southwestern Seminary. Students have recalled that he would saunter into the sauna, sit down, and open conversations about the latest book he was reading while folks were sitting on the cedar benches in the steam. Also, when he was past eighty years of age, he wrote to Huber Martin, commending him for arranging a daily salad bar to be offered as a dining choice in "Wild Bill's Café" in the Student Center. He said he was watching his health and these were better selections than the fare the dining services normally delivered.

4   Russell Dilday's remarks are reproduced in full in Appendix C.
5   William Tolar, personal interview with the writer, 3 February 2015.
6   James Leo Garrett Jr., interview, 8 December 2014.
7   Scotty Gray, notes to the writer, 17 June 2013. The section Gray referred to is in Newport's *Life's Ultimate Questions*, 563.
8   Bill Tillman, written notes to the writer, 24 June 2013. Steve Lyon, professor of pastoral ministries, also witnessed this fall. It was during the Naylor era, and Mrs. Naylor was not amused at the suppressed laughter around the tables. Lyon also shared that Newport was the kindest man, who never said a word against anyone. The closest his colleagues ever heard him utter something less than positive was when he was asked to give a recommendation for a very poor student. All Newport could say was, "If you knew this man as I know this man, you would feel the same way about this man as I do." Steve Lyon, interview with the writer, 10 August 2020.
9   Yandall Woodfin's written notes to the writer through Leta, his wife, 18 June 2013.
10 A corroborating tale from the faculty lounge, which was retold in John's hearing many times and which he never denied, was of his brief flirtation with a green Porsche automobile in the mid-1960s. Supposedly, when stopped by a trooper on a West Texas highway for going eighty miles an hour, John said quite sincerely, "I couldn't possibly have been going eighty. I never go faster than seventy when I'm reading."

11 Harry Leon McBeth, eminent storyteller and Baptist historian, joined the faculty in 1960 and served for forty-five years. He and John were good friends.
12 Keith Putt, interview with the writer, 23 June 2013. Renowned as a master teacher and postmodern Christian philosopher, as of 2020, Putt, like others in this section, has written and published extensively. Collectively, the students listed here have published hundreds of books, chapters in books, and journal articles.
13 Steve Lemke, interview with the writer, 23 June 2013.
14 In the early days, the continental approach was more hermeneutically based, more existentialist, while the analytical approach was more narrow, rigid, logic-centered, with its own highly developed vocabulary. Some degree of animosity existed between proponents of the two approaches, but Newport did not fit neatly into either pattern. Half a century later, the continental approach is now come to be associated with the postmodernists, while the analytical is linked to the theists. Ted Cabal, interview with the writer, 24 June 2013.
15 Dennis Sansom, written notes to the writer, 18 August 2013.
16 Reagan White, written notes to the writer, 20 October 2013.
17 Jim Denison, written notes to the writer, 1 July 2013.
18 Richard W. Harmon, written notes to the writer, 24 June 2013.
19 Martha Newport Shimkus, written notes to the writer across the years from 2012 to 2020. Martha earned her B.A. in 1967 from Baylor University in English and Elementary Education. She was named one of twelve Outstanding Senior Baylor Women. She then earned her M.A. in 1970 from the University of Texas in Diagnostic Remedial Reading and did further mathematics coursework at the University of Houston from 1980–1984.

She taught at the Lucy Read Elementary School in Austin, 1967–1968; the Ortega Elementary School in Austin, 1969–1971; the Cypress Fairbanks High School in Houston, 1971–1972; the River Oaks Baptist School in Houston, 1977–1980; the St. John's School in Houston, 1980–1984; and the Episcopal High School in Houston, where she served as department head and founding teacher, 1984–1999. She then taught at the Brearley School in New York, where she served as math department head from 1999 to 2006 and math teacher from 1999 to 2015. Martha won the Apple Award for Outstanding Teaching, Peabody College of Vanderbilt University, 1983; Master Teacher at Episcopal High School, 1997; and the Sabbatical Award for Outstanding Teaching at the Brearley School, 2012.

Martha married Stanley John Shimkus on 9 August 2013, who graduated from St. Lawrence University in 1969 and taught mathematics in several independent high schools in Florida, New York, and Massachusetts. He currently teaches mathematics at the Buckley School, an independent school in New York City. The fall of 2020 marks his fifty-second year to teach mathematics.

Martha's son, Nicholas Newport Bailey, was born 12 July 1974 and graduated from St. John's High School in Houston. He then graduated from Northwestern University with a major in civil engineering and the University of Houston Law School with a law degree. He currently practices civil engineering in the Houston area and is married to Miranda Bailey. They have four children, Nina, Emerson, Joyce, and Benjamin, all of whom were adopted from China and are wonderful, spirited children with interests in piano, guitar, sports, and schoolwork.

20 Frank M. Newport, written notes to the writer between 2012 and 2020. Frank earned his B.A. at Baylor University in Oral Communications, Radio and Television in 1970. He then earned his M.A. in Sociology at the University of Michigan in 1972, where he also earned his Ph.D. He served on faculty from 1975 to 1979 as an assistant professor at the University of Missouri, St. Louis, in the department of sociology. His specialty was the social stratification and sociology of religion. Frank also served in the Texas Army National Guard, Airborne Infantry, in Marlin, Texas (near Waco, Texas) and in the U.S. Army Reserve Public Information Detachment in Ann Arbor, Michigan, while he was in school.

Just weeks after his father left Rice University to return to Southwestern Seminary, Frank took the post as talk show host and news director at KTRH Radio in Houston from 1979 to 1981. He then served as vice president and partner for the firm, Tarrance, Hill, Newport, and Ryan, Inc. in Houston until 1988, when he moved to Gallup, Inc., still in Houston, as vice president. In 1990, Frank was named Gallup editor-in-chief. He moved his family to Princeton, New Jersey, and also had an office in Washington, D.C., serving in that role until 2018, at which time he was named Gallup senior scientist.

Frank's publication list is lengthy. With six books and numerous chapters in books, articles, *The Gallup Poll: Public Opinion* volumes published between 2004 and 2014, non-scholarly articles, and more than a thousand blogs, research analyses, and op-eds in national, regional, and local publications, his work is extensive and spans more than two decades. He has also appeared hundreds of times on most major television news networks and network programs. He pioneered CNN's remote "flash" studio concept, appearing live from Princeton studios hundreds of times on CNN U.S. and CNN International, and pioneered Gallup video webcasts and Gallup Poll podcasts. Today, Frank is the host of "Objective Religion" podcasts and is the primary polling and town hall debate consultant to the Commission on Presidential Debates; he also assisted in planning the Fall 2020 general election presidential debates. He has served in this capacity since 1992. He has served variously as president, vice president, and conference chair of the American Association for Public Opinion Research and, since 1994, as a board member and vice president for the Roper Center for Public Opinion Research, as well as a board member of the National Council on Public Polls.

In 1976, Frank married Kim Newport, who earned her B.A. at Albion College in Albion, Michigan. She earned an M.A. at Washington University in St. Louis, Missouri, and has served as a flight attendant for TWA, a data administrator for the University of Michigan Institute for Social Research, a systems analyst for St. Louis County, Clayton, Missouri, and other entities. She currently serves as the president of the Hopewell Regional School District Board, a member of the board of deacons, an elder, and a committee chair at the Pennington Presbyterian Church in Pennington, New Jersey. Frank and Kim have four children and nine grandchildren.

Their son, Christopher Newport, has distinguished himself in the Navy, serving currently as the senior resident inspector of the Diablo Canyon Power Station at U.S. Nuclear Regulatory Commission in Morro Bay, California. He spent many years as a nuclear submarine officer after graduating from the U.S. Naval Academy in 2002 with a major in control systems engineering, later earning a master's degree in engineering from the Catholic University of the Americas in Washington, D.C., in 2008. Christopher is married to Kate, and they have a son, Jack.

Their next son, Cal Newport, graduated from Dartmouth College in 2004 and earned his Ph.D. in electrical engineering and computer science at MIT in 2009. After a two-year postdoctorate study, also at MIT, he joined the faculty in 2011 as an assistant professor of computer science at Georgetown University. He earned tenure in the spring of 2016 and is now the provost's distinguished professor of computer science. He specializes in the theory of distributed systems and to date has published more than sixty peer-reviewed papers and six books, which have consistently earned best-seller status. He is also famous for his long-running blog, "Study Hacks," and is on the leading edge of teaching humans how to live smarter with less technology by adopting "deep work." He lives in Takoma Park, Maryland, with his wife, Julie, and three sons, Max, Asa, and Joshua.

Sarah Newport Mustin graduated from the U.S. Naval Academy, where she earned a B.S. in political science and government. She then earned a master's degree in engineering management. She spent many years as a U.S. Navy nuclear surface warfare officer after in-depth operational training in a land-based nuclear power plant and advanced coursework in mathematics, electrical engineering, chemistry, physics, materials, thermodynamics, and plant operations. She specialized in the recruitment and training of the Naval Nuclear Power Propulsion Program. As of 2020, Sarah works at Booz, Allen, Hamilton in Washington, D.C. Sarah and her husband have three children: Frank, Tag, and Lelia.

Emily Newport Hegamyer earned her B.A. in 2009 in anthropology with honors from the University of Notre Dame in South Bend, Indiana, and took a second major in pre-professional studies. She then earned her master's degree in public health from Bloomberg School of Public Health at the

Johns Hopkins University in Baltimore, Maryland, in 2013, concentrating in children and adolescent health. In 2014, she completed her M.D. at Rutgers University at the Robert Wood Johnson Medical School in New Brunswick. Emily has a lengthy publication and research portfolio on public health and is a noted speaker in the medical field. She is married to Kyle Hegamyer and they have two children, Cooper and Cora.

21 John Paul Newport Jr., written notes to the writer between 2012 and 2020. John P. Newport Jr. graduated from Harvard University in 1977 with an honors degree in English literature, after which he worked for the *Fort Worth Star Telegram* as a widely published freelance writer. While on the job there, he once foiled an act of performance terrorism involving Molotov cocktails at an art museum. Since the 1980s, he has been writing for magazines and newspapers. His stories have appeared in *Men's Journal, GQ, Details, Golf, Golf Digest, Sports Illustrated, The New York Times Magazine*, and many other national publications. He was executive editor of *Travel+Leisure Golf* for two years before he joined *Wall Street Journal* as the weekly golf journal columnist from 2006 to 2015.

An avid golfer for many years, he continues to write occasionally for the *Journal* and other outlets while working on a golf-related novel and a history of golf instruction. He has written feature stories about the Reagan military buildup, junk bonds, Wall Street in the wake of the 1987 crash, and black urban poverty. His topics included in-depth feature articles about nuns, financiers, and bare-fist fighters; profiles of John Irving, Joe Montana, Greg Norman, and others; and travel pieces that have taken him literally around the world, including Mongolia. Newport's story about bush-league professional golf was sold to Warner Brothers.

John Paul's first book, *The Fine Green Line*, was published in 2000 by Broadway Books. It is a narrative of the year he spent competing on the pro golf mini-tours, from the Nike Tour to the Hooters Tour, to even lesser-known tours in an effort to qualify for the PGA Tour. The book brings to life the gonzo underbelly of professional golf and sheds light on the riddle of what separates the very finest golfers from all the rest.

John Paul currently lives in Nyack, New York, with his wife, Polly King, a painter. Polly loved John Newport, and he and Polly had rich conversations about art of all kinds. John Paul and Polly's daughter, Anna Belle, was born in 1994 and graduated from the University of Chicago in 2016 in political science. She has recently been a researcher with the U.S. Department of State Fulbright Program in Amman, Jordan, and serves as an Arab American family advocate.

22 John Paul had served as chairman of the religious council while he was a student. This was when he was a roommate of Bob Garrett, the son of James Leo and Myrta Ann Garrett. The elder John Newport related the story to Ken and Paula Hemphill about his son, John Paul. Soon after John Paul

graduated, Newport was asked to preach in the Harvard chapel. In introducing Newport, the university minister said that John Newport needed no introduction to the students because he was the father of John Newport Jr. "This meant a great deal to me, as you can imagine," he wrote. See John Newport letter to Ken and Paula Hemphill, 22 September 1997, in Newport Papers, "Personal Correspondence," Bullock's Newport Biography Reference Box, The Texas Collection.

Epilogue

1 Robert Dalziel Cumming (1871–1958) was a Scots-born newspaperman whose family immigrated to Canada and purchased *The Ashcroft Journal* in Ashcroft, British Columbia in 1912. This quote comes from "Through the Microscope," in *The Skookum Chuck Fables: Bits of History through the Microscope, some of which appeared in The Ashcroft Journal* (British Columbia: Public domain book, Kindle ed., 1915), 80.
2 Revelation 22:1–5: "Then the angel showed me the river of the water of life, as clear as crystal, flowing from the throne of God and of the Lamb down the middle of the great street of the city. On each side of the river stood the tree of life, bearing twelve crops of fruit, yielding its fruit every month. And the leaves of the tree are for the healing of the nations. No longer will there be any curse. The throne of God and of the Lamb will be in the city, and his servants will serve him. They will see his face, and his name will be on their foreheads. There will be no more night. They will not need the light of a lamp or the light of the sun, for the Lord God will give them light. And they will reign for ever and ever" (NIV).
3 One of the last events that John Newport attended was the National Association of Evangelicals meeting in Boston in the spring of 2000.
4 Alford, "John Newport Leaving Legacy," 1–2.
5 William Tolar, Roy Fish, James Leo Garrett, and many other senior faculty may also be considered "builders." Remaining connected to both the denomination in which they had invested their entire lives and preserving their own integrity, these giants of faith chose to stay with the Southwestern they had built and tried to influence her future days as best they could.
6 Philippians 1:21 (NIV).

Bibliography

Reference

Ashcraft, J. Morris. "James McKee Adams." In *Encyclopedia of Southern Baptists*, vol. 1, 2–3. Nashville: Broadman, 1958.
Baker, D. L. "Biblical Theology." In *New Dictionary of Theology: A Concise and Authoritative Resource*, edited by Sinclair B. Ferguson, David F. Wright, and J. I. Packer, 96–99. Downers Grove, Ill.: InterVarsity Press, 1988.
Brackney, William H. "Curtis Lee Laws (1868–1946)." In *Dictionary of Christianity in America*, edited by D. G. Reid, Robert D. Linder, Bruce L. Shelley, Harry S. Stout, and Craig A. Noll, 634. Downers Grove, Ill.: InterVarsity Press, 1990.
Briend, Jacques. "Roland de Vaux." In *Encyclopedia of the Dead Sea Scrolls*, vol. 1, edited by Lawrence H. Schiffman and James C. VanderKam, 202–3. Oxford: Oxford University Press, 2000.
Carson, D. A. "Systematic Theology and Biblical Theology." In *New Dictionary of Biblical Theology*, edited by T. Desmond Alexander and Brian S. Rosner, 89–104. Downers Grove, Ill.: InterVarsity, 2000.
Cox, Norman Wade, ed. "Authority and the Bible." In *Encyclopedia of Southern Baptists*, vol. 1, 161–62. Nashville: Broadman, 1958.
Davies, G. Henton. *Genesis*. In *Broadman Bible Commentary*, vol. 1, edited by Clifton J. Allen. Nashville: Broadman, 1969.
Eskridge, Larry. "Jesus People." In *Encyclopedia of Christianity*, vol. 3, edited by Erwin Fahlbusch, Geoffrey William Bromiley, and David B. Barrett, 912. Grand Rapids: Eerdmans, 1999.
Jones, J. Estill. "William Hersey Davis." In *Encyclopedia of Southern Baptists*, vol. 1, 350–51. Nashville: Broadman, 1958.
Marsden, George. "The Fundamentals." In *Dictionary of Christianity in America*, edited by D. G. Reid, Robert D. Linder, Bruce L. Shelley, Harry S. Stout, and Craig A. Noll, 468–69. Downers Grove, Ill.: InterVarsity Press, 1990.

Marsden, George, and B. J. Longfield. "Fundamentalist-Modernist Controversy." In *Dictionary of Christianity in America*, edited by D. G. Reid, Robert D. Linder, Bruce L. Shelley, Harry S. Stout, and Craig A. Noll, 466–68. Downers Grove, Ill.: InterVarsity Press, 1990.

Neely, Alan. "Carver, William Owen." In *Biographical Dictionary of Christian Missions*, edited by Gerald H. Anderson, 118. New York: Macmillan Reference USA, 1998.

Preston, William Hall. "Frank Hartwell Leavell." In *Encyclopedia of Southern Baptists*, vol. 2, 781–82. Nashville: Broadman, 1958.

Weber, T. P. "Fundamentalism." In *Dictionary of Christianity in America*, edited by D. G. Reid, Robert D. Linder, Bruce L. Shelley, Harry S. Stout, and Craig A. Noll, 461–65. Downers Grove, Ill.: InterVarsity Press, 1990.

Periodicals

Alford, Chip. "John Newport Leaving Legacy of Scholarship at Southwestern." *Baptist Press*, 30 July 1990.

"Arts Festival Launch." *The Scotsman*, 25 August 1947.

Auld, Graeme. Obituary of Norman Porteous. *The Scotsman*, 9 September 2003.

British Weekly: A Journal of Social and Christian Progress, 7 November 1946.

Brown, Joe David, ed. "The Hippies: Philosophy of a Subculture." *Time Magazine*, 7 July 1967.

Bush, L. Russ. "John Paul Newport: A Man for All Seasons." *Southwestern Journal of Theology* 29, no. 3 (1987): 5.

Collier, Keith. "Goldie Naylor, 100, Dies." *Baptist Press*, 2 February 2010.

Craft, Robert H. "Help for the Man in the Pew and in the Pulpit." *Baptist Standard*, 10 January 1962, 7.

Deusing, Jason G. "Luther Russ Bush III." *Southwestern Journal of Theology* 1, no. 50 (2007): 4.

Dilday, Russell H. "John Newport and Revelation." *Perspectives in Religious Studies* 32, no. 1 (2005): 11–24.

———. "Practical Apologist: Faith Seeking Understanding." *Southwestern Journal of Theology* 29, no. 3 (1987): 12–18.

Fea, John. "Understanding the Changing Façade of Twentieth-Century American Protestant Fundamentalism: Toward a Historical Definition." *Trinity Journal* 15, no. 2 (1994): 181–99.

"A Firing at a Southern Baptist Seminary." *The Chronicle of Higher Education*, 30 March 1994.

"George Arthur Buttrick, 87, Dies; Presbyterian Pastor and Scholar." *New York Times*, 24 January 1980.

Hailey, Cory J. "John Newport, Longtime Professor and Religion Expert, Dies at 82." *Baptist Press*, 21 August 2000.

Henry, Carl F. H. "What Is This Fundamentalism?" *United Evangelical Action*, 15 July 1955.
Jones, Jim, and Bill Teeter. "Baptist Theological Newport, 83, Dies." *Fort Worth Star Telegram*, 19 August 2020.
Kirkpatrick, David. "John's Newport's Apologetic of Complementarity: Cults, Consciousness, and Cosmic Evil." *Perspectives on Christian Apologetics* 32, no. 1 (2005): 51–58.
Klinefelter, Donald S. "The Theology of John Baillie: A Biographical Introduction." *Scottish Journal of Theology* (December 1969): 419–36.
MacKay, John A. "John Baillie, a Lyrical Tribute and Appraisal." *Scottish Journal of Theology* (June 1956): 226–27.
Macquarrie, John. "Christianity and Other Faiths." *Union Seminary Quarterly Review* 20, no. 1 (1964): 39–48.
Martin, Dan. "*Glorieta Statement* Discussion." *Baptist Press*, 7 November 1987.
Mauldin, Frank Louis. "John Newport and a Biblical Worldview." *Southwestern Journal of Theology* 29, no. 3 (1987): 33–45.
Obituary of Eddie Belle Newport. *Fort Worth Star Telegram*, 3 October 2012.
Obituary of Olofson Stendahl. *New York Times*, 16 April 2008.
Obituary of William Manson. *Glasgow Herald*, 5 April 1958.
Patterson, Bob E. "Editorial Introduction." *Perspectives in Religious Studies* 32, no. 1 (2005): 5.
Proceedings. Baptist General Convention of Texas (BGCT), 1913.
"Professor's Death Mourned." *The Daily Skiff*, 28 April 1973.
"Retired Missionary Tucker Calloway Dies." *Foreign Mission News*, 27 January 1987. SBC Archives, Nashville, Tennessee.
"The Very Rev James Stewart." *The Times* (London), 10 July 1990.
White, K. Owen. "Death in the Pot." *Arkansas Baptist*, 1 February 1962.

Primary Articles

Newport, John Paul. "The American Dream: Religion, Religious Liberty and the Public Schools." *Missouri Schools* 51 (1985): 22–26.
———. "America's Continuing Controversy Over Humanism." *Liberal and Fine Arts Review* 3 (1983): 87–98.
———. "The Arts and Their Worth." *Baptist Student* 42 (1963): 4–8, 33.
———. "The Arts from a Conservative Perspective." In *Arts in Society*, edited by Edward Kamarck, 56–57. Madison: University of Wisconsin Extension Division, 1976.
———. "The Arts in Worship." *Review and Expositor* 80 (1983): 71–83.
———. "The Baptist Journey." *Christianity Today*, 7 August 1981.
———. "Biblical Interpretation and Eschatological-Holy History." *Southwestern Journal of Theology* 4 (1961): 83–110.

———. "Biblical Philosophy and the Modern Mind." *Baptist Faculty Paper* 6 (1963): 1–4.

———. "The Biblical Worldview and Church-Related Colleges." *Southern Baptist Educator* 53 (August 1989): 3–20.

———. "Called to Life Commitment." *Young People's Teacher* (April 1962): 4–5.

———. "Christianity and Contemporary Art Forms." *Baptist Program* (August 1963): 10–11.

———. "Christianity and the Arts." In *At the Edge of Hope: Christian Laity in Paradox*, edited by Howard E. Butt Jr., 102–16. New York: Seabury, 1978.

———. "The Church Member." In *J. Howard Williams: Prophet of God and Friend of Man*, edited by H. C. Brown Jr. and Charles P. Johnson, 121–29. San Antonio, Tex.: Naylor, 1963.

———. "Communicating the Gospel through Contemporary Art Forms." *Journal of the Southern Baptist Church Music Conference* (1962–1963): 18–25.

———. "Cults, Religious Conflict, Religious Liberty, and Frameworks of Order." *Journal of Police Crisis Negotiations* 2, no. 1 (2002): 5–29.

———. "Falando em Linguas." *Home Missions* (May 1965).

———. "The Future Church Faces Radical New Religions." In *Future Church*, edited by Ralph Neighbor Jr., 187–205. Nashville: Broadman, 1980.

———. "God, Man, and Redemption in Modern Art." *Review and Expositor* 61 (1964): 142–55.

———. "Guest Editorial: The Musical Heritage of Baptists." *Baptist History and Heritage* 19 (1984): 2–3.

———. "Humanism and the Future: A Tentative Proposal for an American Solution." *Liberal and Fine Arts Review* 4 (1984): 53–61.

———. "Interpreting the Bible." In *Broadman Bible Commentary*, edited by Clifton J. Allen, 25–33. Vol. 1. Nashville: Broadman, 1969.

———. "Is the Theory of Human Evolution in Conflict with the Christian Faith?" *Baptist Student* 42 (1963): 5–7.

———. "The Jewish Messiah of the Apocrypha and the Pseudepigrapha." Th.D. diss., Southern Baptist Theological Seminary, 1944.

———. "Living in Two Worlds." *The Student* 60 (1980): 4–6.

———. "Man Seeking God: Religion." *Baptist Student* (November 1960): 7–9.

———. "The Mystery of Immortality and the Life Beyond." In *The Miracle of Easter*, edited by Floyd Thatcher, 115–23. Waco, Tex.: Word, 1980.

———. "New Developments in New Testament Theology." *Review and Expositor* 49 (1952): 41–56.

———. "The Odyssey of an Evangelical Mind." *Southwestern Journal of Theology* 37 (1995): 38–42.

———. "The Pastor and the Local Church." *Baptist Standard*, 10 October 1984.

———. "Philosophy of History." *Southwestern News* (June 1954), 6.

———. "The Problem of Demonic Power and the Nature of the Christian Response." *Ogbomoso Journal of Theology* 3 (1988): 27–31.
———. "Religion and Morals." *Baptist Student* 39 (1959): 21–33.
———. "Representative Contemporary Approaches to the Use of Philosophy in Christian Thought." *Review and Expositor* 82 (1985): 507–19.
———. "Representative Historical and Contemporary Approaches to Biblical Interpretation." *Faith and Mission* (Spring 1986): 32–48.
———. "Response." In *Demon Possession: A Medical, Historical, Anthropological and Theological Symposium*, edited by John Warwick Montgomery, 58–61. Minneapolis, Minn.: Bethany Fellowship, 1976.
———. "Satan and Demons: A Theological Perspective." In *Demon Possession: A Medical, Historical, Anthropological and Theological Symposium*, edited by John Warwick Montgomery, 325–45. Minneapolis, Minn.: Bethany Fellowship, 1976.
———. "Satanism and Demonism." *Baptist Standard*, 6 July 1983.
———. "Skeptic and Apologist." *Baptist Student* (December 1956): 36–52.
———. "Some Thoughts about Miracles." *Baptist Student* (May 1965): 2–4, 39.
———. "Speaking with Tongues." *Home Missions* (May 1965): 7–9, 21–26.
———. "Student Shapers." *Baptist Student* (December 1967): 14–20.
———. "The Theology and Experience of Salvation." *Greek Orthodox Theological Review* 22, no. 4 (1977): 393–404.
———. "Understanding, Evaluating, and Learning from the Contemporary Glossolalia Movement." In *Tongues*, edited by Luther B. Dyer, 105–27. Jefferson City, Mo.: Le Roi Publishers, 1971.
———. "The Unique Nature of the Bible in Light of Recent Attacks." *Southwestern Journal of Theology* 6 (1963): 93–106.
———. "Updating the American Dream." *Report from the Capital* 41 (1986): 4–5, 7.
———. "Who Is a Faithful Teacher?" *Baptist Training Union Magazine*, June 1949.
———. "The World: A Tangled Web and a Scarlet Thread." In *Waiting in the Wings*, edited by Porter W. Routh, 117–24. Nashville: Broadman, 1978.

Books

Newport, John. *Life's Ultimate Questions: A Contemporary Philosophy of Religion*. Galena Park, Tex.: Galena Park Institute, 1989.
———. *The New Age Movement and the Biblical Worldview: Conflict and Dialogue*. Grand Rapids: Eerdmans, 1998.
———. *Paul Tillich*. Edited by Bob Patterson. Makers of the Modern Theological Mind Series. Waco, Tex.: Word Books, 1984.
———. Preface to *Introduction to Solzhenitsyn's Religion* by Niels Nielsen Jr. Nashville: Thomas Nelson, 1975.

———. *Theology and Contemporary Art Forms*. Waco, Tex.: Word, 1971.
Newport, John, and William Cannon. *Why Christians Fight Over the Bible*. Nashville: Thomas Nelson, 1974.

Secondary

Ammerman, Nancy Tatom. *Baptist Battles: Social Change and Religious Conflict in the Southern Baptist Convention*. New Brunswick, N.J.: Rutgers University Press, 1990.

Augustine, Aurelius. *The Confessions of St. Augustine*. Harvard Classics. Translated by Edward Pusey. New York: P. F. Collier & Son, 1909–1914.

Ayer, A. J. *Language, Truth, and Logic*. New York: Dover Publications, 1952.

Baker, Robert A. *Tell the Generations Following: A History of Southwestern Baptist Theological Seminary, 1908–1983*. Nashville: Broadman, 1983.

Barnhart, Joe Edward. *The Southern Baptist Holy War*. Austin, Tex.: Texas Monthly Press, 1986.

Baugh, John F. *The Battle for Baptist Integrity*. Austin, Tex.: Battle for Baptist Integrity, 1995.

Bonhoeffer, Dietrich. *The Cost of Discipleship*. New York: Macmillan Publishers, 1937.

Borges, Jorge Francisco Isidoro Luis. *Twenty-Four Conversations with Jorge Luis Borges: Interviews by Roberto Alifano, 1981–1983*. Altamira Inter-American Series. Edited by Roberto Alifano. Translated by Willis Barnstone and Noemi Escandell. Housatonic, Mass.: Lascaux Publishers, 1984.

Brasseaux, Carl A. *In Search of Evangeline: Birth and Evolution of the Evangeline Myth*. Thibodaux, La.: Blue Heron Press, 1988.

Busch, Eberhard. *Karl Barth: His Life from Letters and Autobiographical Texts*. Eugene, Ore.: Wipf & Stock, 2005.

Calloway, Tucker N. *Zen Way, Jesus Way*. Clarendon, Vt.: Tuttle Publishing, 1976.

Childs, Brevard. *Biblical Theology in Crisis*. Philadelphia: Westminster, 1970.

Coleman, Robert. *One Divine Moment: The Account of the Asbury Revival of 1970*. 2nd ed. Wilmore, Ky.: First Fruits Press, 2013.

Cross, Frank. *The Ancient Library of Qumran*. 3rd ed. Sheffield: Sheffield Academic Press, 1995.

Cumming, Robert Dalziel. "Through the Microscope." In *The Skookum Chuck Fables: Bits of History through the Microscope, some of which appeared in The Ashcroft Journal*. British Columbia: Public domain book, Kindle ed., 1915.

Daniels, Roger. *Franklin D. Roosevelt: Road to the New Deal, 1882–1939*. Champaign: University of Illinois Press, 2016.

Dilday, Russell H. *Columns: Glimpses of a Seminary Under Assault*. Macon, Ga.: Smyth and Helwys, 2004.

———. *The Doctrine of Biblical Authority*. Nashville: Sunday School Board, 1982.
———. *E. Y. Mullins: Shaper of Theology*. Southern Baptist Heritage Series. Nashville: Southern Baptist Historical Commission, 1987.
———. *Higher Ground: A Call for Christian Civility*. Macon, Ga.: Smyth and Helwys, 2019.
———. *Personal Computers: A New Tool for Ministers*. Nashville: Baptist Sunday School Board, 1986.
Dixon, A. C., and R. A. Torrey, eds. *The Fundamentals*. Chicago: Testimony Publishing, 1910–1915.
Dockery, David S. *Southern Baptist Identity: An Evangelical Denomination Faces the Future*. Wheaton, Ill.: Crossway Books, 2009.
———. *Southern Baptists and American Evangelicals: The Conversation Continues*. Nashville: Broadman and Holman, 1993.
Douglas, J. D. *Let the Earth Hear His Voice: International Congress on World Evangelization, Lausanne, Switzerland*. Internet Archive: World Wide Publications, 1975.
Draper, James. *Authority: The Critical Issue for Southern Baptists*. Ada, Mich.: Revell, 1984.
Elliott, Ralph. *The Message of Genesis*. Nashville: Broadman, 1961.
Erasmus, Desiderius. *Spongia Adversus Aspergines Hutteni*. In *Collected Works of Erasmus*, edited by Manfred Hoffman, vol. 78. Toronto: University of Toronto Press, 2011.
Frank, Anne. *Tales from the Secret Annex: A Collection of Her Short Stories, Fables, and Lesser-Known Writings*. Edited by Gerrold van der Stooms. Translated by Susan Massoty. Basel: Anne Frank-Fonds, 2003.
Garnett, Arthur Campbell. *Reality and Value: An Introduction to Metaphysics and an Essay on the Theory of Value*. London: Taylor and Francis, 1937, 2020.
Geach, P., ed., and M. Black, trans. *Translations from the Philosophical Writings of Gottlob Frege*. 3rd ed. Oxford: Blackwell, 1980.
Harrell, David Edwin Jr. *Oral Roberts: An American Life*. Bloomington: Indiana University Press, 1985.
Havergal, Frances Ridley. "Perfect Peace." Published originally in *Hymns of Consecration and Faith*. Public domain, 1876.
Hoffmeier, James K., and Dennis R. Magary, eds. *Do Historical Matters Matter to Faith?* Wheaton, Ill.: Crossway, 2012.
Hugo, Victor. Œuvres complètes. Edition chronologique publiée sous la direction de Jean Massin. Vol. 4 (1838–1843). Paris: Club Français du Livre, 1968.
Hutchison, W. R. *The Modernist Impulse in American Protestantism*. Cambridge, Mass.: Harvard University Press, 1976.
Israel, Charles Alan. *Before Scopes: Evangelicalism, Education, and Evolution in Tennessee, 1870–1925*. Athens: University of Georgia Press, 2004.

Jaffe, Aniela. Foreword to *Memories, Dreams, Reflections*, by Carl Jung. Edited by Aniela Jaffe. Translated by Clara Winston. New York: Vintage Books, 1961.

Kaplan, Edward K. *Prophetic Witness & Spiritual Radical: Abraham Joshua Heschel in America, 1940–1972*. New Haven: Yale University Press, 2009.

Kemp, Daren. *New Age: A Guide*. Edinburgh: Edinburgh University Press, 2004.

Lau, Stella. *Popular Music in Evangelical Youth Culture*. Abingdon: Routledge, 2013.

Leavell, Charlotte Henry. *Genealogy of Nine Leavell Brothers of Oxford, Mississippi*. Charlottesville, Va.: Private printing, 1957.

Leonard, Bill. *God's Last and Only Hope: The Fragmentation of the Southern Baptist Convention*. Grand Rapids: Eerdmans, 1990.

Locke, John. "Of the Conduct of the Understanding." In *The Posthumous Works of Mr. John Locke*, edited by Peter King, 60. London: W.B., 1706; Amazon classic reprint by the same title: Saskatoon: Hardpress, 2018.

Longman, Tremper. *Old Testament Commentary Survey*. 2nd ed. Grand Rapids: Baker, 1999.

MacCulloch, Diarmaid. *Silence: A Christian History*. New York: Penguin Random House, 2014.

Marr, Ron W. *Explorer's Guide, Ozarks: Includes Branson, Springfield, & Northwest Arkansas*. Explorer's Complete Guide Series. 2nd ed. Taftsville, Vt.: Countryman Press, 2012.

Marsden, George. *Evangelicalism and Modern America*. Grand Rapids: Eerdmans, 1984.

———. *Fundamentalism and the American Culture: The Shaping of Twentieth-Century Evangelicalism*. New York: Oxford University Press, 1980, 2006.

———. *Reforming Fundamentalism: Fuller Seminary and the New Evangelicalism*. Grand Rapids: Eerdmans, 1987, 1995.

———. *Understanding Fundamentalism and Evangelicalism*. Grand Rapids: Eerdmans, 1990.

Marty, Martin. *Modern American Religion: The Irony of it All, 1893–1919*. Chicago: University of Chicago Press, 1986.

Mauldin, Frank Louis. "John Paul Newport: Philosophy of Religion." In *The Legacy of Southwestern: Writings that Shaped a Tradition*, edited by James Leo Garrett Jr., 208–10. North Richland Hills, Tex.: Smithfield Press, 2002.

———. "John Paul Newport." In *Tell the Generations Following: A History of Southwestern Baptist Theological Seminary, 1908–1983*. Nashville: Broadman, 1983.

McBeth, Leon. *Baptist Heritage: Four Centuries of Baptist Witness*. Nashville: Broadman, 1987.

McBeth, Leon. *Texas Baptists: A Sesquicentennial History*. Dallas: BaptistWay Press, 1998.

McGrath, Alister E. *Thomas F. Torrance: An Intellectual Biography*. Edinburgh: T&T Clark, 1999.
McLaren, Brian. *Everything Must Change: When the World's Biggest Problems and Jesus' Good News Collide*. Nashville: Thomas Nelson, 2009.
McLoughlin, William H. *American Evangelicals, 1800–1900*. Gloucester, Mass.: Peter Smith Publishers, 1968.
Meckel, Daniel J., and Robert L. Moore. *Jung and Christianity in Dialogue: Faith, Feminism, and Hermeneutics*. New York: Paulist Press, 1990.
Metaxas, Eric. *Bonhoeffer: Prophet, Pastor, Martyr, Spy*. Danvers, Mass.: Thomas Nelson, 2011.
Miles, Barry. *Hippie*. New York: Sterling, 2004.
Moore, G. E. *Some Main Problems of Philosophy*. New York: Humanities Press, 1953.
Nelson, Alvin Fredolph. *Inquiry and Reality: Discourse in Pragmatic Synthesis*. Fort Worth: Texas Christian University Press, 1978.
———. *Primary Questions, Historical Answers: Problems of Philosophy*. Boston: Christopher Press, 1968.
Newman, Stewart A. *W. T. Conner: Theologian of the Southwest*. Nashville: Broadman, 1964.
Newport, John Paul Jr. *The Fine Green Line*. New York: Random House, 1999.
Noll, Mark A., David W. Bebbington, and George M. Marsden. *Evangelicals: Who They Have Been, Are Now, and Could Have Been*. Grand Rapids: Eerdmans, 2019.
Overton, Patrick Miles. *The Leaning Tree*. Bloomington, Minn.: Bethany, 1975.
Owen, Jane. *New Harmony, Indiana: Like a River, Not a Lake: A Memoir*. Edited by Nancy Mangum McCaslin. Bloomington: University of Indiana Press, 2015.
Phelps, Austin. *The Theory of Preaching: Lectures on Homiletics*. New York: C. Scribner's Sons, 1882; reproduction published by Wentworth Press, 2019.
Pressler, Paul. *A Hill on Which to Die*. Nashville: Broadman and Holman, 1999.
Prucha, Francis Paul. *American Indian Treaties*. Berkeley: University of California Press, 1997.
Read, Herbert, Michael Fordham, and Gerhard Adler, eds. *The Collected Works of C. G. Jung*. Translated by R. F. C. Hull. 20 vols. 2nd ed. Princeton: Princeton University Press, 1966–1979.
Readers' Digest Book of Facts. Pleasantville, N.Y.: Readers' Digest Association, 1987.
A Reminiscent History of the Ozark Region: Comprising a Condensed General History, A Brief Descriptive History of Each County, and Numerous Biographical Sketches of Prominent Citizens of Such Counties. Chicago: Goodspeed Brothers, 1894.

Russell, Bertrand. *The Art of Philosophizing.* New York: Philosophical Library, 1968.

Sandeen, Ernest R. *Roots of Fundamentalism.* Chicago: University of Chicago Press, 1970.

Sawyer, Dana. *Huston Smith: Wisdom-keeper, Living the World's Religions, the Authorized Biography of a 21st Century Spiritual Giant.* Louisville, Ky.: Fons Vitae, 2014.

Shelly, Bruce L. *The Gospel and the American Dream.* Sisters, Ore.: Multnomah Books, 1989.

Southern Baptist Convention. *Annual,* 1952.

Stewart, James Stuart, and H. R. Mackintosh, eds. *The Christian Faith* (1928). English translation of Friedrich Schleiermacher, *Der christliche Glaube nach den Grundsätzen der evangelischen Kirche im Zusammenhange dargestellt.* Repr. Berlin: G. Reimer, 1884.

Sutton, Jerry. *The Baptist Reformation: The Conservative Resurgence in the Southern Baptist Convention.* Nashville: Broadman and Holman, 2000.

Sweet, Leonard I. *The Evangelical Tradition in America.* Macon, Ga.: Mercer, 1984.

Szasz, Ferrenc Morton. *The Divided Mind of American Protestantism, 1880–1930.* Montgomery: University of Alabama Press, 1982.

Torrance, T. F. *Calvin's Doctrine of Man.* Eugene, Ore.: Wipf & Stock, 1997.

Vaux, Roland de. "Method in the Study of Early Hebrew History." In *The Bible in Modern Scholarship,* edited by J. P. Hyatt. Nashville: Abingdon Press, 1965.

Wallis, Frank, ed. *Ribbons of Time: World History Year by Year Since 1492.* New York: Weidenfeld and Nicolson, 1988.

Wenham, Gordon. *History, Criticism, and Faith: Four Explanatory Studies.* Edited by Colin Brown. Leicester: InterVarsity Press, 1976.

Wilkinson, John. *The Bible and Healing: A Medical and Theological Commentary.* Grand Rapids: Eerdmans, 1998.

Wilson, Edwin H. *Genius of a Humanist Manifesto.* Washington, D.C.: Humanist Press, 1995.

Wittgenstein, Ludwig. *Philosophical Investigations: The English Text of the Third Edition.* Translated by G. E. M. Anscombe. New York: Prentice Hall, 1958.

Wolterstorff, Nicholas. *Art in Action: Toward a Christian Aesthetic.* Grand Rapids: Eerdmans, 1997.

Woolf, Virginia. *The Letters of Virginia Woolf, 1923–1928.* Vol. 3. Edited by Nigel Nicolson and Joanne Trautmann. Boston: Mariner Books, 1980.

Wright, G. Ernest. *The God Who Acts: Biblical Theology as Recital.* Naperville, Ill.: Alec R. Allenson, 1952.

Zweig, Stefan, Eden Paul, and Cedar Paul. *Erasmus of Rotterdam.* New York: Plunkett Lake Press, 1934.

Archival and Unpublished Sources

Cabal, Ted. "Problems and Promise in a Biblical Worldview with Special Reference to John Paul Newport." Ph.D. diss., Southwestern Baptist Theological Seminary, 1995.
Cabal, Ted. Written notes from interview with the writer, 24 June 2013.
Denison, Jim. Written notes from interview with the writer, 1 July 2013.
Dilday, Russell H. Written notes from interview with the writer, 12 June 2013.
Estep, William R. "Three Days at Southwestern." Newport Papers. "Autobiographical Materials." Bullock's Newport Biography Reference Box, The Texas Collection and University Archives, Baylor University, Waco, Texas.
Garrett, James Leo. Written notes from interview with the writer, 8 December 2014.
Gray, Scotty. Written notes from interview with the writer, 17 June 2013.
Hanan, Robert F. Letter to John Newport. 1 February 1976. Newport Papers. "Personal Correspondence." Bullock's Newport Biography Reference Box, The Texas Collection.
Harmon, Richard W. Written notes from interview with the writer, 24 June 2013.
Hunt, Harry. Letter to John Newport. 19 November 1976. Newport Papers. "Personal Correspondence." Bullock's Newport Biography Reference Box, The Texas Collection.
Lemke, Steve. Written notes from interview with the writer, 23 June 2013.
Lyon, Steve. Interview with the writer, 10 August 2020.
McDonald, John Daniel. "Toward a Baptist View of Metaphilosophy: An Analysis of E. Y. Mullins, John Newport, Richard Cunningham, and L. Russ Bush." Ph.D. diss., Southern Baptist Theological Seminary, 2014.
Naylor, Robert Ernest. Letter to John Newport. 6 November 1978. Newport Papers. "Personal Correspondence." Bullock's Newport Biography Reference Box, The Texas Collection.
Newport Files. Southwestern Baptist Theological Seminary Archives. Located by Jill Botticelli, archivist, on 13 July 2020 and sent to author via electronic copy.
Newport, Frank M. Written notes from interview with the writer, 2012–2020.

> For the following section, see Bullock's Newport Biography Reference Box for this volume in the Newport Papers, The Texas Collection, Baylor University, Waco, Texas.

> Newport, John. "Baptist Thought and Philosophy." Paper presented at the Conference on Teaching Philosophy in Southern Baptist Colleges and Universities, Ouachita Baptist University, Arkadelphia, Arkansas, April 1986.
> ———. "Christmas Greetings from the John Newports." 1998 and 1999.

———. "Columbus, Cultural and Religious Self-Understanding, and the Caribbean."
———. "The Forging of an Evangelical Mind and Heart in the Twentieth Century Cultural and Religious Cauldron."
———. "Founder's Day Address, 9 March 2000" manuscript.
———. "Inerrancy."
———. "Lessons from the Odyssey of an Evolving Baptist Theologian." An address presented to the North American Baptist Professors of Religion, 1992.
———. Letters to Bill Nichols, "Mars Hill" and "New Age Conference."
———. Letter to daughter Martha. 22 March 2000.
———. Letter to Dr. Gerald Mann. 10 January 2000.
———. Letter to Dr. Russell Dilday. 23 March 1978.
———. Letter to Eddie Belle and his parents. 28 December 1946.
———. Letter to his brother Russell Newport. 25 September 1989.
———. Letter to his mother. 20 September 1946.
———. Letter to his parents. 15 December 1946.
———. Letter to his parents. 5 January 1947.
———. Letter to his parents. 28 April 1947.
———. Letter to his parents. 13–14 September 1947.
———. Letter to his parents. 12 April 1951.
———. Letter to Jenkins and Virginia Garrett. 17 April 2000.
———. Letter to Ken and Paula Hemphill. 22 September 1997.
———. Letter to Mrs. Evelyn Hudson. 3 March 1997.
———. Letter to son Frank. 21 June 1977.
———. "Letters to John McNaughton." Newport Papers. "Inerrancy."
———. Memo to the Faculty. "Concerning Ordination and Baptist Polity." 2 October 1998.
———. Memo to President Ken Hemphill. 5 May 2000.
———. "Memoirs." A copy in the hand of the writer.
———. "Memorandum" to Doug Blount and Paul Sands regarding the Wheaton Trip, 10 April 2000.
———. "Odyssey of an Evangelical Mind."
———. "Recollections."
———. "Russell Dilday and Constructive Conservative Theological Education at Southwestern Baptist Theological Seminary, 1978–1995."
———. "Sarah Brown Morrow Genealogy" file.
———. Small Notebook. Newport Papers.
———. "Testimony."
Newport, John Paul, Jr. Personal diary entries. Sent to the writer, 30 July 2020.
———. Written notes from interview with the writer. 2012–2020.

Newport, Mark. Written notes from son of Russell Newport, John's brother, from interview with the writer. Family information. 27 June 2020.

Order of Service for the Funeral of Eddie Belle Leavell Newport. Newport Papers. "Autobiographical Materials." Bullock's Newport Biography Reference Box, The Texas Collection and University Archives, Baylor University, Waco, Texas.

Order of Service for the Funeral of John Paul Newport. Newport Papers. "Autobiographical Materials." Bullock's Newport Biography Reference Box, The Texas Collection and University Archives, Baylor University, Waco, Texas.

Program for Roast/Toast of Dr. John Newport. "Ephemera." "Autobiographical Materials." Bullock's Newport Biography Reference Box, The Texas Collection and University Archives, Baylor University, Waco, Texas.

Putt, Keith. Written notes from interviews with the writer, 23 June 2013 and 10 December 2014.

Ravi, N. S. R. K. Letter to John Newport. 28 March 2000. Newport Papers. "Personal Correspondence." Bullock's Newport Biography Reference Box, The Texas Collection, Baylor University.

Sansom, Dennis. Written notes from interview with the writer, 18 August 2013.

"SBC Peace Committee 1985–1988." SBC Historical Collection. Southern Baptist Historical Library and Archives. Nashville, Texas.

Shimkus, Martha Newport. "Family Notes and Photos." 20 June 2013. Newport Papers. "Autobiographical Materials." Bullock's Newport Biography Reference Box, The Texas Collection and University Archives, Baylor University, Waco, Texas.

———. Handwritten notes to the writer. "Newport Family Memories." 20 June 2013.

———. Handwritten notes to the writer, 2012–2020.

Tillman, Bill. Written notes from interview with the writer, 24 June 2013.

Tolar, William. Written notes from interview with the writer, 3 February 2015.

Walker, Kevin. Southwestern Baptist Theological Seminary. "Recollection." 1982–2005. Newport Papers. Bullock's Newport Biography Reference Box, The Texas Collection.

White, Reagan. Written notes from interview with the writer, 20 October 2013.

Woodfin, Yandall. Written notes from interview with the writer through Leta, his wife, 18 June 2013.

Online Repositories and Citations

Aberdeenshire Council. Online museum. Accessed 9 February 2022. https://online.aberdeenshire.gov.uk/smrpub/master/detail.aspx?Authority=ASH&refno=NJ66SE0007.

Bristo Baptist Church. Accessed 9 February 2022. https://www.bristobaptist.org/history-of-bristo.

Cheyne, A. C. *The Spirit of New College: New College, Edinburgh, 1846–1996.* New College, Edinburgh: 1996. Accessed 9 February 2022. https://www.ed.ac.uk/divinity/about/history/new-college.

Driver, Tom. "Tom Driver on Paul Tillich." Accessed 23 February 2015. http://theological-geography.net/?p=4183.

"Edgar Young Mullins." Southern Baptist Historical Library and Archives. Accessed 6 December 2014. http://www.sbhla.org/bio_eymullins.htm.

FamilySearch.org. Accessed 28 June 2020. https://familysearch.org/ark:/61903/1:1:MDZ4-7RC. 9 November 2014. Margaret Wollard in household of Nathaniel Wollard. Dallas County, Dallas, Missouri, United States. Citing family 384. NARA microfilm publication M432. Washington, D.C.: National Archives and Records Administration, n.d.

"Gaines Stanley Dobbins Papers." Southern Baptist Historical Library and Archives. Accessed 9 February 2022. https://sbhla.org, Gaines Stanley Dobbins Papers, AR 795-281, PDF available at https://sbhla.org/wp-content/uploads/795-281.pdf.

Hancock, Brannon. "John Macmurray." Gifford Lectures Online. Accessed 16 December 2014. http://www.giffordlectures.org/lecturers/john-macmurray.

———. "The Self as Agent." The Gifford Lectures Online. Accessed 9 February 2022. https://www.giffordlectures.org/books/persons-relation.

"Henry Cornell Goerner Historical Collection." Southern Baptist Historical Library and Archives, Nashville, Tennessee, 2006. Accessed 6 December 2014. http://www.sbhla.org/downloads/805.pdf.

Meredith College. "Oak Leaves." 1940 yearbook. Digitized by the North Carolina Digital Heritage Center. North Carolina Collection at the University of North Carolina at Chapel Hill. Accessed 9 February 2022. https://lib.digitalnc.org/record/27416#?c=0&m=0&s=0&cv=3&r=0&xywh=-189%2C0%2C4464%2C2898.

MyHeritage.com. Accessed 27 June 2020. https://www.myheritage.com/research/record-1-392943-3-2465/harriet-narcisses-newport-born-burnett-in-myheritage-family-trees?s=763394271.

MyHeritage.com. Accessed 27 June 2020. https://www.myheritage.com/research/record-40001-781206975/john-barrick-in-familysearch-family-tree?s=763394271.

Obituary of John Dewey. *New York Times*, 2 June 1952. Accessed 9 February 2022. https://archive.nytimes.com/www.nytimes.com/learning/general/onthisday/bday/1020.html.

Schlesinger, Arthur, Jr. Centennial Memorial of Reinhold Niebuhr's Birth. *New York Times*, 22 June 1992. Accessed 23 February 2015. http://www.nytimes.com/1992/06/22/opinion/reinhold-niebuhr-s-long-shadow.html.

Southern Baptist Convention (SBC). "Memorial Resolution." Accessed 9 February 2022. https://www.sbc.net/resource-library/resolutions/resolution-on-memorial-resolution/.

The Southern Baptist Theological Seminary Archives and Special Collection. Accessed 6 December 2014. http://archives.sbts.edu/the-history-of-the-sbts/our-professors/w-hersey-davis/.

Steinfels, Peter. Obituary of Joseph Fletcher. *New York Times*, 30 October 1991. Accessed 18 February 2015. http://www.nytimes.com/1991/10/30/us/dr-joseph-f-fletcher-86-dies-pioneer-in-field-of-medical-ethics.html.

Stout, David. Obituary of John C. Bennett. *New York Times*, 2 May 1995. Accessed 17 February 2015. http://www.nytimes.com/1995/05/02/obituaries/john-c-bennett-a-theologian-of-outspoken-views-dies-at-92.html.

Ward-Belmont College. "Milestones." 1938 Yearbook. Digitized by Internet Archive. Accessed 4 December 2014. https://archive.org/stream/milestones1938ward# page/n135/mode/2up/search/Eddie+Belle+Leavell.

"William L. Morrow." *The History of Dallas County, Missouri*. Chicago: Goodspeed, 1889, 956. http://www.mygenealogyhound.com/missouri-biographies/mo-dallas-county-biographies/w-l-morrow-genealogy-dallas-county-missouri-buffalo-mo.html.

Whitman, Alden. Obituary of Reinhold Niebuhr. *New York Times*, 2 June 1971. Accessed 23 February 2015. http://www.nytimes.com/packages/html/books/niebuhr.pdf.

CPSIA information can be obtained
at www.ICGtesting.com
Printed in the USA
LVHW042121281022
731820LV00002B/183